HAGIA SOPHIA

HAGIA SOPHIA

SOUND, SPACE, AND SPIRIT IN BYZANTIUM

Bissera V. Pentcheva

The Pennsylvania State University Press
University Park, Pennsylvania

Publication of this book was aided by funds from
the Ruth Levison Halperin Fund in the Department
of Art & Art History at Stanford University

Library of Congress Cataloging-in-Publication Data
Names: Pentcheva, Bissera V., author.
Title: Hagia Sophia : sound, space, and spirit
in Byzantium / Bissera Pentcheva.
Description: University Park, Pennsylvania :
The Pennsylvania State University Press, [2017] |
Includes bibliographical references and index.
Summary: "Examines the aesthetic principles and
spiritual operations at work in Hagia Sophia. Drawing
on art and architectural history, liturgy, musicology,
and acoustics, explores the Byzantine paradigm of
animation"—Provided by publisher.
Identifiers: LCCN 2016055895 | ISBN 9780271077253
(cloth : alk. paper)
Subjects: LCSH: Ayasofya Mèuzesi—History. | Church
buildings—Acoustics—Turkey—Istanbul—History. |
Interior architecture—Turkey—Istanbul—History. |
Byzantine chants—History and criticism. | Sacred
space—Turkey—Istanbul—History.
Classification: LCC NA5870.A9 P46 2017 |
DDC 726.6094961/8—dc23
LC record available at https://lccn.loc.gov/2016055895

The Pennsylvania State University Press is a member of
the Association of American University Presses.

It is the policy of The Pennsylvania State University
Press to use acid-free paper. Publications on uncoated
stock satisfy the minimum requirements of American
National Standard for Information Sciences—
Permanence of Paper for Printed Library Material,
ANSI Z39.48–1992.

CONTENTS

ILLUSTRATIONS

ACKNOWLEDGMENTS

To find time to concentrate, to live and to breathe ideas—this harmonizing experience has become such a luxury in our lives. This is a book written without a sabbatical, composed in moments of peace, carved out and treasured. It is dedicated to my mother, Olga Zaharieva, and my father, Vladimir Pentchev. I lost my father when I was still in college. I owe it to him that I became a Byzantinist. And I owe it to my mother that I discovered this intersection of humanities and sciences. She shared in the enthusiasm and excitement of the early stages of this study, and had she lived to see its completion, she would have been very happy.

The research behind this book owes much to the friendship and support of many scholars: Jonathan Abel in acoustics at the Center for Computer Research in Music and Acoustics, Stanford University, Alexander Lingas and Christian Troelsgård in Byzantine musicology, Christina Maranci in Armenian architecture, Anthony Kaldellis in Byzantine philosophy and history, Herbert Kessler and Lisa Reilly in medieval art, Richard Neer in Greek art, Sepp Gumbrecht in comparative literature, Vincent Barletta in Iberian studies, Peter Schreiner in Byzantine history, Kim Haines-Eitzen in sound studies and Early Christian spirituality, Nina Ergin in Ottoman architecture, George Demacopoulos in Byzantine Orthodoxy, Robert Taft and Steven Hawkes-Teeples in Byzantine liturgy, Branislav Jakovljevic in drama, and Federica Ciccolella in Byzantine poetry.

I thank Ellie Goodman, editor at the Pennsylvania State University Press, for her staunch support and insight, leading this project to maturity. My gratitude also goes to the two excellent readers who steered this manuscript to clarity and strength. I thank also my colleagues at the Department of Art and Art History at Stanford University and the graduate students I have been fortunate to work with—Ravinder Binning, Lora Webb, Laura Steenberge, and Joshua Gentzke—and the undergraduates John Newcomb and Konstantine Buhler. I thank Jennifer Hsieh (from the Department of Anthropology) and Justin Tackett (from the Department of English), the two graduate-student coordinators with whom I founded and for the past three years have run the interdisciplinary workshop Material Imagination: Sound, Space, and Human Consciousness. My gratitude goes to all the scholars who came and shared their research at this forum.

I thank the Onassis Foundation (USA) and Dr. Maria Sereti for funding and helping me run the Aural Architecture seminar at Stanford in 2013–14, which grew to become a forum for interdisciplinary discourse on music, acoustics, and ritual in Byzantium.

At Stanford I thank my colleagues who served as chairs of the Department of Art and Art History in this period and supported my research: Kris Samuelson, Richard Vinograd, Nancy Troy, and Alexander Nemerov. I owe deep gratitude to Bryan Wolf and Jonathan Berger, who as directors of the Arts Institute at Stanford funded the early stages of this work; to Stephen Hinton, who as dean of humanities awarded the seed grant to the interdisciplinary project Icons of Sound; and to Jenny Bilfield at Stanford Live, who steered Cappella

Romana's first Bing concert to success in 2013. Additionally, Provost John Etchemendy and Associate Dean for the Advancement of the Arts Matthew Tiews have propelled a new phase for Icons of Sound by funding a Cappella Romana concert, auralization, and recording in 2016.

In Istanbul I thank Melike Ozcan and Dr. Haluk Dursun, director of Ayasofya Müzësi in 2010. For their work on the film made to accompany this book, viewable at https://hagiasophia.stanford.edu, I thank Charlene Music, Ben Wu, and Will Rogers.

The completion of this project would not have been possible without the continual support of my family: Stephen and Olivia Atkinson.

Introduction

Hagia Sophia, the church dedicated to Holy Wisdom, is the single most important monument from Byzantium (fig. 1). Currently a museum, this building opens its doors to visitors in bright daylight—nine o'clock at the earliest. The strong midmorning light holds no lyricism or magic. Neither lurking shadows nor flickering lights respond to the drafts of air stirred by the opening of the doors and the masses of people pouring in. The dust and soot covering the marble revetments subdue the variegated colors of the stone under a film of gray. The clunky modern metal skeleton of the scaffolding, erected for the cleaning of the Ottoman shields, continuously expands to include ever more surfaces, thus blocking the view and tampering with the aesthetic effect of the interior. The introduction of electric light has been equally detrimental, as the wires and electric light bulbs strangle the elegant lines of the Ottoman chandeliers. With their steady network of light spreading right above the heads of the viewers, they disrupt the gaze seeking a continuum from floor to ceiling.

Unlike us, however, the Byzantines experienced this majestic building when it was at the peak of its beauty. They felt the enchantment of the transitions at dawn and dusk, which coincided with the offices of *orthros* (matins, or morning office) and *hesperinos* (vespers). Worshippers gathered in the atrium of Hagia Sophia, sometimes after they had walked for several hours in a religious procession through the streets of the city, carrying torches and candles and singing refrains to the psalms performed by the choirs. Upon seeing the many doors of the Great Church open, the faithful—tired, hungry, dehydrated, and pressed into cramped spaces—were moved with awe by the spacious interior. The surface of the marble floor would have been luminescent in the half-light of the sun rising in the east, while silver disks, suspended on chains from the rim of the dome, reached almost to the level of human height; they captured and reflected the light of myriad glass vials filled with oil. Once inside Hagia Sophia, the faithful stood on their feet for the duration of the service, at times enveloped in the smoke and perfume of incense, responding with refrains to the chanting of the psalms.[1]

FIG. 1

Aerial view of Hagia Sophia, south façade; in the distance, the Golden Horn and the Bosporus. The Byzantine Institute and Dumbarton Oaks Fieldwork Records and Papers, ca. late 1930s–1960s, MS.BZ.004.

Still to this day, at dusk and dawn the light in Hagia Sophia penetrates and illuminates the interior in segments, gliding across the surface of walls covered in marble slabs and gold.[2] The sun's ray catch on the carved stone frames of the revetments and transform the marble into incandescent matter, making it appear liquid rather than solid. Similarly, the slabs of marble consuming the light of sunrise present a warm and fleshlike surface, as if the sun were performing a metamorphosis, turning stone into a living body. The Byzantines called such surfaces "full of grace" (*kecharitōmenē*), for grace (*charis*) expressed Spirit descending into matter and indwelling there.

Very few people today can experience this transformative vision. There is also hardly any impetus to seek it, because we do not expect the inert to be alive. Our response to this building is shaped by an architectural history concerned with the facts about architectural form, engineering technology, and patronage. The difference between the modern and the medieval approaches to Hagia Sophia is a difference between a gathering of facts and a cultivation of transcendent spiritual experience.

In its unprecedented scale, shape, and lavish decoration, Hagia Sophia rose as a man-made artifact that articulated a cosmic vision of empire and religion. It thus palpably expressed claims for both economic and spiritual superiority, which were important for Constantinople at the time.[3] Although the capital had been the seat of imperial and patriarchal power since 324, it lacked an apostolic foundation. By contrast, the other four cities of the pentarchy each claimed a special relation to the sacred:[4] Jerusalem was the hallowed ground where Christ lived, died, and was resurrected; Antioch boasted the mission of the apostle Paul and the first use of the name "Christian" (Acts 11:26); Alexandria's church was founded by the Evangelist Mark; and Rome had a claim on both saints Peter and Paul. Built in a swift campaign from 532 to 537 by Emperor Justinian (r. 527–65), Hagia Sophia reversed the new capital's inferior prestige, bestowing new spiritual powers on Constantinople.

Situated on high ground and overlooking three bodies of water—the Bosporus to the east, the Golden Horn to the north, and the Sea of Marmara to the south—Hagia Sophia's exterior emerges as a cascade of semidomes from a central dome, all held up by robust buttresses (fig. 1). In the interior, the dome rises over a square foundation defined by the four large piers that are hidden from view behind variegated marble revetments (fig. 2). The piers support four large arches. The corners are filled by continuous pendentives that make the transition from the square below into the circular rim of the dome above.[5] A ring of windows at the drum conveys a sense of lightness, as if the masonry cupola hangs suspended on a chain from heaven (fig. 3).[6]

This architectural vision, expressed through the massing of the cupola and semidomes, maintains a geometric simplicity and visual unity while at the same time enabling a spacious interior.[7] Excluding the narthexes and the projecting apse, the footprint of Hagia Sophia forms a rectangle about 71 meters in width and 77 meters in length (fig. 4).[8] The space under the dome forms a square, defined by the four piers, with a side of 31 meters. The dome rises 56.60 meters above the floor and has a maximum diameter of 31.87 meters.[9] The height of this space thus exceeds by far the tallest medieval cathedrals of Western Europe.[10] The vast interior volume of the nave is 255,800 cubic meters and can accommodate roughly sixteen thousand people.[11] Cladding the walls and floor, lavish expanses of marble, gold, and glass enhance the engineering virtuosity of the architecture. The awe that this building inspired in its viewers was enhanced by the impressive staff of five hundred who officiated as clergy, choirs, and doorkeepers during the liturgy.[12]

Byzantine artistic production was not concerned with either a separation or a fusion of art and life but rather with the transcendence of both. A space such as Hagia Sophia and its ritual had the capacity to trigger this transcendence. Through the visual effects of vibrant and glittering materiality, reverberant acoustics, and thick and redolent incense, the participants in the liturgy were led to experience a space in between earth and heaven, identified in Greek as *metaxu*. When in 987 Prince Vladimir of Kievan Rus sent ambassadors to Constantinople to explore a possible conversion to Orthodox Christianity, his men witnessed the liturgy in the Great Church and exclaimed: "We knew not whether we were in heaven or on earth. For on earth there is no such splendor or such beauty and we are at a loss how to describe it. We only know that God dwells there among men, and their service is fairer than the ceremonies of other nations. For we cannot forget that beauty."[13] For the ambassadors who saw the Justinianic church,

FIG. 2

Hagia Sophia, 532–37 and 562, interior.

it was the liturgy celebrated in that building that precipitated the experience of transcendence. They witnessed the Eucharist, the most important rite celebrated in the Great Church. The medieval interpretation of its significance focuses on how

FIG. 3

Hagia Sophia, 532–37 and 562, interior, view of the dome and semidomes.

it enables humanity to reach beyond the earthly bounds and partake in the divine, and this meaning echoes the experience, recorded by the Kiev source, of being in a place in between heaven and earth. The Byzantine theologian and exegete Maximus the Confessor (580–662) writes further about this uplifting effect:[14] "and he [God] will assimilate humanity to himself and elevate us to a position above all the heavens. It is to this exalted position that the natural magnitude of God's grace summons lowly humanity, out of a goodness that is infinite."[15] Maximus speaks of the liturgical reality opening before humanity, allowing it to partake in the divine and, in turn, to become divinized.[16] This transcendence is achieved through the Eucharist, which offers tactile and gustatory access to the divine. The faithful partake in a multisensory experience whose intensity is magnified by the splendor of the ceremony, the staggering numbers of staff and participants gathered in the immense interior. During the performance of the ritual, vision initiates the sensual encounter. Sound and smell give spatial and temporal dimensions to this experience. The fragrance of burning incense spreads through the air, the same air in which the sound waves travel. Chant as a voice exhaling and inhaling fills the void of space, activating both the body of the worshipper and the architectural aurality.

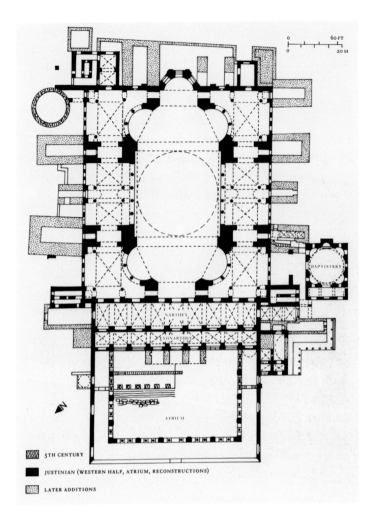

FIG. 4

Plan of Hagia Sophia, after Richard Krautheimer, *Early Christian and Byzantine Architecture*, 4th ed. (New Haven: Yale University Press, 1986), fig. 164.

In a radical departure from the traditional studies of Hagia Sophia, this book does not focus on the architectural form of the building, the materiality of its fabric, the technology of its construction, or the political ideology of its decoration. Instead, it argues for the performativity of this space—the void, or air, under the dome—activated during the liturgy by light and sonic energy (see the frontispiece). It explains how the experience of Hagia Sophia allowed the Byzantine participants in the liturgical ritual to be filled with the Spirit of God, and indeed to become his image on earth. In exploring the process of inspiriting, this analysis uncovers the deep connections between sight and sound produced by the architectural aurality during the Byzantine cathedral liturgy.[17]

Sensual Experience

Since 1990, studies in art history, religion, and anthropology have engaged questions of sensation and cognition in the analysis of religious experience.[18] Liz James, Nadine

Schibille, and Nicoletta Isar, who have worked on aesthetics and the senses in Hagia Sophia, have targeted their analyses on the role of sight and sought to integrate it into the Byzantine philosophical and religious hermeneutics.[19] By contrast, this book introduces the sonic dimension of Hagia Sophia and studies it as a phenomenon linked to the other senses. Reverberation, an enveloping nonintimate sound field, and dissolution of the intelligibility of speech are some of the most prominent sonic phenomena in the interior. Human breath in the form of chant activates the aurality of the building, animating both the worshipper and the space. The Byzantines, I argue, believed this inspiriting produced a nonrepresentational image of God. Thus an attention to sound and acoustics opens for examination and redefinition major art-historical questions about animation and iconicity, which function beyond anthropomorphic figuration.

Through the study of architectural aurality, this book initiates an art history by means other than representational art. Further examples of the synergy of sound and sight uncover how the acoustic phenomena of reverberation and aural obfuscation are correlated to the visual: glitter and shadow. This analysis makes a distinction between the "visible" (which identifies the shapes that light makes accessible to sight) and the "visual" (which moves beyond form and identifies phenomena of form dissolution and darkness as aspects of vision). The recognition of the importance of the visual in the construction of a multisensory phenomenon inside Hagia Sophia is what distinguishes this study from earlier engagements with sight and the visible. I argue that the medieval perception of nearness to the divine manifested itself in both the dissolution of the visible and the blurring of semantic word chains in the sonic.

The book foregrounds sensual experience in the same way as it is privileged in the words of Maximus the Confessor, who argues that a direct knowledge of God can be gained most directly through sensations elicited by participation in the liturgy:

> The Word knows of two kinds of knowledge of the divine, a relative one rooted only in reason and ideas, and lacking in the kind of sensual perception gained through the energies of knowledge through experience; such relative knowledge is what we use to order our affairs in our present life. On the other hand, there is that truly authentic knowledge, gained only by actual experience, apart from reason and ideas, which provides a total [sensual] perception of the known object through a participation by grace. By this latter knowledge, we attain, in the future state, the supernatural deification that remains unceasingly in effect.[20]

Experience (*peira*) of God gained through the sensorium (*aisthēsis*) is privileged over abstract knowledge. This corporeal gnosis is reached by a total sensual immersion; the practitioner is able to participate in the divine energies (*energeiai*) through the intervention of grace (*charis*). *Energeia* acts as the quickening force that "inspirits" matter. In using *energeia* together with the verb *metechō* (to partake) and *charis*, Maximus the Confessor targets the corporeal memory of partaking in the Eucharist. He emphasizes that sensual experience is acquired in a ritual practice. By consuming the Eucharist, the faithful partake physically in the divine.[21]

In this study the term "experience" denotes the sensorial regimes available to a Byzantine audience participating in the cathedral rite. But whose experience is analyzed here? The relationship between surviving sources and social stratification makes an inclusive account from this period impossible. Using hagiography and chronicles as his sources, Robert Taft has sought to expand our understanding of the participants beyond the elite and identify aspects of what the congregation witnessed. Yet his approach still ends up focusing on the pontifical and imperial experience, because the richest data (especially as recorded in the tenth-century *Book of Ceremonies*) concentrate on the highest level of society.[22] Nor do the Byzantine mystagogical texts, which interpret the liturgy, provide adequate evidence on which to build a nuanced analysis. Instead, these texts communicate a general meaning of the liturgical rites to those who performed and participated in them. Given the nature of the evidence, this study recognizes that the "experience" accessible through the written sources is that of subjects at the highest level in Byzantine culture.

In the effort to uncover the character of medieval experience of Hagia Sophia, this study turns to the liturgy. Art history has long been invested in context, but ritual adds dimension to the spatiotemporal character of artworks, enabling the art historian to view them as imprinted artifacts of past practices, rather than just documents of information and discourse. Unlike theological treatises, whose intention rarely coincides with a desire to explicate public performance or the use of objects in it, the liturgy is envisioned from the start as a public theater that activates objects and people. By performing a corpus of texts, the liturgy embeds them into a specific material fabric of a building, time of day, movement, and gesture. It thus offers, through written and visual sources, the ability to recuperate historically locatable performance and original conditions of display.[23] The analysis in this book draws on texts pertaining to the liturgy, such as *euchologia* (prayer books), *typika* (liturgical ordinals), *psaltika* (collections of the chants for the soloist, or *domestikos*), and *asmatika* (collections of the chants for the elite choir of *psaltai*, or cantors).

While these texts help in reconstructing the order and content of the services, they are not illustrated and thus do not indicate what visions the liturgical actions and gestures elicited when publicly performed. In order to access fragments of what was envisioned in the socially shared Byzantine imagination, this study turns to the miniatures of the so-called marginal Psalters of the ninth and the eleventh centuries.[24] These images were the first to illustrate the very passages sung in the cathedral liturgy as *koinōnika* (Communion verses), *allēlouïai* (the singing of praise), or *prokeimena* (psalm verses sung as an introduction to the scriptural readings, similar to the gradual in the Latin West).[25] Since the miniatures bear a clear link to the liturgy, they give access to the visions that these texts elicited in their elite audience.

My analysis considers many textual passages that discuss the space in Hagia Sophia and its liturgy and imply a high level of learning in their writers, but in all cases a reconstruction of the full experience from them is not possible. As such, this inquiry can offer only a variety of hypotheses based on the extant record. But the analysis also pushes in new directions to expand beyond the limits of the written record. Acoustic measurements and digital reconstructions of some of the music performed in Hagia Sophia serve the imagination in reconstructing the sensual impact of this space, taking "experience" beyond the language and text of the learned elite. As a result, this book integrates five areas of exploration: (1) the material fabric of Hagia Sophia, (2) the written stage directions of the liturgy, (3) the musical design of some of the chants, (4) the visualization accessible through the miniatures of the marginal Psalters, and (5) digital reconstructions of the performance of chant in the Great Church.

Phenomenology

In combining traditional textual and visual analysis with digital audial examination, this book uncovers two operative dynamics through which sacred space emerges in Hagia Sophia: inspiriting (*empsychōsis*) and mirroring (*esoptron*). Both are produced by participation in the liturgy. Inspiriting marks the descent of the Spirit into matter, activated by an invocation spoken by the patriarch (or an officiating priest). This pneumatic descent in turn engenders the figural dynamic of the horizontal mirror, which causes the celestial to enter the visual realm of the terrestrial and become a reflection in a material surface. The mirror is identified here not as an object or a metaphor but as a visual and sonic phenomenon for structuring a religious and poetic mode of being. Hagia Sophia abounds visually and acoustically in mirroring structures. Optically, they emerge in the book-matched marble plaques and the reflected light from the gold mosaics. Sonically, they are reified in the reverberant acoustics of the resonant interior, in the chiastic form of the psalms intoned during services, and in the reflexivity of the iterative root *marmar-* in the Greek words for marble (*marmaron*) and glitter (*marmarygma*).[26]

By focusing on the ephemeral and immaterial such as reflection, reverberation, and breath, this analysis charts a new poetics of viewership and experience in Byzantium. Semiotics cannot fully explain the spatial and temporal dynamics underlying the sensual phenomenon of divine nearness. Therefore, this study proposes a new method that draws on both Heideggerian philosophy and sensory archaeology.[27] Heidegger's essay "The Thing" offers a platform for understanding the interaction between matter and Spirit, which emerges through mirroring. Heidegger's earthen jug filled with water or wine presents the conditions that can ingather the celestial in the liquid's reflective surface. Mirroring as a spatial phenomenon creates a sensory nearness of the divine that is visual but not tactile. The immaterial reflection of the sky dissolves as easily as it comes into existence when the wind riffles the liquid's surface. The ephemerality of reflection attests to the ineffability of gathering earth, water, and air and of rendering the celestial present in the terrestrial. "[The Thing] is the presencing of nearness," writes Heidegger. "Thinging gathers. Appropriating the fourfold, it gathers the fourfold's stay, its while, into something that stays for a while."[28] Nearness and ingathering are immaterial, ephemeral; they emerge as modes of appearing in the visual; they are not essences.

In the Heideggerian model, materiality offers the foil against which the metaphysical can leave a fleeting trace in the sensorial. Heidegger does not use the word "spirit," but his concept of "divine nearness" captures its sense. Nearness of the celestial in the terrestrial emerges in what is fleeting, phenomenal, and ungraspable—the reflection on a liquid's surface. It is this phenomenological manifestation of Spirit in matter that underscores this book's engagement with materiality. As such, this study expands the platform of semiotics, with its current focus on material signs, into the realm of phenomenology and spirituality.

Historians and philologists have led this neomaterialist turn in the humanities,[29] and art historians of the Middle Ages have reclaimed ground for the primacy of their field in engaging questions of materiality.[30] But while this research has demonstrated the rich variety of symbolism invested in materials, it has yet to recognize the performance of what I call "material flux," such as glitter, shadow, reverberation, and scent—phenomena produced in and through matter but remaining ungraspable and ineffable. It is here, in the material flux, that Byzantium offers a corrective to the limits of the semiotics of materiality and elevates phenomenology in defining the aesthetic of the spiritual. I make the case that current material studies, in their engagement with materiality in general and Heidegger's essay "The Thing" in particular, fail to recognize that medieval materiality is not an end in and of itself but just a medium through which Spirit becomes manifest in the sensorial. In recognizing matter as a medium of the metaphysical, the phenomenological approach of my project remedies that failing.

Phenomenology focuses the attention on the object's mode of appearing, not on its essence.[31] Since Byzantine art itself invests animation into material flux—identified here as a series of changing appearances unfolding in time—the kinesthetic aspect of the medieval artwork and space demands a phenomenological analytical model that draws on aesthetic considerations in order to render its temporality apparent. My earlier book *The Sensual Icon* has shaped the analytical framework of the current project. Focusing on the synergy of ambience, object, and subject, this previous work explores how changing appearances, caused by shifting environmental conditions, produced in the viewing subject the perception of liveliness in the artwork. The current study of Hagia Sophia takes the model of animation in the Byzantine image and applies it to the Byzantine architectural space.

Focusing attention on the phenomena of glitter and reverberation, this book uncovers the transient presence of the metaphysical in the material and temporal. The material flux foregrounds realms of contiguity, which dissolve the separation of subject and object, leading to an intertwining and transcendence. This phenomenon is captured in Merleau-Ponty's concept of chiasm: "A human body is present when, between the see-er and the visible, between touching and touched, between one eye and the other, between hand and hand a kind of crossover occurs."[32] Merleau-Ponty's revelation of flesh and the sensorial establishes the connectivity of body and world. It is on the surface, I contend, that Byzantine inspiriting occurs, transforming matter into a vibrant flux. What Merleau-Ponty perceives further as a chiastic reflexivity and reversal between self and world, expressed in the paintings of Matisse and Cézanne, among other artists, is the interchange of visible and invisible worlds: the hand of the artist restores to visibility the original invisible impact of the world on visual perception.

If chiasm in Merleau-Ponty's conceptualization is identified with artistic activity and creativity, in the Byzantine model it is the participant in the ritual who generates this restoration of the metaphysical in the sensorial and thus embodies the chiasm. This process is accomplished through the mouth, more specifically through speech, chant, and consumption of the Eucharist. One Greek term designates both the Holy Spirit and the generic breath—*pneuma*. In what follows, I capitalize "Pneuma" to denote the Holy Spirit; in all other instances the term refers to breath. It is divine Pneuma that inspired Adam (Gen. 1:26–28 and 2:7), transforming him into an "image of God." The Eucharist engenders a similar process. As the Spirit descends over the gifts at the altar and begins its indwelling in matter, the inert transforms into the body and blood of Christ. It thus restores to visibility the original impact of the divine in the world. The Eucharist produces presence that functions beyond representational iconicity. In consuming the gifts, the faithful become "inspired" and return to a state of being "an image of God." I designate this nonrepresentational image performative. It is a product of the mouth and breath. In appearing and perduring, however briefly, it allows humanity to partake in the divine.

Sound

The focus on pneuma has led this study to transcend the visible and enter the realm of chant and architectural aurality. The sonic aspect of the Byzantine "image of God" and its performative nonrepresentational character have not been recognized and explored in scholarship. This book not only turns attention to what is overlooked but also situates this sonic iconicity in space. The vast interior volume and reflective materials of Hagia Sophia produce reverberant acoustics, enabling a single note exhaled in space to last more than ten seconds. This resonant chamber dissolves the intelligibility of speech but enhances melismatic chant.[33] The aurality of Hagia Sophia presents alternative, nontextual evidence that can expand our access to the Byzantine "experience" of sacred space.

In pursuing this course, the present study turns to sensory archaeology, which aims to reconstruct, by means of digital media, some of the original conditions influencing interactions between subject, object, and space.[34] In this particular study the attention focuses on the fleeting visual and aural phenomena inside Hagia Sophia. *The Sensual Icon* implemented this method in exploring the optical manifestation of inspiriting in the Byzantine relief icon. The short video I produced to accompany that volume shows how moving candlelight causes phenomenal shadows to give the impression of movement in the eyes of an iconic archangel's face.[35] For Hagia Sophia I have worked collaboratively with engineers to reconstruct digitally the acoustics of the Great Church and have used this acoustic model in a video that traces the changing manifestations of marble and gold mosaic in the interior at dusk and dawn. The film is a phenomenological exploration; it reveals how solid marble and gold mosaic start to resemble molten metal and how this liquidity of appearance, which I call "liquescent aesthetic," finds an aural correlate in the reverberant, or "wet," acoustics of the Great Church.[36]

Through its focus on sound, this book draws attention to the paradoxical phenomenon of the void—the airy interior—which acquires an aural materiality as the sonic energy exhaled in chant continues to reflect and propagate (see the frontispiece). This aggregation and decay of sound is called reverberation. Hagia Sophia's vast marble-revetted interior quickly mixes the reflected sound energy, especially at the wavelengths in the range of the human voice. It stays full and well mixed for a reverberation time upwards of ten seconds. The dome and semidomes contribute to the production of an enveloping sound as they redirect and scatter the sound energy. They also stir the sensation of multiple waterfalls staggered at different times and places as the sounds reach the listener. While listening to sound under the dome is more uniform, further away from the dome the complexity of these staggered waterfalls increases.[37] This book explores how these acoustic and visual phenomena of brightness and liquescence engender the experience of divine presence. With reference to the acoustic phenomena, the term "aural architecture," which concerns the properties of a building that pertain to the ear, appears frequently.[38]

In Hagia Sophia, the aurality of the interior has undergone many changes throughout the ages. The building's original interior furnishings are gone, as are the state-sponsored choirs who sang during the liturgy. The building has lost its voice. Today it is a museum, where no vocal performance is allowed. This is the reason the current project has turned to new media to seek alternative ways to experience Hagia Sophia's aural architecture. Toward that end, Jonathan Abel, electrical engineer at Stanford University's Center for Computer Research in Music and Acoustics, and I have developed the project Icons of Sound.

Established in 2008, Icons of Sound has helped define a new integrated study of acoustics, architecture, and aesthetics in Byzantium. It uses digital technology to imprint the resonant acoustics of Hagia Sophia on recorded or live performances of Byzantine chant.[39] This process of rendering audio data by digital means in order to recreate the aural experience of a particular space is called auralization. The method employed here, using an algorithm to imprint Hagia Sophia's acoustic signature on a live or recorded sound, is called convolution.[40] Since 2014 UCLA and USC have pursued an acoustic project, focusing on Byzantine Thessaloniki, led by Sharon Gerstel and Chris Kyriakakis. The UCLA/USC team, just like the Stanford group, includes acousticians, architectural historians, art historians, and musicologists. The Stanford and the UCLA/USC projects are closely linked and offer a lot of potential for the future of Byzantine studies and, more specifically, the soundscapes of Byzantium.[41]

These auralizations are not a reconstruction of the sixth-century liturgy, however. The model that digital technology offers of the sound of voice unaccompanied by musical instruments in the Great Church is based only on the current physical conditions of the building. It therefore misses the effects that curtains, liturgical furnishings, and many bodies in this space would have had in the medieval period, dampening some of the reverberation.[42] Just as the architectural historian records and studies the material remains of a building to propose a reconstruction, the acoustician approaches the extant material fabric in order to offer an acoustic model. The value of these auralizations is to give modern audiences an opportunity to hear baseline acoustics for a space and to help them recognize the contrast between the resonant aural architecture of the medieval "concert hall" and the much "drier" acoustics (with shorter reverberation time) of performance spaces today.

In merging humanist exploration with digital technology and acoustics, this book follows Deborah Howard and Laura Moretti's *Sound and Space in Renaissance Venice: a pioneering study of aural architecture and polyphony in Counter-Reformation Venice.*[43] Inspired by this model, the analysis here draws on acoustic measurements and auralizations. At the same time, I do not let the digital become an end in itself. I employ auralizations in conjunction with textual and visual evidence in order to marshal a thesis that is historically grounded and sheds light on the cultural circumscription and aesthetic experience of image and sound in the Great Church. Auralizations, however, open a new domain of exploration: that of the phenomenology of sound. The focus is on the prosody of the Constantinopolitan cathedral singing, but I also consider the role played by the intercalation of aspiratory, nonsemantic sounds in creating the sensorial experience of a space in between heaven and earth: the *metaxu*. Contemporary discourse in musicology has advocated for the importance of sensual experience in the perception of art and the need for moments of release from questions about intentionality and meaning.[44] This study approaches the nonsemantic intercalation in the cathedral chant as an aural manifestation of such a release from the register of human speech, pushing beyond the borders of the rational.

Since the turn of the century, sound studies have emerged as an interdisciplinary domain, outside strictly musicological research.[45] As the communications scholar Jonathan Sterne observes, sound studies are based on the premise that there is no set epistemology and method and that there are many competing systems of knowledge of what constitutes sound.[46] This is the approach taken by the current project.

Interest in the spatial aspect of sound may be traced to the origins of the term "soundscape." Introduced by the musician R. Murray Schafer, the term originally signified a sonic ecology. Taking the study of sound outside the domain of music, Schafer placed it into the larger realm of aurality: sounds of nature, of animals, of humans, and of machines. According to him, music and noise together establish a field of interaction that constitutes a soundscape.[47] His analysis draws on a variety of fields, including acoustics, architecture, musicology, and psychology. But his primary concern is with sonic ecology, especially with how to reduce noise pollution and to counteract the increasing human insensitivity to the disappearing diversity in the sounds of nature.[48]

Emily Thompson has expanded Murray Schafer's original definition of soundscape as an acoustics environment, arguing that, just like landscape, soundscape is produced by the interaction of multiple societal forces. She argues that the twentieth-century rise of the science of acoustics had effects on the development of sound technologies and architectural design, which ultimately led to changes in the culture of listening and to the privileging of dry sound.[49]

The musicologist Alexander Lingas has brought the concept of "soundscape" to the study of Byzantium. He applies it, in more strictly musicological terms, to the exploration of the chant in Constantinople and Jerusalem. Lingas explains how the idiosyncratic character of cathedral chant was used to broadcast each city's identity and thus to territorialize and to establish its soundscape of authority.[50] In the process, Lingas has shown that the complex relationship between Constantinople and Jerusalem is reflected in the development of their music, ranging from synergy to antagonism.[51]

Taking Lingas's conclusions, this project explores further how the architecture, acoustics, and liturgy of Hagia Sophia plastically articulated a particular sensual encounter with the divine. Using the concept of soundscape and drawing on art history, musicology, liturgy, and acoustics, it uncovers an underlying aesthetic system in which the visual and the sonic phenomena in Hagia Sophia such as glitter, shadow, and reverberation produce the experience of being inspirited with divine Pneuma and thus transformed into an image of God. This sustained engagement with acoustics and Byzantine chant brings to art history concepts of image and animation in Byzantium that function outside the domain of pictorial naturalism; these icons of sound are products of the architectural aurality stirred by chant.

Sterne's work on artificial reverberation connects directly with the goals of this engagement.[52] Artificial reverberation is the process of recreating by physical or mathematical modeling the acoustic signature of a space and then imprinting it on prerecorded or live sound. Sterne calls this acoustic signature a "detachable echo" and recognizes that reattaching it to any sound introduces the possibility of manipulating the experience of space and producing the effect of plurispatiality. Sterne's ideas relate directly to the use Icons of Sound has made of digital technology, more specifically, auralization to imprint the "detached echo" of Hagia Sophia on a live performance of Cappella Romana.[53] Through this process contemporary audiences have been immersed in the reverberant sound field of the current acoustic environment of the Great Church. The aesthetic act invested in this modern performance allows current audiences sensually to encounter aspects of the distant past and thus develop empathy for what is irretrievably lost.

But what makes Sterne's analysis of artificial reverberation even more significant for the current project is that he draws attention to the spatial dimension of sound. Sound studies have opened this alternative way of analyzing sound through space, rather than through the traditional value of time. This transformation of thinking about sound through space has a reciprocal potential to reshape visual studies, introducing the dimension of temporality to the study of the image. This book pursues this chiastic engagement of sound through space and image through time. I argue that Byzantine chant structures sacred space, allowing the Byzantine image, or *eikōn*, to unfold in a temporal performance.

Chapters

The present book consists of seven chapters. The first one, "*Sophia* and *Choros:* The Making of Sacred Space in Byzantium," explores how the Justinianic Hagia Sophia gives a plastic articulation of Christianized Neoplatonic ideas about divine wisdom (*sophia*) as sacred space. While previous scholarship has focused on the optical dimension of *sophia,* this study uncovers its sonic aspect. In showing synergy between the spatial and aural, the chapter exemplifies sound studies' shift in analyzing sound through space. At the same time, the chapter does not lose sight of the visual material; it gathers a series of Middle Byzantine miniatures that have never heretofore been recognized as carrying traces of *choros* and *sophia.* They use multiplanarity (the layering of different viewing perspectives in an otherwise flat, two-dimensional pictorial surface) in order to express how chant produces sacred space and how the liturgical performance allows for the paradoxical commingling of time and eternity, mortal and divine.

Although *sophia* expresses the incarnation of Christ, this moment of Spirit's entering flesh (*sarkōsis*) is first ritually enacted in the inspiriting of the altar at the consecration rites. The second chapter, entitled "Inspiriting in the Byzantine Consecration (*Kathierōsis*) Rite," thus focuses on the dynamic of this process by drawing on the evidence of the late eighth-century Vatican City manuscript Barberini gr. 336. While the analysis relies on the comparative studies of the liturgists Michael Findikyan, Vincenzo Ruggieri, and Vitalijs Permjakovs, it shifts the research emphasis from the origin of the rite to how it engenders animation and how this inspiriting is sensorially imprinted in the space and time of the participants. By bringing in Psalter miniatures that illustrate passages performed in the liturgy, this chapter explores further what images are brought to consciousness in a Byzantine audience when these words are performed. The analysis focuses in particular on the mid-ninth-century marginal Psalters that bear evidence of the cathedral liturgy of Hagia Sophia.[54] By including their eleventh-century copies, such as the Theodore Psalter, this study shows the stability of the pictorial associations articulated by the cathedral liturgy.

The consecration of the altar ensures the continual incarnation of the divine in the liturgical ritual and, more specifically, in the Eucharist. This embodiment of Spirit, I argue, has an aural manifestation in the expelling of breath in chant and in the reflection of this sonic energy by the acoustics of the space. The elaborate *allēlouïa* refrains chanted in the cathedral liturgy use melismas and intercalations of nonsemantic syllables as devices to break free from the register of human speech and produce this mixing of human and divine voices.

Chapter 3, "Icons of Breath," turns to a study of the processes by which mirroring and inspiriting define a mode of iconicity in Byzantium that functions outside representation and pictorial mimesis. The image formed by these processes is what I call "the performative icon." Scripture and apostolic and patristic writings attest to the development of this concept in the Late Antique period. The stylite saints (named for *stylos,* "column," on top of which each of these holy men spent his life) offer further examples of the performative icon. Their bodies, like newly consecrated church buildings, become spaces for the continuous process of inspiriting. Pneuma indwells and overshadows them, enabling them to heal by exhaling this vivifying Spirit on the faithful. The chapter then uncovers the ways in which this performative iconicity, produced through an action of the mouth and breath, relate to chant and more specifically to the aspiratory nonsemantic syllables intercalated in the Communion verses (*koinōnika*) of the cathedral office.

The first three chapters introduce examples of the cathedral chant and explore the melodic structure of these pieces and their aural effect when sung in the resonant interior of Hagia Sophia. In order to ground this analysis of music in the particular material fabric of the building, the fourth chapter, "Aural Architecture," addresses the acoustics of the Great Church and explains the role of digital technology employed by Stanford's project Icons of Sound. The study of how space imprints itself on sound focuses the discourse on the aural aspect of the ritual and leads to questions about soundscape, especially how Byzantine culture responded to resonant interiors.

These aural aspects of the celestial, emerging from water metaphors and resonant acoustics, are then channeled back to the realm of the visual and material in chapter 5, "Material Flux: Marble, Water, and Chant." The analysis here focuses on the image of moving waters evoked by the wave pattern of veins in the book-matched marble floors. The chapter considers how the medieval epistemology of marble as petrified water responds to the phenomenology of vibrant matter and to the prophetic visions of divinity. The analysis explores further how the concept of animation, invested in the liquescent aesthetic of the material flux, finds an expression in the ekphrasis of Hagia Sophia written by Paul the Silentiary.

Chapter 6, "The Horizontal Mirror and the Poetics of the Imaginary," returns to the *esoptron* phenomenon and focuses on how it ingathers the real and the imagined, allowing the metaphysical to dwell in the sensorial. The analysis uncovers the sonic manifestation of this mirroring process expressed in the way the angelic voices of the Trisagion appear as melodic fragments in the Cheroubikon. Drawing on primary textual sources, the chapter shows a Late Antique shared cultural understanding that the singing of psalmody produces an immaterial acoustic mirror in which the faithful can see themselves and adjust their image to return to being *eikones tou Theou*. These sonic *esoptra* work synaesthetically with the liturgical ritual, as when the mirroring surfaces of the vessels of the Eucharist ingather the visage of the faithful with the metamorphic substance of the gifts. These mirroring phenomena—performative, nonmimetic, and nondiscursive—respond, I argue, to the nonnarrative and aniconic character of Justinian's monumental mosaic program inside the Great Church. The *esoptron* performances inside this aniconic interior thus draw attention to the poetics of the imaginary. These poetics emerge in a compelling way in the sung sermon, or *kontakion,* of the Justinianic age. The chapter ends with an analysis of the mirroring dynamics in Romanos Melodos's *kontakion* on the Prodigal Son, which, by recalling the liturgical ritual in Hagia Sophia, specifically the Eucharist, trains the faithful to mirror the characters of the liturgical drama. The singing of the *kontakion* thus offers another example of the performative iconicity elicited by the liturgical ritual.

Chapter 7, "Empathy and the Making of Art in Byzantium," reads the forms and modalities of paganizing literature into the aesthetic sensibility of Hagia Sophia and the Justinianic age as a whole. The analysis uncovers the resonances between the ekphrasis of Paul the Silentiary and the Late Antique sympotic Anacreontics. Mirroring and inspiriting emerge as the dynamics through which divine presence is established in the poetics of both Holy Pneuma and Zephyr. Yet, despite a shared poetic empathy between

Christian ekphrasis and the paganizing literature of Anacreontea, this artistic impulse does not translate into the visual programs, confirming this Byzantine tendency to privilege the performative over the mimetic *eikōn*. To show the significance of this selective empathetic response, the analysis turns to the Italian Renaissance, whose poets discover and emulate the pagan erotic and sympotic literature and whose artists concordantly build an equally expressive visual tradition, drawing inspiration from the ancient figural models. The chapter ends with a question about the role of empathy in bringing past forms to life, engaging with Aby Warburg's concept of *Pathosformel.*

The conclusion considers the main themes of the book and addresses the implications of the nonrepresentational iconicity for a modern understanding of animation in medieval art. Equally important in this discussion is the sonic dimension of architecture and the role modern technology and performance can play in establishing new ways of thinking about cultural heritage and historic preservation.

Glitter, shadow, and reverberation—these passing phenomena restore the metaphysical to the sensorially perceptible. In bringing attention to these fleeting traces of Spirit in matter through both traditional visual and textual analysis as well as the medium of film and digital auralization, this study draws attention to the overlooked: animation that functions beyond representational mimesis. Opening with the phenomenon of sacred space and consecration rites, this book proceeds to trace the continual imprinting of Pneuma in matter across the sensorium: an *empsychōsis* that transforms bodies and buildings into *eikones tou Theou.*

1.

Sophia and Choros

THE MAKING OF SACRED SPACE IN BYZANTIUM

The concept of sacred space in Hagia Sophia, invested in the Greek terms *sophia* (wisdom) and *choros* (dance, chant, choir, choral movement, circular motility, and choir/dance floor), is expressed in three ways: plastically, in the architecture of Hagia Sophia; textually, in the anonymous *enkaineia* (inauguration) *kontakion* and the ekphraseis of Procopius and Paul the Silentiary; and visually, in a series of Middle Byzantine miniatures. My reading identifies a Byzantine concept of sacred space, showing that *chōra*, *pace* Nicoletta Isar, is not embraced as a term in Byzantine theology. Yet many of Isar's insightful conclusions about the Byzantine perception of sacred space as simultaneously a movement and changing perceptual phenomena hold as long as *sophia* and *choros* are brought in as two of several cultural terms naming these phenomena.

Studies on the sacred have insisted on the role of place in producing the *hieros* (sacred), viewing sacrality as emplacement.[1] By contrast, I insist on the *hieros* as a process of becoming, identified with space rather than place. It is the liturgy that brings about the sacred in Hagia Sophia, especially since the site is not inherently sacred; the church was not originally linked to illustrious saintly relics.[2] Hagia Sophia thus differs from the pilgrimage churches of Rome, with their focus on relics, and from the sanctuaries in the Holy Land, with their possession of the Cross and the sanctity of the soil trodden by Christ.[3] In other words, the sacred in Hagia Sophia cannot simply be defined by the church as place, for it is linked to the ephemeral phenomena occurring in the interior, such as the movement of natural light, the sway of the circular *choros* formation of *polykandēlia* suspended on chains from the rim of the dome, and the reverberant sound of chant enveloping the space under the dome, called *kallichoros* (see the frontispiece).

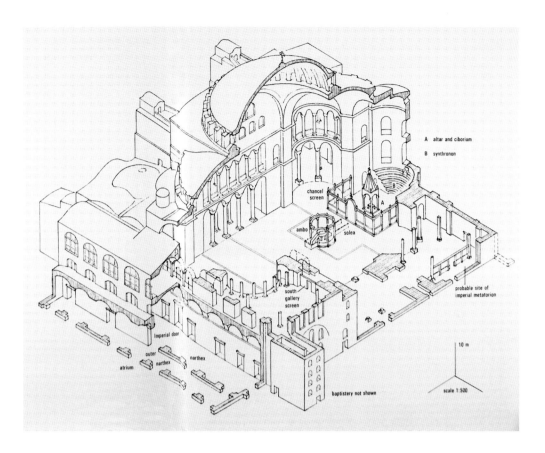

A altar and ciborium

B synthronon

chancel
screen

ambo   solea

south
gallery
screen

probable site of
imperial metatorion

Imperial door

outer
atrium   narthex   narthex

10 m

baptistery not shown   scale 1:500

FIG. 5

Hagia Sophia, 537, axonometric drawing of the interior. From
Rowland J. Mainstone, *Hagia Sophia: Architecture, Structure,
and Liturgy of Justinian's Great Church* (London: Thames &
Hudson, 1988), fig. 252.

The production of sacred space in the Great Church is anchored in two centers: (1) the altar, where the Eucharist is performed, and (2) the ambo, the platform in the space under the dome, where the chanting is performed (figs. 5–6). The ambo is the focus of this chapter, while the consecration of the altar is explored in the next. The Byzantines called the open area under the dome *kallichoros,* or "beautiful *choros.*"[4] The Justinianic building made the *kallichoros* prominent in the way the cupola drew attention to the luminous void above and its golden-clad heavens (figs. 2–3). Although light has been the focus of numerous studies, the sonic aspect of this void and its relation to sacred space have not been explored heretofore.[5] I argue that the *kallichoros* honed a perception of the *hieros* not only as light but as sound, expressed in the synergy of chant and reverberant acoustics. Traces of this sonic experience of *sophia* and *choros* are preserved in a series of Middle Byzantine miniatures.

Rather than insist on the sanctity of the building and identify this concept with the concrete structure and its architecture, an approach taken by Robert Ousterhout in his engagement with Hagia Sophia,[6] I argue that the *hieros* is space, which cannot be solely

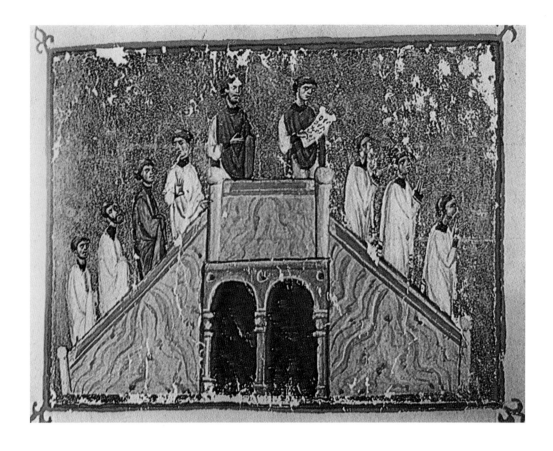

FIG. 6

Mt. Athos, Dionysiou, MS gr. 587, eleventh century, fol. 43r, showing the ambo with soloist and choir. From Neil Moran, *Singers in Late Byzantine and Slavonic Painting* (Leiden: Brill, 1986), plate I.

identified with the container/material fabric of the Great Church but should include the elusive void, or *kallichoros,* it shapes and its capacity to ingather optical and sonic energy. What is important here is not so much the materiality of the container and its semiotics as the phenomena—reflection and reverberation—that are instrumentalized by this materiality.

The *kallichoros* can be identified as a Heideggerian "thing" that creates a sensorial field in which the metaphysical can be experienced in the phenomenal. In Heidegger's essay "The Thing," the focus is not the clay of the jug or its semiotics, as neomaterialist studies may claim, but on how the "thing" mediates the appearance of the metaphysical in the sensorial. In his particular example, the jug containing wine or water ingathers the celestial in the ephemeral reflection of the sky on the surface of the liquid. By ingathering the celestial and terrestrial, divine and mortal, it brings the fourfold into the phenomenal onefold as a reflection. It is this spiritual aspect of Heidegger's essay that has escaped the attention of neomaterialist studies.[7]

As this chapter reveals, the sacred space in Hagia Sophia emerges in the *kallichoros* through horizontal mirroring. The mirror, identifying the concept of *sophia,* is called in Greek *esoptron* or *katoptron*. It creates two views: looking up, *enōpion,* and looking down, *katōpion.* Drawing on a series of Middle Byzantine miniatures that heretofore have not been explored in terms of choral movement, I argue that these images employ a multiplanar mode in order to show the ordered movement of renewal, or *choros,* through which *sophia* enters the physical space of experience. The miniatures visualize these spiritual dynamics by showing the simultaneity of views from above (*katōpion*) and from below (*enōpion*). Although the first meaning of *enōpion* is "facing, to the front," to see and look at God frontally, or face to face, in a space like Hagia Sophia means as much following the horizontal axis toward the altar as following the vertical axis toward the dome. Staying with the vertical axis, *enōpion* designates the heavenward gaze toward the golden cupola. The Pantheon offers another cogent example of the same visual dynamic; its oculus directs mortals' gaze skyward, a frontality before the gods, manifested in the craned necks and upturned faces of the worshippers.

Chōra Is Not a Byzantine Theological Term

Nicoletta Isar has revitalized the Byzantine concept of sacred space in her numerous studies on *chōra.*[8] Her major contribution is in revealing the synergy between building and performer in the creation of sacred space:

> Thus, in a space of liturgical experience, the movement performed [*choros*], the faithful him/herself, and the sacred space [*chōra* or *chōros*] thus created were intimately bound together and impossible to be conceived as detached, independent, and abstract entities or concepts. The final outcome of such experience was a living space of presence and participation into the divine, a personified space, identical and continuous with the self (*persona*) and with the divine—an event, one may say, of the ontological continuity between being and becoming.[9]

In this beautiful summary, Isar recognizes how sacred space is produced by the interaction of the faithful and the material container in which ritual unfolds. Sacred space has no audience; all are performers. The energy produced by the participants and reflected by the material structure simultaneously brings into being the *hieros.* Isar correctly defines this generative dynamic as *choros,* and this dance or choral movement has a long tradition in both pagan and Christian philosophies of renewal and partaking in the divine.[10]

Yet Isar transforms the word *chōra,* as well as its cognate *chōros,* into a reified theological term designating sacred space. No such reading finds confirmation in the patristic writers, in the mystagogies of Pseudo-Dionysius, Maximus the Confessor, and Patriarch Germanus, or in the ekphraseis of Procopius and Paul the Silentiary: the main figures whose writings shed light on the spiritual operations of Hagia Sophia.[11] It is not surprising that such a meaning of *chōra* as a sacred space, manifesting itself in movement, does not feature in the entries of the Greek dictionaries compiled by Liddell and Scott, Lampe, and Chantraine.[12]

Plato's *Timaeus* is the main source for Isar's *chōra* as space and movement.[13] In *Timaeus* 52a–53a Plato defines *chōra* as the receptacle of creation, receiving all things that have birth; *chōra* is moved by and moves them. Its *kinēsis* is compared to that of winnowing, a shaking through which grain is separated from chaff. It is the movement of *chōra* that has allowed John Sallis and Isar to connect the noun to the verb, and thus to identify *chōra* with the action of *chōreō*.[14]

Yet *chōra* is not picked up either in Christian theological discourse or among the Neoplatonists; it offers a model, but not a name, for the concept of the vessel, or *hypodochē*, that instrumentalizes the theurgic process.[15] In Iamblichus (ca. 250–325), deification is perceived as a process of becoming a vessel for the divine: "He who propitiates all these [divine] powers and offers to each gifts that are pleasing and as similar to them as possible will remain secure and free from error since he has completed, perfect and whole, the receptacle [*hypodochē*] of the divine choir [*choros*]."[16] The word χώρα also does not develop as a technical term in Neoplatonic discourse, yet the verb *chōreō* plays an important role in the theurgic vision of achieving divinization, becoming a vessel (*hypodochē*) of the divine.[17]

Although *chōra* as a term does not appear in Platonic discourse beyond the *Timaeus,* its traces persist in other terms—*sophia* and *choros*—identifying respectively the movement-producing renewal and the incarnate Logos (*sophia*) and the choir/ chant and the circling motion (*choros*); both words are textually attested as theological terms in Byzantine sources. Further aspects of the Platonic *chōra* are manifest in the dream spaces created by the reverberant acoustics that cancel the register of human speech and in the pleasure-filled world of love and drink of the Anacreontea, which transcends the symposiac setting and resurfaces in the sensual imagery of Paul the Silentiary's ekphrasis of the Great Church.

Movement in the *Kallichoros*

While Isar's *chōra* is not a Byzantine theological term, many of her insights about the operation of sacred space still hold, because the word *chōra* and its cognate *chōros* are used by Procopius and Paul the Silentiary to designate the area of the dome as well as the ambo, and these writers see in the spaces shaped by these two architectural structures a vital, energy-producing movement.[18] Isar argues that space and movement are interconnected, producing the sacred through a complex *kinēsis*.[19] The ekphraseis of Procopius and Paul the Silentiary both render the central space under Hagia Sophia's dome as endowed with such a special motility (see figs. 2–3), but they do not express this concept with the word *chōra* or *chōros*.[20] Procopius describes the *kallichoros* as follows: "And whenever anyone enters this church to pray, he understands at once that it is not by any human power or skill, but by the influence of God, that this work has been so finely turned (*apotetorneutai*). And so his mind is lifted up toward (*epairomenos aerobatei*) God and exalted, feeling that He cannot be far away, but must especially love to dwell (*emphilochōrein*) in this place, which He has chosen."[21] The passage starts with the faithful, who upon entering the church are in awe and perceive how this structure could not have been produced by human power and skill but has been shaped by divine force descending to earth. The word *ropē*—meaning "fall of the scale pan," "weight," and, by extension, "influence"—captures this pull of gravity, rendering the descent of the divine to earth. The building is then described as being sculpted as if on the potter's wheel, *apotetorneutai*, from *torneuō*, "to turn." It carries in its shape the trace of a whirling, circular motility that has brought into being two new energies: a human ascent, or *anabasis*, propelled by the centripetal movement and expressed in the way the mind travels upward toward the luminous dome (*epairomenos aerobatei*), and simultaneously a *katabasis*, indicated by a vector descending from heaven to earth as divinity has gladly chosen to dwell (*emphilochōrein*) among humans.

Paul's ekphrasis of the dome further reveals this interconnection between space and movement. He perceives the dome as imbued with energy that shapes the air and produces a complex motility: "A helmet rising above into the boundless air / spins [*elissetai*] it from both sides into a sphere; / radiant as the heavens, it bestrides the roof of the church."[22] Paul's ekphrasis describes how the radiant helmet-dome has created a whirling motion, from the verb *elissomai*, "to whirl in a dance," which shapes the air into a luminous sphere. It is significant that both Procopius and Paul the Silentiary write about the architectural form of the dome and the empty space it encompasses as permeated with a whirling dynamic, yet both writers use neither *chōra* nor *chōreō* to describe this *kinēsis*; even *choros* does not feature here. Instead, the verbs associated with this phenomenon are *apotorneuō* and *elissomai*. It is this whirling movement present in the *kallichoros* that I trace through the theological terms *sophia* and *choros*, as it pertains to human singing.

Procopius uses *choros* metaphorically to describe the colonnades lining the nave as a frozen dance.[23] When he refers to the dome, he uses the word "circle," or *kyklos*, yet *kyklos* and *stephanos* ("ring" and "crown") function as synonyms of *choros*.[24] Paul the Silentiary identifies the space under the dome as *kallichoros*.[25] He calls *choros* the overall round formation of numerous *polykandēlia*, suspended on chains from the rim of the dome.[26] Further, he uses the cognate *choreia*, which signifies dance and circling motion, to identify the vocalization of the ekphrasis, the imagined dance of the stars envisioned in the golden dome, and the hymnody.[27] Paul uses *choros* as choir only once.[28] Both Procopius and Paul the Silentiary attest that the Byzantines saw the manifestation of *choros* in the imagined circular (*kyklos*) motility of the dome and the dance of stars; in the petrification of this motion as realized by the columns of the ground-level arcades; in the circular spatial configurations formed by the *polykandēlia*; and finally in the vocalization of the ekphrasis and that of chant, performed by the elite choir.[29]

Choros as the Circular Motility That Triggers Linear and Helicoidal *Kinēsis*

The dome crowning the *kallichoros* visualizes the round shape of *choros*, a term with a long tradition in Greek culture. The *choros* denotes the circling motion of the stars,

of the Muses, of a swarm of bees, and of the human propitiation of the divinity performed as choral dance and song. It is this ordered choral movement that solicits and
has the power to bring about divine response. Thus *choros* offers the most tangible image
of unity with the divine.[30] Patristic writers received the concept from their pre-Christian
forebears and associated *choros* with the church and communal singing.[31] Similarly, the
Neoplatonists perceived *choros* as a means of achieving unity with the divine.[32] Pseudo-
Dionysius reconciles the theurgic understanding of *choros* among the Neoplatonists
with the mystagogy of the sacraments.[33] The following passage illustrates how the choral dance of the heavenly beings around the divinity at the center is transmitted and
imitated by mortals, who enact it as choral chant:

> This, so far as I know, is the first rank of heavenly beings, positioned *in a circle*
> around God [Isa. 6:2, Rev. 4:4] in immediate proximity to him. Simply and cease-
> lessly, it dances around [*perichoreousa*] an eternal knowledge of him according to
> its [the angels'] highest rank, as the angelic nature [is] ever moving. It [this highest
> rank of angels] has purely seen numerous blessed visions, has been enlightened in
> a simple and immediate quivering shimmer, and has been filled with much divine
> nourishment through one initial stream. . . . Hence theology has transmitted to
> the men of earth those hymns sung by the first rank of angels, whose gloriously
> transcendent enlightenment/clear sound is thereby made manifest. Some of these
> hymns, if one can use perceptible things, are like *the sound of many waters* [Ezek.
> 1:24, Rev. 14:2, 19:6] as they proclaim: *"Blessed be the glory of the Lord from his place"*
> [Ezek. 3:12].[34]

The beginning builds an image of a whirling dance; the first rank of celestial beings
moves in a circle (*kyklō*) around God at the center. Although the word *choros* is not
used here, the concept is manifested by its cognate, the verb *perichoreō* (from *peri-*,
"around," and *choreō-*, "to sing and dance"), and the synonym *kyklos*.[35] These heavenly
choruses receive the divine enlightenment directly and transmit it to the beings of the
lower ranks.[36] Some of these emanations, synaesthetically defined as bright light and
sound, have reached humanity in the form of hymns. Pseudo-Dionysius thus conceives
the cosmic order as moving in a choral dance around the divinity. This *choros* produces
reflections that are embodied and enacted by mortals as choral chant. Thus the human
choros, or the way mortals mirror the movement of the cosmos, comes to be identified
exclusively with singing; the modulation of breath replaces what in the ancient tradition
was both dance and song.[37]

The bright sound/light transmitted from heaven to earth forms a *katabasis*. In turn
chant constitutes an *anabasis* of sonic energy rising to the dome. An overall triple kinetic
structure emerges: whirling, linear (ascending and descending), and helicoidal. This
structure is explained further by Pseudo-Dionysius in chapter 4 of his *De divinis nominibus*, whose motility model of the *cosmos* is comparable to the complex *kinēsis* of Hagia
Sophia's *kallichoros* as described by Paul the Silentiary and Procopius.

Pseudo-Dionysius defines celestial *kinēsis* as spinning, ascending and descending, and moving in a spiral:

> The divine intelligences [*theioi noes*] are said to move as follows. First they move in a circle [*kyklikos*] while they are at one with those illuminations which, without beginning and without end, emerge from the Good and the Beautiful. Then they move in a straight line when, out of Providence, they come to offer unerring guidance to all those below them. Finally they move in a spiral [*elikoeidos*], for even while they are providing for those beneath them they continue to remain what they are and they turn unceasingly around [*perichoreuontes*] the Beautiful and the Good from which all identity comes.
>
> The soul too has movement. First it moves in a circle, that is, it turns within itself and away from what is outside and there is an inner concentration of its intellectual powers. A sort of fixed revolution causes it to return from the multiplicity of externals, to gather in upon itself and then, in this undispersed condition, to join those who are themselves in a powerful union. From there the revolution brings the soul to the Beautiful and the Good, which is beyond all things, is one and the same, and has neither beginning nor end. But whenever the soul receives, in accordance with its capacities, the enlightenment of divine knowledge and does so not by way of the mind nor in some mode arising out of its identity, but rather through discursive reasoning, in mixed and changeable activities, then it moves in a spiral fashion. And its movement is in a straight line when, instead of circling in upon its own intelligent unity (for this is the circular), it proceeds to the things around it, and is uplifted from external things, as from certain variegated [*pepoikilmenōn*] and pluralized [*peplēthysmenōn*] symbols, to the simple and united contemplations [*theōrias*].[38]

The divine intelligences simultaneously perform a tripartite movement: circular (*kyklō, kyklikōs*), linear (upward and downward: *proiasis,* related to *proodos,* "emanation"), and helicoidal (*helikoeidōs*). This celestial motility is mirrored by mortals. The soul, revolving around itself, closes into itself, performing the whirling dynamic. In this state it can receive the energy (emanations) that moves in accordance with a linear up-and-down dynamic and transmits the reflected brightness of the higher celestial orders. Finally, the soul moves spirally, desiring a union with God.[39]

The Sonic and Visual Inscription of *Choros*

Pseudo-Dionysius's mystagogical revelations of the complex motility that structures the cosmos is not just an abstract concept. This *kinēsis* finds expression in the melodic structure of the singing of several psalms. The last antiphon for Pentecost vespers— "antiphon" here signifying an elaborate performance of a psalm, introduced with a prayer and completed by a doxology—Psalm 18 (19), sung according to the tradition of the Great Church, reveals this sonic inscription of the triple motility initiated by the *choros*.[40] Being the last antiphon, it is further identified as *teleutaion*, "last," and is performed during the kneeling, or *gonyklisia,* vespers.[41] The musically notated *teleutaion* is transmitted in a single manuscript, Florence, Biblioteca Laurenziana, MS gr. Ashburnhamensis 64, fols. 258r–264v, dated to 1289 (see figs. 32–33).[42] Although this is a manuscript produced in Southern Italy, its liturgy incorporates the music of Constantinople's Great Church for all major feasts, Pentecost among them.[43] My analysis relies on Ioannis Arvanitis's transcription from the manuscript, Alexander Lingas's analysis of the melodic structure, and its performance and recording by Cappella Romana.[44]

The antiphon starts with the prayer (litany), interrupted by the foundation melody, which Lingas designates as A (see fig. 34).[45] Next comes the triple repetition of the refrain, "Alleluia," in variants B, C, D. This is then followed by the completion of the litany. The singing of the verses (*stichologia*) of Psalm 18 follows; here each half line, sung according to the musical setting A, is coupled with a variation of the refrain, following the order B, C, D, and thus completing a round structure. The *stichologia* culminates in a *doxologia* (singing praise), using the musical setting of A and intercalating it with the repeated refrains "Alleluia" set in an alternating order to the variant melodies of B, C, D.

The circularity of the structure is most evident in the combination of verse and refrain: each hemistich is chanted to A but completed with the refrain set to the melodies of B, C, or D, strictly following the order of succession. Thus each half-verse and refrain form a circlet that is strung onto a larger necklace formed by all the successive verses completed with the appropriate refrains (AB, AC, AD). The combination of A with the refrains yields a structure that is both repeating and advancing, the repetition exemplified by the A and the advancement by the successive inclusion of the refrain melodies B, C, D. At the same time, the progression of the *ritornello* from B to D shows a rise in pitch, a gradual ascent in vocal register (tessitura) to a sixth above the starting pitch.[46] As a result, the circular melodic shape is also anagogical. The tessitura conveys the sense of upward flight and soaring.[47]

During the daily liturgy, Psalm 18 (19) was sung at *orthros,* or matins, on Mondays in the narthex of Hagia Sophia; it was part of the third psalmodic unit of the morning preparation service, known as antiphon 8, comprising Psalms 18–20 (19–21) ("antiphon" here signifying a grouping of several psalms that form a unit of the "distributed" Psalter of the Constantinopolitan cathedral rite).[48] In the ferial version, Psalm 18 was chanted responsorially, with the congregation joining in with the refrain "Hear me, O Lord" (ἐπάκουσόν μου, κύριε).[49]

Yet for Pentecost vespers, Psalm 18 acquired a special ceremonial prominence. It was performed by the elite choir of the *psaltai,* singing from the ambo (figs. 5–6). The singing of the psalm was thus transposed from the narthex to the *kallichoros;* here the chant centered the attention on the space under the dome. Similarly, in the Pentecost vespers performance, the psalm's usual refrain was replaced with the melodically elaborate "Alleluia," expressive of an aural ascent in its progression in pitch from variants

B to D (see fig. 34). The performance of Psalm 18 (19) as part of the festal *teleutaion* thus sonically embodied a motility both circular and ascending, reminiscent of what Pseudo-Dionysius defines as the movement of the cosmic bodies and the soul. The melodic structure of the *teleutaion* shows how chant can aurally inscribe in the *kallichoros* under the dome the complex motility initiated by *choros*.

I further propose that aspects of this triple *kinēsis*, which structures the cosmos and finds manifestation in the melodic contour of some of the cathedral chants, is also pictorialized in Byzantine culture. A miniature on folio 63v of Cosmas Indicopleustes's *Christian Topography* depicts the circular and linear progressions (fig. 7).[50] This manuscript was produced in the ninth century, but the text and its original illustrations date back to the sixth. The Middle Byzantine manuscript appears to follow this original closely, providing access to the sixth-century pictorial vision of Cosmas's treatise. The image illustrates David as the inspired writer of the Psalms and the organizer of the singing of psalmody by the human choirs.[51] He occupies the center of the miniature. Above him, the prophet Samuel emerges in a medallion; he conveys a visual reference to the act of anointing, by means of which David becomes inspirited and thus "moved" (*kinoumenos*) to compose the Psalms.[52] Two dancing figures appear below David. Identified as *orchēsis*, or "dance," they embody the process of being moved by divine force. The vertical alignment thus shows how the inspired prophet produces the poetry to be performed/danced in praise of God. The image presents a vertical axis of *katabasis* that inspirits, leading to the incarnation of Pneuma in David and its further embodiment and performance in the human dance, or *orchēsis*. Since the archaic roots of *choros* are linked to dance, the image carries the imprint of this archaic tradition and thus further supports the hypothesis about the sixth-century date of the original composition.[53]

Yet the miniature also shows how *orchēsis* as dance movement is superseded by *choros* identified as choral chant. This idea is developed in the flanks. Here the choirs appear in six rotating wheels, three on each side, vertically arranged. Each group is identified by name: "the *chōros* of Asaph," "of Idithoum," "of the sons of Kore" (two), "of Aitham the Israelite," and "of Moses the man of God."[54] The planarity of the miniature changes in the sides; no longer depicted as parallel to the picture plane, the way David is represented in the center, the choruses are seen from above, embodying the divine gaze—*katōpion*—over humanity. At the same time, the center of each circle has a disk of blue, suggestive of the heavens and thus reversing the *katōpion* view by simultaneously presenting the human gaze upward—*enōpion*—toward heaven. This conflation of the *katōpion* and *enōpion* conveys a linear movement along a vertical axis. By employing multiplanarity, each spinning wheel visualizes a whirling dynamic that triggers the linear movement along the *katōpion-enōpion* axis. The circular and the up-and-down movements form two of the three energies in the imagined motility of the *kallichoros* (as described by the sixth-century ekphraseis of Hagia Sophia) and in the *kinēsis* of the angelic choirs and the soul as defined by Pseudo-Dionysius. The miniature presents in a diagram form the mystical operations of the *kallichoros*, activated by chant and plastically expressed in the circular shape of the dome. Further, the sonic energy

FIG. 7
Vatican City, BAV, MS gr. 699, ninth century, fol. 63v, showing
the prophets David, Solomon, and Samuel and the six choirs
and a pair of dancers. Photo © 2015 Biblioteca Apostolica
Vaticana.

rising from the ambo to the dome when the elite choir sang produced a sonic pole, immaterial and invisible, centering the imagined whirling movement of the *kallichoros* and articulating the desire to connect the terrestrial with the celestial.[55]

Sophia in the *Kallichoros*

If *choros*'s circular *kinēsis* emerges concomitantly with the linear (up and down) and the spiral, the Byzantines identified the force that engenders this tripartite motility with *sophia*. They conceptualized wisdom as a dynamic energy that permeates creation, causing the creature to desire and thus to move to and receive emanation from the Creator.[56] Wisdom of Solomon 7:24 calls it "more dynamic than all movements; it pervades and moves (*chōrei*) through everything because of its purity."[57] Like a quickening force, *sophia* endows the inert with life. Aspects of this Christianized Neoplatonic understanding appear in Pseudo-Dionysius's description of the angelic choirs revolving around the Lord and receiving the linear emanations of knowledge from the center.[58]

By naming the Great Church Hagia Sophia, Constantine "placed the concept and the term 'Wisdom' at the center of the Greek Christian religious consciousness and civilization."[59] As a generative force, *sophia* identifies the Incarnation. This concept finds a direct expression in the sixth-century consecration *kontakion*, or sung sermon, written for Hagia Sophia's reinauguration (*enkaineia*) in 562.[60] Such an understanding of wisdom/*sophia* derives from Proverbs 9:1—"Wisdom built herself a temple"—a verse that has been viewed as signifying the incarnation of Christ. The *kontakion* makes this idea even more explicit in its first stanza: "for in truth the Wisdom of the Father built for herself a house of Incarnation [Prov. 9:1] and dwelt among us, above understanding: [Refrain] *Life and Resurrection of All!*"[61] The first line makes the meaning of Proverbs 9:1 translucid by defining the built house as that of the Incarnation (*sarkōsis*). Similarly, the passage presents a reciprocal for this paradoxical dwelling of the divine in the terrestrial by placing the action of living *oikodomēō* (in a building) in the here and now of a supercelestial power that is otherwise *hyper noun*, above the Divine Intellect.

The *kontakion*'s fourth stanza further elaborates the definition of *sophia* in Proverbs 9:1–5, identifying wisdom with the Eucharist and thus linking *sophia* to the altar and the liturgical reality of the Great Church:

Having assumed dwelling in flesh, [Christ] decided to come down and dwell in
    temples made by human hands [*cheiropoietos*]
through the energy of the Spirit;
binding his presence in the mystical rites,
he resides together with mortals in grace,
the one who is uncontainable [*achōrētos*] and unapproachable [*aprositos*].
And not only [this], but the one who dwells under the same roof with the heavenly [creatures] is [now dwelling] on earth,

and welcomes [mortals] as fellows to the banquet table and entertains with
the sumptuous feast of his own flesh, [a feast] which Christ set before the
faithful.
Life and Resurrection of All![62]

The *kontakion* presents the paradox of the supercelestial lowering itself to reside on
earth, expressed in the pairing of *enoikeō* (dwell) and *katoikeō* (settle). It identifies this
process with the Incarnation of Christ and with its iteration in the Eucharist through
the energies of the Holy Spirit. The Greek demonstrates this paradox in both content and form. The sentence starts with a reversal; Christ lowers himself to dwell on
earth, and only at the end of the sentence is his true supercelestial identity revealed as
"the one who is uncontainable [*achōrētos*] and unapproachable [*aprositos*]." The next
sentence connects the *sarkōsis* with the Eucharist; Christ, who shares "with the heavenly
[creatures]" the same supercelestial realm, has descended to reside on earth and has
welcomed humanity as guests to partake in the *koinōnia* of his own flesh and blood.
The *kontakion* ultimately shows how *sophia* becomes coextensive with the Incarnation
and Communion; both acquire material presence in the performance of the liturgy and
specifically at the altar.

The Radiant *Sophia* as the Spotless *Esoptron*

An Apocryphal definition of *sophia* finds a plastic embodiment in the Justinianic *kallichoros*. Wisdom of Solomon 7:26 states that "no blemish creeps into her [Wisdom], for
[she] is the radiance of ineffable light and a spotless mirror of the divine energies and
its most sacred image."[63] Wisdom as light is a major concept in Neoplatonic philosophy
and Christian mystagogy.[64] Late Antique church architecture and interior decor strive to
express this radiant *sophia*. Large expanses of window glass channel natural light abundantly; this luminosity is further reflected by the polished marbles and gold mosaics.
Numerous *polykandēlia* would bring illumination at night.[65] Yet while the production of
luminous interiors is a guiding principle in Late Antique church architecture, a domed
building, as opposed to the boxlike basilica, creates a second focus on light, in the dome.
The cupola and double-shelled structure was introduced in Christian architecture
in the mid-fourth century by Emperor Constantius II. The Golden Church of Antioch,
which no longer exists, must have offered an important precedent.[66] Justinian's Hagia
Sophia incorporates this idiom and fuses it harmoniously with the longitudinal basilica.
As a result, it formulates two competing centers: one along the horizontal axis, which
focuses attention on the altar, and a second, even more powerful, extending from the
ambo on a vertical axis toward the golden-clad dome (see figs. 2–3, 5).[67] The cupola
shapes the central void—the *kallichoros*—into a luminous sphere of air (see the frontispiece).[68] The radiant dome has a whirling form echoed in the exedrae and semidomes,
which cumulatively simulate a revolving motility (see fig. 79).[69] The coiling shapes of

FIG. 8

Mt. Athos, Pantokrator MS gr. 61, fol. 93v, whose illumination illustrates Ps. 71 (72): 1: "O God, give thy judgment to
the king, and thy righteousness to the king's son," and 6:
"He shall come down as rain upon a fleece; and as drops
falling upon the earth."

the *kallichoros* give reality to the existing anagogical explanations of Christian worship as a reflection of the perpetual angelic liturgy revolving around the Lord's throne.[70]

The way in which Wisdom of Solomon 7:26 links *sophia* to both a mirror (*esoptron*) and an icon (*eikōn*) and Hagia Sophia's *kallichoros* plastically expresses this linkage is reflected in a miniature on folio 93v of a ninth-century marginal Psalter from Mt. Athos, which depicts a golden disk that serves both as an *esoptron* and as the truest *eikōn* of God (fig. 8).[71] Both mirror and icon directly engage the definitions of *sophia* in Wisdom of Solomon 7:26. In a golden medallion icon at the top of the folio, the pre-eternal Logos is depicted in the supercelestial realm. Below is the golden disk-mirror, positioned to receive the reflection of the pre-eternal Logos. This *esoptron* can then transmit the reflection in the form of abundant streams of rays flowing toward the medallion of the Theotokos at the bottom.

The central disk attracts notice; it is larger in size, and its blinding luminosity focuses attention on its potential to transmit and to incarnate the pre-eternal *eikōn* of Christ. The viewer is drawn to the threshold of this incarnation. The miniature visualizes a potential, a process of becoming suspended in time without actually depicting the final moment. But in centering visual attention on the golden mirror, it articulates the mirror's power to ingather the metaphysical in the phenomenal.

The dome as reflective mirror embodies just such power, conceptualized as hierarchy in the writings of Pseudo-Dionysius:[72] "A hierarchy bears in itself the mark of God. Hierarchy causes its members to be images of God in all respects, to be clear and spotless mirrors reflecting the glow of primordial light and indeed of God himself. It ensures that when its members have received this full and divine splendor, they can then pass on this light generously and in accordance with God's will to beings further down the scale."[73] The celestial *choroi* reflect the Lord's light with diminishing intensity the further they are from the center. The diminution of brightness of the reflected divine light becomes expressive of the distance from the Lord down the vertical axis.

The Sonic Dimension of Sophia

The optical manifestation of *sophia* as a spotless mirror draws on the natural light reflected by the dome of the Great Church.[74] Light reflection is a capacity of the shapes and materials of the interior; the process does not involve human participation. By contrast, human action—the singer's breath expelled in chant—stirs the cupola to become an aural mirror. It is this synergy between participant and building, I argue, that distinguishes the dome's sonic *esoptron* from the optical one.[75]

Wisdom's sonic aspect is attested in the scriptural tradition but is not explored in scholarship. Proverbs 8 defines *sophia* through a series of verbs and nouns expressing the processes of vocalization and annunciation: *sophia* "hymns at the gates," "utters her voice," "opens her lips to speak"; "her throat practices the truth"; "the words of her mouth are in righteousness."[76] Wisdom thus manifests herself in the flowing word emerging as breath from the mouth. Her words allow mortals to stand *enōpion*, "in front of," God.[77]

The golden dome attracts this *enōpion* view, becoming a collector and reflector of sonic energy. Wisdom of Solomon 7:25 intertwines the optical with the sonic in calling *sophia* the "breath of God's power and the effusion of the pure glory of the Pantokrator" ("glory" [*doxa*] understood as radiance, Exod. 24:17).[78] Moreover, though passages of the *enkaineia kontakion* identify *sophia* with the Incarnation and locate it in the Eucharist, this *sarkōsis* finds a second manifest vessel in the great dome, as attested in another stanza of the poem. Here the *kontakion* projects a similar synergy of visual and acoustic energy into the dome:

> In this most sacred and most praiseworthy house
> We truly behold the eye of the whole church.
> Therefore "we shall be filled with his good things,"
> As is written, singing to God:
> "Holy indeed is thy temple, marvelous in righteousness."
> It is known to be an impression [*ektypōma*] of the liturgy of those on high.
> Here is the voice [*phōnē*] [of joyfulness] and salvation
> And the refrain-reverberation [*ēchos*] of those making festival in the Spirit,
> Which [*phōnē* and *ēchos*] God [composed] as a harmony in voices:
> *Life and Resurrection of All!*[79]

The first lines draw attention to the radiant dome, which like a sleepless eye remains always awake. Then the seal (*ektypōma*) of the Spirit is imprinted on the *kallichoros,* making it reflect the celestial liturgy.[80] The *katabasis* of the divine Pneuma, expressed through the act of sealing, is immediately interlinked with the *anabasis* of the monodic chant of the human masses rising toward the divine.

That sound can produce the psychological effect of *anabasis* is already attested in patristic writings long before the building of the Justinianic Hagia Sophia. The material shape of the sixth-century building just gave these ideas an eloquent plastic embodiment in the ambo and dome (see figs. 2–3, 5–6). This is how John Chrysostom writes about the power of communal singing to produce this sensation of being lifted to the Creator:

> When God saw that the majority of men were slothful, and that they approached spiritual reading with reluctance and submitted to the effort involved without pleasure—wishing to make the task more agreeable and to relieve the sense of laboriousness—he mixed melody with prophecy, so that enticed by the rhythm and melody, all might raise sacred hymns to him with great eagerness. For nothing so arouses the soul, gives it [wings], sets it free from the earth, releases it from the prison of the body, teaches it to love wisdom, and to condemn all the things of this life, as concordant melody and sacred song composed in rhythm.[81]

FIG. 9

Hagia Sophia, reconstruction of the Justinianic liturgy unfolding in the interior.

John states that song can lift the soul heavenward and explains that this is the reason the Christian ritual combines prophecy with melody, singing the sacred mysteries. This anagogical power of chant is also present in Patriarch Germanus's depiction of the lips of priests as wings: "with their two lips like wings, they keep singing hymns."[82]

While the perception that singing produces an *anabasis* is stated long before the Justinianic rebuilding of Hagia Sophia and was most likely preached in basilica buildings, it is the idiom of the dome that gave this idea a plastic and acoustic reality. The pairing of cupola and ambo in the Great Church articulated this *anabasis* as both optical and aural brightness. Recent acoustic measurements in that space have shown how high-frequency sound waves concentrate in the current dome, creating, along with the natural light streaming in through the drum, a synaesthetic sonic and optical brightness.[83] Simultaneously, the dome produces an acoustic *katabasis,* "raining" some of the reflected sonic energy on the *kallichoros*.[84] Thus the cupola brings the two vectors of ascent and descent (the emanations) together as a sonic experience. This dynamic of *anabasis* and *katabasis,* energizing the air under the dome, recalls the linear up-and-down movements identified by Paul the Silentiary and Procopius in the triple *kinēsis* of the *kallichoros.*

The *enkaineia kontakion* quoted earlier contains one last piece of evidence concerning the aural manifestation of *sophia* in the great dome. The lines read: "Here is the voice [*phōnē*] [of joyfulness] and salvation / And the refrain-reverberation [*ēchos*] of those making festival in the Spirit, / Which [*phōnē* and *ēchos*] God [composed] as a harmony in voices."[85] The text pairs *phōnē* and *ēchos*, which, I argue, marks this participatory aspect of the aural *sophia.* The coupling can identify respectively the *phōnē* (voice/solo of the choir) and *ēchos* (the refrain sung by the congregation) or the human voice and the reverberant reply of the building. The aural *sophia* thus emerges as a back-and-forth between call (solo) and response (congregation) and as *empsychōsis,* in which the animate (human voice) imbues the inanimate (the *kallichoros*) with pneuma.

Ambo and Choirs

By virtue of its architecture and central location, the ambo gave prominence to the elite choir known as *psaltai*. Their voices, rising from the ground to the dome, in turn activated the "reactive" voice of the church, filling the space with sonic energy. The large size of the choirs singing the verses of the psalmody contributed to the aggregation of sonic energy that characterized Hagia Sophia's aurality and propelled the spiritual experience of transcendence (fig. 9). The *psaltai* centered this sonicscape (fig. 6). The elite choir, whose number was not to exceed twenty-five, consisted of two groups, each with its own soloist, or *domestikos*. Each group took turns to perform for a weeklong rotation. The *psaltai* were led by a choir director, whose name is identified with various terms throughout the centuries: *primikērios, protopsaltēs,* and *archōn tōn kontakiōn.*[86] Additional choirs, known as *anagnōstai,* situated inside the area east of the green marble band fourth from the entrance, joined in the responsorial singing of the psalms.[87] Because they did not have an architectural platform on which to perform, they were less of a visual focus, but their singing helped in the aggregation of sonic energy.[88] A Justinianic decree of 535 sets their number at 110; by 612 their size had grown to 160.[89] Just like the *psaltai,* only half of the *anagnōstai* performed on a given occasion.[90]

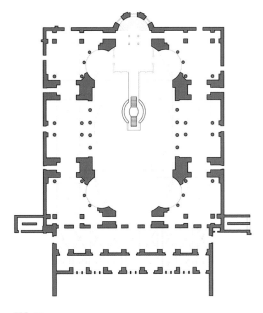

FIG. 10

Hagia Sophia, ca. 562, ground plan showing the ambo and solea. Drawing by James Huemoeller.

The *psaltai* stood at the ambo, an imposing structure that focused the visual and sonic attention of the participant in the liturgy. It was an oval marble platform raised on eight columns; the top was reached by two ascending ramps aligned on the west-east axis (figs. 5–6, 10).[91] Some reconstructions give it a round shape (figs. 9, 11–12), but this form does not correspond fully to the description in Paul the Silentiary.[92] An open circulation corridor circled around the ambo; this feature would have allowed the *psaltai* and clergy to move around the platform (fig. 10).[93]

The elite choir of the *psaltai* stood in the cavity under the ambo or lined at its sides.[94] Yet when they sang their solo parts, they ascended the steps. Their position in such special moments would have been reminiscent of that taken by deacons and priests when they lined the ambo's stairs. A miniature in the eleventh-century Mt. Athos lectionary recording the patriarchal liturgy shows the celebration of the Sunday of the feast of Orthodoxy (first Sunday of Lent) in Hagia Sophia (fig. 6).[95] Lining the left-hand ramp are four tonsured members of the lower clergy; the figure approaching the

FIG. 11

Hagia Sophia, ca. 562, reconstruction of the interior, showing the ambo, solea, and sanctuary barrier.

top turns his head and raises his hand in a gesture calling for silence; he and the two figures standing at the top of the ambo have been identified as cantors.[96] The *anagnōstai* were positioned further back, in the eastern *exedrae* within the marble-parapet enclosure marked on the floor by the fourth green marble band (figs. 5, 13).[97]

The ambo played an important role in negotiating the border between the worshippers and the sanctuary. Yet the exact location cannot be determined with certainty. Different sites have been offered. George Majeska reconstructs the ambo further to the east (fig. 14).[98] Studying Robert Van Nice's precise drawings of the stone blocks in the pavement of Hagia Sophia, Majeska has pointed out that the fourth green marble band marks a π-shaped perimeter that might indicate the area separated from the nave and reserved for the choirs and officiating clergy (fig. 13).[99] Majeska and later on Mainstone both place the ambo on the western edge of this perimeter, aligned with the two main eastern piers supporting the dome (figs. 5, 14).

By contrast, Stephen Xydis and Nino Zchomelidse have placed the ambo closer to the space under the dome, nearer the north-south axis running through the middle of the nave (fig. 10).[100] We do not have enough evidence to weigh in the reconstruction of the exact location.[101] Paul the Silentiary's description states that the ambo stood under the dome, though slightly to the east.[102]

Situated at the eastern periphery or under the umbrella of the dome, the ambo formed a counterpoint to and vied for attention with the altar to the east. Germanus identifies the ambo as a marker of the round stone over the tomb of Christ,

FIG. 12

Hagia Sophia, ca. 562, reconstruction of the interior, showing the ambo, solea, and sanctuary barrier, close-up.

which rolled off at his Anastasis. The angel sat on this stone as he announced the Resurrection.[103] Paul the Silentiary builds a metaphoric seascape in which the ambo rises as an island breaking the waves of the faithful.[104] Syriac sources, including the sixth-century inauguration anthem (*sogitha*) for the Hagia Sophia reconstructed in the 540s–550s by Justinian in Edessa, expand this envelope of symbolic associations.[105] The hymn's fifteenth strophe states: "Set in the middle of the temple is a platform (*bēma*), evoking the Upper Room in Sion; for just as the eleven Apostles hid there, so there are eleven columns under the platform."[106] The first hemistich identifies the *bēma* as a Holy Sion, the place where the apostles hid but also the site of the Last Supper and the descent of Pneuma at Pentecost. The word *bēma* in the East Syrian *sogitha* is equivalent to the Greek *ambo*.[107] This Edessan church exhibited architecture, ritual, and interior furnishings that self-consciously emulated those of the cathedral in Constantinople.[108] The symbolic significance of the *bēma* of Edessa therefore suggests that Hagia Sophia's ambo could also have been perceived as a terrestrial Jerusalem, a Holy Sion where the Spirit descended.[109] As such, the ambo anchored a terrestrial Jerusalem under the umbrella of the dome, while the altar on the east formed the heavenly Jerusalem. This reciprocal and mirroring dynamic was articulated architecturally: the raised platform of the ambo offset the ciborium of the altar. The two architectural structures thus echoed a vertical axis: of sonic energy rising *enōpion* from earth to heaven at the ambo, and a visual one descending *katōpion* from heaven to earth at the altar.

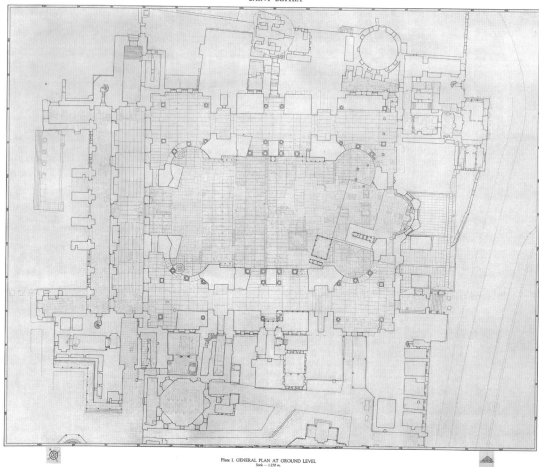

Plate 1. GENERAL PLAN AT GROUND LEVEL
Scale — 1:250 m.

FIG. 13 (*above*)

Hagia Sophia, drawing of the pavement. From Robert L.
Van Nice, *Saint Sophia in Istanbul: An Architectural Survey*
(Washington, D.C.: Dumbarton Oaks Center for Byzantine
Studies, 1965), plate 1 (DBI. Folio NA 5870.A9 V36 1965,
"General Plan at Ground Level").

FIG. 14 (*right*)

Hagia Sophia, plan showing the position of the ambo and
four green marble bands. From George P. Majeska, "Notes on
the Archaeology of St. Sophia at Constantinople: The Green
Marble Bands on the Floor," *Dumbarton Oaks Papers* 32
(1978): fig. A.

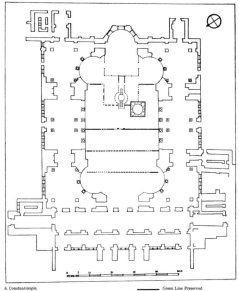

A. Constantinople,
St. Sophia, Ground Plan

———— Green Line Preserved
- - - - - Line of Strip Preserved in Pavement
· · · · · · Conjectural Continuation of Strip

The Macrocosm and Microcosm of the *Esoptron*

The Justinianic *kallichoros* shapes a radiant spherical void, which embodies the Neoplatonic luminous sphere: the vehicle capable of receiving the Demiurge.[110] This void is the space in which the *esoptron* dynamic operates. Again the *enkaineia kontakion* preserves traces of this Byzantine perception of the *kallichoros*:

> And this miraculous temple [*temenos*] shall become known
> above all others as the most sacred dwelling place [*endiaitēma*] of God,
> the one which manifestly exhibits a quality worthy of God,
> since it surpasses the whole of mankind's knowledge of building.
> Both in its material form [*morphōmati*] and in its worship [liturgy, *latreia*] it is
>   seen to be—yes,
> and proclaimed—a kind of heaven on earth [*ouranos epigeios*],
> which God has chosen for his own habitation;
> and in the Spirit hast thou buttressed it, thou:
> *Life and Resurrection of All!*[111]

The building elicits marvel both in form and in the metaphysical energy it is capable of gathering. The miraculous is first identified with the man-made, stirring the hearer to marvel at the architecture that surpasses all existing buildings. But then the poem turns to the metaphysical, vesseled in this material shell (*morphōma*) and activated by the liturgy (*latreia*). The building ingathers the divine; it is filled with Pneuma. Paradoxically, as the poem argues, it is the Holy Spirit that sustains the material structure.

The Justinianic radiant void of the *kallichoros* is evocative of the rotating celestial bodies. A monumental mosaic cross, which no longer survives, sealed the apex of the inverted hemisphere.[112] The same visual pattern formed in the dome can be traced in the cross-in-a-circle designs in many of the vaults of the aisles and galleries (fig. 15).[113] I find a connection between this large-scale design in the dome and the same configuration attested on the microscale in the bowls of some of the Eucharist chalices. The Attarouthi chalice, dated to the second half of the sixth and early seventh centuries, offers a compelling example. Its silver bowl is decorated with four standing figures in bas relief (fig. 16). When viewed from the top, the inside of the hemispherical bowl is marked by the pattern of the cross (fig. 17). The chalice functions as an inverted counterpart to the great dome: it is a microscopic mirror image of the great cupola (fig. 3). The result of this inverted parallelism is that the great dome and its association with the celestial appear in the nearness of the chalice's interior.[114] The *esoptron* instrumentalizes this process by which what is otherwise far off is brought paradoxically close.

The same process is at work in the perception of the paten for the bread. For instance, Germanus, in his *Mystagogia*, sees the paten, called *diskos*, as vesseling Christ, the spiritual sun, marked by the cross: "The *diskos* represents the hands of Joseph and Nicodemus, who buried Christ. The *diskos* on which Christ is carried is also interpreted

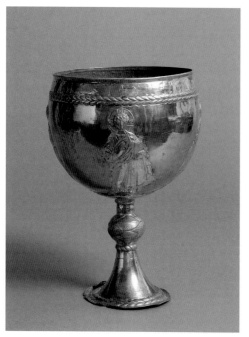

as the sphere of Heaven, manifesting to us in miniature the spiritual Sun, Christ, and containing him visibly in the bread."[115] The passage starts with an image of two pairs of hands, forming a cross-shaped structure; they hold the body of Christ and bury it in the ground. The vision describes a downward-facing dynamic, which is immediately paired with an *enōpion* view toward the spiritual sun, or Christ. At the end both the *katōpion* (downward, Crucifixion and Anastasis) and the *enōpion* (upward, Christ, the spiritual sun) are made visible in the round shape of the *diskos* marked by the trace of the cross. This cross-in-a-circle shape contains (*chōrei*) Christ/Eucharist. An inversion occurs: by looking down at the *diskos* the faithful come in contact with an *enōpion* vision—seeing God—which paradoxically gives access to what experience has taught the faithful to identify as the view upward, toward the dome/spiritual sun. In performing this inversion, the participant experiences the reification of the macrocosm in the circular microcosm of the *diskos* and plunges into shifting *katōpion* and *enōpion* views.[116]

A miniature on folio 101v from the Khludov Psalter further exemplifies how these micro- and macrocosmic connections are brought to consciousness (fig. 18). The illumination visualizes Psalm 101 (102): 25: "In the beginning thou, O Lord, didst lay the foundation of the earth; and the heavens are the works of thine hands." The earth is depicted in the miniature as a flat *diskos*. Two axes form a cross inscribed in the circle; they are known as *poloi*.[117]

Paul the Silentiary further calls attention to *poloi* and *choros* by describing the elite choir as *hymnopoloi*.[118] *Poloi* can be translated as both "singers" and "universal axes, or pivots," around which the earth or celestial bodies revolve.[119] The *psaltai* formed a center around which the other choirs were distributed. When they sang, they produced a "pivot," or *polos*, of sonic energy, rising from earth to heaven. They thus inspirited matter with their breath, a process marked by the sign of a cross, or *polos*, inside a *choros*. This *empsychōsis* formula decorated the apex of the cupola and the domical vaults, as well as the Eucharist chalices. It also appears in variant configuration in Cosmas Indicopleustes's representation of the choirs of David as the pivots of the spinning wheels (see fig. 7).

The combination of *poloi* inside a *choros*, I argue, visualizes *sophia*. Consider the texts performed at the feast of the Exaltation of the Holy Cross in Hagia Sophia, which include 1 Corinthians 1:18–24, read before the Divine Liturgy:[120]

> For the preaching of the cross is to them that perish foolishness; but unto us which are saved it is the power of God. For it is written, I will destroy the wisdom of the wise, and will bring to nothing the understanding of the prudent. Where is the wise? where is the scribe? where is the disputer of this world? hath not God made foolish the wisdom of this world? For after that in the wisdom of God the world by wisdom knew not God, it pleased God by the foolishness of preaching to save them that believe. For the Jews require a sign, and the Greeks seek after wisdom: But we preach Christ crucified, unto the Jews a stumbling block, and unto the Greeks foolishness. (KJV)[121]

FIG. 18

Khludov Psalter, Moscow, State Historical Museum,
MS gr. 129, fol. 101v, whose illumination illustrates Ps. 101
(102): 25: "In the beginning thou, O Lord, didst lay the foundation of the earth; and the heavens are the works of thine
hands." From M. V. Shchepkina, *Miniatjury Khludovskoi
psaltyri* (Moscow: Iskusstvo, 1977), n.p.

The text explains how the cross has superseded the wisdom of the pagans and the signs of the Jews. The ritual setting in which this text was performed suggests an interconnection between the domed *kallichoros* and the Holy Cross raised by the patriarch from the ambo, the former encompassing the latter. In fact, verse 17 of Psalm 85 (86), sung as part of this fixed psalm for vespers on the eve (*paramonē*) of the feast of the Exaltation, is illustrated on folio 86r of the Khludov manuscript with a Golgotha Cross, at whose center is a medallion with the face of Christ; the cross in the nimbus suggests the presence of the *poloi* inside the golden *choros*. The cross-in-a-circle formula marks *sophia*, the generative force that can give life. The structuring of the architectural space, the liturgical objects, and the chants and scriptural texts performed at the liturgy ensured the lodging of this *sēmeion* in the cultural consciousness of Byzantium.[122]

The cross-in-a-circle arrangement simultaneously presences the *katōpion* view the faithful cast at the Eucharist chalice and the *enōpion* view toward the great dome in the interior of Hagia Sophia.[123] This configuration, I argue, signifies the cosmic structure unfolding on the macro and micro levels. The cross at the center is like a propeller that has the potential to spin the wheel, gradually lifting the structure heavenward. This simultaneously circular and anagogical motility characterizes the sacred space emerging in the void of the *kallichoros,* as Paul the Silentiary defines it.[124] The dome and its inversion in the Eucharist chalice constitute mirroring halves—one macrocosmic, the other microcosmic—separated by a great distance, a distance breached by the mirror reflection.

Can this separation be overcome? Maximus the Confessor sheds light on this question. He explains how an intellective being, driven by divine force (*sophia*), transcends the limits of the self as it fuses with a greater force and thus reaches deification (*theōsis*).

> For from God come both our general power of motion (for He is our beginning), and the particular way that we move toward Him (for He is our end). If an intellective being is moved intellectively that is in a manner appropriate to itself, then it will necessarily become a knowing intellect. But if it knows, it surely loves that which it knows; and if it loves, it certainly suffers an ecstasy toward it as an object of love. If it suffers this ecstasy, it obviously urges itself onward, and if it urges itself onward, it surely intensifies and greatly accelerates its motion. And if its motion is intensified in this way [1073D], it will not cease until it is wholly present in the whole, beloved and wholly encompassed by it, willingly receiving the whole, saving circumscription by its own choice, so that it might be wholly qualified by the whole circumscriber and, being wholly circumscribed, [1076A] will no longer be able to wish to be known from its own qualities, but rather from those of the circumscriber, in the same way that air is thoroughly permeated by light, or iron in a forge is completely penetrated by the fire, or anything else of this sort.[125]

Maximus conveys the experience of the intellective being driven by the divine force and burning in a desire to be suffused with it.[126] What is segmented and partial becomes complete, defined by the term *perigraphē* (circumscription). In a way, the hemisphere of the dome and its micro-inversion as the Eucharist chalice strive for a similar completion. This process of temporal *perigraphē* occurs in the daily performance of the liturgy; it is synergistic, pulling performers and building into a dynamic of action and reaction: singing and reverberation, light and reflection, together producing sacred space.

Inspiriting in the Byzantine Consecration (*Kathierōsis*) Rite

If sacred space emerges in the formation of nearness to the *enōpion* view—for instance, in the way the Eucharist chalice brings near the otherwise distant view toward the dome—how is the reverse, *katōpion,* or the descent of the divine, mobilized by the liturgy? This emanation from the divine is activated in the church consecration ritual. When the construction of a new ecclesiastical building is completed, this man-made house is not yet a sacred space; it needs to be activated through a consecration ceremony in order to transform from a material fabric into an instrument of Pneuma: a site where the Holy Spirit would continually descend at the celebration of the Eucharist.

Of foremost importance in this transformation is what I shall call inspiriting, or *empsychōsis,* in the Byzantine consecration rites. Inspiriting denotes the process by which Holy Pneuma descends into and activates matter; it is targeted by the *kathierōsis* and activated by sacerdotal *epiklēsis,* or invocation. The prayers and litanies do not use the term *empsychōsis* specifically, but they employ synonyms such as "hovering"/ *epiphoitēsis* and "overshadowing"/*episkiasis* to denote the descent into matter and animation of the inert.[1]

Michael Findikyan, Vincenzo Ruggieri, and Vitalijs Permjakovs have greatly expanded our understanding of the Eastern consecration rites.[2] Ruggieri and Permjakovs have assembled and explored the surviving texts from the perspective of comparative liturgy, aiming to situate the Byzantine rite in the Eastern Christian family, tracing its similarities with and differences from the liturgy of Jerusalem and the Armenian, the Georgian, the West Syrian Antiochene, and the Coptic rites.[3] While drawing on the insights of the liturgists' comparative study, my analysis of the Byzantine consecration ritual shifts the research emphasis from the origin of the rite to how it engenders inspir-iting and how this *empsychōsis* is sensorially imprinted in the space and time of the participants.

In addition to the liturgical studies, the method used here finds further inspira-tion in Christina Maranci's exploration of the medieval churches at Mren (ca. 638), Mazdara (640–50), and Zuart'noc' (641–61) with respect to the early Armenian conse-cration ritual. Maranci examines relief sculpture, epigraphy, and architectural settings in relation to the *kathierōsis,* demonstrating the hagiopolite meanings produced through a liturgical encounter with the Armenian church façade.[4] In a similar approach, this chapter confronts the Justinianic Hagia Sophia with the stage directions of a generic liturgical rite, dated to the sixth century but recorded in the eight-century euchologion, or prayer book, Vatican City manuscript Barberini gr. 336.[5] There is an inherent differ-ence between the abstract presentation of the rite in this written document and the way the same stage directions were executed in each instantiation of the rite. But rather than cast this text aside because it cannot be grafted perfectly onto a specific monument, I turn to it in order to gain access to the culturally shared framework of prayers and gestures that the *kathierōsis* liturgy employed in shaping the sensual encounter with the divine. This body of liturgical texts functions like a Jaussian "horizon of expectations," establishing the parameters of the cultural memory and imagination that the Byzantine faithful brought to the liturgy.[6] Containing the prayers and the script of the consecration liturgy, Barberini 336 is read here for its temporal, spatial, and sensual language.

The prayers and ritual actions and gestures are intercalated with excerpts from the Psalms. Are there specific images that came to consciousness when these very passages were voiced during the *kathierōsis?* What role do these same excerpts play when they appear inscribed in the apses of Byzantine churches? To answer these questions, I turn to the miniatures of the marginal Psalters, more specifically the mid-ninth-century Khludov Psalter (Moscow, State Historical Museum, MS gr. 129), for several reasons. The Khludov is the best preserved of the three ninth-century examples, and many of its miniatures illustrate passages performed in the liturgy. These images thus offer partial access to a pictorial imagination elicited by the ritual in the consciousness of its elite audience.

The division of psalms in the Khludov bears witness to both the cathedral (Con-stantinopolitan) and the monastic practices (which harken back to the services per-formed at the monastery of St. Sabas in Jerusalem, which were introduced in Constan-tinople in the ninth century by the Stoudios monastery).[7] Yet both the cathedral and monastic rites remained similar in the selection of psalm verses for major feasts.[8] This fact alone justifies using the miniatures of the Khludov to explore how certain passages of the *kathierōsis* ceremony, one of the major rites, were pictorially envisioned by a Constantinopolitan elite audience. The Theodore Psalter offers further visual evidence. This eleventh-century marginal Psalter reproduces many of the miniatures of its ninth-century predecessors despite the fact that, unlike them, it is firmly embedded in just the monastic liturgy. This continuity of the visual tradition provides access to a cultural imagination shared by the users of these books.[9]

In order to expand the visual further into the realm of the aural, this chapter brings forth evidence from the elaborate melismatic *allēlouïas* chanted for the annual commemoration of the *kathierōsis*. These music samples, one of which is performed and recorded by Cappella Romana, exhibit melodic structures expressive of a spiritual dynamic of ascent. If the *kathierōsis* conveys a descent of Spirit into matter, the melismatic *allēlouïas* sung at the annual commemoration of the rite suggest the opposite— an anagogical dynamic.

The Structure of the *Kathierōsis* Rite in Byzantium

The Justinianic consecration rite in Hagia Sophia both in 537 and 562 would have offered an impressive spectacle. Fragments of this ceremony are described in Paul the Silentiary's ekphrasis of Hagia Sophia, the *enkaineia kontakion,* and the much later *Narratio de S. Sophiae* (eighth–ninth centuries).[10] Extant Byzantine liturgical sources instead document a generic ceremony of consecration. In turning to this evidence, the present study momentarily puts aside the specific material fabric of Hagia Sophia.

The late eight-century euchologion Barberini 336 offers access to the script of the Byzantine consecration rites; it is the earliest Byzantine document preserving the structure of the Constantinopolitan rite.[11] The manuscript records a consecration ceremony comprising two parts: (1) a *kathierōsis,* or consecration, of the altar performed by the elite clergy behind closed doors—which is the focus of the analysis here—and (2) a public inauguration, or *enkaineia,* of the building, which consists of a procession depositing relics followed by the celebration of the Eucharist. The texts documenting the *kathierōsis* rite reflect sixth-century practices in the Byzantine capital and thus bear witness to aspects of the consecration of the Justinianic Great Church. The *enkaineia,* by contrast, is more recent; it has been dated to the late eighth century because the ritual with relics it introduces responds to one of the clauses of the second, iconophile Council of Nikaia (Nicaea), in 787, that stipulates that churches consecrated without relics need to supply them.[12] The *kathierōsis* starts with patriarchal and diaconal prayers.

A. PATRIARCHAL AND DIACONAL PRAYERS

After setting the altar, the masons leave. The clergy come in and lock the gates. The patriarch advances and kneels before the doors of the sanctuary. While the sequence preserved in Barberini 336 switches the order at this point and first gives the petitions of the deacon, it is the patriarchal prayer that inaugurates the rite.[13] His prayer first calls on the book of Genesis, specifically the story of Creation, and addresses God:

> O Lord, without beginning, eternal, who brought all from nonbeing to being. [You who] inhabit unapproachable light, having the heavens as your throne, and the earth as your footrest; [you] who, in giving Moses the command and the model and in inspiriting Beseleēl, enabled them to complete the tabernacle of the testament,

in which [were deposited] the ordinances of truth, the images and tablets; [you who] granted Solomon breadth and largeness of heart, and through whom [you] raised the Temple of old; but established through the all-laudatory apostles the worship in the Holy Spirit, and renewed the grace of the true tabernacle . . . through them you established your churches and altars, O Lord of Powers, so that noetic and bloodless sacrifices may be offered to you, who is also pleased for this new temple to be built in the name of X.[14]

By evoking Genesis, recalling specifically how God created living forms from nonbeing, the patriarch targets the Lord's power to animate inert matter. This parallel acquires immediacy in the ritual, since the new altar is still incomplete and inert, or *apsychos* (from *a-,* "without," and *psychē-,* "spirit," "soul"). The patriarch then enlists important Old and New Testament precedents that show how divine inspiration transforms inert matter into a conduit for divine nearness: the tabernacle made by the inspirited Beseleēl after the plan God revealed to Moses at Sinai and then Solomon's First Temple at Jerusalem. In turn, both are now superseded by the coming of Christ and the establishment of the new worship (*latreia*) in Holy Pneuma. Here the prayer evokes Pentecost as the moment when the Holy Spirit descends on the apostles, inspiriting them to establish churches, officiate the mysteries, and transmit the New Law. By evoking these old and new acts of *empsychōsis,* the patriarch conceives the current consecration of the altar as part of a prefigured series of events, coming as their direct successor.

He then invokes inspiriting: "Send down to us your all-holy, venerated, and all-powerful *Pneuma* and sanctify this house! Fill it with eternal light, choose it for your dwelling on earth; make in this tent the abode of your glory!"[15] Two of the verbs appear with the prefix *kata-,* meaning "down," expressive of the downward pull from heaven to earth that this prayer aims to activate: the *katōpion.* This inspiriting is imagined visually as a burst of light (figs. 19–20). In using the words *phōs* (light) and *doxa* (glory), the prayer evokes the luminous divine presence in Genesis 1:3 and in Exodus 3:2–3 and 24:17, where Moses encounters God in the burning bush and in the fiery peaks of the mountain at Sinai.[16]

Then, following the model of Solomon's prayer at the First Temple of Jerusalem (3 Kings 8:29),[17] the patriarch prays to God to set his eyes and ears on this church and keep them always open to the requests of the faithful: "let your eyes remain open on this church night and day, and . . . your ears [be] turned to the ones fearful of you."[18] This request introduces a new consciousness about being in the interior of the church (see figs. 2–3). The subject (the faithful) will constantly appear exposed to the eye and ear of the Lord, becoming an object of divine judgment. All the windows and doors puncturing the walls of the physical building could thus be likened to the slits in a mask: openings in a material membrane through which the discerning gaze and voice of God becomes manifest (see the frontispiece). Matter serves as the medium through which God reaches down to the human being.

Toward the end of his prayer, the patriarch repeats his request to God to activate the altar with the energy of the Holy Spirit: "Preserve it unshaken until the End of

FIG. 19

Hagia Sophia, interior. The Byzantine Institute and
Dumbarton Oaks Fieldwork Records and Papers, ca. late
1920s–2000s.

FIG. 20

Hagia Sophia, interior, apse, sunrise, December 6, 2010.

Time and show the altar that is in it [the church] as the Holy of Holies by means of the power and energy of the all-holy Pneuma; glorify it more than the mercy seat of the [Old] Law, so that the sacred services performed upon it may reach unto your holy, supercelestial, and noetic sanctuary and bring down [to it] the grace of your unblemished overshadowings/epiphanies [*episkiaseis*]."[19] As the prayer specifies, the act of consecration through the descent of the Holy Spirit will be the first, bringing in its wake an uninterrupted line of successive inspiritings, and this should be identified with the repeated performance of the Eucharist.

The ending of this excerpt also draws attention to the way inspiriting produces divine nearness. By means of *empsychōsis* two energies, upward and downward movements, are brought into synergistic action: the human action "reaches out" to the supercelestial altar, while the divine "brings down" the pneumatic "overshadowing." In a similar way, once the altar is consecrated, it becomes the site of a regular *empsychōsis* when the Eucharist is performed. Through these two liturgical practices—*kathierōsis* and Eucharist—God's supercelestial abode is brought down to the perceptible. Divinity descends to overshadow and give grace, while humanity has the potential, through the reception and consumption of the Eucharist, to ascend and taste what dwelling in the celestial courts could be.

But in order for this phenomenon to take place, the new altar needs to be activated. Thus, while the patriarch rises, the deacon starts a second petition, which already in its fifth line targets *empsychōsis:* "Let us pray to the Lord that this house and the altar that is in it may be sanctified by the overshadowing [*epiphoitēsis*] and power and energy of the Holy Spirit."[20] Invoking the Holy Spirit, the deacon asks the Lord to let Pneuma overshadow, empower, and energize the new altar, transforming the profane marble into a sacred table for the mystical communion with God.

As in the patriarchal prayer, overshadowing (*epiphoitēsis* or *episkiasis*) marks the descent of Spirit into matter, reminiscent of the Eucharist. The verb *epiphoitaō* also evokes the Genesis narrative, where the Holy Spirit hovers (*epipherō*) over the primordial ocean (Gen. 1:2), and the Incarnation, where Pneuma overshadows Mary. A miniature introduced in the first chapter, on folio 93v of Mt. Athos, Pantokrator MS gr. 61, depicts this understanding of the Incarnation as a *katabasis*/descent (see fig. 8).[21] The image interprets Psalm 71 (72): 6: "He shall come down as rain upon a fleece; and as drops falling upon the earth." At the top of the composition the pre-eternal Logos appears in a golden medallion icon containing the face of Christ. The flowing waters forming an arch below suggest that the medallion icon of Christ is to be understood as existing in the supercelestial realm. Below these supercelestial waters is another disk of gold, from whose blank but luminous surface a ray of light emerges. It conveys a downward-facing dove—Pneuma—which inspirits a third golden disk, containing an image of the Virgin. The composition presents a mirroring structure: at the center is the large empty disk of heaven; at the antipodes are the medallions with Christ above, in the supercelestial realm, and Mary below, in the terrestrial domain. By its overshadowings the Spirit allows what is invisible and set above the supercelestial waters to enter the visible and become incarnate and sensorial through the body of the Theotokos. The horizontal mirroring structures this process through which the divine emerges in the sensorial.

The miniature in Pantokrator 61 also establishes a connection between inspiriting and water, which echoes the patriarch's and the deacon's prayers. The latter, in asking for the Spirit to descend, recalls the story of Genesis and more specifically Pneuma's riffling the surface of the primordial sea. This in turn conjures in one's consciousness a vision of waters enlivened by a breeze. As such, a vision of moving waters marks the process of inspiriting. The prayers not only stir this culturally shared image but place it in the dynamic of ritual mirroring; just as God quickened matter with his vital inbreathing in Genesis, so too Pneuma, activated by the call (*epiklēsis*) of the patriarch, would come down to overshadow and to inspirit the new altar.

These anamnestic intertextual references, starting with Genesis and ending with Pentecost, control a visual regime. Be it the image of the Spirit floating over the primordial ocean or the Marian body overshadowed by Pneuma or the apostles inspirited by tongues of fire at Pentecost, these imagined scenes visually inform and shape the perception of the liturgical actions and gestures executed in space during the *kathierōsis* of the new temple.

Beyond the concept of vivifying power that links Genesis and Pentecost, inspiriting is evocative of a particular place: Jerusalem. The dedication of the Holy Sepulchre in 335 and its commemoration on the octave beginning with September 13 establish the model of church consecration throughout the Mediterranean.[22] In addition, two other hagiopolite sites had a particular bearing on *empsychōsis* and church consecration. The altar of Golgotha was dedicated on the feast of Pentecost, and the church of Holy Sion marked the Pentecost site where the Holy Spirit descended on the apostles.[23] The consecration of Holy Sion was commemorated on the third day, September 15, of the octave of *enkaineia* of the Holy Sepulchre.[24]

FIG. 21

Khludov Psalter, Moscow, State Historical Museum, MS gr.
129, fol. 79r, whose illumination illustrates Ps. 77 (78):
68–69: "but [he] chose the tribe of Juda, the mount Sion
which he loved. And he built his sanctuary [*hagiasma*]
as [the place] of [the unicorn (Christ)]; he founded it
forever on the earth." From M. V. Shchepkina, *Miniatjury
Khludovskoi psaltyri* (Moscow: Iskusstvo, 1977), n.p.

FIG. 22

Khludov Psalter, Moscow, State Historical Museum, MS gr.
129, fol. 86v, whose illumination illustrates Ps. 86 (87): 5:
"A man shall say, Sion [is my] mother; and [such] a man
was born in her; and the Highest himself has founded her."
From M. V. Shchepkina, *Miniatjury Khludovskoi psaltyri*
(Moscow: Iskusstvo, 1977), n.p.

Only fragments remain of the hymnography composed for Holy Sion's commemoration. As Permjakovs has suggested, a couple of *troparia* (hymns) listed in the section for the Holy Sepulchre's *enkaineia* may have been composed originally for the commemoration of Holy Sion's foundation. These hymns identify Sion as the place where the agentive power of the Spirit descended on the apostles at Pentecost (Acts 2). The texts survive in a Georgian recension,[25] two fragments of which are pertinent to this analysis. First: "May the Holy Church [Sion] and the assembly of great multitudes rejoice, in which the Holy Spirit was revealed and said to the apostles: Raise up the voice of your praise in Sion and give glory to God in it!"[26] As the hymn states, Holy Sion is recognized as the place where Pneuma descended, thus inspiriting the site. The Spirit's *katabasis* prompts the human voice to produce the opposite dynamic: that of an ascent to heaven through the exhalation of breath in chant.

The same concept of *empsychōsis* is recorded in the next *troparion:* "Surround Sion, O people, and encompass her and give glory to God in her, for she is the mother of all the churches in whom the Holy Spirit came to dwell."[27] The text establishes a connection between Holy Sion and the body of Mary: both attain the paradoxical virginal

FIG. 23

Altar front, Constantinople or Ravenna, ca. 540–600, marble. The Cleveland Museum of Art, John L. Severance Fund 1948.25.

motherhood once they are overshadowed by the Holy Spirit. The miniatures of the marginal Psalters bring out the same connection, as they represent the Virgin and Child emerging from the foundations of Holy Sion. Folio 79r of the Khludov Psalter pairs Mary with the church of Holy Sion in its illustration of Psalm 77 (78): 68–69: "but he chose the tribe of Juda, the mount Sion which he loved. And he built his sanctuary [*hagiasma*] as [the place] of [the unicorn (Christ)]; he founded it for ever on the earth" (fig. 21). The church of Holy Sion stands on top of a steep rock, while the bust images of the Mother and Child emerge from the architectural enclosure. The inscription "Holy Sion" stands next to Mary's head. The image and its inscription clearly identify Holy Sion with the virginal body of Mary. The same concept appears also on folio 86v, which illustrates Psalm 86 (87): 5: "A man shall say, Sion [is my] mother; and [such] a man was born in her; and the Highest himself has founded her" (fig. 22). The text prophesies the Incarnation, while the miniature depicts David before the open gate of Sion, lifting his hand toward an icon of the Virgin and Child. The inscription "Holy Sion" stands above the tall architectural complex. The very presence of Mary with the Christ Child inflects the perception of the church of Sion as inspirited: a dwelling place of Pneuma.

An altar front now at the Cleveland Museum of Art visually expresses this identification of the altar with Sion as an inspirited site (fig. 23). A parted curtain underneath the central pediment billows as if moved by wind (fig. 24). The deeply undercut marble appears like a pliable, pregnant membrane. It paradoxically gives shape to a void that the human imagination wants to fill in with the presence of the Holy Spirit. Being the altar

front, this composition draws attention to the divine energy that has the power to animate matter. The play of shadow and light, void and matter, articulates this *empsychōsis*. The physical shadow envelops the center and alludes to the divine energy emptying out in matter. By contrast, the highlights moving across the surface of the billowing drapery express the result of this impregnation. Pairing form and content, this altar front inscribes *empsychōsis* in image and in ritual practice.

Holy Sion emerges as the model for the *empsychōsis* through which all subsequent churches are produced. This localization and containment of Pneuma is expressed ritually through the circumambulation: "Surround Sion, O people, and encompass her." This call may refer to an annual procession around the walls of Holy Sion in Jerusalem or just serve as an evocation of Psalm 47 (48):12: "Go round about Sion, and encompass her." Put together, the two Georgian *troparia* give insights into the ritual performed at Holy Sion. The annual commemoration there targeted the memory of Pentecost, recognized how inspiriting produces a simultaneous *katabasis* and *anabasis,* and suggests how this sacred energy can be localized and contained through ritual circumambulation. The Khludov miniatures on folios 50v and 51r further secure the association between Sion and the Incarnation as a descent of Spirit into matter. At the same time, both miniatures—in perching Holy Sion at the top of steep rock and inviting the viewer to climb a small ladder to the great heights—manage to express an ascent. Divinity descends in order to allow humanity to ascend: Holy Sion becomes the center where these opposing vectors meet.

As the site of Pentecost, of the Last Supper, and of the appearance of Christ among his disciples after the Resurrection (John 20:19, 26), Holy Sion marks sacred ground inspirited by Pneuma. The image of Sion identifies the incarnation of Spirit in matter. For this reason, both the Eucharist and the *kathierōsis* rites seek a connection with this hagiopolite site. While the Eucharist is observed to produce a daily *empsychōsis,* the *kathierōsis* prepares the ground for this observance as it activates the altar for the celebration of the daily liturgy. Not surprisingly, the Byzantine patriarchal prayer at the *kathierōsis* taps into the same core associations between Pneuma and Holy Sion as it consecrates the altar for its ritual function.

FIG. 25

Khludov Psalter, Moscow, State Historical Museum, MS gr. 129, fol. 50v, whose upper illumination illustrates Ps. 50 (51): 7–8: "Thou shalt sprinkle me with hyssop, and I shall be purified: thou shalt wash me, and I shall be made whiter than snow. Thou shalt cause me to hear gladness and joy: the afflicted bones shall rejoice." The lower illumination illustrates Ps. 50 (51): 11: "Cast me not away from thy presence; and remove not thy holy Spirit from me." From M. V. Shchepkina, *Miniatjury Khludovskoi psaltyri* (Moscow: Iskusstvo, 1977), n.p.

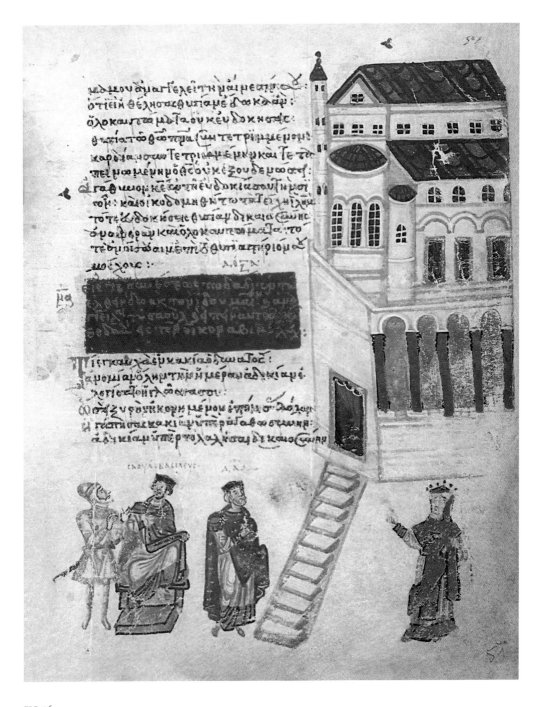

FIG. 26

Khludov Psalter, Moscow, State Historical Museum,
MS gr. 129, fol. 51r, whose illumination illustrates Ps. 50
(51): 18: "Do good, O Lord, to Sion in thy good pleasure; and
let the walls of Jerusalem be built." From M. V. Shchepkina, *Miniatjury Khludovskoi psaltyri* (Moscow: Iskusstvo,
1977), n.p.

B. RITUAL ACTIONS AND THE SINGING OF PSALMS

1. Cleansing

Following the patriarch's prayer, Barberini 336 records a series of actions involving the cleaning, lustration, anointing, and dressing of the altar. The patriarch receives sodium carbonate, which he throws crosswise on the altar; he then takes up a vessel with warm water. The text specifies that this container is usually used in the rituals of holy baptism. The allusion to Christ's baptism is sustained in the first sentence of the new prayer the patriarch commences with as he inclines his head to the altar: "Lord, our God, who has sanctified the streams of Jordan through your salvific epiphany, bless this water for the consecration and perfection of this altar of yours!"[28] In awaking the memory of the Spirit's descending on Christ in the waters of Jordan, the patriarch effectively establishes how the new table will become the body of Christ through the *kathierōsis*. The words "consecration" (*hagiasmos*) and "perfection" (*teleiōsis*) quote the formula of the Eucharist anaphora and thus further strengthen the identification of the new altar with Christ. The *anamnēsis*, or commemoration, of the opening lines of the prayer also reveals the connection between the consecration of the altar and the anointing of the waters of the baptismal font with oil, since the vessel specified in the liturgical script is the one usually used in baptism. The *kathierōsis* as recorded in Barberini 336 exhibits genetic links with the rites of Eucharist and baptism, and in all three *empsychōsis* constitutes the core.[29]

2. Wiping

The patriarch then wipes down the altar and its columns, first with his hands and then with a clean sponge. As he performs this rite, he sings, accompanied by the clergy, Psalm 83 (84): 1–3, which begins: "How amiable are thy tabernacles, O Lord of hosts! My soul longs and faints for the courts of the Lord: my heart and my flesh have exulted in the living God. Yea, the sparrow has found himself a home, and the turtle-dove a nest for herself, where she may lay her young, [even] thine altars, O Lord of hosts, my King, and my God."[30] The entire psalm is sung repeatedly until the wiping is completed.

3. Wine Libation

Next the patriarch takes a vessel with wine and pours it three times over the altar, making the shape of the cross. He accompanies this action with the singing of Psalm 50 (51): 7–8: "Thou shalt sprinkle me with hyssop, and I shall be purified: thou shalt wash me, and I shall be made whiter than snow. Thou shalt cause me to hear gladness and joy: the afflicted bones shall rejoice" (fig. 25).[31] And he sings the psalm to its end and repeats it as many times as necessary to reach the completion of the pouring.

Psalm 50 connects ritual cleansing (vv. 7–8, illuminated in the Khludov Psalter with the washing of feet) with inspiriting (v. 11, illuminated in the Khludov Psalter with the dove descending on David) and thus enforces the aim of the *kathierōsis*. The poetry communicates the process of renewal and recalibration that allows humanity to enter into a new covenant with divinity. This is accomplished through inspiriting invested in a chiastic structure. "Chiasm" refers to a mirroring composition that collapses down to a center. Repetition of the same words establishes a frame for the composition.[32] Psalm 50 has been recognized as carrying a chiastic structure.[33] The verb "rejoice," *agaliaō,* and its noun, *agaliasis,* define the frame; they appear in lines 8, 12, and 14 and are here marked in bold. The center falls either on verse 11, considering the largest frame, verses 8–14, or on verse 10, considering the smaller frame, verses 8–12. Each of the center lines 10–12 has the word *pneuma* in its second hemistich:

8 ἀκουτιεῖς μοι **ἀγαλλίασιν** καὶ εὐφροσύνην, **ἀγαλλιάσονται** ὀστέα τεταπεινωμένα.

9 ἀπόστρεψον τὸ πρόσωπόν σου ἀπὸ τῶν ἁμαρτιῶν μου καὶ πάσας τὰς ἀνομίας μου ἐξάλειψον.

10 καρδίαν καθαρὰν κτίσον ἐν ἐμοί, ὁ Θεός, καὶ <u>πνεῦμα</u> εὐθὲς ἐγκαίνισον ἐν τοῖς ἐγκάτοις μου.

11 μὴ ἀπορρίψῃς με ἀπὸ τοῦ προσώπου σου καὶ τὸ <u>πνεῦμά</u> σου τὸ ἅγιον μὴ ἀντανέλῃς ἀπ᾿ ἐμοῦ.

12 ἀπόδος μοι τὴν **ἀγαλλίασιν** τοῦ σωτηρίου σου καὶ <u>πνεύματι</u> ἡγεμονικῷ στήριξόν με.

13 διδάξω ἀνόμους τὰς ὁδούς σου, καὶ ἀσεβεῖς ἐπὶ σὲ ἐπιστρέψουσι.

14 ῥῦσαί με ἐξ αἱμάτων, ὁ Θεὸς ὁ Θεὸς τῆς σωτηρίας μου· **ἀγαλλιάσεται** ἡ γλῶσσά μου τὴν δικαιοσύνην σου.[34]

These second hemistichs read: verse 10, "and renew a right spirit in my inward parts"; verse 11, "and remove not thy holy Spirit from me"; and verse 12, "establish me with thy directing Spirit." Verses 10–12 capture the human plea to God to establish his vivifying Spirit in the mortal and thus save him or her.

A miniature from the Khludov Psalter illustrates verse 11 with the dove descending on David (fig. 25). The image offers evidence that the medieval viewer recognized the meaning of this line as *empsychōsis.* The stability of this link is supported by a later copy of the Khludov, the Theodore Psalter, of the second half of the eleventh century, which reproduces the same composition; it shows a ray of light descending from the arc of heaven and overshadowing David (fig. 27). The image illustrates verse 12, "establish me with thy directing Spirit." While the reason for the switch from verse 11 to verse 12 as the subject for illustration remains unclear, it is evident that the medieval viewer recognized that the message of this segment was inspiriting. Whether as dove or ray of light, both miniatures render the descent of Pneuma into matter. The efficacy of Psalm 50 in expressing content—*empsychōsis*—through a chiastic form recommends it to rituals targeting inspiriting.

Although the ceremony of *kathierōsis* was performed behind closed doors and the congregation did not witness it, the miniatures of the Khludov and Theodore Psalters illustrating Psalm 50 show a shared cultural understanding that these lines of poetry evoke inspiriting for a Byzantine audience.[35] The congregation would have experienced this *empsychōsis* as they participated in the annual commemoration of the inauguration of Hagia Sophia, on December 23. *Orthros* started at the ambo with the *psaltai* singing Psalm 50.[36] In addition, all major feasts in the Great Church began with the singing of Psalm 50 from the ambo as the first light of dawn touched the ring of windows in the apse and the dome (figs. 19–20).[37] This psalm thus became linked in Byzantine consciousness with the call of penitent humanity to be renewed in the Spirit of God at *orthros.*

The inspiriting in Psalm 50 is immediately connected to Holy Sion both through the text and the miniatures. Verse 18 contains a plea on behalf of Holy Sion: "Do good, O Lord, to Sion in thy good pleasure; and let the walls of Jerusalem be built." The Khludov

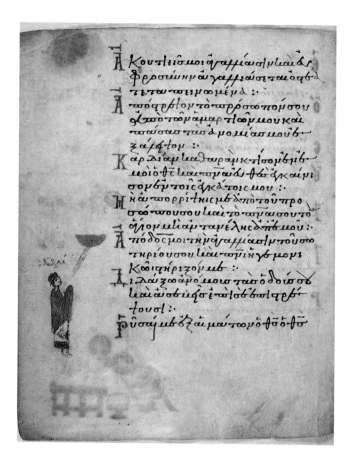

FIG. 27

Theodore Psalter, London, British Library, Add MS 19352, mid-eleventh century, fol. 64v, showing inspiriting as a ray of light descending on King David, thereby illustrating Ps. 50 (51): 12: "Restore to me the joy of thy salvation: establish me with thy directing Spirit."

Psalter visualizes this idea with the church of Holy Sion raised on high. A steep staircase gives access to its lofty courts. Below it stands the personification of Jerusalem, dressed like a Byzantine empress (fig. 26).

5. Vesting of the Altar

After the ritual libation with wine, the patriarch places a new cloth on the freshly wiped altar, accompanied by the singing of Psalm 131 (132): 2–8:

> How he sware to the Lord, [and] vowed to the God of Jacob, [saying], I will not go into the tabernacle of my house; I will not go up to the couch of my bed; I will not give sleep to mine eyes, nor slumber to mine eyelids, nor rest to my temples, until I find a place for the Lord, a tabernacle for the God of Jacob. Behold, we heard of it in Ephratha; we found it in the fields of the wood. Let us enter into his tabernacles: let us worship at the place where his feet stood. Arise, O Lord, into thy rest; thou, and the ark of thine holiness.[38]

The poetry illustrates the human zeal to establish a space for the divine. The Khludov Psalter identifies David's vision with the exterior of a Christian basilica (fig. 28).

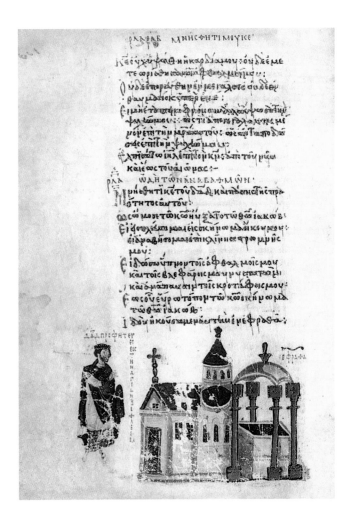

FIG. 28

Khludov Psalter, Moscow, State Historical Museum, MS gr. 129, fol. 131v, whose illumination illustrates Ps. 131 (132): 6–8: "Behold, we heard of it in Ephratha; we found it in the fields of the wood. Let us enter into his tabernacles: let us worship at the place where his feet stood. Arise, O Lord, into thy rest; thou, and the ark of thine holiness." From M. V. Shchepkina, *Miniatjury Khludovskoi psaltyri* (Moscow: Iskusstvo, 1977), n.p.

Lodged next to the church's eastern wall, the miniature depicts an interior view showing a close-up of a ciborium and an altar table. Magnified in scale, the ciborium dwarfs the church exterior, focusing the reader's attention on the altar. Its prominence argues visually for the connection between this psalm and the consecration of an altar. The Theodore Psalter confirms this semantic identification, here connecting the tabernacle at Ephratha with the altar, as its miniature compresses the exterior of the church in order to expand the view to the altar (fig. 29). Though folio 132r of the Khludov, that which faces the folio shown in figure 28, is mutilated, the iconography of its miniatures can be recuperated from the surviving example of the Theodore Psalter. Two more scenes appear below the altar at Ephratha: a Crucifixion that visualizes verse 7, "Let us enter into his tabernacles: let us worship at the place where his feet stood," and Christ enthroned, illustrating verse 11, "The Lord sware [in] truth to David, and he will not annul it, [saying], Of the fruit of thy body will I set [a king] upon thy throne."[39] The vertical alignment of images in the Theodore Psalter establishes the shared identity between altar, Cross, and enthroned Christ. All three are understood as figures expressing the same divine energy. Likewise, the inspiriting of the *kathierōsis* rite ensures the shared identity of altar and body of Christ. *Empsychōsis* triggers these metamorphic manifestations of Christ visualized in the Theodore Psalter miniatures. Attention to *empsychōsis* is also drawn by the way Psalm 131 (132): 10—"For the sake of thy servant David turn not away the face of thine anointed"—echoes the language of the chiastic center of Psalm 50 and thus stirs the memory of inspiriting targeted by the *kathierōsis* rite.[40]

6. Chrismation: The Climax Inscribing *Empsychōsis* in the Sensorial

Psalm 131 leads to the climax of the rite as the patriarch takes the vessel with chrism and pours *myron* (chrism) over the cleansed table. He pours three times; in each instance he traces the shape of the cross, for inspiriting is engendered by the figure of the cross made in the gesture of blessing.[41] And it is this ritual pouring of *myron* that evokes the consecration with holy oil of the waters of the baptismal font.[42] The patriarch then traces with *myron* three crosses on the surface of the table and with his anointed hands imprints the same mark on the columns supporting the altar. He accompanies his action with the singing of Psalm 132 (133): "See now! what is so good, or what so pleasant, as for brethren to dwell together? [It is] as ointment on the head, that ran down to the beard, [even] the beard of Aaron; that ran down to the fringe of his clothing. As the dew of Aermon, that comes down on the mountains of Sion: for there the Lord commanded

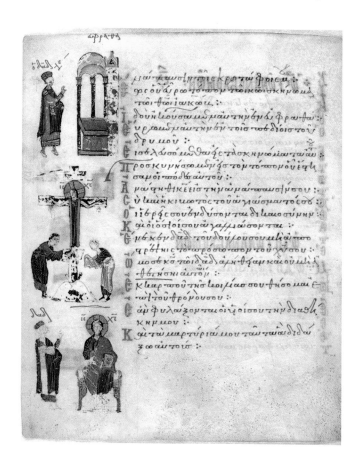

FIG. 29

Theodore Psalter, London, British Library, Add MS 19352, mid-eleventh century, fol. 172v, whose illuminations illustrate Ps. 131 (132): 6, 7, 11. David standing before a church and altar illustrates verse 6: "Behold, we heard of it in Ephratha; we found it in the fields of the wood." A Crucifixion illustrates verse 7: "Let us enter into his tabernacles: let us worship at the place where his feet stood." An enthroned Christ illustrates verse 11: "The Lord sware [in] truth to David, and he will not annul it, [saying,] Of the fruit of thy body will I set [a king] upon thy throne."

the blessing, even life for ever."[43] The poem gives meaning to the ritual act; it explains how the drops of *myron*, soaking into matter, manifest the penetration of sacred energy into matter. This act ensures salvation. Psalm 132 also enables its audience to draw a connection between the drops of *myron* and the dew of Sion.

Myron expresses divine blessing, which marks the penetration of Spirit into matter. The ritual aspect of this mingling of Pneuma and *hylē* (matter) is marked by smell: immaterial, invisible, and unlocatable, yet sensual. The anointing releases perfume, which signals *empsychōsis*.[44] A fourteenth-century Coptic source that transmits the *enkaineia* of the *lavra* (ascetic monastic community) of St. Makarios at Scetis in the period 645–47 suggests how this process conveys the presence of Pneuma.[45] The text records a chrismation that bears traces of the Constantinopolitan and Antiochene practices.[46]

> And when I [Patriarch Benjamin of Alexandria, r. 622/26–665] took the *myron* in order to pour it slowly upon the holy altar, I heard a voice saying, "Be attentive, O bishop!" As I turned slowly toward the table, I saw the hand of the Savior anointing the altar, while I was seized by great fear and trembling. . . .
>
> We [the concelebrant clergy], looking at him [Benjamin], saw him all enflamed, his face glistening with light. [Benjamin then quotes Ps. 83:1–3.] And when he [Benjamin] consecrated the altar, he went out toward the people and [consecrated the pillars] and the walls. [When he returned to his seat in the sanctuary, he said,] "Believe me brothers, I saw the glory of Christ today filling the tabernacle, and I saw with my sinful eyes the invisible arm and the exalted hand of our Savior Jesus Christ anointing the table of the holy place."[47]

The performance of the chrismation leads to an ecstatic vision, enabling the officiating patriarch to encounter the Savior. Benjamin sees Christ anointing the altar. The human action causes a reciprocal divine reaction, mirroring the human. And through this mirroring, the divine emerges in the material and manifests its presence through scent.

The central role chrismation plays in engendering *empsychōsis* can also be gleaned from West Syrian prayers pronounced at the anointing: "[A]nd now vouchsafe to overshadow this place, and to sanctify it for the praise to your all-honored name . . . and fulfill the promise of your all-holy Spirit, so that it may dwell and work, and move the word of the Gospel, and complete every deed and word that comes to pass in this place."[48] This patriarchal prayer said at the chrismation expresses the causal relationship between anointing and inspiriting. Through chrismation, the Holy Spirit is activated in the new temple, ensuring that every word exhaled over the new altar will produce a divine response, transforming breath into action.

The importance of the chrismation is further confirmed by Patriarch Germanus (r. 715–30), who writes: "She [the church] is cleansed by the waters of his baptism [no. 1 above]; sprinkled by the blood [no. 3]; clothed in bridal garments [no. 7]; and sealed with the *myron* of the Holy Spirit [no. 6]."[49] By switching the order of vesting and anointing, Germanus establishes a hierarchy, treating the chrismation as the culminating action through which Pneuma enters the sensorial.

7. Dressing of the Altar

The altar is now activated. The patriarch takes a cloth to cover it while singing Psalm 92 (93) as many times as necessary to complete the ritual action: "The Lord reigns; he has clothed himself with honour: the Lord has clothed and girded himself with strength; for he has established the world, which shall not be moved. Thy throne is prepared of old: thou art from everlasting. The rivers have lifted up, O Lord, the rivers have lifted up their voices, at the voices of many waters: the billows of the sea are wonderful: the Lord is wonderful in high places. Thy testimonies are made very sure: holiness becomes thine house, O Lord, for ever."[50] The imagery of these few lines is extremely rich; it links the beauty and attraction of the royal dress to the image of Creation, specifically to the waters that rise. It culminates with a glimpse of the supercelestial house of God. The cloth spread over the altar harmonizes with the evocation of the royal attire, while the *anamnēsis* of Genesis and the waters rising to reach the supercelestial throne connect the two abodes of God: the terrestrial and the supercelestial. Through the act of inspiriting and mirroring, a reciprocity is established between the earthly temple and the divine sphere. Aspects of this dynamic recall the patriarchal prayer at the beginning of the *kathierōsis*, which states: "so that the sacred services performed upon it may reach unto your holy, supercelestial, and noetic sanctuary and bring down [to it] the grace of your unblemished overshadowings/epiphanies."[51] Inspiriting engenders mirroring; thus through *empsychōsis* the terrestrial altar becomes a mirror in which the supercelestial divine altar emerges in the mortal field of vision. The earthly temple has given humanity a medium, a reflective surface, through which the mortal may commune with the celestial. Through the process of inspiriting, which manifests itself in scent and Pneuma overshadowing the altar, the faithful can experience the inscription of divine nearness in the spatiotemporal frame of their own corporeal existence.

8. Incensing and the Circumambulatory Procession

After the vesting of the newly consecrated altar, the patriarch incenses the table and the entire church, whereby he ensures the presence of Pneuma through smell.[52] Psalm 25 (26) is sung during the incensing: "I will wash my hands in innocency, and compass [*kyklōsō*] thine altar, O Lord: to hear the voice of praise, and to declare all thy wonderful works. O Lord, I have loved the beauty of thy house, and the place of the tabernacle of thy glory."[53] The psalm uses the word *kyklōsō*, which suggests a circumambulation. Yet is this possibility indicated in the stage direction recorded in Barberini 336? The latter states: "While the patriarch incenses, one of the bishops, present with him and carrying the vessel of the *chrism*, follows him and makes crosses with *myron* upon every column and pillar."[54] The generic "every column and pillar" suggests a circumambulation of the interior of the temple. This interpretation finds parallels in the Georgian sources that record circumambulation.

The same sequence of psalms—83 (84), 131 (132), and 25 (26)—has survived in the Georgian *iadgari*, or book of hymns, Tbilisi A86, which transmits, albeit in fragmentary shape, the liturgy of Jerusalem from the fifth to the seventh centuries.[55] Permjakovs has suggested that this sequence of psalms may have originated in the hagiopolite rite.[56] In the Georgian material, Psalms 83, 131, and 25 appear in the rite for consecration of a moveable altar and mark each of three circumambulations of the altar. The Georgian evidence about circular procession suggests that the vague Byzantine stage directions in Barberini 336 specifying the marking of every column with *myron* imply a procession that rotates around the sanctuary and/or nave of the church.

Furthermore, the mid-seventh-century Coptic account of Patriarch Benjamin's consecration of the *lavra* of St. Makarios at Scetis quoted earlier attests to the practice of several circumambulation processions: three performed around the altar after the chrismation and one around the nave, during which the patriarch anoints the columns and the walls of the church.[57] What is significant in executing these circumambulations is the spread of fragrance in the entire church through incensing and chrismation. The rite thus intensifies the sensation of Pneuma through smell.

C. CONCLUDING PRAYERS

At the conclusion of the *kathierōsis* the patriarch inclines his head toward the consecrated altar and pronounces his final prayer. His opening lines again affirm the interpenetration of celestial and terrestrial temples: "Lord of the heavens and of earth, who has established in wisdom your ineffable holy church in heaven, and as its antitype of the angelic liturgy you have put together the order (*taxis*) [of the liturgy on earth]."[58] As the prayer states, God has ensured that the divine temple and its angelic liturgy become manifest on earth through the terrestrial liturgy. Since this prayer comes at the completion of the *kathierōsis,* it shows how the ritual actions that set the conditions for *empsychōsis* have resulted in the transformation of the newly consecrated temple into a mirror image of the divine. The combination of both *empsychōsis* and mirroring—which never fully resolve themselves in the visible but activate other sensory modes such as smell—enable humanity to experience nearness to the divine.

The prayer proceeds to enumerate the moments of Christ's life marked by the descent of Holy Pneuma—the Incarnation, baptism, and Resurrection: "you have granted the coming in the flesh of your only-begotten Son—who, appearing on earth and shining to those in darkness the light of salvation, offered himself for us as a sacrifice and became the propitiation (*ilastērion*) of the whole world, making us the partakers in his own resurrection."[59] As the office draws to a close, the prayer ensures a continual *empsychōsis,* which comes with partaking in the Eucharist.

Then, evoking 3 Kings 8:11, the patriarch beseeches God as follows: "[to] fill with your divine glory this house built up for your hymnody, and . . . [to] manifest the altar present in it as the holy of holies, so that standing before it as before the awesome throne of your kingdom, we may without condemnation worship you."[60] He begs that the glory of God descend into the temple, so that it can transform the altar table into the divine throne. The miniature of the Theodore Psalter has already visualized this connection between altar, Cross, and throne in its illustration of Psalm 131 (132) (fig. 29), but it is the patriarchal prayer that suggests how the connection is established in Byzantine consciousness.

The deacon, who steps in after the patriarchal prayer, reinforces the same connection and expresses a hope that the newly consecrated altar will continuously produce *empsychōsis:* "so that the bloodless sacrifices offered in it [this temple/altar], may be changed into the pure body and precious blood of our great God and Savior Jesus Christ."[61] Both the diaconal and the patriarch prayers conclude with the plea for the continual *empsychōsis,* which will be produced by the performance of the Eucharist on the new altar.

The Sonic Dimension of Sacred Space: *Empsychōsis* in the Singing of *Allēlouïa*

The last prayer of the patriarch at the *kathierōsis* mentions the chanting of hymnody. Singing is an exhalation of breath, a form of human reciprocation for the gift of Holy Pneuma. An Armenian hymn that carries fragments of the church consecration rites in Jerusalem attests to an interlinking of Holy Spirit and human breath: "You established your church on your word, O Christ, upon the apostolic rock, in order to sing spiritual songs in her."[62] The hymn recognizes the church as a vessel of the Logos and breath; it is a material chamber for the prayers and hymns of the faithful, performed in order to elicit divine response. Though the *kathierōsis* rite was executed behind closed doors by the officiating priesthood and centered on the descent of Pneuma into matter, the annual commemoration was public and conveyed an opposite, anagogical dynamic, which elevated humanity to the celestial. This ascent is inscribed in the melodic structure of the *allēlouïas* sung at the annual commemoration ceremony.

Elaborate *allēlouïas* were sung in the Eucharistic liturgy before the reading of the Gospels.[63] The word expresses the singing of praise to God. According to Byzantine etymology: *al* stands for "God" or "the one appearing," *ēl* for "God" or "powerful," and *ouïa* for "mighty" or "sing" or "praise the living God."[64] Christian Thodberg's systematic study of the scores has made this material more accessible. According to his analysis, verses 1b–2 and 3–4a of Psalm 86 (87) (A8 in Thodberg's system) and verses 2, 5c–d, and 12 of Psalm 64 (65) (A32 in Thodberg's system) were chosen for the annual commemoration of a church consecration. The soloist known as *domestikos* sang the *allēlouïa* refrain and the line "psalm of David." The deacon next called everyone to attention. The *allēlouïa* model melody was sung again (by the soloist, as suggested by Thodberg, or possibly by the choir/congregation). The *psaltai* then began the chanting of the verses. At the end of each line the choir/congregation came in with the *allēlouïa* melody.[65] Hagia Eirēnē, one of the three churches (Hagia Sophia, Hagia Eirēnē, and the Theotokos Chakoprateia) served by the staff of Hagia Sophia, displays Psalm 64:4–5 as a mosaic inscription in the bema.[66] This suggests that the words sung as an *allēlouïa* of the annual commemoration ceremony were visible and accessible throughout the year for all who participated in the liturgy of this church. Dormant and visible, the epigram would have become inspirited, transformed into the sound of chant at the annual commemoration.

A. THE BYZANTINE *ALLĒLOUÏARION*

Thodberg focuses on the syllabic style, the so-called short *Psaltikon* style, and, more specifically, on the melodic contours of the psalm verses without their paired *allēlouïa*

1. melisma on final syllable

αλ – λη – λου – ι – α

2. similar melody as line 1, but melisma shifts to middle syllable

αλ – λη – λου   –   ι – α

3. similar structure as line 2, but with melodic variation

αλ – λη – λου   –   ι – α

4. greatly expanded melisma, additional melisma on intercalated nonsense syllable νου

αλ – λη   –   λου   –   –   νου   –   –   ι – α

FIG. 30

Transcription of the sung announcement of *allēlouïa* and verses in the long *Psaltikon* style from MS Vat. gr. 1606, thirteenth and fourteenth centuries. © Laura Steenberge.

refrains. Thus he includes the melody for one of the two psalms (Ps. 86: 1b–2, 3–4a; A8 in Thodberg's system) sung for the annual commemoration but without the refrain.[67] He records six other *allēlouïa* refrains in the short *Psaltikon* style, transmitted by Patmos gr. 221, dated to the 1177.[68] Yet it is the long *Psaltikon* style that is linked to the cathedral liturgy. Thodberg records one such refrain transmitted by Vat. gr. 1606 (thirteenth–fourteenth century). The melodic form is provided in an appendix and refers to the sung announcement of *allēlouïa* plus verses (fig. 30).[69] Being a unicum, this evidence does not lend itself to a definite interpretation, but it still offers important information about what the singing of such refrains in the Great Church would have sounded like and how it would have interacted with the acoustics of this interior. The melody of the *allēlouïa* is given in four variants, which progress from a syllabic to a melismatic form. The first three are mostly syllabic, with one five-note melisma set on the final *a* in the first example and on *lou* in the second and third examples. By contrast, the fourth is floridly melismatic; not only does a nine-note melisma appear on *lou*, but it is extended even further with an additional eight-note melisma set on the intercalated syllable *nou*. This last melismatic version, ornamented with intercalated letters, can be viewed as a record of how an *allēlouïa* in the long *Psaltikon* style would have been sung in the Great Church. The melismas concentrate in the middle of the melodic structure, which is expanded even further with the intercalation. The melisma pushes the melody to a higher register, to rise to an upper F.

B. *O KYRIOS* AND THE *EMPSYCHŌSIS* EXPRESSED BY THE WAVES OF WATER

The musical design of this melismatic version in Vat. gr. 1606 attests to a difference between the Byzantine approach to elaborating the *allēlouïa* and the approach found in

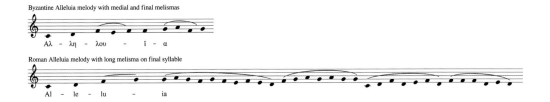

Byzantine Alleluia melody with medial and final melismas

Αλ – λη – λου – ï – α

Roman Alleluia melody with long melisma on final syllable

Al – le – lu – ia

FIG. 31

Transcription of the sung *Allēlouïa* from the *O Kyrios* in MS Vat. lat. 5319, late eleventh century. © Laura Steenberge.

the better-known examples preserved in the papal liturgy. In the latter the melisma forms an extended cadence on the last vowel, *a,* which is known as *jubilus.*

O Kyrios (Ps. 92 [93]: 1) is one of three Byzantine *allēlouïa* melodies imported into the papal liturgy.[70] It is transmitted in the manuscript Vat. lat. 5319, from the late eleventh century and recorded by Marcel Pérès and his Ensemble Organum.[71] *O Kyrios* has the form of ABA: A. melismatic *allēlouïa*—B. Psalm 92 (93): 1—A. melismatic *allēlouïa.* *O Kyrios* was chanted by the papal chapel at Easter vigil and the Pentecostal periods. The transcribed record shows a move from the syllabic singing of *al-* and *lē-* to the melismatic *lou-ï,* reaching the extremely elaborate singing of the final vowel in what is known as the melismatic *jubilus* (fig. 31). The *jubilus* has four phrases: each one exhibits melodic ripples, or oscillations, between adjacent notes, which sometimes leap by a third. The first phrase begins at the top of the range, cascading down a fifth through a sequence of alternating seconds. The following three parts are more static, with a rippling ascending and descending melodic behavior within a narrower range. A broader undulating behavior can be detected in the overall contour composed of the four sections, emphasized by the leaps between them as well as the melodic direction of each.

The image of water can be applied to this melodic form. The association with water is present in the very psalm sung with this *allēlouïa.* Psalm 92 (93) speaks of the rising waters in verses 3 and 4. Thus the extended melisma fosters associations with water poured out of a container (phrase 1), splashing up (phrase 2), settling and subsiding (parts 3 and 4). Section 4 begins with three Fs in a row, which generates stillness. This, coupled with the narrowing of the range from a fourth in section 3 to a third in section 4, implies the settling of water. A similar wave pattern occurs in all the musical settings of the *allēlouïas* recorded in Vat. lat. 5319 and performed by Pérès and his Ensemble Organum.[72] These ascending and descending ripples sonically convey a compelling link between water and voices.

C. THE *ALLĒLOUÏA* OF THE *TELEUTAION* ANTIPHON OF THE CATHEDRAL VESPERS

If the *jubilus,* with its rippling contour, defines the Latin character of the melismatic *allēlouïa,* the Byzantine examples of the Great Church distinguish themselves with the intercalations of nonsemantic syllables. An eloquent example, written in diastematic Middle Byzantine notation, is presented by the *allēlouïa* refrains for Psalm 18 (19), sung in Hagia Sophia as part of the last antiphon of the cathedral vespers on Pentecost (figs. 32–33). The rubric at the beginning of the *teleutaion* specifies that the soloist,

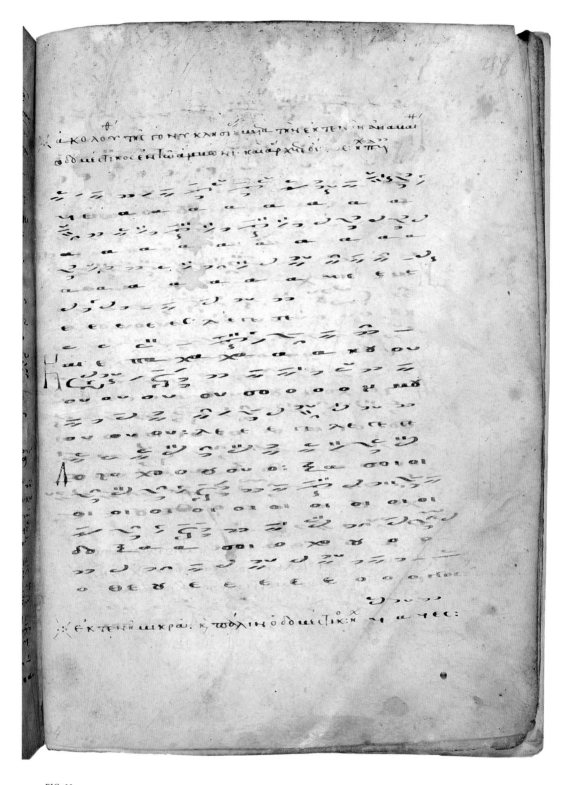

FIG. 32

Florence, Biblioteca Laurenziana, MS gr. Ashburnhamen-

sis 64, dated to 1289, fol. 258r, showing the beginning of

the *teleutaion* antiphon for Pentecost vespers known as the

gonyklisia service.

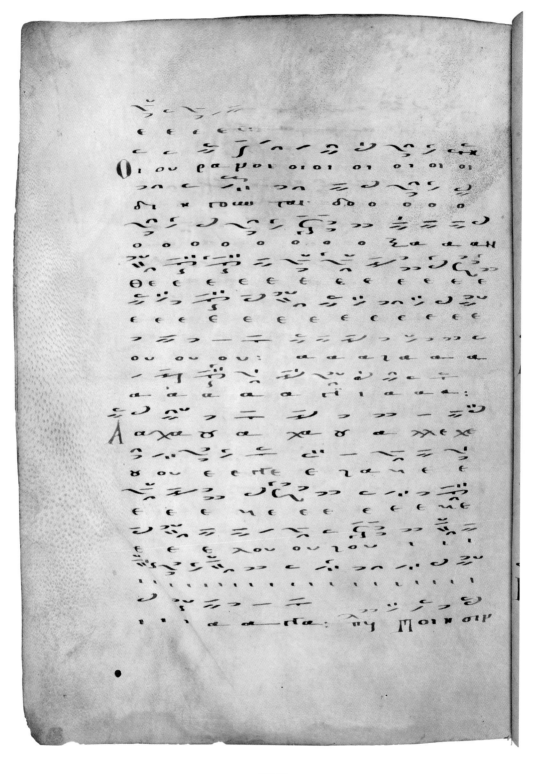

or *domestikos,* ascends the ambo, the ceremonial center for the choir and officiating clergy in the interior of Hagia Sophia (see figs. 5–6, 9–10).[73] The singing then unfolds responsorially between the soloist and the elite choir known as *psaltai.* The heightened solemnity of the feast of Pentecost is expressed in the extreme technical sophistication of the vocal tradition recorded in the stage directions given in the lemma.

The melodic contour for the *allēlouïa* refrain here offers the closest approximation to the elaborate melismatic chants originally designed for Hagia Sophia. Although this piece was performed during the celebration of Pentecost, no evidence links it to the annual consecration rituals of Hagia Sophia. But I use it as a model to gain insight into the elaborate *allēlouïai* sung on important occasions. Many challenges hinder the entry into Byzantine music: a limited number of extant manuscripts in diastematic notation, a lack of adequate transmission of information regarding tempo and phrasing, and a musicology that has privileged the study of syllabic over melismatic styles.[74] But these obstacles should not prevent an exploration into the sonic, because music plays a crucial role in the structuring of sacred space and mystical experience.

As described in the previous chapter, the *allēlouïa* refrains are sung according to three variants, defined by Lingas as types B, C, and D (fig. 34). All three attest to the intercalation of nonsemantic syllables that stretch the semantic chains of the word *allēlouïa:*[75]

Variant B
Ἀχαουαχαουαλλεχεουεγγεενανενεεελουνονϊαγγα (choir) (fig. 33)

Variant C
Ἀλλενανενεουενενανελούνονϊα (choir)

Variant D
Ἀναουα ανaναουα ανaναουα (choir)
Νεανες (soloist)
Ἀναλλεχεουεενεχενεουεχεουελούνονϊνια (choir).

I have marked in bold the intercalated extra-semeiosic letters. The way the word is parsed, a-lē-lou-ï-a, does not coincide with the division (al-ēl-ouïa) in the etymologies of the Byzantine mystagogical tradition.[76] Yet it is clear from this intercalation that variant D reaches an excess. For example, the contiguity between *lē* and *ouïa* dissolves under the pressure of the elaborate pattern of *he-ou-e-e-ne-he-ne-ou-e-he-ou-e;* these intercalated syllables disintegrate the linear composition of meaning in order to produce a sound that functions outside the register of human speech and semantics. The melismatic performance of variant D takes Cappella Romana more than two minutes to sing, exemplifying how the temporal aspect of melismatic singing further enhances this dissolution of meaning.

The intercalations of nonsemantic sounds in the shape of an established word produce the effect of strangeness. Meaning and nonmeaning converge to form something

THE FINAL ANTIPHON ('TELEUTAION') PRIOR TO THE LAMPLIGHTING PSALMS AS SUNG AT THE ASMATIC 'KNEELING' VESPERS OF PENTECOST ACCORDING TO THE PSALTIKON MS FLORENCE ASHBURNHAMENSIS 64

With additional rubrics from the Euchologion MS Grottaferrata Γ.β. 35 (GROT) and the Typikon MS Florence di San Salvatore di Messina MS Mess. gr. 115(MES)[1]

Liturgical Unit and Additional Rubrics	Musical Style	Vocal Range (relative pitch)	Musical Form	Greek Text with Intonations and Asmatic Letters from MS Ashb. 64	Translation (Intonations and asmatic letters omitted)
1. Continuation of Small Litany	Improvised cantillation			Ὁ Διάκονος. Ἀντιλαβοῦ, σῶσον, ἐλέησον καὶ διαφύλαξον ἡμᾶς, ὁ Θεός, τῇ σῇ χάριτι.	Deacon: Help us, save us, have mercy on us, and keep us, O God, by your grace.
2. Antiphon Solo Intonation #1	Melismatic chant	d–c'	A	Ὁ Δομέστικος. Νεανενανο. Τὴν οἰκουμέ-νε-νενενηγην. Αναγια·	The Choir Leader: The Universe.
		c–b	B	Αχαουα χαουα· λεχεουευγε- ευανε νευε· ελουνουϊα· Αναγια.	Alleluia.
		d–c'	C	Αλλεναυενεουε· νευανελουια· αγγα. Νεανες·	Alleluia
		e–d' g–e'	D(ab)	Αναγγα· αουαναναουα· αυαναουαναουα. (Νεανες·)[2] Αναλλεχεουγγε· ενεχενεουεουε·λουνουϊαγγα.	Alleluia
3. Conclusion of the Litany, Prayer and Ecphonesis	Improvised cantillation and congregational response			Ὁ Διάκονος. Τῆς Παναγίας...Χριστῷ τῷ Θεῷ παραθώμεθα. Ὁ Λαός. Σοί, Κύριε. Ὁ Ἱερεύς. ...νῦν καὶ ἀεὶ καὶ εἰς τοὺς αἰῶνας τῶν αἰώνων.	Deacon: Commemorating...to Christ our God. People: To you, O Lord. Priest ...now and for ever, and to the ages of ages.
4. Antiphon Solo Intonation #2 = Ps 18:1a	Melismatic chant	d–d'	A'	Ὁ Δομέστικος. [Αμήν.] Νεανες. Οἱ οὐρανοὶ διηγοῦνται δόξαν Θεοῦ. Αναγια.	The Choir Leader: Amen. The heavens declare the glory of God
GROT and MES: The choir of psaltai enters at 'διηγοῦνται'		c–b	B'	Αχαουα χαουα λλεχεουευγε ευανε.νευε ελουνουϊαγγα. (Νεχεανες.)	Alleluia
5. Antiphon Stichologia		d–b	A''	Ποίησιν δὲ χειρῶν αὐτοῦ ἀναγγέλει τὸ	The firmament proclaims the work of his hands.

[1] C. Høeg, ed., *Contacarium Ashburnhamense: Codex Bibl. Laurentianae Ashburnhamense: Codex Ashburnhamensis 64 phototypice depictus*, Monumenta Musicae Byzantinae 4 (Copenhagen, 1956), fols. 259r–64v; O. Strunk, ed., *Specimina notationum antiquiorum: Folia selecta ex variis codicibus saec. x, xi, & xii phototypice depicta*, Monumenta musicae Byzantinae, 7 (Copenhagen, 1966), plates 38–42; and M. Arranz, *Le Typicon du monastère du Saint-Sauveur à Messine: Codex Messinensis gr. 115*, Orientalia Christiana Analecta 185 (Rome, 1969), p. 279.
[2] Intonations in parentheses are indicated in the manuscript by *martyriai* (intonation signs).

FIG. 34

Structure of the *teleutaion* for Pentecost vespers.

© Alexander Lingas.

Structure of the *teleutaion* for Pentecost vespers.

Section		Form	Greek	English
	d–c'	C'	στερέωνονομαγγα. Ἀναγία Ἀλλεναναγενεουε· νεvανε· λούνουία.	Alleluia.
	d–b	A'''	(Νεχεανες.) Ἡμέρα τῇ ἡμέρᾳ ἐρεύγεται ῥῆμα καὶ νὺξ νυκτὶ ἀναγγέλει γνῶνονονοαττγιν. Νεανες;	Day to day produces speech and night to night proclaims knowledge
	e–d' g–e'	D(a'b')'	Αναουα αναναουα αναναουα (Νεανες;) αναλλεχεουε ενεχεουε χεουε λούνουῖνια	Alleluia.
	d–c'	A''''	(Νεχεανες.) Οὐκ εἰσὶ λαλιαί, οὐδὲ λόγοι, ὧν οὐχὶ ἀκούονται αἱ φωναὶ ἀναυτῶγγων. Ἀναγῖα.	There are no sayings or words in which their voices are not heard:
	c–b	B''	Αχαουα χαουα λεχεουεγγε εναvε vε λούνουία. (Νεχεανες;)	Alleluia
	d–c'	A'''''	Εἰς πᾶσαν τὴν γῆν ἐξῆλθεν ὁ φθόγγος αὐτῶν, καὶ εἰς τὰ πέρατα τῆς οἰκουμένης τὰ ῥήματα αναναναυτῶγγυν.	Their sound has gone out into all the earth, and their words to the ends of the world:
	d–b	C''	Αλλεναναγενεουε· νεvανε λούνουῖνιαγγα.	Alleluia.
	d–c'	A''''''	(Νεχεανες;) Εν τῷ ἡλίῳ ἔθετο τὸ σκήνωμα αὐτοῦ, καὶ αὐτὸς ὡς νυμφίος, ἐκπορευόμενος ἐκ παστοῦ ἀναναῦτοῦ. (Νεχεανες;)	He has pitched his tent in the sun; and he is like a bridegroom who comes out of his marriage chamber.
	e–d' g–e'	D(a''b'')''	Αναουαναναουα· αναναουα (Νεανες;) Αναλεχεουε ενεχεουε χεουε λούνουῖνιαγγα.	Alleluia.
(5a. Optional continuation of the Stichologia)	(c–e')	(ABCD(ab))ˣ	*Εἶτα στιχολογεῖται τὸ ἐπίλοιπον τοῦ ψαλμοῦ* [MES (=GROT): *Καὶ λέγει στίχους ὅσους θέλει.*]	*And then the stichologia of the rest of the psalm is performed* [or, in MES and GROT: *And he performs as many verses as he wishes.*]
6. Doxology and Coda	d–c'	A''''''	(Νεχεανες;) Δόξα Πατρί, καὶ Υἱῷ, καὶ Ἁγίῳ Πνεὐμαναττγι.	Glory to the Father and to the Son and to the Holy Spirit.
	c–b	B'''	Αχαουα χαουα αλλεχεουεγγε εναvε vενενελούνουῖαγγα.	Alleluia.
	d–c'	A'''''''	(Νεχεανες;) Καὶ νῦν, καὶ εἰ, καὶ εἰς τοὺς αἰῶνας τῶν αἰώνων. Αναναναμῆγγην. Ἀναγῖα.	Both now and ever and to the ages of ages. Amen.
	d–c'	C'''	Αλλεναναγενεουε εναvε λούνουῖνιναγγα Νεανες;	Alleluia
	e–d' g–e'	D(a'''b''')'''	Αναναουαναναουα αναναουα Νεανες Αναλλεχεουεγγε ενεχεουε χεουε λούνουῖαγγα.	Alleluia.

FIG. 34 (*cont'd*)

Structure of the *teleutaion* for Pentecost vespers.

FIG. 35
Rossano Gospel book,
Biblioteca arcivescovile,
MS gr. 042, sixth century,
fol. 2v, showing the
parable of the ten virgins.

that exceeds the power of human speech to signify. If the semantics of words are linked to representation, then the intercalation of nonsemantic patterns such as *he-ou-e-e-ne-he-ne-ou-e-he-ou-e* creates presence without representation. This excess in form and meaning enables the sonic to reify the metaphysical without being the divine voice itself and to evoke the music of the cosmic spheres without being the celestial bodies themselves.[77]

The dissolution of meaning is essential, and it is connected to the temporal aspect of melismatic chant and to the reverberant acoustics of the interior space. Hagia Sophia produces an extremely long reverberation time (RT); it is more than ten seconds for frequencies in the range of the singing human voice, 200–2,000 Hz.[78] This RT helps to blur the semantic chains further, to obscure the human register of speech, and to produce a sound evocative of the celestial spheres. The experience of divine nearness is thus sonically inscribed in the physical fabric of the building and made acoustically accessible to the faithful.

Hagia Sophia's long reverberation and melismatic blurring of the intelligibility of words can be heard as "wet" sound, as opposed to the "dry" and clear sound of nonre-verberant spaces.[79] The evocation of water in this "wet" sound connects it with the act of consecration and the establishment of the new altar, as a miniature from the sixth-century Rossano Gospels demonstrates (fig. 35).[80] The image illustrates the Parable of the Wise and Unwise Virgins. Christ guards the golden gate, which will remain forever shut to the five unwise maidens. By contrast, the elect have passed through this door and arrived in the interior of the temple. The architectural body has paradoxically transformed into a garden with an abundant spring. The Rossano miniature equates the sacred, in this case the church interior, to waters flowing in a garden. They lustrate and sanctify the ground; this process is called *hagiasmos,* and the same term appears in the patriarchal prayer pronounced at the *kathierōsis:* "Lord, our God, who has sanctified the streams of Jordan through your salvific epiphany, bless this water for the sanctification (*hagiasmos*) and perfection of this altar of yours!"[81] *Hagiasma,* the product of the lustration, is identified with the altar.[82] The same word appears in Psalm 92 (93): 5, which accompanies the vesting of the sanctuary.

In addition to its power to purify, water smooths surfaces and dissolves the solid. I suggest that an acoustic equivalent of this natural phenomenon resides in the performance of variant D. The singing of the intercalated syllables dissolves the meaning and form of the word *allēlouïa.* The stretched semantic chains thus produce a sonic *metaxu,* set in between the intelligibility of human speech and the incommensurability of the divine.

D. MYSTICAL EXPERIENCE THROUGH THE ACOUSTICS OF ASCENT

Singing inside the resonant interior of Hagia Sophia produces synaesthetic aural and optical phenomena. When activated by chant, the space sustains high-frequency harmonics in all ranges of the human voice; they concentrate in the dome and then are scattered, thus evoking both a soaring, upward movement and an acoustic waterfall.[83] The musical contour of variant D of the *teleutaion's allēlouïa* shows how the intercalations push the melody into the upper ranges.

For the sake of clarity, my analysis of the refrain in variant D refers to the line numbering in Arvanitis's transcription (fig. 36). The entire middle section (*le he ou e e ne he ne ou e he ou e lou*) creates a chiastic center with three peaks reached at the second *he* and *lou.*[84] Flanking these peaks is an opening melody (*a a na a le he ou e*) and an elaborate melismatic variant of the same at the end of line 7 (*nou ou ï*), but transposed by a third. The highest number of intercalated syllables occurs in lines 6 and 7; here the florid melismatic activity spans from G to upper F (a seventh). By contrast, the number of intercalations drops dramatically in lines 8 and 9, and the passage travels from A to upper D (a fourth). Variant D shows clearly how the intercalations help push the range upward and thereby articulate an ascent. The next chapter explores how such aspiratory sounds represented by *he* (in the *teleutaion*), *ho,* and *ha* (in other examples) produce some of these peaks. I contend that these aspiratory sounds draw attention to breath and are frequently set in larger chiastic structures. The latter activate sonic phenomena that are expressive of how, in entering matter, divine energy precipitates a human ascent to the celestial.

The ascent produced by the singing of variant D conveys a mystical transcendence—a sense of liberation from gravity and human affairs, attuning the faithful to the imagined cosmic sound of the rotating celestial spheres. It is fitting to end this chapter in this realm of the sonic, as it sustains the invisibility of divinity. Animation

in Byzantium is incarnate: at a site cir-

FIG. 36

Teleutaion for Pentecost vespers, transcription of the melody after Ioannis Arvanitis. © Laura Steenberge.

cumscribed in time and space, the Holy Spirit enters the phenomenal world as a visual memory stirred by intertextual references, as a diffusing scent, and as a reverberant sound blurring the intelligibility of human speech. Through the ritual proceedings of the *kathierōsis* and its annual commemoration, the consecrated building emerges as a zone for the continual imprinting of Pneuma across the human sensorium and opens the possibility for the experience of ascent and transcendence.

3.

Icons of Breath

Inspiriting, then, as characterized in the previous chapter, is a phenomenon targeted by the Byzantine *kathierōsis* rite and aimed at transforming the newly built and *apsychos* (inert) temple into an *empsychos naos* (animate temple). This animation of the inert manifests itself in the visual, olfactory, and sonic realms of perception. This chapter broadens the exploration of medieval animation by showing how inspiriting produces an *eikōn*, an image engendered through a participation in the liturgy, especially chant. By partaking in the religious rite and singing, the faithful can recuperate, albeit ephemerally, a lost capacity to become an "image of God": in Greek *eikōn tou Theou*. I identify this process of becoming an image with the exhalation and inhalation of breath in singing and use the term "performative *eikōn*" to designate this nonrepresentational image in order to distinguish it from the traditional representational image. This performative icon is the product of the mouth and breath; and it is invested in the collective body of the singers, listeners, and architectural space (fig. 37). While the term "performative" originates in speech-act theory and, later, gender studies,[1] here I use it specifically with reference to inspiriting.

The architectural shell acts as an instrument of the human voice. A deep connection runs between the *eikōn tou Theou* and the building consecrated by the *kathierōsis* rite. Both are *empsychos* matter transformed by the grace of the Holy Spirit. In the same way that *empsychōsis* activates the new altar, so too inspiriting engenders the performative image in the participant. The link between the inspirited building and iconicity can enrich our understanding of the phrase "architecture as icon." Up to this point scholars have identified its meaning with the pictorial representations of buildings.[2] By contrast, this analysis demonstrates how iconicity expands beyond representation to encompass the transformation of the body of the faithful and the architectural space in the course of the liturgical ritual.

FIG. 37

Eastern Orthodox monks chant *Christos Anesti* during an
Easter midnight vigil, 2009.

In highlighting the concept of the
performative *eikōn,* this chapter brings to
the fore an aspect of Late Antique image
theory that has not been recognized and
sufficiently explored. The *eikōn tou Theou*
offers a novel manifestation of an essentialist theory: the icon shares in the nature of
the prototype—because it partakes in Pneuma—without tying this participation,
or *methexis,* to pictorial representation. The Eucharist exemplifies this phenomenon; it is
an *eikōn* of Christ without being a representational image; its ontology is tied to the liturgical ritual. This insight sheds new light on Byzantine Iconoclasm (726–843).[3] It shows
that the performative image existed alongside the representational one (figs. 37–38) and
that the ensuing crisis about the image focused on which of the two definitions—the
performative or the representational—should underscore the meaning of what an image
is.[4] In fact, the so-called Iconoclasts did not reject the concept of image altogether; they
only rejected the representational icon, but embraced the performative *eikōn. Perigraphē*
is another heavily contested term. For Maximus the Confessor, *perigraphē* means this
final state of *henōsis* (union) with the divine that leads to the faithful's deification; it is
perigraphē that resolves the separateness of the two halves—the hemisphere of the dome
and the bowl of the Eucharist chalice—in the unity of participation in the divine.[5]

The church fathers introduced the performative image in order to articulate a difference between the new religion and its pagan predecessors.[6] This nonrepresentational
iconicity allows us to approach the body of the faithful and the material fabric of the

FIG. 38

Icon of Christ, mid-sixth century, encaustic paint on wood board. Monastery of Saint Catherine, Sinai, Egypt.

building as instruments of breath and expand the discourse on the Byzantine image beyond art history and into music and ritual. What we distinguish today as two separate entities—"image" and "sound"—were much more complexly interlinked in Byzantium. During the liturgical performance modulated breath exhaled in chant stirred the acoustics of the ecclesiastical space, producing a sensorial yet nonrepresentational manifestation of divinity. The structure and prosody of the sung poetry aided this process. In foregrounding a chiastic form and an aspiratory sound, the performance of the psalmody in the cathedral rite, I argue, produced an acoustic equivalent to the vital inbreathing of Adam that had transformed him before the Fall into an "image of God." By turning to a phenomenology of sound in Hagia Sophia, this chapter demonstrates how singing engenders the sacred, transforming both performers and listeners into *eikones tou Theou*.

The Performative *Eikōn* in the Textual Record

Adam's story in Genesis indicates the two processes through which the performative *eikōn* emerges. The first is mirroring linked to sustaining likeness, *homoiōsis;* it marks a nonessentialist model because the copy does not share in the nature of the prototype. The second process is inspiriting. It presents an essentialist model; the copy and the prototype share essence because they partake in Pneuma. Both processes occur in the *kathierōsis* liturgy; inspiriting makes the new altar *empsychos* and capable of mirroring the supercelestial table.

A. *EIKŌN TOU THEOU* IN GENESIS

The origins of the performative *eikōn* can be traced back to Genesis 1:26–28, with their mention of three concepts: image (*eikōn*), likeness (*homoiōsis*), and blessing (*eulogia*). Together, these lines transform Adam into an image of God: "Let us make man according to our image and likeness. . . . And God made man, according to the image of God he made them, male and female he made them. And God blessed them."[7] God makes Adam according to the Lord's form (*eikōn*). Adam is given a capacity to reflect divine likeness (*homoiōsis*), which allows him to sustain being an *eikōn* of God. As evident also in later texts, divine blessing (*eulogeō*) plays an important role in maintaining this mirroring process.

The function of this *eulogia* becomes clearer in Genesis 2:7, where it introduces inspiriting as engendering the *eikōn tou Theou*: "And God formed the man of dust of the earth and breathed upon his face the breath of life and the man became a living soul."[8] In this second version of the story, God forms Adam out of the dust of the earth and animates the inert by breathing life into him. Genesis 2:7 uses *emphysaō,* denoting the act of breathing in a life-giving Spirit. Is this descent of Spirit into matter connected to the act of blessing (*eulogeō*) in Genesis 1:28? A similar pairing occurs in the *kathierōsis* rite, where the gesture of blessing the altar performed at the cleansing, wine libation, chrismation, and incensing ultimately activates Pneuma to descend and to sanctify the new sanctuary.[9] The blessing gesture brings about *empsychōsis.*

Together, the two accounts in Genesis compose a definition of the performative image as the human being infused with divine breath (*pneuma* and *pnoē* are synonyms denoting both "breath" and "spirit") through vital inspiriting (*emphysaō*) and divine blessing (*eulogeō*).

B. THE *EIKŌN* IN THE NEW TESTAMENT AND PAUL'S LETTERS

The word "image" in the New Testament identifies only the mimetic representation: the portrait of the emperor on coins.[10] Yet Christ himself presents an alternative model that develops in the subsequent apostolic and patristic writings as the performative *eikōn*. In the Gospel accounts, inspiriting marks the epiphanic moments in Christ's life: baptism and Transfiguration. At these two events, two familiar forces make their appearance, blessing and inspiriting, which were operative earlier in Genesis 1:28 and 2:7. They cause the metaphysical to manifest itself in the phenomenal as bright light and sound: "Jesus, when he was baptized, went up straightway out of the water: and, lo, the heavens were opened unto him, and he saw the Spirit of God descending like a dove, and lighting upon him. And lo a voice from heavens, saying, 'This is my beloved Son, in whom I am well pleased'" (Matt. 3:16–17, KJV).[11] The resplendent light and sound mark this inspiriting, through which Christ's divinity manifests itself in the phenomenal. Similarly, the descent of Pneuma over Christ at his Transfiguration unfolds as a visual and aural phenomenon in the form of a bright cloud and a voice: "While he yet spake, behold, a bright cloud overshadowed them: and behold a voice out of the cloud, which said, 'This is my beloved Son, in whom I am well pleased, hear ye him!'" (Matt. 17:5, KJV).[12] Christ is overshadowed by the bright cloud and inspirited through the aural manifestation of divine Pneuma. The Son of God transmits these spiritual energies further when he performs his miracles. He implants the Spirit's vivifying power in those who seek his help.[13]

Interpreting the Gospel accounts, the apostle Paul identifies Christ with the *eikōn tou Theou*: "[God the Father] hath delivered us from the power of darkness, and hath translated us into the kingdom of his dear Son. In whom we have redemption through his blood, even the forgiveness of sins. Who is the image of the invisible God, the firstborn of every creature" (Col. 1:13–15, KJV).[14] He further states, in Romans 8:29, that the saints share an essential link with him and have the capacity to become such *eikones:* "For whom he did foreknow [the saints], he also did predestinate [them] to be conformed [*symmorphoi*] to the image of his Son, that he might be the firstborn among many brethren" (KJV).[15] The saints are born into Christ and sustain this link by being *symmorphoi,* meaning continuously mirroring the form of Christ. The fact that they are also called brethren of the firstborn, or offspring, shows that their reflexive, nonanalogue iconicity is incarnational, and as such it should be viewed as engendered by the grace of Pneuma: inspiriting.

C. THE PERFORMATIVE *EIKŌN* IN PATRISTIC WRITING: MIRRORING AND INSPIRITING

The patristic literature further develops the concept of the performative iconicity.[16] Anca Vasiliu, in her study of the icon, points to a change from what she defines as an "ancient" conceptualization of the *eikōn* to a "medieval" conceptualization. The early church fathers work with an ancient paradigm, which identifies image with a mimetic and pictorial representation; this analogue image is considered an open book that one can read. By contrast, the medieval model, articulated in the writings of Basil of Caesarea (ca. 329–371), Gregory of Nyssa (ca. 335–395), and John Chrysostom (ca. 349–407), defines the image as a reflexive entity. An *eikōn* is a mirror—*esoptron* or *katoptron*—that continuously models itself on Christ. This *eikōn tou Theou* originates with Adam, who forms a special link between the uncreated and created. This original *eikōn* is ontologically different from the representational image; it does not derive from the Platonic concept of image as representation.[17] It has an other agentive aspect, which comes into being through the incarnation of divine breath.[18]

Basil of Caesarea expounds these ideas in his homilies 10 and 11, "On the Creation of the Human Being." God bestowed iconicity on humanity at the Creation. But since the Fall humanity has been challenged to sustain this likeness (*homoiōsis*) to the original form. *Homoiōsis* captures the continuous and arduous process of performing a nonrepresentational iconicity:

"Let us make the human being according to our image [*eikona*] and likeness [*homoiōsin*]"; we possess the former through creation, and the latter we acquire through our will. According to the first, it is given that we be born in the *eikōn tou Theou,* but according to the will, a being is formed in us after the likeness of God. The latter part [likeness], according to choice, is in our power, and we bring it to vividness for ourselves. In creating us, would the Lord have anticipated the precaution, saying "create" and "in likeness," if he had not simultaneously given us the power to arrive at likeness, and if he had not been our proper power to acquire likeness to God? And so God created us with the power to achieve likeness of him. And given the power to model ourselves in a likeness of God, we are the artists producing likeness to God, [a likeness] unlike a portrait produced by the hand of the artist, and eventually receive the recompense for our efforts. In the end, our likeness results in praise, not for someone else [some artist], creating vainly, but for us. For regarding a portrait, you do not praise the image itself but marvel at the painter who produced it. As opposed to the object of praise being I and not someone else, I have let myself become a likeness of God. In *eikōn* I have the rational essence, and in likeness I become Christian.[19]

Likeness, *homoiōsis,* is achieved by will, through which one sustains the original *eikōn tou Theou.* Likeness is inscribed in the structure of the living through the action of modeling. The success of this performance is determined by the strength of the human will. Sustaining likeness to God is the reason to shower praise on the individual human being. Basil separates this nonrepresentational iconicity from the representational, artifactual image. The man-made portrait is an inanimate object, which bestows praise on the artist for his skill to depict likeness. The representational image never brings praise to the human being whose likeness is being portrayed.

Gregory of Nyssa also contends that image making is dependent on achieving likeness, for both the representational and performative images: "for the [image/icon] is properly so called if it keeps its [likeness] to the prototype; but if imitation be perverted from its subject, the thing is something else, and no longer an image of the subject."[20] If likeness is lost, the "image of X" can no longer claim to be an image of X. The human being achieves likeness to God through a mirroring process independent from pictorial *mimēsis.* The mind (*nous*) acts as such a mirror. If this *esoptron* is set wrongly or dimmed, it will no longer be capable of reflecting the divine. Likeness will be lost, and with it the possibility of sustaining the *eikōn tou Theou:*

> The mind [*nous*] is decorated by the likeness of the prototype's beauty in the way that a mirror is shaped from the reflection of the person who appears in it; by this analogy the nature managed by the mind is set up in a similar way: it is adorned by the beauty at hand, like some mirror of a mirror. . . . and so the transmission of the ugliness of matter reaches through nature to the mind, so that the image of God is no longer seen in the reflected figure expressed by that which was molded according to it; for the mind, setting the idea of good like a mirror behind the back, turns off the incident rays of the effulgence of the good, and it receives into itself the impress of the shapelessness of matter.[21]

As Gregory of Nyssa states, *nous* is a mirror that reflects the divine; if the mirror is damaged or wrongly positioned, the power to reflect the divine is lost, and with it are gone *homoiōsis* and the possibility of recuperating the state of being an *eikōn tou Theou.* As analyzed in the first chapter, the dome of Hagia Sophia, like an enormous *esoptron,* visualizes this mirroring process, channeling the divine *katabasis* and the mortals' *anabasis.* And as Maximus the Confessor asserts, the intellective being desiring the divine urges itself onward, accelerating its motion, until it is wholly encompassed by the beloved. This *kinēsis,* underlying the complex motility of the *kallichoros* and of the faithful, sustains *homoiōsis.* The ultimate stage is to complete the circuit, *perigraphē,* which in the ritual setting meant the *methexis* (partaking) in the divine. The iconicity produced through this theurgic understanding of *perigraphē* is that of partaking in Pneuma, producing inspirited, *empsychōs,* matter.[22]

The *kathierōsis* rite can help shed light on this mirroring process. At least in the context of consecration, mirroring is made possible by inspiriting. *Empsychōsis* causes the new altar to become a terrestrial mirror reflective of the supercelestial one.[23] The consecrated table thus serves triply as altar, suffering Christ, and resurrected Christ. The Theodore Psalter shows all three in a vertical succession (see fig. 29). What these three miniatures convey expands beyond pictorial representations; they allude to the Eucharist as nonanalogue *eikōn tou Theou,* mixing human with divine, matter with Spirit. The miniatures thus direct the imagination to a metaphysical dimension that can only be experienced in the liturgical ritual.

The *empsychos eikōn* emerges most clearly in the Eucharistic rite; it is incarnate Spirit: divinely human Logos continuously inscribing itself in the aural. It is this capacity to speak that distinguishes the *eikōn tou Theou* from the mute and *apsychos* representational icon produced by the artist's hands. John Chrysostom lends further support to this identification of the performative icon with the sacraments. He views the bride and groom coming together in Christian marriage as producing a performative *eikōn:* "Rather, when they [the bride and groom] come together, they make not a inanimate icon [*apsychos eikōn*] or the image of an earthly creature, but the image of God himself."[24] In coming together in Christ, the bride and groom form a living image, *eikōn* of God, in which they recover, albeit temporarily, a prelapsarian perfection. Their *empsychos* iconicity is contrasted to an *apsychos* icon, produced by the painter's or the sculptor's hand. The set of opposites juxtaposes speech with muteness, Spirit with lifelessness. The performative *eikōn* is ritually produced and engendered by inspiriting. More specifically, blessing triggers the *empsychōsis;* this is the very gesture performed by the priest over the new couple. The *eulogeō* produces *empsychōsis,* underscoring the connection established between vital inbreathing and blessing in Genesis 1:26–28 and 2:7.

D. INSPIRITING IN THE EUCHARIST AND THE COLUMN SAINTS

Medieval exegetes discuss the sacraments as engendered by inspiriting.[25] Thus the sacrament of the Eucharist exemplifies this performative iconicity. In the 740s the iconoclast emperor Constantine V (r. 741–75) wrote in his *Peuseis* (Inquires) that "[a]n *eikōn* of his [Christ's] body is the bread, which we accept, as it morphs [*morphazōn*] into his flesh, so as to become a *typos* of his body."[26] The Eucharist as a performative *eikōn* exemplifies essentialist image theory. This nonrepresentational image partakes in the prototype; through the descent of Pneuma into matter, the bread and wine morph into Christ's body and blood and are infused with his divinely human nature.

Moreover, the passage presents a couple of other terms that help articulate this incarnational definition of *eikōn* as a product of the sacraments. The Greek *typos* (referring to both "sealing" and "imprint") marks the branding of matter with the energies of the Holy Spirit. It is also related to the way in which the Eucharist bread is produced: the dough is set in a mold that carries the negative image of the cross (fig. 39): this figure is imprinted on the bread through fire and sealing. A second imprinting of fire on matter takes place when, after the sacerdotal *epiklēsis,* the Holy Spirit descends onto and brands (*typoō*) the bread, infusing sacred energies in the process.[27] The faithful then receive the Eucharist through their mouths, and in consuming it, they partake in Pneuma.

FIG. 39

Terra-cotta bread mold, Byzantine, fifth–sixth centuries. Royal Ontario Museum, ROM 986.181.122.

By extension, the communicants become, albeit ephemerally, *eikones tou Theou. Empsychōsis* is marked by the sign of the cross, as indicated by the bread mold that has the cross in its center. The same figure is invested in the gesture of blessing, which endows Adam with life and ensures that the bride and groom become *eikones tou Theou.*

The Iconoclast writings show how Byzantine Iconoclasm was not a simple rejection of artifacts but a philosophical debate concerning the ontology of image. A major question was whether the concept of image should be identified with a pictorial *mimēsis* or with a performative/sacramental paradigm lodged in inspiriting and *methexis.* The Iconoclasts supported the latter. This nonrepresentational iconicity had a significant base in the period before Iconoclasm. In addition to the sacraments, it included the cult of the so-called pillar saints, or *stylites* (from *stylos,* "pillar"), of the fifth and sixth centuries, who lived on top of columns (fig. 40).[28]

Starting in Syria with Saint Symeon the Stylite the Elder (d. 459), the pillar saints quickly gained a following in the course of the sixth century. Large monastic complexes and pilgrimage churches rose at the sites of their columns, while a profusion of hagiographic literature commemorated their extraordinary lives.[29] Their sanctity issued from a continuous *empsychōsis;* Pneuma descended into and dwelled in their bodies, allowing them to heal by exhaling its salvific energies on the stricken and afflicted. This occurrence is captured well in the vita of Saint Symeon the Stylite the Younger (521–592):[30]

> And as he was praying, the Holy Spirit descended into his heart and filled him with wisdom and knowledge, as the saint had demanded. . . . For truly Symeon was the lamp of the Holy Spirit. . . . [A]nd holding the incense in his right hand,

FIG. 40

Gilded silver plaque, fifth–early seventh centuries, showing

Saint Symeon Stylites. Musée du Louvre, inv. Bj 2180.

he offered it to God, and suddenly, like flame, the smoke of perfume rose up. . . . Again some [people] brought before [the saint] a blind man, and [Symeon], blowing/*emphysēsa* toward [the blind man's] eyes, said: "In the name of our Lord Jesus Christ, the son of God, acquire sight!" And immediately, straining his eye, [the blind man] started to see everyone, and raising his hands toward the sky, he glorified God and his holy servant, and for many years he was able to see the light.[31]

Through prayer, the stylite activates the descent of the Holy Spirit into his body. As a result of this *empsychōsis,* he can burn incense without the use of fire, and by extension he can heal by exhaling this divine Pneuma. Much as the wafting perfume of burning incense at the end of the *kathierōsis* rites marks Pneuma's presence, so the stylite's burning of *thymiama* without real fire manifests the Holy Spirit's infusion of his body. His *empsychos* body acquires the identity of a consecrated altar.

Like the newly consecrated altar, which doubles as Christ (fig. 29), the stylite acquires the same powers through *empsychōsis.* Pneuma coursing in his body transforms the stylite into an *eikōn tou Theou.* A text attributed to Leontius of Neapolis in the seventh century or to George of Cyprus in the eight century attests to this fact; it equates the saintly body with the ecclesiastical space; both present matter continually inspirited by the Holy Ghost:[32] "an *eikōn* of God is the human being who has transformed himself according to the image of God, and especially the one who has received the indwelling of the Holy Spirit. I justly give honor to the image of the servants of God and veneration to the house of the Holy Spirit."[33] In this essentialist definition, *eikōn tou Theou* emerges as the living body of the saint, where the Holy Spirit finds its dwelling. The identification of the performative *eikōn* with both the saint and the ecclesiastical building shows that this concept has temporal and spatial dimensions.

E. THE CHURCH AS A PERFORMATIVE *EIKŌN*

The mystagogical texts that record the Byzantine interpretation, or exegesis, of the liturgy further develop this spatial and temporal paradigm of the performative *eikōn.*[34] Maximus the Confessor, in his *Mystagogia,* written ca. 630, identifies the concept of the church with the material structure, the corporate body of the faithful, and the site of unfolding mystical rituals.[35] Rooting his analysis in the mystagogy of Pseudo-Dionysius, Maximus states: "According to the first principle of his theory, the venerable old man [Pseudo-Dionysius] said that indeed the holy church is the *typos* and *eikōn* of God, sharing in his [God's] [spiritual] energy through mirroring [*mimēsin*] and inspiriting [*typon*]."[36] Maximus uses *eikōn* and *typos* to define the church's space and its relationship with the divine. *Typos* identifies inspiriting, the process through which the energies of Pneuma descend into matter. *Eikōn* as the church emerges through *mimēsis,* which I identify with the *esoptron* phenomenon in the *kallichoros* of the Great Church (see fig. 2); this idea is also manifested in the Mt. Athos miniature on folio 93v (analyzed in the first chapter; see fig. 8). Through mirroring, the *kallichoros* sustains itself as a vessel of the divine, and through *typōsis,* it ingathers divine energy.

Chiasm: The Performative *Eikōn* as a Textual Structure

As shown in the first chapter, Byzantine culture developed a visual formula to mark *empsychōsis:* the cross-in-a-circle configuration manifested in the cupola, the Eucharist chalice, the imagined form and movement of the earth, and the shape of the Eucharist bread (see figs. 3, 5, 17–18, 39).[37] This structure identifies a *typos* and renders it graphically as a cross in a circle. The shape is symmetrical and reflective both along its vertical and horizontal axes. Placed in this graphic form, matter transforms into an *eikōn tou Theou* during the Eucharist liturgy. I propose that the graphic formula of the *typos* identifies what textual studies have defined as chiasm, or inverted parallelism.

Chiasm in literature operates through the repetition of a word or a phrase in a mirroring structure that establishes a frame arranged centripetally about a center. As a result, the structure focuses attention on the center, which, in a chiasm occupying several lines, embodies the main idea, understood as a premeditated action, a counsel, or a promise. Chiasm is attested in many prominent texts: the Old and New Testaments, Homer, the Gospel of John, and some of Paul's letters.[38] New in my analysis of chiasm is the recognition that this textual structure can inscribe Pneuma at its center and thus use the form to enact *empsychōsis.* To show this occurrence, I focus on psalms that place Pneuma or man at the center of the chiastic structure. These texts were also chanted in the liturgy of Hagia Sophia; thus the *empsychōsis* they generated through their use of chiasm, I argue, acquired spatial and temporal dimensions in the ritual.

Nils Lund has established the foundation for the study of chiasm in the Psalms.[39] His analysis focuses on the original Hebrew version of the Psalms and uncovers the chiastic structure underlying the composition of entire psalms, blocks of psalms (such as the grouping of Psalms 1 and 2), and single strophes. In its basic form the structure assumes the pattern ABCB'A'. Within the chiastic unit, the shape and length of the strophe, as well as its rhythm, could vary. This is how Lund identifies the chiasm in Psalm 66 (67), using his own literal English translation from the Hebrew original:

A v. 1 *God* be merciful onto us, and bless us,
　　　　May he cause his face to shine upon us.
　　v. 2 That may be known upon the *earth* thy way,
　　　　among all nations thy salvation.

　　　B v. 3 Let the *peoples* give thee thanks, O *God*
　　　　　　Let the *peoples* give thee thanks, *all of them.*

Chiastic center, C v. 4 Let the *nations* be glad and sing for joy
　　　　　　　For thou will judge the *peoples* in equity,
　　　　　　　And the *nations* upon the earth thou wilt lead.

　　　B' v. 5 Let the *peoples* give thee thanks, O *God*
　　　　　　Let the *peoples* give thee thanks, *all of them.*

　A' v. 6 The *earth* hath yielded her increase;
　　　　May *God* bless us
　　　　Our own God;
　　v. 7 May *God* bless us
　　　　and all the ends of the *earth* shall fear him.

As Lund has predicted, the chiasm follows an ABCB'A' pattern. Contentwise this structure proceeds from a plea to God (A) to the performance of the prayer at the center of the chiasm (C) and the disbursement of God's grace on the earth and his people at the end (A'). Strophes B and B' are identical in form and content, focusing attention on the center (C). In addition to structuring the overall composition, the chiasm also appears in a miniature version in strophes C and A'. C is chiastic in its repetition of "nations," defining the frame, around "people," which stands at the center. In A' the phrase "Our own God" stands at the center of another group displaying inverted parallelism. Further, subtler patterns of correspondences run through the chiastic structure of this psalm. The word "God" opens A, while the same word appears in the second hemistich of A'. This relationship is inverted in the use of "earth"; the word appears in the second verse of A but opens A'. The word "peoples" appears in the odd verses 1, 3, and 5, while "nations" appears in the even verses 2 and 4. "God" is also used in strophes A, B, B', and A' but not in C, and "earth" is found in A, C, and A' but not in B or B'. According to Lund, this frequently recurring arrangement distributes similar or antithetical terms in the center and in extremes of chiastic structures.[40]

John Breck has developed Lund's work further by engaging the Greek Septuagint, the Gospels, and the Pauline letters.[41] Drawing on this research, I present two examples of chiasm that put "man" and "Spirit" at the center of the inverted parallelism. The first is Psalm 50 (51): 8–14 (already analyzed in the previous chapter). As the larger outer frame (vv. 8–14) is arranged centripetally about a center (v. 11), it identifies the heart of the chiasm as a request to God not to turn his face away from the faithful but to implant in them instead his vivifying Spirit. In this case, the meaning of the passage is fully embodied in the shape of the poetry: form and content mutually reinforce the desire for inspiriting. The recognition of *empsychōsis* is further confirmed by the illustration of this very verse in the Khludov Psalter, showing the Holy Spirit as a dove descending over the prophet David (see fig. 25).

If the chiasm of Psalm 50 inscribes *empsychōsis* in the center, the inverted parallelism of Psalm 8 (9) draws attention to the spiritual operations of mirroring inherent in the form. The chiasm of Psalm 8 places man at the center of the cosmos. I have marked this center with the sign of *empsychōsis*, ⊗:

A 1. **O Lord, our Lord, how majestic is thy name in all the earth,**

   B 2. Thou whose glory above the heavens is chanted by the mouths of babes and infants,

      C 3. Thou hast founded a bulwark because of thy foes to still the enemy and the avenger.

         D 4. When I look at thy heavens, the work of thy fingers, the moon and the stars, which thou hast established;

            ⊗ **E 5. What is man that thou art mindful of him, and the son of man that thou dost care for him?**

            ⊗ **E 6. Yet thou hast made him a little less than God, and dost crown him with glory and honor.**

         D' 7. Thou hast given him dominion over the works of thy hands, thou hast put all things under his feet,

      C' 8. All sheep and oxen, and also the beasts of the field,

   B' 9. The birds of the air, and the fish of the sea, whatever passes along the paths of the sea.

A' 10. **O Lord, our Lord, how majestic is thy name in all the earth.**[42]

                                                 (RSV)

The first and last lines form the frame (A, A'): extolling the greatness of God's name; at the center is man, the perfect reflection of divine greatness, who is endowed with powers to rule over the earth and the sea (E, E). Above him rise the heavens and the firmament; below are the earth and the seas offering their bounty at his feet. The content of the poem—of divinity reflected in man—is perfectly embodied by the chiasm. Its mirroring structure captures the *esoptron* of the divine-human dynamic. Psalm 8 becomes an alternative rendition of Genesis 1:26–28 and 2:7. Its chiastic structure places Adam at the center, transforming him into a mirror of the divine and thus an *eikōn tou Theou*.

The Spatial Dimension of *Typos* and *Chiasm* in Hagia Sophia

As the psalmody is performed in Hagia Sophia, where it unfolds in time and space, does the textual chiasm of its poetry translate into a spatial, three-dimensional construction? The answer to this question can be found, I argue, by exploring the connection between the chiasm and the graphic formula of the sign of the cross inscribed on objects and in the interior of Hagia Sophia.

FIG. 41

Cross of Justin II (r. 565–78), relic of the True Cross, gold, pearls, and gems. St. Peter's Treasury, Vatican City.

Christianity gave impetus to the use of chiasm because the new religion promoted the chiastic structure of the cross as the sign of its identity. The center of this visual formula is recognized as the locus of spiritual energies. The *staurothēkē* of Emperor Justin II (r. 565–78) exemplifies this model (fig. 41).[43] Fragments of the True Cross are placed in the center. The cross-shaped opening in the middle of the silver disk, through which the relics of the True Cross are visible, configures the cross-in-a-circle formula of *empsychōsis*. This core is integrated in a larger cross-shaped container made of gold and decorated with gems and pearls. The arms of the outer *typos* present a two-line dedicatory inscription. The verse on the vertical axis announces that Christ defeated his enemies by means of the Cross (Crucifixion). The horizontal bar expands on this idea by announcing that the emperor Justinian, in offering this relic to Rome, secures the protection of the city, while his wife dutifully embellishes the relic.[44] The arrangement of components visualizes the belief that the powers of the *staurothēkē* issue from its center. Form and content fully align: the miniature fragments of the True Cross infused with Pneuma shape an *empsychōsis* cross-in-a-circle formula, which is in turn engulfed by a larger cross.

The structuring of elements in Justin II's *staurothēkē* attests to a perception that divine energies reside in the center of the chiastic structure. Not surprisingly, the same graphic formula is adapted as a marker of Christ's name. Χρίστος is configured as a Christogram (a letter configuration from *Christos-*, "Christ," and *gramma-*, "letter") using the first two letters of his name: the Chi-Rho (☧). This chiasm decorates many surfaces; a beautiful golden object today at the Cleveland Museum of Art displays the basic shape (fig. 42). The crossing of the two bars along the diagonal lines establishes the shape of the X, while the sinusoidal attachment at the top of the sole vertical bar forms the letter P. Together, they inscribe the Chi-Rho (☧) of Χρίστος. This Christogram originally had a circular frame, which has since been lost. The resulting form would have reproduced the cross-in-a-circle sign of *empsychōsis*. Since Christ is an *eikōn tou Theou*, his Christogram identifies both a performative *eikōn* and a *typos*.

Some Christograms add the letters alpha and omega to the diagonal cross bars. This development, I argue, intensifies the chiasm and its power to identify Christ and *empsychōsis*. Alpha and omega introduce an alternative graphic formula to designate the Christogram's inverted parallelism. These two letters mark the beginning and end of the Greek alphabet. Their presence is related both to the ancient practice of learning the alphabet and to its symbolic significance. Children in the ancient Mediterranean studied the alphabet not just as a linear progression of letters, the way we do today, but chiastically; they paired the first with the last letter, the second with the second to last, the third with the third to last, and so on: *alpha* with *ōmega, bēta* with *psi, gamma* with *chi,* and so forth, all the way to *mu* and *nu* at the center.[45] *Mu* and *nu* give the consonants to the word *monos,* meaning "one." Christianity identified this *monos* with Christ. Thus the alpha and omega became an alternative way to signify Christ at the center of a chiasm.

The Christograms on the lid and front of the fifth-century bishop Theodorus's sarcophagus display this composition (fig. 43). A Chi-Rho and an α-ω appear enclosed in two roundels, one on the lid and the other on the face of the container. The alpha and omega implicitly bring to the fore *monos* and thus intensify an awareness of the chiasm and the cross as a source of inspiriting. This inscription of *empsychōsis* is quite appropriate given the context; as a decoration on a sarcophagus, the Christogram expresses a desire for salvation and resurrection. The two peacocks flanking the monogram and the circular vine rinceaux allude to renewal of life and resurrection. The Christogram stands at the center of this visual field as a source of vivifying energy.

As discussed in the first chapter, variants of this chiastic figure mark the Justinianic decor in Hagia Sophia. Examples in mosaic can be found in the keys of the domical vaults in the aisles on the ground level (see fig. 15).[46] Each manifestation shows two intersecting crosses. They are surrounded by an outer rim with miniature roundels in which other tiny crosses alternate with swastikas. The succession from center to rim shows a reproduction and miniaturization of the main cross-in-circle motif. Not only does power reside in the center of the chiasm, but, as this composition shows, it also triggers a cloning process. This dynamic, I argue, structures the visual field in Hagia Sophia: a monumental cross executed in mosaic originally graced the apex of main dome, but it has since disappeared (see figs. 2–3).[47] Paul the Silentiary, in his ekphrasis of Hagia Sophia, mentions this cross on a number of occasions.[48] In the first (a passage quoted in the first chapter), he writes: "A helmet rising above into the boundless air / spins it from both sides into a sphere; / radiant as the heavens, it bestrides the roof of the church. / Art has depicted at its summit a cross, / protector of the city. . . . in the navel inside the circle the form of the cross is shaped / in small mosaic tesserae, so that the Savior / of the whole world may forever protect the temple."[49] In Paul's ekphrasis the dome is animate, a helmet that has come to life; its whirling motion shapes the air into a sphere that evokes the resplendent skies. A cross is inscribed at its heavenly apex. This figure is enclosed in a circle, producing the visual formula of a cross in a circle, which marks *empsychōsis*. Paul qualifies the cross in the dome with the Homeric adjective *erysiptolis,* which is used in the Iliad to define the protective powers of the goddess

FIG. 42
Monogram of Christ (chrismon), Syria, 500s. The Cleveland
Museum of Art, Gift of Lillian M. Kern 1965.551.

FIG. 43

The sarcophagus of Bishop Theodorus, fifth century. Basilica of Sant'Apollinare in Classe, near Ravenna.

Athena.[50] Hagia Sophia's mosaic cross is thus seen as lending divine protection to the city much as Justin II's *staurothēkē* secures the same for Rome. On another occasion the same cross is called "propitious" (*ilaos*), again implying its miraculous powers.[51] Paul's ekphrasis suggests that a medieval viewer looking at the mosaic cross in the cupola recognized the presence of divine energies in this *typos*.

Paul ascribes animacy further to the marble carvings displaying cross-in-a-circle designs (fig. 44). The pattern shows four petals forming a cross. Most prominently, this motif frames the discs of red stone in the spandrels of the ground-level arcade (fig. 45). These roundels are set in vibrant acanthus rinceaux. In the spandrels of the gallery level of the exedrae we encounter porphyry disks, which originally had a cross in their centers (fig. 46). These crosses must have been removed in the Ottoman period. Paul the Silentiary animates both the acanthus and the stone roundels:

> And above the high-crested columns underneath the projecting stone edge
> the swirl of a lacy acanthus, spreading pliantly,
> swirls, a roving chain golden,
> full of yearning, winding its sharp needles;
> it encloses marble roundels like disks,
> flashing an enchanting *charis* of stone.[52]

FIG. 44 (*below*)

Hagia Sophia, 532–37 and 562, carved marble frame with flowers and leaves set in roundels.

FIG. 45 (*right*)

Hagia Sophia, 532–37 and 562, spandrel with a red stone roundel and deeply undercarved acanthus rinceaux.

FIG. 46 (*bottom*)

Hagia Sophia, 532–37 and 562, spandrel of the gallery level of the exedrae, showing porphyry disks that originally held crosses.

A series of synonyms builds the image of a revolving, whirling movement, at whose center matter has become *kecharitomenē*, imbued with the grace of the Holy Spirit. The chiastic designs constituting the marble frame both signify *empsychōsis* and produce *empsychōsis* at the center of the larger structure they enframe. The graphic formula is performative; it circumscribes (*perigraphē*) Christ nonanthropomorphically in time and space. The chiasm not only identifies an *eikōn tou Theou* but configures it nonrepresentationally and spatially in the architectural space and can multiply and reproduce it in infinity both materially and ritually.

The Performative *Eikōn* as Chant

By virtue of its place in the dome, the *typos* (cross in a circle) structures the visual field, in which a sonic inspiriting unfolds. In the first chapter, I identified this sonic *empsychōsis* with the singing (exhalation of breath) of the elite choir stationed in the perimeter of the ambo, under the dome (see figs. 5–6, 10, 47). Singing embodies a collective human voice in space. In this process the incarnate pneuma activates the reverberant acoustics making what appears as a void—the air under the dome—sonically luminous. Although this aural *empsychōsis* is generated by any chant sung in Hagia Sophia, it becomes particularly poignant and expressive when the form and content of the poetry is chiastic. This is the case, I argue, with the singing of the fixed Psalm 50 (51): 8–14;[53] its chiastic structure gives form to *empsychōsis* as content. That *empsychōsis* is recognized as the meaning

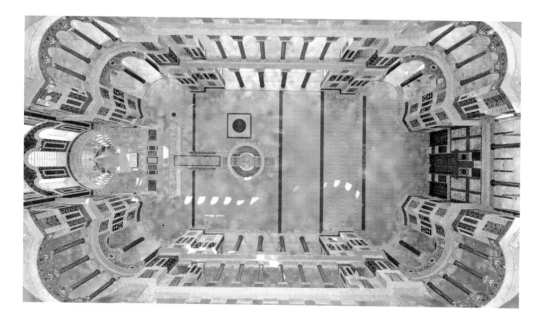

FIG. 47

Hagia Sophia, reconstruction of the *katōpion* view from the dome down to the pavement.

FIG. 48

Teleutaion for Pentecost vespers showing the two peaks, based on Ioannis Arvanitis's transcription of the melody.

© Laura Steenberge.

of Psalm 50 (51): 11 is clear by the way the Khludov miniature illustrates this verse (see fig. 25). Furthermore, as a fixed psalm, it was performed daily at *orthros* and sung by the *psaltai* from the ambo under the dome.[54] When combined with the spatial and temporal dimensions of the performance of Psalm 50, the evidence of the textual chiasm shows how the great dome of Hagia Sophia became the mise-en-scène for this sonic *empsychōsis*. In performance, the chiasm of the text became an embodied voice, inspiriting matter and generating in its own way a sonic *eikōn tou Theou*.

The example of Psalm 50 leads to the aural manifestation of *empsychōsis* in the cathedral chant. Inspiriting, as this study has noted, identifies the action of breath: inhaling and exhaling. Aspiratory sounds draw attention to this process. *Chi* is an example of this phenomenon. Its graphic form presents the initial letter of Christ's name and thus identifies him, and it also figures the basic shape of chiasm. In its aural dimension, the pronunciation of *chi* produces an aspiratory sound, which has the potential to inspirit. The intercalations of nonsemantic syllables in the cathedral chant frequently use the aspiratory *ho, he,* and *ha.* This leads to the following questions: Are these intercalations engaged in structures that produce inspiriting or mirroring, the two processes that engender the performative *eikōn*? How does Hagia Sophia's acoustic dimension of *empsychōsis* manifest itself?

I have already considered intercalations in the singing of the *allēlouïa* refrains of the *teleutaion* (analyzed in the previous chapter; see fig. 36). In that instance, the nonsemantic additions helped push the melody into the upper registers, thus producing a form of spiritual ascent. The melody reaches an upper F at two peaks, on *he* and *lou* (fig. 48). These heights form, I argue, the musical equivalent of the textual and visual chiastic structure: they shape an inverted parallelism. In the case of *he,* the chiasm also imprints an aspiratory sound at the center, thus engendering through the prosody a form of aural *empsychōsis.* The acoustics of the dome concentrate these high-frequency waves in the curvature of the cupola, only to reflect and scatter them; this dynamic causes a form of sonic waterfall,[55] essentially an aural *enōpion* and *katōpion.* The sonic *empsychōsis* articulated at the ascent of the *he* and the *lou* activates the acoustic rain, enabling some of its energy to penetrate and thus inspirit the faithful standing under the dome. The chiasm framing *he* and *lou* thus can be viewed as an example of how chant can trigger *empsychōsis,* producing *eikones tou Theou* by activating the acoustics of the interior.

Inspiriting and mirroring are interrelated, producing *typos* and *eikōn.*[56] Both dynamics can transform a material body into a performative icon of God. In the next musical

example, the communion verse known as *koinōnikon* sung for Pentecost, the melodic structure articulates the mirroring.[57] The melody is recorded in two thirteenth-century Grottaferrata manuscripts: MS gr. Γ γ 1, folio 195v, and MS gr.

FIG. 49

Communion verse for Pentecost recorded in Middle Byzantine diastematic musical notation, from Grottaferrata, MS gr. Γ γ 7, thirteenth century, fols. 67v–68r.

Γ γ 7, folios 67v–68r (fig. 49). These two manuscripts are known as *asmatika* because they contain the chants (*asmata*) for the elite choir.[58] While the Constantinopolitan Typikon of the Great Church records the inclusion of this particular *koinōnikon* in the period 800–850, its melody is not recorded until the thirteenth century.[59] This incongruity raises a legitimate concern: to what extent are the South Italian *asmatika* reliable as a source on which to reconstruct the Constantinopolitan cathedral liturgy? The South Italian monasteries in which the two Grottaferrata manuscripts were used employed the cathedral rite of Hagia Sophia for major feasts, Pentecost among them. The melody recorded in Grottaferrata Γ γ 7 has further a close correspondence with the material preserved in Slavonic *kondakaria,* which transmit Middle Byzantine melodies of the period 800–1050.[60] Thus the Grottaferrata evidence offers the closest possible approximation of the type of chant originally composed for Hagia Sophia, for which we have no other direct information.

What is special about this particular communion verse and its relation to *empsychōsis* is the fact that it is chanted on the feast of Pentecost for the Eucharist liturgy; the coincidence of this double descent of Pneuma intensifies the expectation of inspiriting. The verse is a variation on Psalm 142 (143): 10, announcing: "Your good Spirit shall guide me [in the straight way], *allēlouïa*" (τὸ πνεῦμα σου τὸ ἀγαθὸν, Κύριε, ὁδηγήσει με [ἐν γῇ εὐθείᾳ], ἀλλελούϊα). The line is then intercalated with the extra-semeiosic χο, χε, χα, γγα, γγο, γγε, να, νε, and the vowels α, ου, ε. So the verse appears as follows (with the intercalations marked in bold): τὸ πνεῦμα σου τὸ **χο χο** ἀγα-**γγα**-θὸ-**χο ου ο γγο**-ν, Κύριε, **γγε χε χε**, ὁ-**γγο**-δηγή-**γγη**-ή-σει με, **α α α α ου α ου α α χα χα α ου α** ἀ-λλε-**ου ε γγε ε νε ου ε νε ου ε να νε ε** ε-λούϊ-α, **γγα γγα**. Transcribed into the Latin alphabet, the phrase emerges as: *to pneuma sou to* **ho ho** *aga-tho-***ho ou o ngo**-*n, Kyrie,* **nge he he**, *o-***ngo** *dē-gē-***ngē**-*ē-sei me,* **a a a a ou a ou a a ha ha a ou a** *a-lle-***ou e nge e ne ou e ne ou e na ne e** *e-loui-a,* **nga nga**.[61]

My analysis of the melodic structure of this *koinōnikon* is colored by projecting into the text a play between human and divine: a model melody for the divine, in the words "Pneuma" and "Kyrie" and the vowels *a ou a,* and for a mortal's striving to imitate it, in the intercalated aspiratory χο χο, χε χε, χα χα marking human breath.[62] The pairing of divine and mortal unfolds through melodic mirroring. The piece is set in the fourth plagal mode, which translates roughly into a G-major scale (fig. 50).[63] The melody starts on D and quickly rises F–F–G (πνεῦ-) G–G–a–a–b–a–G–a–b (-μα).[64] The melismatic fragment on -μα is repeated but inverted as a–b–a–G–G–a in the singing of the first intercalated χο χο. This mirroring of the melodic fragments in -μα and χο χο establishes a relationship between Spirit and human breath: the former leads, the latter follows.

Similarly in ἀγαθὸν, the melodic fragment G–G–F–E–F–G on α- is first repeated and inverted from a descent into an ascent on -θο- as a–b–a–b–c–b–c; it is this high pitch that the following χο tries to match as b–c–b–a–G–a–b, which mirrors the original melodic pattern on α- but transposes it by a third, following the model on θο; χο attempts to rise to c but does that just as a grace note.

Then the melody rises quickly at Κύριε, reaching a high E. After that the melody descends gradually to G. Human breath expressed with the next aspiratory χε χε (a–a–G–a) repeats in a simplified form the melody of -μα and χο χο but cannot rise to b.

Three jumps of a fifth (G to c, c to G, G to c) follow in the singing of ὁδηγήσει με ("guide"). The next intercalation of the vowels α α α ου α ου echoes the melodic fragment on Κύριε. Through this repetition of the melodic structure, the tune conveys the return of the divine. Its nearness injects new energy, resulting in two new jumps of a fifth at α α, propelling human breath at χα χα to reach a high D. The α- following this *ha ha* extends the rise to a high F, the highest pitch reached in the entire composition. The synergy of Pneuma and breath established through mirroring melodic fragments has enabled human breath at χα χα to reach to the divine and embody the high D of Κύριε and push beyond it to a high F.

This dynamic intertwining of human and divine takes place in the interplay between semantic and asemantic registers. As shown, the melody of *Kyrie* repeated in α α α α ου α ου gives human breath the energy to rise to the divine in the singing of χα χα. The terrestrial voice has learned how to follow its celestial guide. Maximus the Confessor defined the church space as *eikōn* and *typos,* the former produced through

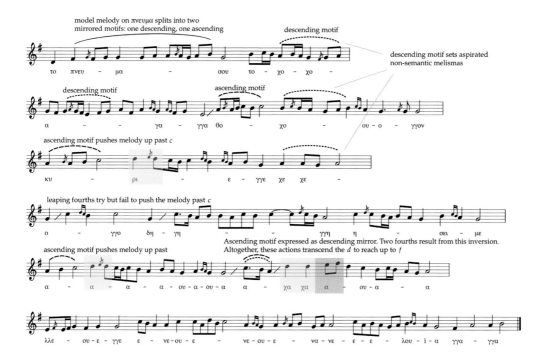

mimēsis and the latter through inspiriting. The *koinōnikon* for Pentecost in Grottaferrata Γ γ 7 performs the mirroring in the dynamic between the divine (πνεῦμα, ἀγαθόν, Κύριε) and mortal (χο χο, χε χε, χα χα). But it is these very aspiratory sounds that miraculously produce inspiriting as they draw attention to the passage of breath and the act of inspiriting (ἐμφυσάω, ἐμπνεύω, εὐλογέω).

FIG. 50

Communion verse for Pentecost, from Grottaferrata, MS gr. Γ γ 7, thirteenth century, fols. 67v–68, reconstruction of the melody based on Ioannis Arvanitis's transcription. © Laura Steenberge.

The mirroring in the melodic fragments fulfills the desire lodged in the chiastic center of Psalm 50 (51): 10–12: "Create in me a clean heart, O God; and renew a right spirit in my inward parts. Cast me not away from thy presence; and remove not thy holy Spirit from me. Restore to me the joy of thy salvation: establish me with thy directing Spirit." Sung under the dome of the *kallichoros* at *orthros,* the chiasm in Psalm 50 would have triggered the ascent, reflection, and showering down of sonic energy over the people gathered under the cupola. This sonic and visual experience would have engendered the nonrepresentational iconicity in the participant and the space. Through both devices— sonic mirroring of melodic fragments and aspiratory sounds sung in a reverberant *kallichoros*—the *koinōnikon* imprinted Pneuma in material bodies, transforming them into performative *eikones tou Theou.* Since exhalation causes the reverberant response and engenders the nonrepresentational iconicity, I call the product "icons of breath."

Tied to reverberation, the experience of this sonic *empsychōsis* becomes more poignant with the blurring of the semantics of the chanted poetry. The modern listener can hear the difference in four recordings of Cappella Romana singing the *koinōnikon*. The first is performed in the Cathedral of St. Mary in Portland and carries the acoustics of that space.[65] The second is the dry studio recording done at Stanford's Stage at the Center for Computer Research in Music and Acoustics (CCRMA).[66] This recording is then auralized from two different listener's positions inside Hagia Sophia.[67] One captures a listener's position close to the choir,[68] and the other a position at the back of the nave, far from the choristers.[69] This variation in the auralizations manifests the changing intelligibility of the chanted poetry: the further away from the choir, the less clear the sung words are; their meaning dissolves into the wet acoustics of the space. In inverse proportion, the decreased intelligibility comes with an increased awareness of the wet sound produced by the late field reverberation. As a result, the listener perceives the interior of Hagia Sophia in the second auralization as a more resonant and thus a livelier space. The perception of this nonrepresentational animation is tied to the joint psycho-acoustic effect produced by the reverberation and blurring (enhanced further by the use of melismas and intercalation). The next chapter offers a more sustained engagement with the acoustics of the Great Church and explores further what modern technology can bring to the study of wet sound.

Aural Architecture

The acoustics of the Great Church and its cathedral chant facilitated the sensation of divine nearness as an aural phenomenon. To avoid analyzing this acoustic experience merely in texts, tables, and graphs, scholar-singers have performed Byzantine chants and thereby gained deeper understanding and done some very insightful work.[1] In order to strengthen this direction of research, which combines scholarship with experience and performance, Icons of Sound has made use of auralizations. They were produced through the process known as convolution. The latter is an algorithm that imprints the impulse response (acoustic signature) of the space being modeled onto an input audio signal, which can be a recording or live sound.[2] Auralizations allow a prerecorded, dry sound to be "placed" effectively in a particular space, revealing, in the case of the Hagia Sophia experiments, the interaction between voice and acoustics.

Auralizations have become a means to experience aural architecture. The term "aural architecture" designates those features of a building that can be perceived through listening.[3] In situations where either the building is no longer extant or vocal or instrumental performances are forbidden, auralizations are an important tool.[4] This is the case with Hagia Sophia, where auralizations offer the only means to a listening experience that is otherwise impossible because of the restrictions on the use of the interior as a secular museum. In re-creating aspects of this lost aural dimension, the digital renderings of chanted vocalization have enabled this study to address larger questions about performative iconicity and spiritual experience of transcendence and to recognize how both phenomena are established through the synergy of the acoustics, the melodic design of the chants, and their prosody. Yet these auralizations are not a transparent window to the real; they are based on certain assumptions and limitations that shape the work of acoustic engineers.

Reverberation stands at the core of understanding room acoustics and auralizations. In common parlance "reverberation" is a synonym of "echo," but in terms of acoustics, the two mark different physical phenomena. Echo is a series of distinct returns or partial repetitions of the original sound due to reflection off a distant surface, such as, for instance, the chain of staggered repetitions of the word "echo" when shouted from a mountain peak in a craggy landscape.[5] By contrast, "reverberation" is used by acousticians to identify the residual sound energy that accumulates in an enclosed space from a collection of reflections from surfaces after an original sound has been fired. These sonic reflections arrive by the millions, densely compacted in time, each with minimal loudness and thus inaudible by itself; yet as a group they build what acousticians consider the reverberation of a space.[6] Long reverberation is the by-product of any large enclosed space whose walls, ceiling, and floor are faced with highly reflective surfaces. The typical Late Antique church, with its spacious acoustically coupled volumes (nave, aisles, galleries) and marble revetments, constitutes such a reverberant chamber.[7]

Reverberation can be engineered through electroacoustics or computational algorithms; the result is artificial reverberation. Because this measured room signature can be imprinted on any recorded or live sound, artificial reverberation has the power to manipulate the perception of space.[8] But in addition to representing and constructing space, reverberation also affects the perception of time. As Barry Blesser and Linda-Ruth Salter have argued, "reverberation destroys the temporal fine structure of sound."[9] What this observation means is that if a sequence of pure notes is played in a reverberant space, the time units between them will be manipulated and changed by the reverberation. This phenomenon emerges because each note produces a specific wavelength. The sound wavelength of each frequency is reflected with different amplitude and reverberation time by the acoustics of the space. For instance, low frequencies might linger longer compared to high tones. In this process every spectral component "acquires a statistically random time relationship to every other component."[10] Reverberation thus relativizes time. Reverberation's effect on time can thus play, I argue, a role in stimulating the spiritual experience of *metaxu* as a sensation of being in between time and timelessness.

The Acoustics of Hagia Sophia

Measuring the acoustics of Hagia Sophia started in 2000–2003 with the CAHRISMA (Conservation of Acoustical Heritage by the Revival and Identification of Sinan's Mosque Acoustics) project, which included a research group from the Technical University of Denmark in whose ranks were the acoustic engineers Jens Rindel, Claus Christensen, Anders Gade, and Christoffer Weitze.[11] Stanford's Icons of Sound repeated some of their measurements in 2010 and again in 2014–15.[12] In 2013 Wiesław Woszczyk conducted a third set of measurements.[13] These measurements offer a starting point for what is an evolving field of exploration; new data about how the material shell of

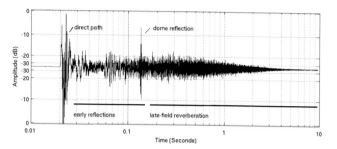

FIG. 51

Reverberation (T_{30}) plotted

as a wave.

FIG. 52

Spectrogram of a balloon

popping in Hagia Sophia.

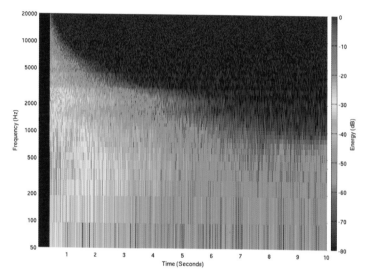

Hagia Sophia responds to sound continues to be collected and will modify and enrich this initial understanding.[14]

The experience of listening to sound is as much a function of what the source emits as it is about the space in which the sound travels. When a sound is made by a source in a room, an acoustic wave is produced, which propagates in all directions. The sound first heard at the listener's position is called the *direct sound,* or *path* (fig. 51). As other portions of the propagating wave front interact with obstacles and surfaces, some of their energy is absorbed, and some is reflected back into the space. This reflected energy reaches the listener's position slightly later. The delayed arrivals are called *early reflections.* As the sound reflections continue to be reflected by the surfaces and objects in the room, their staggered arrivals create what is called the *late field reverberation.* The sound will continue to be reflected until all the energy is absorbed by the air and the objects/ boundaries of the space. This collection and decay of reflected energy is heard as reverberation in a room (fig. 52). A characteristic of room acoustics called reverberation time (RT or T_{60}) is defined as the time it takes for a sound level in a room to decrease by 60 decibels after a continuous sound source has been shut off.[15] When the initial amplitude is less than 60 decibels, the reverberation time can be extrapolated from a shorter rate of decay. T_{60} can be extrapolated from T_{30}, which measures the rate of decay experienced

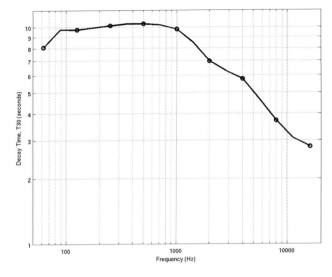

FIG. 53 (*left*)

A graph of the reverberation time (T$_{30}$) as a function of frequency.

FIG. 54 (*below*)

Reverberation time (T$_{30}$) measured with broadband sources at eight positions in Hagia Sophia.

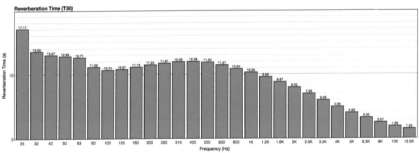

by sound after it has decayed thirty decibels from its initial amplitude (from −5 dB to −35 dB), and then multiplies that to arrive at the value of T$_{60}$.[16] Together, the staggered arrivals and different energies of the direct sound, the early reflections, and the late field reverberation enable the listener to perceive the imprint of space on sound. This imprint is called the *impulse response* (IR).[17]

The measured reverberation time in Hagia Sophia is about ten seconds for a sound source in the apse and slightly over eleven seconds for a sound source in the space under the dome when the church is empty.[18] The long reverberation time is due to many elements, among which are the immense interior volume of 255,800 cubic meters, the dome and semidomes, the nesting of architectural volumes, and the reflective surfaces of marble and gold mosaic.[19] This long reverberation remains uniform across a vast spectrum of frequencies in the range of the singing human voice, from 200 Hz to 2,000 Hz (figs. 53–55).[20] It reaches a peak of twelve seconds at frequencies of 250–500 Hz and reduces to ten and eight seconds respectively for frequencies of 1 and 2 kHz (fig. 54).[21] Envelopment of the *kallichoros* by aisles and galleries enables the space under the dome to mix the reflected sound energy quickly and to remain full for a long time. The enveloping sound of the *kallichoros* is a characteristic shared by some of the best concert halls. Yet the extremely long duration of this reverberation in the Great Church

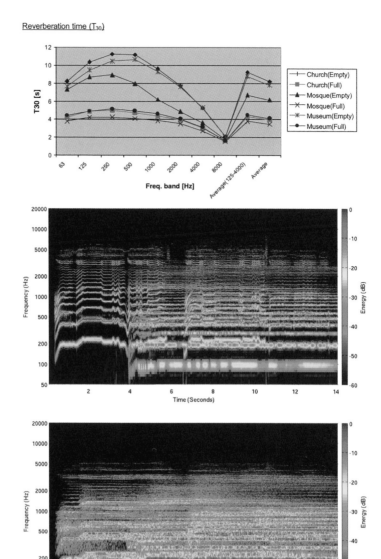

sets it apart from the modern performance spaces; their RT, by contrast, is often less than two seconds.[22] Because of this, clarity and intelligibility of speech in Hagia Sophia are poor overall, even in the space under the dome.[23]

The enveloping sound and long sustain of the late field reverberation present room acoustics well suited for sung vocalization and especially monody.[24] The *kalli-choros* responds to the chant in the entire range of the human voice by sustaining high-frequency harmonics; thus the singers' notes smeared over time end up harmonizing with themselves (figs. 56–57). The choristers can use the space as a musical instrument that gives body and fullness to their voices. They can interact further with the high-frequency harmonics subtended by the space and create a form of polyphony from the synergy of the singers' output and the resonant subtended return of the chamber.

The interior causes two important acoustic effects. The first is amplification as the sung notes are sustained for a long time. The volume gradually builds up as more sound energy is continually added, outpacing its slow absorption. This phenomenon produces a fuller and richer sound. The second effect is that of overlapping and dissolving of notes. The building responds to the monody by prolonging high-frequency harmonics that interact and may gradually evolve from dissonant to consonant harmonics.[25] This second effect leads to a brighter sound, a phenomenon enhanced by the domes and semidomes. Raised almost fifty-seven meters above the floor, the cupola reflects and scatters the sound waves, producing an acoustic "waterfall" over a much wider area of the floor.[26] The dome causes the high-frequency short wavelengths of the harmonics that the space sustains to concentrate here and reflect and scatter continuously. This phenomenon stirs the synaesthetic effect of aural and optical brightness as it combines the acoustic reflection with the visual reflection of light off the gold mosaics. As a result, the sonic brightness acts like a mirror reflecting the human vocal energy and, in the process, producing a radiant vision of the imagined splendor of the angelic choirs.[27] This luminous celestial voice is more prominent when the building is full. At these moments people and their clothing absorb most of the reflections off the polished surface of the floor. This enhances the experience of an ephemeral concentration of sonic energy in the golden superstructure. In its volatile state, it quickly transforms into a golden sonic "waterfall."[28]

A comparison of two spectrograms from an anechoic recording and its auralization in a virtual Hagia Sophia clearly demonstrates the two effects—amplification and sonic brightness—produced by the resonant acoustics of the Great Church (figs. 56–57).[29] They show the first few seconds of the soloist, John Boyer, and Cappella Romana performing a *prokeimenon,* or gradual, for the feast of Saint Basil. In the dry performance one can clearly see how the soloist's voice peaks at around 200 Hz, triggering harmonics ranging between 300 Hz and 5,000 Hz. The drone (*ison*) hovers around 100 Hz, with harmonics reaching 2,000 Hz and above (fig. 57). When the same performance is auralized in Hagia Sophia (auralized, or convolved digitally, with the room acoustics of the empty interior), the resonant returns of the building and the overlapping transition of voices together produce a richer, fuller, and brighter sound, visualized in the spectrograph as the smeared and swollen waves (fig. 52). Melodic progressions appear suspended over time; they collide tonally or harmonize with the newly sung pitches, increasing the perceived loudness of the sound but decreasing the clarity of speech.[30]

Melismatic singing by the elite choir of the *psaltai* must have skillfully manipulated this lack of clarity produced by Hagia Sophia's wet acoustics. This type of melodic stretching of semantic chains articulates a desire to break free from information and the semantics of language, transcending to a domain where sound functions in some prelinguistic manner. As noted in the previous chapters, the intercalations of nonsemantic syllables and melismas deepen this sensation. And the total effect is further enhanced by the manner in which long reverberation randomizes time.

Artificial Reverberation and Hagia Sophia

The spatial imprint on sound indicates an important psychological dimension of aural architecture—more specifically, that the psychoacoustic effect a piece of music has on the singer and on the listener will depend on the space in which it is performed.[31] Artificial reverberation offers the means to manipulate the perception of space and thus elicit a variety of emotional responses. Several different processes exist to produce artificial reverberation.[32] The oldest uses a device called an electric reverberator; one version consists of coils that reverberate when the sound signal passes through them. This device only approximates the reverberation of a given space, simplifying the human ear's perception of it.[33] The electric reverberator's link to the acoustics of the real space is abstract and symbolic; it reproduces the effect but not the behavior of a specific space.[34]

Convolution, a form of digital artificial reverberation, uses at its core the room's IR, an imprint of the acoustic behavior of a particular space when excited by a starter signal; the latter can be produced, for example, by a pistol, or a sinusoidal sweep, or balloon pops (used by Icons of Sound). Convolution reimprints this IR on a prerecorded or live signal through an algorithmic computational process. Convolution, unlike methods using electroacoustic or digital reverberators, is indexical.[35] It is causally connected to the space, whose acoustic imprint it carries and reproduces. This is the reason why the designers of convolutions/auralizations have claimed that this process is somehow superior to and more authentic than the other forms of creating artificial reverberation. Yet it is important to bear in mind that all artificial reverberation works with a relatively small sample of IRs, despite its claims on the real.[36] It is still not computationally possible to measure how all air molecules in a space will respond to the propagating sound waves. Further, convolution assumes that humidity and temperature are constant, while in fact both values fluctuate from moment to moment.[37] Blesser and Salter have stated that complex architectural interiors such as concert halls "cannot be fully and accurately characterized with any technology that is currently available."[38] But despite their limitations, convolutions offer good approximations for the acoustics of a building such as Hagia Sophia.

Auralizations at Stanford University

Auralization has been the only process used in the digital re-creation of Hagia Sophia's acoustics. The group from the Technical University of Denmark used three sound sources and twelve receivers to measure a standard reverberation time (T_{60}) and to determine a set of impulse responses. This data assisted Rindel and Christensen in the development of computer software that offers predictive modeling of room acoustics for general architectural and engineering purposes.[39] Using this software, the Danish group auralized a couple of anechoic recordings of Byzantine chant and Qur'ānic readings in a virtual Hagia Sophia.[40]

Because the Danish group did not publish their measured impulse responses, I obtained that value by gathering acoustic data in situ. In May and December of 2010, using a set of portable omnidirectional microphones affixed close to my ears, I recorded four balloon pops in Hagia Sophia with the balloon exploding under the dome and the listener's position under the cupola and in the west end (see fig. 52). Balloons are cheap and easy to use. In exploding, they radiate rather uniformly and produce a simple but compact acoustic pulse, which contains the entire frequency range of human hearing.[41] Knowing how a particular space imprints itself on a simple pulse, such as a balloon pop, allows researchers to study and reproduce more complex processes such as human speech or singing, which may be thought of as composed of a series of pulses.[42]

Jonathan Abel, an acoustic engineer and a codirector of the Icons of Sound project, extracted impulse responses from the balloon-pop recordings in Hagia Sophia; the IRs were in turn convolved with an existing recording of the Cheroubikon hymn.[43] This first auralization was based on the sound pulse recorded directly in Hagia Sophia, not relying on an entirely synthesized IR using computer software that assigns relative values to materials and architectural shapes.[44] It was also adjusted to account for the acoustics of Fontevraud Abbey's refectory, where this recording of the Cheroubikon was performed.

In 2011, Icons of Sound invited Cappella Romana to participate in the collaboration. Our choice was guided by the fact that this established choir specializes in the performance of early music and has developed an impressive repertoire of Byzantine chant.[45] We recorded them in the Stage at CCRMA singing the First Kontakion on the Nativity by Romanos Melodos, a *prokeimenon* (gradual) for the feast of Saint Basil, and Psalm 140, which was a fixed psalm sung for vespers in Hagia Sophia. These anechoic recordings were then convolved with the impulse response of Hagia Sophia. In the process, the voice of each singer was captured dry on a separate track. At the same time, each chorister received live feedback via earbuds, auralizing his or her and the chorus's performance in Hagia Sophia.

This real-time feedback enabled the performers to hear themselves sing in the Great Church and to explore its timbre during the recording session rather than defer the interaction to postproduction.[46] The Danish auralizations of Byzantine chant, on the other hand, were done as a postproduction process. The singer, who is the philologist and musicologist Christian Troelsgård, was recorded anechoically in a studio; the track was then imprinted with Hagia Sophia's IR. Troelsgård did not have the chance to "play" the acoustics of the building like a musical instrument while singing. Icons of Sound has helped with this "play." In receiving live feedback, Cappella Romana had the chance to interact with the interior of the Great Church and to align pitch with the maximum resonance of the building. As a result, the choristers dramatically slowed their tempo. They also adjusted their pitch to activate the high-frequency resonances sustained by the building.

Abel tested the validity of his recording method at Stanford University's Memorial Church. It offers a good control sample as the building has a dome and a sizable overall volume, which produce reverberant acoustics. Here Abel recorded a singer in situ and with a "close mic," a microphone positioned close to the mouth so that it does not get sound reflections from the space surrounding the singer; close miking allows dry recordings. Then Abel measured the impulse response of Memorial Church by recording a balloon exploded at the singer's position. Abel then convolved the dry recording with the measured impulse response. The auralization was found to be sonically very similar to the recorded live performance in Memorial Church.[47]

Live Auralization at Bing Hall

Abel's use of live feedback marks a departure from the traditional method of producing auralizations and led to the experiment with convolution of a live performance of Cappella Romana. He accomplished this first at the Stage at CCRMA and then at Stanford's Bing Concert Hall.[48] The auralizations of the *teleutaion* and the *koinōnikon* for Pentecost analyzed in the previous three chapters come from the live performances of Cappella Romana at the Stage at CCRMA.

An inspiration for how to auralize a live performance was found in the Virtual Acoustics Technology (VAT) developed by Wiesław Woszczyk at McGill University. The VAT system is based on low-latency multichannel convolution, which allows the acoustics of different concert halls to be activated in a studio, enabling the performers to interact during their performance with a specific acoustic chamber, digitally re-created and sustained.[49] A similar principle was explored by Icons of Sound in the live auralization of Byzantine chant at Stanford's Bing Concert Hall.[50] At the foundation of the Stanford experiment was the balloon-pop recording, from which were generated a large number of statistically independent impulse responses based on the echo density and amplitude-envelope model of the reference response.[51] These decorrelated impulse responses were randomly assigned and imprinted on the signals carried by the individual microphones. A total of forty-eight statistically independent IRs, each twelve seconds long at 48 kHz sampling frequency, were used to stimulate the enveloping sound of Hagia Sophia.[52]

By itself, the Bing Concert Hall has an RT of about 2.5 seconds when all curtains are in place. In this auralization, the direct sound and early decay time is that of the Bing. But the late field reverberation is that of Hagia Sophia; it is played by loudspeakers placed in the hall, which transmit the voices of the choristers converted into a digital signal and convolved with Hagia Sophia's late field reverberation.[53] As a result, the audience is immersed in a dual sound field that has combined the Bing's early reverb with Hagia Sophia's late field reverb.[54] Enhancing this bispatiality is the architecture of Bing Hall, which, with its terraced seating encircling the stage, is reminiscent of the central domed space of the Great Church, surrounded by aisles and galleries (fig. 58).[55]

In overlaying the early reflections of the Bing Concert Hall with the late field reverberation of Hagia Sophia, the live auralization created a hybrid environment of direct sound produced by the concert hall but imprinted with the late field reverberation of the imagined and unseen vastness of Hagia Sophia. Media scholar Lev Manovich has called such mixed environments, in which dynamically changing information overlays the real, "augmented space." Jonathan Sterne has subsequently used this concept to address the multispatiality, or complex subjectivity, produced by artificial reverberation.[56] In contradistinction to virtual reality, which is all about full immersion, the

FIG. 58

Bing Hall, Stanford University, 2013.

augmented space never fully releases its hold on the real. It creates multidimensional space.[57]

Reverberation (artificial in the modern world and natural in the medieval) draws a strange but compelling connection between the new and the old. Manovich's insight about augmented space for the contemporary world speaks to the power of the synaesthetic saturated phenomenon: "the power lies in the interaction between the two spaces—between vision and hearing (what users are seeing and hearing), and between present and past (the time of the user's walk versus the audio narration, which, like any media recording, belongs to some undefined time in the past)."[58] The live auralization of Cappella Romana's concert immersed its audience aurally both in the Bing and in the simplified version of Hagia Sophia. People could hear the aurality of Hagia Sophia without seeing it. Perhaps this is a modern poetic gesture imitating the way the Byzantine participant in the liturgy could participate in the divine without seeing a mimetic representation of heaven. The example of bispatiality in the Bing implies the existence of a form of bispatiality at play in the reverberant interiors of Late Antique churches. These resonant ecclesiastical spaces and the melismatic monodic chant allowed the faithful to transcend the register of human speech and the linearity of time, finding themselves in an aural and visual *metaxu* between terrestrial and celestial, invoked by the interaction of voice and acoustics and light and reflective surfaces. The melismatic chant and the randomization of time stirred by the long reverberation ephemerally interconnected time and timelessness.

Early Twentieth-Century Acoustics and the Demise of Reverberation

Yet what happened with reverberation in the modern period? The development of acoustics and aural architecture in the early twentieth century led to the privileging of dry spaces, direct sound, and information, which cumulatively contributed to the flattening of the experience of sound. While on the one hand the science of acoustics rose to the fore during the 1900s, on the other it immediately set out to eliminate reverberation, now regarded as unwanted noise that interferes with the intelligibility of speech.[59] Wallace Sabine became the founder of the modern science of room acoustics when he developed the mathematical formula for measuring the reverberation time of an interior. His equation established a relationship between reverberation and the interior volume and materials of a room. In manipulating the materials and interior dimensions, one could change the length of the room's reverberation time.[60] Sabine's discoveries sparked interest in the invention of building materials with increased absorption qualities that muffled and controlled sound, reducing the reverberation.

St. Thomas Church at Fifth Avenue and Fifty-Third Street in New York City offers a good example of this trend in introducing new acoustically engineered building materials that sever the visual experience of architecture from the aural; the interior has a cladding that resembles stone but does not produce the long reverberation associated with masonry construction (fig. 59). St. Thomas was rebuilt in 1913 after the original structure burned down in 1905.[61] In the process, new acoustically engineered materials were used: absorptive Rumford tiles. Designed by the Gustavino brothers with porous interiors, these tiles significantly muffled the reverberation of the interior.[62] Thus, while the architectural style and materials reaffirmed a Gothic look (figs. 60–61), the building no longer sounded like a traditional Gothic church.[63] With a reverberation time of 2.5 seconds for sound waves of 500 Hz in the empty building, St. Thomas's dry interior is well suited for the transmission of speech but inadequate for the sound of chanting or organ.[64] This building exemplifies the early twentieth-century trend to diminish reverberation and thus to privilege the intelligibility of human speech, of anechoic (dry) sound, over the wet sound of chant. As Thompson concludes: "The desire for clear, controlled, signal-like sound became pervasive, and anything that interfered with this goal

FIG. 59

St. Thomas Church, Fifty-Third Street and Fifth Avenue, New York City, exterior from the sidewalk.

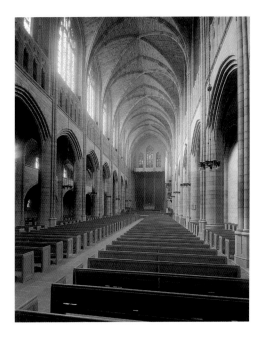

FIG. 60

St. Thomas Church, Fifty-Third Street and Fifth Avenue, New
York City, interior toward the altar.

FIG. 61

St. Thomas Church, Fifty-Third Street and Fifth Avenue, New
York City, interior, view through the north aisle.

was now engineered out of existence."[65] The introduction of acoustically modified construction materials in the early twentieth century disrupted the link between reverberation and reflective, hard surfaces.[66]

The trend toward increasingly dry interiors reached an extreme in the design and construction of Radio City Music Hall in New York City (fig. 62). Completed in 1932, its interior exemplifies the excess pursued in order to satisfy a desire for absorbing reverberation and privileging direct, clear sound. What the audience hears here is the electroacoustic signal of what is said and sung on stage, recorded and transmitted by loudspeakers to the auditorium.[67] Sound as an artificial signal is no longer connected to the architecture or to the bodies that produce it, but to the technology that reproduces and transmits it. Radio City Music Hall also employs absorptive materials to increase the dry acoustics; the arches over the stage are made of Kalite, a sound-absorbing plaster, and the same material covers the rear walls, resulting in a reverberation time of less than one second.[68] Reverberation as the natural product of the space and its materials is here replaced by the "radio voice" of electroacoustics, producing and amplifying a clear and anechoic sound.[69]

The privileging of dry sound in the early twentieth century has led to the flattening of the experience of space. As Thompson remarks, "the sound was issued directly toward the listeners with little opportunity to reflect and reverberate off the surfaces of the room in which it was generated."[70] This tendency is well exemplified in the design of modern concert halls.[71] The stage tends to be constructed with reflective materials,

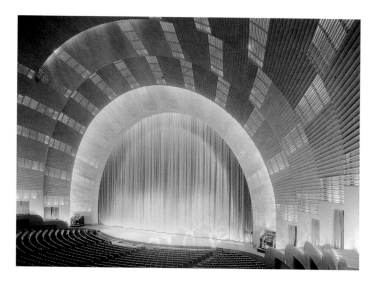

FIG. 62
Radio City Music Hall,
1932, view of the stage
with the curtain down.

but the auditorium is built with highly absorbent ones. Since the stage occupies the mouthpiece of a large horn, the sound produced there reflects once off the sidewalls but has little opportunity to develop late field reverberation (a phenomenon prominent in Hagia Sophia's interior), because it is quickly absorbed by the auditorium. As a result, sound is efficiently and uniformly transmitted to the extended seating area, confirming the tendency to privilege frontality and clarity of sound and increase the intelligibility of speech. The use of microphones and loudspeakers further enhances the reception of this direct, clear, nonreverberant sound.[72] Compare the modern frontal arrangement to the medieval, where the elite choir sings from the ambo in the nave, activating the enveloping acoustics of the central *kallichoros*.

The *Empsychos Naos*

What is lost in the process when intelligibility rises and reverberation decreases? I would argue that with the loss of wet sound visitors lose the ability to experience a building as alive—*empsychos*. This liveliness I see both in the synergy between building and human voice (movement) and in bodies' immersion in and absorption of the energy of an enveloping sound field. On the former, Blesser and Salter comment: "Reverberation gives rise to an interactive experience, with the space entering into an acoustic dialogue with its occupants. It is difficult to enter a reverberant space surreptitiously because the sound of your footsteps produces an acoustic reaction for all to hear. Metaphorically, the reverberated sound of footsteps is the reactive voice of the space; the spatial acoustics of a reverberant space announce the presence of active life by responding with an audible hello, as either a whisper or a shout."[73] The animation emerges from the sonic interaction of call and response. Human movement and voice transform what appears initially as inanimate into an animate entity.

The second form of inspiriting occurs when an enveloping sound field places visitors inside the sphere of reflecting and refracting sonic energy: "with localized sound, the instrument is external to the listener, whereas with enveloping reverberation, the listener is inside the sound generation process, within the mass of air holding the sonic energy."[74] This is especially true of the space under the dome of Hagia Sophia, where the ambo and the elite choir stood. This building's reverberant and enveloping sound field places the faithful standing in the *kallichoros* (nave) at the center of the air mass holding a continuously reflecting and refracting sonic energy. *Empsychōsis,* I argue, arises from the aurality of the building—more specifically, its reverberation. The acoustics of the Great Church thus engender what Psalms 8 and 50 do by chiastically placing man in the center of a mirroring process and making him *empsychos* through vital inbreathing.

My contention is that wet and nonintimate sound has an inspiriting effect on human consciousness, as the contemporary aural artwork of Yolande Harris indirectly attests. She performed orchestral music in an abandoned nineteenth-century mine and wrote a short statement to accompany this event.[75] In it Harris observes how the acoustics of the mine were extremely reverberant and produced a blurred, wet sound. Its resonant quality had a defamiliarizing effect on the audience, estranging the classical music from its traditional acoustic format of the drier concert hall. Harris remarked how "attacks do not behave like attacks, sound is put into space and hangs there, like the dust."[76] The lingering reverberant tail changes the way one experiences sound, and in this metaphoric linkage the melodic progressions seemingly suspended in time take on the behavior of dust languorously drifting in space.[77]

Harris's experiment paradoxically gives materiality to the void, transforming it into an aural substance: "The building wasn't answering back—it was substantiating the event, turning the sound into liquid, spreading it so all focal point was lost, leaving it as a container of sound, as an instrument." The resonant sound field of Hagia Sophia exercises a similar effect, giving the huge open space under the dome a certain aural density that has a sensorial, while immaterial, presence. The acoustics of reverberant chambers force sound into a liquid behavior.[78]

The defamiliarization effect that Harris identifies, operative in the acoustics of the mine, could also be considered a property of the reverberant space of Hagia Sophia, in the way it transforms the human voice into an emanation: no longer focused on the intelligibility of words but on their sensual valence.[79] The reflective interior and its immense volume manipulate the listener into experiencing the Logos (Word/Christ) in the bodiless voice of sound reflections. This voice is similar to the cinematic *acousmêtre,* a voice behind the screen that has no face or body displayed that could be taken as the sound source. The *acousmêtre* in film has a disorienting, menacing, and threatening effect, which arises from the visual absence of the source.[80] The *acousmêtre* in Hagia Sophia's aural reflections would have sustained the effect of defamiliarization and disorientation, but frequently this phenomenon was manifested as an aural and optical brightness rather than a menacing darkness. The disorientation it produces also leads to a paradoxical reorientation as the faithful's attention is redirected from the horizontal to the vertical axis, pulled upward toward the dome: the *enōpion*. The *acousmêtre* produced by the synergy of chant and reactive acoustics in Hagia Sophia shows how the architectural aurality gave rise to performative iconicity.

Intentionality: Between Modern Archaeoacoustics and the Medieval Record

Was the building intentionally designed to produce such a long reverberation? This is the question my research usually elicits from audiences. Intentionality is a difficult problem to solve, first, because the medieval written record does not provide clear answers; any information about the architects' interest in acoustics is indirect. The sixth-century Byzantine sources describe the two designers of Hagia Sophia, Anthemius of Tralles and Isidore of Miletus, as *mechanikoi*.[81] In that time period *mechanikoi* were experts in physics, mathematics, astronomy, and engineering.[82] The city of Alexandria played a crucial role in training *mechanikoi*.[83] Yet no evidence suggests what specific knowledge of acoustics Anthemius and Isidore had or if they manipulated it in order to produce special aural effects. The construction of the original flat dome of the Justinianic Hagia Sophia can be attributed to their expertise in optics.[84] This flat cupola reflected and redirected the sonic energy to the ground; the higher apex of the later dome, of 562, directs the raining reflected energy at a point above the ground.[85] The original dome also channeled light through its many windows in such a way as to create a radiant surface not obscured by any shadow that might otherwise have occurred due to the passage of the sun during the day.[86]

While Anthemius and Isidore shared an expertise in optics, it seems Anthemius was also inclined to experiment with acoustics.[87] Since reverberation concerns the reflection of acoustic energy, it is possible that his research in conic structures and mirrors might have led him to insights about the behavior of sound waves.[88] This hypothesis finds support in Agathias, who recounts that Anthemius was able to simulate the sounds of thunder by means of percussion on resonant objects.[89] He also used steam power to create the effect of earthquake in order to torment his neighbor. The record of these two incidents has led Anthony Kaldellis to conclude that Anthemius "specialized in visual, audio, and kinetic special effects."[90]

It is possible that insights about acoustics emerged also out of Isidore's interest in inscribing solids within solids.[91] Coupled or nested volumes are another feature of Hagia Sophia's architecture that has an impact on its acoustics. Nesting of volumes characterizes the configuration of the aisles and galleries enclosing the central domed space, transforming the nave (*kallichoros*) into a room within a room. The inscribing of solids within solids helps sustain an enveloping sound field, characterized by sonic energy that quickly mixes and remains full for a long time.

This indirect evidence is hardly sufficient to allege intentionality. The nested volumes in Hagia Sophia do, however, reflect contemporaneous design practices. Smaller-scale precedents exist in Constantinople: the church of Sts. Sergius and Bacchus (527–32) and Hagia Eirēnē (532–37).[92] These structures suggest a trend toward space free of columns at the center but enclosed with an ambulatory.[93] In addition to the enveloping sound field, the geometry and volume of such connected and nested structures produce desirable acoustic effects such as diffuse reflections and the dispersal of unpleasant echo. But whether these effects followed from any expertise or interest in acoustics—whether an exploration in acoustics was an active pursuit of the *mechanikoi* of Hagia Sophia and their contemporaries, and whether such an interest guided them in the selection and development of the domed shape and coupled volumes—cannot be conclusively determined.

Questions about intentionality have continually challenged the study of acoustics of premodern buildings. In the introduction to the 2006 edited volume on archaeo-acoustics Chris Scarre outlines the conditions based on which intentionality could be evaluated: (1) recurrent pattern and (2) closeness of fit. The former focuses on the morphology of the shape, while the latter requires a multidisciplinary exploration into the interrelation of space, ritual, and human action.[94] Scarre uses the stone vaulting of Romanesque churches as an example of a recurrent pattern, pointing out how this type of ceiling produces a significantly higher reverberation time compared to the timber roofs of Early Christian basilicas.[95] He then links the stone vault to the rise of Gregorian chant.[96] Scarre uses this particular example as a possible ground on which to argue for intentionality and thus to justify archaeoacoustic exploration.[97] One could argue that Hagia Sophia satisfies the requirements both for recurrent pattern and for closeness of fit. The coupled spaces and domes are shared features in Hagia Sophia, Hagia Eirēnē, and Sts. Sergius and Bacchus in Constantinople, as well as San Vitale in Ravenna. Similarly, the reverberant acoustics these spaces produce would have enhanced the monodic and melismatic chant that characterizes cathedral singing. But I am still hesitant to promote the concept of intentionality.

The same caution emerges in the research of the acoustic engineers Ettore Cirillo and Francesco Martellotta. They have measured, collected, and analyzed acoustic data from a large group of churches dating to a span of time from the Late Antique to the modern periods. Both scholars have questioned whether intentionality is a valid concept to apply to premodern aural phenomena. They argue that correlating form to function precisely is a modern concern and not a medieval conceptualization of the relationship of architectural design to acoustics.[98]

Functionalism captures an antagonistic dynamic between engineers and architects today. Some acoustic engineers have seen their role as guiding the creative design process. The development of acoustically predictive software further supports the engineer's drive to leave his or her mark on the design process.[99] With such tools, the acoustics of a new building would supposedly not be accidental but would satisfy the intended purpose of the new interior.

But is this modern approach to architectural design and acoustics traceable to the medieval period? The lack of written sources precludes the construction of a solid argument that acoustics was a major concern for the builders in Late Antiquity. Many of the acoustic properties of ancient buildings appear as "the incidental consequence of unrelated sociocultural forces."[100] As established by Sabine, the founder of the modern science of acoustics, volume and materials are the major elements that determine the acoustics of a space. Both the large interior volumes and the polished marble surfaces of Late Antique churches, which result in long reverberation, are the product of political and economic exigencies, with no further evidence of their selection because of acoustic considerations. Large interiors and marble cladding for the walls and floors characterize the architecture of the basilicas built by Constantine after he proclaimed the legitimacy of the new religion in the Roman Empire in 313.[101] The basilica as a form had five centuries of development before its adaptation for ecclesiastical use in the early fourth century. The availability of Proconnesian marble accounts for its wide use, which in turn led to the development of uniform interior decors with hard, reflective surfaces.[102] The use of large volumes and rigid materials for traditional architectural purposes, therefore, seems to have been opportunistic. The combination of both resulted in very reverberant church interiors.[103] These wet acoustics would have challenged the intelligibility of speech even when these buildings were full to capacity.[104]

Concerning the dome specifically, the best-known early examples are found on the Pantheon in Rome and then the Late Antique imperial mausolea.[105] For instance, the Rotunda of St. George in Thessaloniki was originally conceived as the burial place for Galerius, one of the tetrarchs and junior governor of the East (293–311). It was only converted into a church in the fifth century.[106] Its cupola has an acoustic impact, increasing the reverberation time (five seconds) despite the relatively small interior volume. This long reverberation contrasts with those in the much larger fifth-century basilicas in the same city: the church of the Acheiropoietos, for example, which has preserved its original wooden ceiling, has an RT close to four seconds. Another example is the basilica of Hagios Demetrios, which has an RT around three seconds.[107] The Rotunda of St. George only shows that domes play a role in enhancing reverberation, but this example does not argue for a conscious choice of cupolas in order to increase the reverberation of Late Antique church buildings. After all, the Rotunda of St. George was not originally built to be a church.

Instead of seeking to prove intentionality, it is more productive to redirect the scholarly exploration of aural architecture toward the aesthetic act of listening to what a wet sound afforded in Late Antique ecclesiastical spaces and what meanings came to be associated with this long exposure. Following this line of thinking, I find inspiration in Blesser and Salter's concept of "earcon."[108] They use the term to refer to an aural matrix/imprint created in human consciousness due to repeated exposure to sound in a particular space. Hagia Sophia afforded such long exposure to wet sound framed in religious ritual. This earcon was embedded in a network of social, cultural, and spiritual values. "Earcon" thus becomes an acoustic equivalent to the term "visuality," which identifies the cultural regimes of sight.[109] Even if the human ear presents a certain physiological constancy in its capacity to hear sound, the way the wet sound of Hagia Sophia was conceptualized in Byzantium is different from the way modern audiences perceive and interpret it.

The Aurality of Psalmody

In reconstructing Hagia Sophia's earcon, this analysis draws both on auralizations, which record the phenomenological aspects of hearing, and on medieval texts, which offer access to the cultural perception of wet sound. Since earcon results from repeated exposure to the aurality of a particular space, it should emerge from recitation of the daily office of the psalmody in Hagia Sophia, which structures just such a continuous encounter with the reverberant acoustics of the Great Church and shapes it in spiritual terms as the experience of divine nearness. The singing of the psalms in Hagia Sophia was distributed between a choir—itself divided in two, singing the psalm line by line antiphonally—and the congregation, which came in after each verse and sang the refrain.[110] This responsorial structure mirrors the reverberant acoustics of the space. As stated by Blesser and Salter, a reverberant building has a "reactive voice," which comes to life and responds to the human energy exhaled as chant or to the noise made by steps moving through the space.[111] This reactive voice of Hagia Sophia is mirrored, I argue, in the call-and-response structure of the psalmody.

Yet the singing of psalmody developed independently from the architectural design and predates the Constantinian churches. Textual references place the origins of antiphonal psalmody in the city of Antioch during the second century; from there it was introduced into the cathedral practice of Constantinople by Patriarch John Chrysostom (398–404). The same source also maintains that the antiphonal psalmody imitates what Ignatius, bishop of Antioch (d. ca. 107), saw as a celestial vision of the angels worshipping the Holy Trinity by singing in a responsorial fashion.[112] The antiphonal psalmody was part of the stational liturgy, which consisted of processions that celebrated stations at different churches along the ritual itinerary.[113] The singing of psalmody would have happened both outdoors and indoors. Thus the aurality of the psalms unfolded in two parallel modes: a relatively dry one, when the singing was performed outside, and a wet one, inside the reverberant Constantinian and later churches. This evidence suggests that there is no causal relationship between the singing of psalmody and the reverberant acoustics of the Late Antique churches. Yet the singing of this prayer to God in reverberant interiors gave a new dimension to the poetry; it enhanced the sense that the divine was responding to the worshipper's entreaty, because the building substantiated the human voice, transforming it into a powerful and enveloping *acousmêtre.*

Similarly, while the text of the psalms predates Christianity, the selection of some of these poems for particular moments of the ritual—like the psalms that were always sung at *orthros* (morning office) and *hesperinos* (vespers) at Hagia Sophia, such as Psalms 62 (63) and 140 (141), also known as "fixed" psalms for the cathedral liturgy—tied the semantics of the texts to the occasions for which they were sung.[114] Psalm 62 introduces the notions of divine nearness as water and of the quenching of one's thirst after a night's sleep—ideas that harmonized with the sunrise and with the faithful's waking up and coming to the temple of God. Sung most likely in the narthex of Hagia Sophia, this psalm would have been imprinted with the reverberant signature of the space and would thus have acquired the wet sound of its aquatic semantics. Similarly, Psalm 140 performed its content. Chanted at sunset, at the moment of entry from narthex to naos, it functioned as a processional psalm, carrying the vestige of the Late Antique *lucernarium* (lamp-lighting) ritual.[115] The clergy led the processions as they swayed burning censers. The fragrance and the smoke rising upward produced the very phenomena elicited by the poetry of Psalm 140 (141): 2: "Let my prayer be set forth before thee as incense; the lifting up of my hands [as] an evening sacrifice." The same verse is repeated in the patriarchal prayer after Psalm 140 and at the dismissal of vespers.[116] The visual and olfactory phenomena of smoke enveloping the procession and filling up the space with fragrance were correlates to the singing of this psalm. The slow tempo matched the languor of the spreading smoke, while the reverberant aurality produced by the acoustics of the interior offered a sonic equivalent to the visual and olfactive envelopment.

Reverberation can draw attention to the sound of the poetry but muddles comprehension of the semantics as it randomizes time, disturbing the semantic chains. Perhaps this effect, this obfuscation of language, was welcomed by the worshipper in Hagia Sophia. The exposure to the psalms was daily and repetitive; the entire Psalter was sung in a weeklong rotation, making the faithful intimately familiar with the text in the course of their lives. But hearing these poems muddled by reverberation must have offered an aesthetic experience beyond the semantic. By tuning out, the worshipper could taste the pleasure of sound, allowing its meaning to remain clouded.

This flexibility to tune the semantics in and out existed in an otherwise very controlled system. While the text of the psalmody remained constant, the way individual psalms were grouped in larger units and refrains appended to them varied by region.[117] Constantinople's cathedral liturgy groups the psalms into larger units called antiphons with respective refrains; this is the structure of the so-called distributed Psalter. Middle Byzantine sources attribute this arrangement to Patriarch Anthimos I (535–36), an origin that coincides with the construction of the Justinianic Hagia Sophia and is likely expressive of its territorialization impetus.[118]

Constantinople's distributed Psalter has sixty-eight to seventy-four antiphons, depending on the particular manuscript. The larger number includes the fixed psalms representing the antiphons always performed at *hesperinos*—Psalm 85 and Psalm 140— and at *orthros*: Psalms 3, 62, and 133; Psalm 118; Psalm 50; and Psalms 148–50. It took approximately a week for the distributed Psalter to be sung in its entirety. Fourteen to fifteen antiphons, comprising a total of twenty-five psalms, were performed daily. To keep this number of units constant every day, more antiphons were sung in the morning liturgy during the winter, when the day was short, whereas the reverse occurred in the summer, when the day was long, resulting in the increased duration of the vespers office.[119] The rotation began with Saturday vespers but skipped Sunday as the day of the Eucharist liturgy. The singing of the distributed Psalter resumed on Monday at *orthros*, with all antiphons completed by Friday vespers. *Orthros* on Saturday was dedicated to the singing of the odes.[120]

Orally transmitted, this simple psalmody suddenly appears in musically notated manuscripts of the late thirteenth century.[121] In the case of the melodic structure of

Psalm 140, it survives in two Late Byzantine manuscripts connected to the church of Hagia Sophia in Thessaloniki, which was the last outpost to perform the Constantinopolitan cathedral liturgy.[122] From this repertoire, Cappella Romana has recorded the fixed Psalm 140 in a version reserved for Saturday vespers.[123] In this modern performance, the soloist first starts with the model melody of the refrain, intoning: "We glorify your saving resurrection, *philanthrōpos* [lover of humankind]."[124] This particular refrain is appended to paschal vespers, on the feast of the Elevation of the Holy Cross (September 14), and other festal Saturday and Sunday services.[125] Yet the same characterization of Christ as *philanthrōpos* is frequently stated in the prayers for vespers as recorded in the euchologion Barberini 336.[126] The "congregation" (here composed of the male and female voices of Cappella Romana) then repeats the model refrain. At that point the male choir, divided into two groups, proceeds with the text of Psalm 140, each group singing a hemistich (half a verse). The congregation completes each hemistich by joining in with the refrain. While one group chants a hemistich, the other holds the drone, or *ison*. This rhythmic and repetitive structure ensures that disturbances that are bound to occur at the beginning, as choir and congregation settle into their respective tracks, are eventually smoothed out, transforming the potentially dangerous cacophony of out-of-sync entries into an ordered and rhythmic harmony.

The singing of the refrain in itself produces an effect similar to that of reverberation on time and speech. The refrain breaks the linear progression of the psalm and thus affects the perception of time's passage. Imposing its circularity and timelessness, it can elicit a new state of consciousness: a *metaxu* between the real and the oneiric. The refrain is similar in this respect to incantation, which leads to sonic otherworldly presence and can affect human consciousness.[127] The singing of psalmody in the nave of Hagia Sophia afforded a sustained exposure to the reverberant aurality of the interior. The wash of chanted words filled in the space. As it aggregated, it paradoxically produced the experience of distance and closeness: an aurality that was simultaneously enveloping but nonintimate.

Sonic richness was part of the cathedral psalmody; there was no audience; all became performers/singers by joining the refrains.[128] The combined sonic energy emptied into Hagia Sophia's reverberant interior by the choirs and congregation produced an aural icon of God. Maximus the Confessor, in his mystagogy of the liturgy, explains how such an aggregation of sonic energy brings the presence of Christ: "[t]he sacred ten-stringed harp of the psalter; it stands for the soul whose thoughts respond to the spirit through the other blessed decade of commandments, on which the perfect, harmonious, tuneful music is played, by which God is hymned; this helps me understand what is meant by the decades singing and sung, and how one decade added mystically to another brings Jesus back to Himself, my God and Savior, fulfilled when I am saved."[129]

Maximus the Confessor uses the example of the Psalter as ten-stringed instrument played by the pure soul following the Ten Commandments. In the process, the soul itself becomes an instrument played by God. The layering of sonic materiality of the music produced by the strings of the Psalter and by the soul played by God makes aurally present the music of the spheres. The expression of the decades "singing and sung," which characterizes the music of the rotating spheres, is evocative of the responsorial pattern of call and refrain enacted by the cathedral psalmody as well as the mirroring dynamic of human voice and reverberant "reactive" voice of a building. Circularity, dissolution of the linear dimension of time, and obfuscation of speech are all sonic effects produced by the cathedral psalmody in a reverberant interior, which cumulatively effected Christ as an icon of sound and led to a fleeting sensation of being in a *metaxu*.

Reverberation makes sensorially accessible the interaction between animate and inanimate—singer and interior—and thus exemplifies the two spiritual processes this book identifies as mirroring and inspiriting. The reverberant returns produced by Hagia Sophia's acoustics form sonic mirroring; the building reflects and responds aurally. Similarly, the human breath exhaled in chant leads to the inspiriting of the architectural interior. The circle is completed when the same sonic energy, continuously reflected by the interior, is eventually absorbed by the people and the boundaries of the room, inspiriting both. The intercalated aspiratory sounds in the melismatic chant of the elite choir draw further attention to this *empsychōsis*. Viewed as a system, the synergy between Hagia Sophia's acoustics and melismatic and intercalated chant produces a fuller and brighter enveloping sound field, swelling and ornamented by the resonant returns of the spatial acoustics. This reverberant sound field renders the divine audible and visual in its synaesthetic brightness, but still beyond both tactile grasp and visible anthropomorphic figuration. This is the process I identified earlier with one of the manifestations of the nonrepresentational iconicity.

The reverberant acoustics, together with the use of melismas and intercalations, helped Byzantine cathedral chant push beyond the register of human speech. I draw a connection between this observation and a passage in Maximus the Confessor's *Mystagogia* where the author contemplates the Godhead through a series of paradoxes that interconnect human and divine: the silence of the mind to the silence of the Lord, both paradoxically manifested in sound. The psalmody performed by mortals elicits the reverberant return of the building, and together they produce the imagined sound of the celestial courts: "And he [man] calls through an eloquent and musical silence from the altar of his mind to that other oft-sung silence in the hidden shrines of the Godhead, so resonant, though imperceptible to us and unintelligible."[130] Two silences. One issues from the faithful; it is oxymoronically eloquent (*lalos*) and composed of many voices (*polyphtongos*), alluding to the singing of psalmody, which made the congregation participants in the Late Antique worship. This terrestrial call seeks the response of the divine—the other and greater silence—paradoxically sung continuously in the hidden celestial shrines; it is imperceptible (*aphanos*) and unintelligible (*agnostos*), yet so resonant (*megalophōnia*). The sonic presence emerging out of this paradoxical, resonant silence of the many voices, imperceptible and unintelligible, I argue, operates sensorially and phenomenologically in a space like Hagia Sophia's. Its reverberant acoustics transform human voices into that luminous, unintintelligible sonic emanation that frees itself from the flow of information, escaping the shackles of human speech.

When writing about the same phenomenon in Western cathedrals, scholars and musicians have associated the effect of long reverberation and low clarity and intelligibility with the sound heard by a body immersed in water. Murray Schafer and Peter Doyle further explain this psychoacoustic effect as reminiscent of the experience of being in the womb.[131] Hagia Sophia aurally produced this return to the beginning of life, stimulated by the way its resonant acoustics transformed human voice into emanation. The next chapter seeks the visual correlate to this aural return to Genesis.

Material Flux

Who will sing gaping with the thundering mouths of Homer,
the marble meadows solidly assembled along the walls
or the open plains of the hauntingly high naos?
—Paul the Silentiary, *Descriptio S. Sophiae*, vv. 617–20

Can stones sing? Can a landscape of marble produce the divine *acousmêtre*?[1] Paul's rhetorical question is strangely evocative of the synergy between the human voice and the reactive return of the marble interior that occurs naturally in Hagia Sophia (see figs. 2–3, 19, 63). Human breath and reverberation together can produce the thundering sound of the Great Church, in which Paul discerns echoes of Homer's epic voice. As ascertained in the previous chapter, Hagia Sophia's resonant acoustics push sound further into a "liquid" behavior, creating an enveloping and immersive sound field. This aural perception of "wetness," I argue, is visually substantiated by the wavelike patterns of the marble revetments and by the shifting intensity of sunlight, which causes stone to appear incandescent at certain moments of the day and to take on the appearance of rivers of molten metal (figs. 63–64, 66, 68, 71, 78). These chameleonic surface changes, which I call "material flux," confuse the perception of what is solid and what is liquid. Their emergence coincides with the main daily offices of *orthros* and *hesperinos*. At these times the building becomes *empsychos*, performing what I call a visual and an aural "liquescence," which correlates with the Late Antique aesthetic of *marmar* and *poikilia*.

    The work of the philologists Michael Roberts and Gianfranco Agosti has shown how polymorphy, variety, shimmer, and chiastic structuring represent major aesthetic principles that guide the composition of Late Antique literature.[2] Variation (*varietas* in Latin or *poikilia* in Greek) is fundamental, leading to the increasing conceptualization of poetry as an imaging text, and this process of visualization focuses specifically on the instability and mutability of color.[3] The pairing of variation with the effects of light has led Roberts to name this Late Antique style in Latin literature "the jeweled style."[4] The same artistic trend is present in the sixth-century Greek poetry, an excellent example of which is Paul the Silentiary's ekphrasis of Hagia Sophia.[5] The text has received considerable attention from philologists, historians, and archaeologists.[6] Yet the work that most intensively connects the analysis of this ekphrasis to the Late Antique "jeweled style" has been accomplished by art historians. Both Nadine Schibille and I have delved into the poetry to seek resonances of perceptual experience.[7] My analysis has singled out the terms *aiolomorphos, daidalos,* and *poikilos* as identifying the polymorphy of matter and surface changes. Schibille has continued this work and connected the terminology both to Neoplatonic philosophy and to the epistemology of color in Greek culture. Yet my work differs from that of both other art historians and philologists in that I introduce the reverberant sound field of Hagia Sophia as an aural correlative to the visual material flux and recognize further how this ephemeral *poikilia* marks for a medieval audience the descent of Pneuma into matter and its indwelling there. This pneumatic emphasis opens up both the spiritual dimension of medieval materiality and uncovers the centrality of sound in the liturgical staging of the experience of the divine.[8]

Even more so, my analysis singles out the association with water as the guiding aesthetic principle at work in the poetry and the polymorphic interior decor of Hagia Sophia. This liquescence of sound and sight, I argue, is linguistically invested in the iterative *marmar-* of the Greek words for *marmaron* (marble), *marmarygma* (glitter), and *marmairō* (to quiver, to coruscate). Glitter and reverberation are the optical and aural manifestations of reflection. Sparkle marks a kind of form disintegration that, I argue, functions as a visual correlate to the acoustic blurring of semantic chains produced by melismas and intercalations and the reverberant acoustics of the Great Church. This chapter explores further how the *marmar-* aesthetic sustains the synergy between stone and voice imagining divine presence in the murmuring sound of the quivering sea.

The Liquescent Aesthetic of *Marmar-:* Marble and the Sea

In order to explore how the perception of polymorphy was linked in Byzantine consciousness to coruscating water, this analysis turns to the poetry of Paul the Silentiary and the actual marbles in Hagia Sophia. Paul's ekphrasis was performed during the rededication ceremonies of the Great Church in the period between December 24, 562, and January 6, 563, in the imperial and patriarchal palaces.[9] He writes for an elite audience who rules the world and orders the affairs of men:

> However it is no Attic bean-eater who is [this poetry's] judge,
> but rather men of piety and mercy

in whom both God and the emperor rejoice;
they order cities, they hold the reins
of all things, both words and actions.[10]

Paul consciously addresses the elite, for only such an erudite audience will be capable
of understanding his classicizing style and Homeric vocabulary.[11] His poem deftly plays
with time and timelessness: two prologues composed in iambic trimeter (vv. 1–80,
81–135) and two epilogues in hexameter (vv. 921–66, 967–1029) define the realm of
the political and linear time. They enclose, like bookends, a domain of ritual in which
the hexametric ekphrasis of the Great Church (vv. 136–920) unfolds.[12] The hexameter
harkens back to the Homeric epic and speaks to notions of timelessness and transcendence, while the iambic trimeter, which of all meters is the closest to ordinary speech
and was employed in Byzantium for occasional poetry, strikes with the immediacy of
current events.[13] Thus the perception of time and eternity intertwine in this poetry.
But even the realm of the timeless carries the imprint of the moment as this type of
building panegyric exemplifies a contemporary trend toward imperial-praise poetry
woven entirely out of the description of architecture. Procopius's *De aedificiis,* dated to
the period before 558, offers another example of this development.[14]

    The marble of Hagia Sophia, the other element of this analysis that helps sub-
stantiate the claim for a Late Antique aesthetic of water and liquescence, has attracted
intense scholarly attention: Alessandra Guidobaldi and Claudia Barsanti have recorded
the marble in Hagia Sophia and explored the archaeological evidence for the quarries,
stone carving, and transportation of stone in the Mediterranean.[15] Studying the marble
floor, dado, wall veneer, columns, capitals, and cornices, Eugenio Russo has brought to
the fore the enormous scope of the reconstructions in Hagia Sophia directed by Isidore
the Younger, the nephew of Isidore of Miletus, after the collapse of the first dome in 558.
It was previously thought that just the superstructure was affected by this restoration,
but Russo has conclusively shown that the reconstruction spread all the way down to
the ground-level arcades. In the process, all the original marble decor (dating to the
building campaign of 532–37) was carefully dismantled and then reinstalled following
the repair. As a result, the interior seen today is largely that of Isidore the Younger's
intervention.[16]

    Similarly, Bente Kiilerich's 2012 study has enriched our knowledge of the political
geography mapped by the variegated marbles used in the wall revetments. Kiilerich
also turns to the ekphraseis of Paul and Procopius and detects in them dual modes
of viewing these marbles, which, she argues, correspond to what neuroscience today
defines as global impression and focal attention. The former mode manifests itself in the
spinning and overwhelming vision, while the latter stills the body, directing the mind
to contemplation.[17]

    Fabio Barry's study, however, has the deepest resonance with my project; he focuses
on the Proconnesian marble floors and the metaphor of water.[18] Barry explores the
meaning of marble in the ancient and medieval Mediterranean. Hagia Sophia's pavement is composed of book-matched Proconnesian slabs forming an undulating outline

FIG. 63 (*top*)

Hagia Sophia, 532–37 and 562, view of the Proconnesian floor and south aisle.

FIG. 64 (*bottom*)

Hagia Sophia, 532–37 and 562, view of the Proconnesian pavement of the nave with light creating an opalescent effect.

of waves (figs. 63–64). The field of this dove-gray stone is traversed by the four bands of green marble known as "the rivers of Paradise" (see fig. 13).[19] In its restrained palette and design, the stone floor of the Great Church differs from the colorful opus-sectile geometric patterns known in imperial Rome, such as that in the Pantheon (fig. 65).[20]

Barry has argued that the materiality of marble was tied to water in ancient and medieval thought and that this association was rooted in the language and knowledge of geology and cosmogony.[21] Theophrastus—in his *De lapidibus* (ca. 315–305 B.C.E.), following Aristotle's *Meteorologia,* book 3—writes about marble as composed of earth particles percolated in water and then solidified into stone by the dry exhalation in the earth's depths.[22] This linkage between marble and water found an even more compelling expression in the Late Antique period, when Proconnesian marble replaced green Carystian as the

FIG. 65

Pantheon, Rome, 125–28, interior marble floor.

preferred stone for pavements. The dove color and veins, evoking the undulations of lapping waves, made the materiality of Proconnesian marble more compelling in conjuring up the image of water.[23]

Barry consciously steers his study away from discussion of politics and economy. Yet marble—and more specifically the quarrying, transportation, and trade of Proconnesian marble—is invested in both the political and commercial networks of the Mediterranean.[24] The Proconnesian quarries, situated only 133 kilometers away from Constantinople, came to prominence when Constantine chose the city on the Bosporus as his new capital. The proximity of the capital to the island of Proconnesus and of the quarry to the harbor ensured the availability of large quantities of easily transportable stone.[25] This reduced its price, making it the preferred material for construction and interior decoration. This trend is reflected in the way imperial patronage of Proconnesian marble grew in scope throughout the fifth and early sixth centuries.[26] In fact, the rich archaeological evidence attests to the export and use of this stone in the Black Sea, the eastern Mediterranean, North Africa, and on the western coast of Italy during the early reign of Justinian.[27] The stone was carved at the quarries into cornices, capitals, and plutei and sent on ships for the construction of churches and public buildings throughout the Mediterranean.[28] Concomitantly, the vast quantities,

FIG. 66 (*top*)

Hagia Sophia, 532–37 and 562, north aisle, sunlight glistening on the Proconnesian marble floor.

FIG. 67 (*bottom*)

View of the Bosporus at noon on December 8, 2010.

FIG. 68

Hagia Sophia, 532–37 and 562, marble pavement of the nave acquiring the appearance of molten gold.

easy marine transportation, and low prices of Proconnesian marble led to the establishment of a uniform aesthetic that privileged luminosity and the image of coruscating water evoked through the materiality of the island's stone (figs. 66–68). Greek language made these connections even deeper because the word for marble, *marmaron*, echoes the verb "to quiver," *marmairō*, and the word for glitter, *marmarygma*.[29] Further, this *marmar-* aesthetic becomes expressive of imperial ambitions for a maritime empire of the Mediterranean, unified in the name of a Christian God.

The economy and politics of marble and the semiotics of its materiality establish a strong foundation on which to build a phenomenological analysis.[30] My study posits a connection between the jeweled style of Late Antique literature and the polymorphy of marble. The shifting appearances of Proconnesian marble are activated by moving diurnal light.[31] This polymorphism, I argue, stirs the perception of animation in the stone, which in turn Byzantine culture connected to the image of quivering water.[32] Paul the Silentiary's ekphrasis offers compelling evidence.[33] When describing the floor of Hagia Sophia (see figs. 9, 11, 47, 63–64, 66, 68), he seeks out and dwells on the Proconnesian marble's polymorphy:

> The peak of Proconnesus soothingly spreading over the entire pavement
> has gladly given its back to the life-giving Mistress [the Theotokos / the Church],
> the softly rippling Bosporus appears [as]
> the radiance of a dark metal that has transformed into luminous surface.[34]

Paul attributes animacy to the island of Proconnesus, willingly spreading its back for the Virgin. Its marble, cut into slabs, forms the floor of the Great Church. These radiant polished faces resemble the shimmering surface of the Bosporus (figs. 64, 66–68). Here the poet uses the onomatopoeic *phrissousa,* containing the sound of the wind. An animate, as opposed to static, image emerges in the poetry, and it is based on the memory of coruscating water. The sea's shimmering surface is in constant flux, continually changing its shape. Paul likens the polymorphy of the marble to that of running waters. He traces this metamorphosis of the Proconnesian stone through three metaphors. The stone's radiance transmutes from the deepest darkness of gushing, swollen waters (*akrokelainiōs*) into the softness and shine of sheep's wool (*argennos*), which invests its bright surface with the radiance of metal (*metallon*).[35] The luster of wool shows the transition from darkness to light and from coldness to warmth. It then leads to a material that combines both liquidity and warmth: molten metal (fig. 68). The three substances—water, wool, and metal—evoked by *akrokelainiōs, argennos,* and *metallon* emerge in the imagined polymorphy of sight.[36] The chameleonic figure gathers the paradoxes of murkiness and shine, fluid and solid. It evokes an alchemical process in which stone liquefies into water and has the luminosity of wool and the radiance of molten metal.

The watery, woolen, and metallic polymorphy of stone forms a poetic amplification that draws attention to the materiality of marble and its optical instability. As he calls up the image of the Bosporus, Paul guides his audience to dwell on movement and change: water riffled by winds, light transforming the surface into molten metal. To an extent, this polymorphy of the Proconnesian marble is still observable today but has not attracted scholarly attention. At dawn the stone glows with the luster of mother-of-pearl, which recalls the opalescence of the Bosporus at certain times of the day (figs. 66–68).[37]

Paul's ekphrasis of the Proconnesian pavement recognizes how the polymorphic nature of marble is invested, not in its color, but in the way its surface interacts with the light, and this chameleonic appearance of marble is linked to the shimmer and movement of coruscating waters (fig. 67).[38] The root *marmar-*, as in *marmaron* (marble), *marmarygma* (glitter), and *marmairō* (to quiver), offers the linguistic basis for this unfolding Late Antique aesthetic of liquescence. The frequency of the words' use in literature increases in this period. Although *marmarygma* and *marmairō* have a long tradition in Greek literature, as Homer uses them to describe the sea and the sparkling appearance of metal armor,[39] their presence triples by the time of Nonnus of Panopolis, in the mid- to late fifth century. His *Dionysiaca* uses *marmairō* and *marmarygē* to describe lightning, armor, pearls, textiles, precious stones, and the light of the moon reflected in water.[40] *Marmar-* in Nonnus encompasses the extremes: from the frightening appearance of lightning, fire, and armor in battle to the lyrical luminescence of pearls, tears, dew, and the moon mirrored in a body of water. The optical sparkle identified by *marmar-* simultaneously carries in the pronunciation of the linguistic root the acoustic correlate of an iterative murmuring sound associated with lapping waters. There is no such correspondence in Latin, and despite the fact that the jeweled aesthetic is shared at this time in the East and the West, the *marmar-* aesthetic of water appears to have deeper cultural roots in the Greek-speaking Mediterranean.

The intensified use of *marmar-* in Late Antique literature also resonates with the polymorphic capacity of the materials used in the decor of church interiors and other large public spaces: Proconnesian marble, gold mosaic, and glass are all affected by moving diurnal light, which causes their surfaces to glitter or to become translucent and luminous (figs. 64, 66, 68–72). Just as water has a power to dissolve the solid, so too streams of

light flowing onto the *marmaron* foster the
dissolution of the solid into a multiplicity of sparkling appearances: *marmarygē*.
Marmar- causes the solid to appear liquid,
making the familiar become strange. Paul

FIG. 69

Hagia Sophia, 532–37 and 562, gold mosaic in the south
aisle glittering under the light of the rising sun.

the Silentiary's ekphrasis offers a good example of this deceptive polymorphy. When
the ekphrasis transitions from the pavement as the windswept surface of the Bosporus
to the gold mosaics in the ceiling, it reveals the resemblance of gold and marble, both
acquiring a liquescent presence (figs. 69–72). The gold tesserae metamorphose into rivers of radiant metal, and in the process they activate the entire space in a series of mirror
reflections: "The ceiling encompassing gold-inlaid tesserae, / from which the glittering
gold-streaming ray / irresistibly bounces off the faces of the mortals."[41] The mosaic ceiling liquefies in a gold-streaming (*chrysorrytos*), glittering (*marmairousa*) ray (*aktis*) that
bounces overflowingly (*chydēn*) off the faces of the faithful.[42] The nouns and adjectives
chosen in this description—"streaming," "glittering," and "abundantly flowing"—highlight the liquescent properties of the gold mosaic, which unify the inert with the animate
(fig. 69); the glitter of the gold, stimulated by the sunlight, reflects off and thus visually
imbues the faces of the faithful with energy. Light imagined through the sound and sight
of *marmar-* resembles water, simulating the latter's power to dissolve and to estrange form.
Natural light still manifests its liquescent effects on Hagia Sophia's *marmaron*. At dawn
the first rays cause the tessellated Proconnesian marble to appear like streams of molten gold (fig. 71) or take on the luminescent surface of the Bosporus (figs. 66, 67, 72).

FIG. 70 (top)

Hagia Sophia, 532–37 and 562, Justinianic gold glass mosaic
in the vaulting of the inner narthex.

FIG. 71 (bottom)

Hagia Sophia, 532–37 and 562, sunlight highlighting in gold
the tessellated marble frames of the nave revetment.

The perceptual merging of marble and gold produced by shimmer and translucence asserts the power of a unifying aesthetic of the glittering sea inside Hagia Sophia.

The Polymorphy of Vibrant Matter

The sparkling sea shows movement triggered from within: an animation of the inert.[43] It is this vivifying force that recommends the image of the *marmairousa* water to model the *empsychōsis* associated with the miracle of the Eucharist. Again, Late Antique poetry gives evidence about how polymorphism is perceived as animation. This evidence introduces two other aesthetic terms—*aiolomorphos* (shape changing) and *daidalos* (variegated)—which supplant *marmar-* and express the liveliness of inspirited matter. In the medieval phenomenon of liveliness, animation is seen to resonate with the modern concept of "vibrant matter," which identifies the nonhuman forces that shape modern political reality.[44] Yet, as this analysis uncovers, vital materialism in Byzantium carries in addition a spiritual and metaphysical dimension.

In the *Dionysiaca*, Nonnus uses *marmairō* and *marmarygē* to capture the shining skin, the luminous face, and the sparkle in the eyes, which show how light becomes a marker of life and thus an outer expression of liveliness.[45] Paul draws on the image of

FIG. 72
Hagia Sophia, 532–37 and 562, north aisle, sunlight glistening on the marble revetment.

surging sea in his ekphrasis of the ambo and solea in order to show how this structure transforms as it becomes the focus of spiritual energy during the liturgy:

> and as an island rises amid the waves of the sea
>
> .   .   .   .
>
> so in the middle under the boundless ceiling
> emerges the ambo of stone, built lofty like a stone-faced tower
>
> .   .   .   .
>
> Here the messenger of the Gospels [the reader]
> passes along on his return from the ambo,
> holding aloft the golden book,
> while, desiring to honor mystically the immaculate God
> and to touch the sacred book with their lips and hands,
> the countless waves of surging people break all around.[46]

The image of the ambo emerges through the metaphor of the island washed by the sea. The people pushing to touch the Gospel book resemble the waves surrounding and breaking at its shores. The word *endia,* which means "a place of sojourn in the open air," switches the perception of the dome to that of sky. The concatenated metaphoric images thus enable a move from the man-made interior to the natural exterior: the floor becomes a sea; the pulpit, an island; the dome, a sky; and the people, waves. The borders dissolve: animate and inanimate interchange.

Anthropologists have observed how combining the memory of sensual perception with that of participation in a ritual stimulates vivid imagination.[47] Similarly, Paul draws on his audience's memory of taking part in the liturgy when he describes the ambo and solea (see figs. 5–6, 9–12). Rather than formal analysis of the structure, he engages the architectural furnishings during their use in the liturgy of the Word. The congregation in Paul's ekphrasis transmutes into waves, agitated by a desire to venerate the Gospel book as Christ incarnate. In recalling the embodied experience of the liturgical ritual, the ekphrasis seeks to imbue the inert with life, manifest in the transference of human agency to nonhuman objects:[48] the *kymata* (waves) of *kinymenōn dēmōn* (moving people). Just like *marmaron, marmarygma,* and *marmairō,* the near-phonetic pair of *kyma* and *kinymai* suggests how the inert transforms into a live entity.[49]

Paul recognizes animation in shifts of appearance. Again he chooses the ambo for deployment of terms marking polymorphy and treating it as an outward manifestation of *empsychōsis.* The passage describing the stone of the ambo uses the term *aiolomorphos,* "of changeful form," and connects it to *poikilia* and the ensuing abundance of contrasting sense perceptions.[50]

> and thanks to its changeful form, [the stone] glistens in a variety of modes,
> on its surface revolve transparent figures like eddying whirlpools,
> in some places resembling the infinity of circles,
> in others they stray from the circle into helical shapes.
> In some places [the stone] is seen ruddy mingled with pallor,

or the fair brightness of human fingernails;
in other places the brilliance turns into a soft woolly whiteness,
gently staying or imitating the sheen of yellow boxwood,
or the lovely image of beeswax,
which men oftentimes wash in clear mountain streams
and lay out to dry under the sun's rays;
it turns silver-shining without completely altering its color,
showing traces of gold.[51]

In this ekphrasis the ambo's alabaster or onyx is characterized by its *aiolomorphon,* or changeful form; its surface glistens in a flux of changing appearances. The veining of the stone transmutes from infinite circles to helixes. The alabaster panels in the interior of Hagia Sophia offer the closest illustration of this water-related figuration on the alabaster of the ambo (fig. 73). The circles and helixes appear as if on a water surface, unstable in the way they emerge and dissolve. From the fluid's polymorphic surface, attention switches to chameleonic color. The abundance of metaphors here tries to capture what is beyond containment and definition. The appearance of onyx and alabaster realizes many divergent phenomena: the radiance of dawn, the pallor of death, the luster of fingernails, the warmth of white wool, and the vibrant yellow of boxwood. In particular, Paul mixes opposites: for example, *ereuthros* (ruddy) with *ochros* (sullen, lifeless).[52] Then his attention turns to a malleable substance, wax, which appears in a variety of states: dry, warm, wet, and cold. Washed in the mountain stream, wax displays the sheen of silver while retaining specks of gold. The trope of aporia lurks in this aggregation of metaphors. At the same time, the ever-expanding sphere of metaphors produces an amplifying effect, which in turn conveys how the changing appearances of vibrant matter overwhelm the senses. This poetic figure of amplification recalls the way the acoustics of Hagia Sophia amplify and sustain chanted vocalization.

Paul's ekphrasis of the ambo's alabaster or onyx activates through vivid language (*enargeia*) mental images (*phantasiai*) that are imprints of sense apprehension on the soul.[53] According to Stoic epistemology, these *phantasiai* resurrected by the speaker create in the listener a simulacrum of perception itself, and this process is called perceptual mimesis. As Ruth Webb observes, "it is the act of seeing that is imitated, not the object itself."[54] Paul's vivid language captures the spectator/hearer in a whirl of dualities of sense perception: hard and soft, solid and liquid, wet and dry. This dizzying, *choros*-type movement is essential in building the sense of saturation and disorientation on which transcendence is predicated.[55] Antithesis and syncrisis alternate in this string of metaphors. The quick shifts between extremes convey a sense of evanescence, a surface that is translucent and reflective at the same time, shimmering and polychromatic. The language takes on the very character of the phenomenon it describes: it is chameleonic in order to depict a polymorphy of stone caused by light.

The *aiolomorphos* presence of the ambo, built on a rich array of perceptual experiences, confirms the pivotal role this structure plays inside Hagia Sophia and at the same time conveys how a more direct access to the divine is possible through the senses. In this respect Paul's ekphrasis answers Maximus the Confessor's belief that knowledge

FIG. 73

Hagia Sophia, 532–37 and 562, marble revetments in the
nave, with a horizontal band of onyx/alabaster. The stones
include cipollino (Carystian green marble), porphyry,
marmor celticum (black and white), and Phyrgian marble,
or pavonazzetto (purple and cream in color).

of the divine gained from sensorial experience by far surpasses any other form of
epistemology. He writes: "there is that
truly authentic knowledge, gained only by
actual experience, apart from reason and
ideas, which provides a total [sensual]
perception of the known object through
a participation by grace."[56] According to Maximus's statement, sense perception is direct
and marks a participation in the divine, which is indicated by the word "grace," or *charis*.

It is not haphazard, I believe, that the *aiolomorphos* presence emerges intensively in
the ekphrasis of the ambo, the place where the Gospel book is read and where the *psaltai*
empty their pneuma in chant. The stones become *empsychos* in these moments of performance of the Logos. This swelling of matter by the indwelling (*enoikēsis*) of Pneuma
enables one to participate in the divine without being the divine and to receive the
energies of life without being the possessor of those energies. This phenomenon is
again illustrated in the writings of Maximus the Confessor (*Ambigua*, bk. 7, discussed
in chapter 1), in association with the changeful form of iron plunged in fire. This state
of being *aiolomorphos* is seen as an exterior marker of participation in the divine. The
image of the soul "eagerly pressing" is reminiscent of the crowds in Hagia Sophia striving to reach the Gospel book. Radiance signals attainment of this union or ecstasy, albeit
only for a fleeting moment.[57] In achieving the union, or *perigraphē*, the self dissolves
in something larger than itself; it is suffused by that which embraces it. Incandescence

and luminescence—these accidents of appearance mark this state in which matter is overshadowed by Pneuma, which allows the faithful to dwell ephemerally in the divine.

FIG. 74

Hagia Sophia, 532–37 and 562, north aisle and gallery, marble revetments.

Paul's ekphrasis of Hagia Sophia provides access to the Byzantine conceptualization of inspirited matter as modeled after the Eucharist. The *marmarygma* of water enacted by the stone revetments and gold mosaics in Hagia Sophia's interior create an image of a world in a flux. To this dynamic of molten metal and coruscating water, Paul adds the image of woods and lush meadows in spring, which he projects onto the green Thessalian columns of the nave. The speckled shafts and gilded Proconnesian capitals effuse *marmarygma,* in which Paul discovers *charis* (figs. 74–76):

> In turn four columns firmly resting on the ground lift with their great heads
> 　　[the six columns of the gallery] by unshaken force,
> with gilded capitals they stand effusing grace
> in the shimmer of Thessalian marble.
> They separate the airy and beautiful naos
> along the length of the neighboring aisles.
> Never in the land of the Molossians did they cut such columns,
> high crested, full of grace, blooming in the color-harmony of variegated forests
> and flowers.[58]

FIG. 75

Hagia Sophia, 532–37 and 562, oblique view of the north aisle and gallery, marble revetments.

The four Thessalian marble columns appear as trees or mountain peaks (*karēnoi*) firmly rooted in the ground (figs. 74, 76). Their gilded capitals please the eye with beauty (*charitessi*) and shimmer (see fig. 45).[59] While *charis* suggests beauty and grace, it also stirs the memory of the Eucharist, with its concomitant descent of Pneuma.[60] The sparkle of gold is traced further to the column shafts. Paul describes them as gleaming with *amarygma* (fig. 76). Speckled in green, gray, and white, these Thessalian columns stir the perceptual mimesis of polychromatic forests and flowers. In Greek, *anthos*, "flower," also designates "color"; consequently, the image of a meadow of flowers is juxtaposed to the dynamically contrasted shadowy sacred forest, *alsos*. Again, the play with alliteration in the dative forms of *alsesi* and *anthesi* brings to the fore the paradoxical duality of syncrisis and antithesis—shadow and light. This contrast is pregnant with energy, indicated by *daidalos*, meaning "complex" and "variegated" and expressive of this dynamic multitonality and luster. The speckled Thessalian shafts do not offer a mimetic representation of a landscape. Instead, they simulate the dynamic of a color-infused meadow in spring through the shimmer and variegated palette of the stone's materiality.[61] Yet the optical spectacle has a spiritual dimension; the *amarygma* (sheen) of *marmaron* produces *charis* (grace, beauty).

It is not only that Paul's poetry concentrates on polymorphism, invested in words such as *marmarygma, aiolomorphos, daidalos,* and *poikilos,* but the material production

itself had become more lavish in this period. Marble revetments originated in Hellenistic architecture and became prominent in Late Roman Republican buildings, with a trend that continued to

FIG. 76

Hagia Sophia, 532–37 and 562, south aisle, Thessalian green marble columns.

grow during the imperial age. With Constantine, marble revetments entered the vocabulary of church architecture.[62] What makes the marble of Hagia Sophia exceptional is the quantity and rich variety used in the interior. The design of the revetments uses contrast to highlight the material diversity (figs. 73, 75, 77). Similarly, Paul builds his ekphrasis of the *daidala marmara* by juxtaposing their differences; he describes ten types of marble.[63] My analysis only focuses on the last three stones mentioned: alabaster, Thessalian marble, and Celtic stone:

> And all the precious yellow that Mount Onyx
> produces in its translucent quarries,
> and that which the land of Atrax produces
> in the smooth plains, not the highlands,
> in part with the intense green of spring not unlike emerald,
> in part from the deep green appearing almost blue in form;
> just as shimmering black resembles [glittering] snow:
> an intertwined *charis* has risen from the stone.[64]

FIG. 77

Hagia Sophia, 532–37 and 562, north aisle and gallery, marble revetments with horizontal bands of onyx/alabaster. The stones include cipollino (Carystian green marble), porphyry, *marmor celticum* (black and white), and Phyrgian marble, or pavonazzetto (purple and cream in color).

What Paul calls "onyx" most likely identifies alabaster, which he describes as having a radiance comparable to gold tesserae (*metallon*) (fig. 77).[65] The "stone from Atrax" (*verde antico* or *marmor Thessalicum*) returns to the Thessalian green, which was also used for the columns of the ground-level arcade and the galleries (fig. 76).[66] According to Paul, its surface, mixing green, white, and black, is polymorphic; it simultaneously conjures up the gleam of spring vegetation, the luster of emerald, and the depths of the sea's abyss. Next comes Celtic marble, whose sharp contrast of black and white fuels an ekphrastic passage already rich in antithesis. These lines capture the culturally specific color perception of Byzantium. Rather than hue, color words stress brightness and saturation.[67] Once again an intense contrast is sought between light-reflective and light-absorbing properties of materials.[68] The polymorphy of stone culminates with the image of a pregnant, *kecharitōmenē* body: "intertwined *charis* risen from the stone."

Mirroring and *Poikilia:* Byzantine Animation Versus Abstraction

In an article on the marbles of Hagia Sophia, John Onians has argued that the Late Antique viewer, trained in the culture of ekphrasis and *encomium* (praise), was capable of discovering naturalistic images in increasingly abstract visual representations.[69] Onians sees the increased production of ekphrasis in Late Antiquity as the cause that enabled Late Antique viewers to develop higher imagistic capabilities, allowing them to conjure up naturalistic anthropomorphic forms from the abstract figuration of marble veins. Onians explains that "the imaginative response of the spectator created a new imaginative activity in the artist. The same is even more true of the relationship between the modern artist and his public, with both exploring the frontier of imaginative alertness. Now, as then, the real measure of that alertness is the capacity to see representational reference in what is essentially abstract."[70] Linking medieval abstraction to modern art, Onians believes that ekphrasis helped viewers to imagine anthropomorphic and zoomorphic representation in the marble slabs.

Yet is this really the case in the Justinianic Hagia Sophia, especially given the fact that the monumental mosaic decoration eschews human and animal figuration? Why should we then seek to discover some latent anthropomorphism and indulge a contemporary urge to discover a quasi-Rorschach dynamic operative in the marble revetments? I would argue, instead, that rather than use the imagination to see representational references in what is an abstract pattern, Paul, in his ekphrasis, cognized the polymorphy of the marble and the mirroring symmetries created by the book-matching of the slabs as forms of inspiriting. While the polymorphy of vibrant matter is easier to grasp in the way shifting diurnal light causes the *marmaron* to acquire an incandescent appearance resembling molten metal or coruscating waters (figs. 68, 71), mirroring symmetries as a form of animation are harder to perceive and to explain to a modern audience (fig. 78). Yet mirroring, as observed in chapters 2 and 3, constitutes one of the two operative principles that engender the *eikōn tou Theou*. Paul introduces this topic, the perception of mirroring symmetries in the book-matched marble as being invested with the Spirit, as follows:

> Upon the carved stone walls [of the peristyle atrium] sheeny designs
> glitter everywhere. The chasm [quarry] of sea-girt Proconnesus
> conceived these [stones]. The joining of the finely cut slabs
> is made equal to [the fine lines drawn by] the stylus; here indeed
> on the slabs made of four or eight [book-matched] slicings you would duly rec-
>   ognize a continuous [pattern] of veins; connected in this way
> the plaques imitate the splendor of living figures [*zōotypoi*].[71]

Paul describes the marble revetments on the walls of the peristyle atrium. This Proconnesian *marmaron*, he writes, is imbued with glittering sheen. Its optical brightness is enhanced by the book-matching. Here I propose to translate *tetratomos* and *octatomos* not as terms identifying the cutting-out of shapes, such as rectangle and octagon, but as the number of slabs sawn parallel to the surface of the marble block. Once cut, these Proconnesian panels, the result of four or eight slicings in the thickness of the block, are arranged like the facing leaves of an open book, creating a wavelike, undulating design (fig. 78).

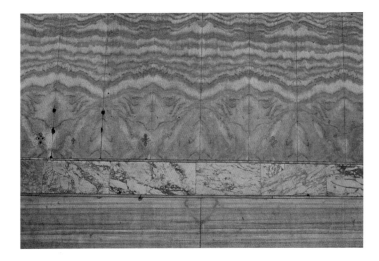

FIG. 78

Hagia Sophia, 532–37
and 562, west gallery,
book-matched marble
revetments.

Paul characterizes this wave pattern with the term *zōotypos*. Why does he call it "full of living figures"? *Zōē* refers to material, physical life, while *typos,* as the earlier chapters have shown, frequently denotes the Eucharist as inspirited matter.[72] In choosing *zōo-typos,* I argue, Paul targets vibrant matter, and for him, this entity is embodied in the perceptual memory of quivering water. Thus in Paul's ekphrasis the wavelike marble pattern points to the reality of living waters as a perceptual earthly memory imbued with metaphysical significance: inert matter brought to life by the energy of the Holy Spirit. This identification of *typos* with the animation of the coruscating surface of the sea conjured by the mirror symmetries of the book-matched marble veins contrasts with what scholars in the past have interpreted as the hidden representational figuration in the abstract pattern of veins on the marble slabs.[73]

This vision of animation engendered by the book-matched patterns of Proconnesian slabs arrests the viewer before the entry into the interior of the church. Paul enhances the liveliness of the *marmairon marmaron* with words for sheen and glitter such as *daidalos, aglaios,* and the verb *astraptō,* "to flash." In effect, he describes an almost blinding sheeny surface that appears as if moving. He recognizes how the rhythm of these repetitive butterfly symmetries manipulates the perception of the otherwise flat surface, making the polished *marmaron* resemble the changing reliefs of quivering water.

Hagia Sophia's marbles present a synergy between two forces that produce the effect of animation: first, the imaging power of such forms and materials as columns and wave-pattern book-matched marble slabs, and second, the phenomenal polymorphy of the material surfaces, together with the visual refrain manifested in the mirror symmetries. Faced with this richness, the medieval audience for the ekphrasis, when visiting the building, was asked to conjure up images of vibrant matter such as quivering water and tie them to the concepts of *charis* and *empsychōsis*. The Byzantine perception of animation arising from the temporal polymorphy and repeated but varied geometric designs is nonanthropomorphic. As such, it is very different from that raised in any previous discussions of abstraction in art. Looking at the frescoes of the fictive marble slabs painted by Fra Angelico (ca. 1395–1455) in San Marco in Florence, Georges Didi-Huberman has argued that their nonfigural designs are apophatic, that they refer to the divine by means of dissemblant figuration.[74] By contrast, the Byzantine example of animation invested in repeated geometric patterns and in phenomenal polymorphy of marble does not stem from an apophatic drive. Rooted in the performance of the liturgy and of ekphrasis, the Byzantine faithful learned to recognize the presence of the metaphysical in the phenomenal and to perceive the *aiolomorphoi* surfaces and mirror symmetries of marble, glass, and gold as vibrant, *empsychos* matter. The visual refrains (like the butterfly symmetries of the book-matched marble) interlock with the sonic ones of the psalmody, breaking the linearity of time and inducing changed states of consciousness.[75] These visual and sonic mirrors (chiasms) produce infinity that is both bounded and boundless, endlessly repeated across the walls and floors of the church.

Sound Reflections of "Many Waters": Divine *Omphē* and Human *Ēchos*

In evoking water, the animation in the Justinianic Hagia Sophia not only eschews anthropomorphic figuration but also works against a narrative sequentiality or a linear perception of time; it captures the imagination in the *marmar-* of coruscating water. As the earlier chapters have revealed, this *empsychōsis,* expressed visually in the *poikilia* of vibrant matter, has an aural dimension in the multiple waterfalls produced by the acoustics of the dome and semidomes and in the water-like effect of the running rever-beration and the intercalation of nonsemantic syllables dissolving the meaning of the chanted poetry. The presence of water manifested in the optical and aural sensations engendered by the interaction of light, reflective surfaces, and human voice in the inte-rior of Hagia Sophia suggests that this sea aesthetic must feature in the epistemology of the divine in this period. This hypothesis finds support in the mystagogical writings of Pseudo-Dionysius, the synergy of divine voice and human breath in Paul the Silen-tiary's ekphrasis of Hagia Sophia, and Saint Ambrose's aural reflections on the effect of congregational singing. What emerges in these texts is the *esoptron* dynamic of call and response: the agency of the divine voice (*omphē*) and its reflection in human voice (*phōnē* and *ēchos*).

The linkage of divine nearness and water appears in many sources already consid-ered: The semantics of Psalm 62, sung at *orthros,* express the desired encounter with God as the sensation of quenching one's thirst. Similarly, the Rossano Gospels min-iature depicting the wise virgins inside the temple renders the sacred space through the image of abundant rivers (see fig. 35). Psalm 92 (93): 3–5, which accompanied the vesting of a newly consecrated altar, also draws on water: "The rivers have lifted up, O Lord, the rivers have lifted up their voices, at the voices of many waters: the billows of the sea are wonderful: the Lord is wonderful in high places. Thy testimonies are made very sure: holiness [*hagiasma*] becomes thine house, O Lord, for ever."[76] The poetry speaks of the aural encounter of the Lord in the thundering sounds of many streams,

FIG. 79

Hagia Sophia, 532–37 and 562, northeast exedra, view of the
coiling shapes revealed as the gaze ascends to the dome.

which rise from the rivers and pour into the billowing sea. The divine is imagined at the crests of these liquid mountains. The ending of the passage on the word *hagiasma,* denoting "holiness," further draws attention to the epiphanic in water, as the word doubles semantically to identify holy waters and asperges. All these references to water and its majestic sound show the Old Testament roots of the concept of the liquescent divine voice. When Christianity became a recognized state religion, the serendipity of Constantine's building large marble-clad basilicas produced the conditions for reverberant and enveloping sound fields, which only enhanced the preexisting Old Testament linkage of the divine with the "sound of many waters." The sensory richness of the Lord's nearness experienced in these interiors could be both nonrepresentational in its aniconicity and yet powerfully audible and optically luminous.

Pseudo-Dionysius, in *De coelesti hierarchia,* chap. 7, sect. 4 (quoted in chapter 1), turns to the concept of the *esoptron* in order to explain how sonic emanation sustains the relationship between divine and human. The celestial *choros* and its bright optical manifestation acquire a sonic dimension, perceptible in the sound of "many waters." This phrase is a quote from Ezekiel 1:24: "I heard the sound of their [seraphim and cherubim] wings when they went, as the sound of much water." The aural epiphany resurfaces twice in the Apocalypse: "and I heard a voice from heaven, as the voice of many waters" (Rev. 14:2, KJV) and "I heard as it were the voice of a great multitude, and as the

voice of many waters" (Rev. 19:6, KJV).[77]
Drawing on the Old and New Testament
conceptualization of divinity as a powerful voice, audible in the streams of many

FIG. 80

Hagia Sophia, 532–37 and 562, narthex.

waters, Pseudo-Dionysius translates this perception into the context of late fifth- to
early sixth-century Christianity. The hymns sung in the ecclesiastical interiors of the
Mediterranean basilicas of marble, gold, and glass must have produced an enveloping
and wet sound field that informed the experience of divine nearness.

The Justinianic Hagia Sophia fine-tuned this model as it architecturally articulated
the prophetic visions echoed by Pseudo-Dionysius: the whirling angelic *choros* reified
in the circular forms of dome, semidomes, and ambo (see figs. 2–3, 5–7, 10, 79). Unlike
the box shape of the typical basilica, the round shape of the Great Church's golden
cupola helped the faithful imagine what Pseudo-Dionysius described as an angelic
chorography dancing incessantly about divinity in the center.[78] As the earlier chapters
have demonstrated, the domed interior enhanced the experience of wet sound and also
focused attention upward to the synaesthetic aural and optical brightness.

Paul the Silentiary, in his ekphrasis of the Great Church, emphasizes this liquescent
theophany as he draws on images of water. He also structures the theophanic experience
as a horizontal-mirror phenomenon. In his passage regarding the singing in the narthex
(fig. 80), Paul distinguishes between two voices: divine (*omphē*) and human (*ēchos*).
The former is agentive; the latter, passive, a mere a reflection of the divine. The synergy
between the two voices then emerges most powerfully in the description of the *psaltai*

singing in the ambo. A mirroring dynamic of *enōpion* and *katōpion* emerges in this passage. The first few lines draw attention to the night and the rising human voices, which aim to beseech the mercy of Christ. This *anabasis* is completed with the introduction of the composer of the psalms, David. Described as "God fearing," *theoudeos,* this epithet brings to the fore David's sin, penance, and punishment, danced out before the Ark.[79] The dark side of David's sin and penance is then paired with its opposite: light, divine response, forgiveness, and renewal. The verses proceed with the light-suffused prophet, now called "gentle of heart," *prēynous,* who composes the psalms and through this creative act initiates the process of renewal and forgiveness, identified with Mary's birth of Christ:

> Along the series of gates extends a long portico
> that receives the ones who enter through the ample gates;
> its length is as long and broad as the naos of the wondrous temple.
> This *chōros* the Greeks call *narthēx.*
> Here at night the ringing melodious sound [*ēchos*], continuously rising, attracts
>   the ears of Christ, the giver of life,
> when, in performing the venerable rites [psalmody] of the God-fearing David,
> the ones communing with the prophetic voice [the elite choir], divided into two
>   streams,
> sing of the gentle-of-heart David, whom the divine voice [*omphē*] praised
> as the wonder of the glorious light, from whom [came into existence] the much-
>   hymned branch [the Virgin],
> [who,] after conceiving in her virgin's womb, blossomed with the divine Christ
>   Child
> in a childbirth that did not come about through a sexual act,
> thus dispensing with the natural laws of procreation through her spermless
>   conception.[80]

In the visual, darkness and light present the energies through which human plea and penance bring about the light of divine mercy and forgiveness. This mirroring reciprocity of *anabasis* and *katabasis* is further manifested in the sonic: the rising voices of psalmody cause the divine response, *antiphōnē,* bringing forgiveness and renewal through Christ. The psalmody produces a melodious *ēchos,* a word simultaneously designating a ringing sound, breathing, echo, and voice. The same aural experience is repeated a few lines later with the verb *iacheein,* "to resound." The *ēchos* of the choir singing responsorially is then juxtaposed to the divine voice, *omphē,* marked by the Homeric word.[81] God's *omphē* inspirits, while the human responds with echoes. Following this dynamic, David receives the *empsychōsis* of the divine *omphē* like a rain of glorious light, which enables him to produce poetry that foretells the miracle of the Virgin's conception and Christ's birth. The miniature on folio 93v of the Mt. Athos Psalter (discussed in chapter 1) beautifully expresses this inspiration as both rays of light and water pouring over the Theotokos (fig. 8).

FIG. 81

Hagia Sophia, 532–37 and 562, northeast exedra, spandrel, carved acanthus rinceaux with porphyry roundel in the center.

When this radiant and wet *omphē* of the divine rains over matter, it marks the site as *omphalos*. As noted in the earlier chapters, Paul uses the term to indicate the dome marked by the cross, the porphyry medallions in the spandrels from which *charis* rises, the ambo, and the fountain in the atrium (see figs. 3, 5–6, 45–46, 81–82).[82] The materials designated as *omphaloi* comprise polymorphous materials such as the gold mosaic of the dome, the alabaster/onyx of the ambo, the porphyry of the medallions in the spandrels, and the Carian marble (*marmor Carium*), or *cipollino rosso* or Jassense, of the fountain (see figs. 3, 73, 81–83).[83] The dome, with its cross-in-a-circle design and sparkle, constitutes a *typos* and thus *empsychos* matter (see figs. 3, 15, 46). Similarly, specks of white glitter with optical liveliness in the deep blood color of the porphyry in the medallions of the spandrels (figs. 46, 81). In Paul's description of the ambo an *aiolomorphōsis* of the alabaster/onyx is apparent in the comparison of its surface figuration to eddying whirlpools, the pallor of fingernails, and the translucence of beeswax (fig. 73).

The fountain in the atrium, the last in this series of *omphaloi,* also combines *daidalos* materiality with the liquescent presence of the divine voice. It was carved out of Carian breccia (*marmor Carium*), or *cipollino rosso* or Jassense, which is red stone with veins of white and black, giving the appearance of opened flesh (figs. 82–83). It performed its *empsychōsis* both in the *poikilia* of its Carian stone and in the temporal *kinēsis* of its rising and subsiding jet of water. This is how Paul describes it:

> In the middle [*omphalon*] of the precious atrium stands
> a most ample fountain, cut from the peak of Iasus,
> in which a sonorous stream [*roos keladōn*] bouncingly springs,
> sending with force from its bronze spout a rebounding jet in the air,
> a jet driving away all sufferings.[84]

The two verbs *anapallō,* "springing up," and *anathrōskō* picture a rebounding movement, going up and down, rising and subsiding, the *ana-* carrying both the upward jet

FIG. 82

Hagia Sophia, 532–37 and 562, reconstruction of the atrium
and its fountain by Tayfun Öner.

and the continuous oscillation between rising and falling. *Keladeō* in turn invites associations with rushing water, loud voices, and the twittering sound of birds. The evocation of these sounds is further intertwined with water because it appears along with the word *roos,* "stream." The water of the fountain thus speaks in an oscillating, twittering, and loud voice, ascending and descending, and with its rhythmical movement, it drives away all suffering. Some of the same words appear in the earlier description of the antiphonal singing of psalmody in the narthex. The twining voices of the choristers are *eukeladoi,* from *kelados,* or "the loud noise of rushing water." The liquescence of the chant is further enhanced by the verb *anerpein,* "to spring up."[85] Thus the image of the water jet becomes a metonym of the human voice rising and falling in psalmody as well as the sexual virility of the divine driving away all suffering. The divine nearness emerges as the *kelados* sound of "many waters."

Paul sees the ambo as perhaps the most important *omphalos,* focusing on the sonic aura it produces (see figs. 5–6, 7, 9–12):

> Then I approach the august place [the ambo],
> which the emperor has recently brought to completion;
> this [is the] supremely beautiful place for the [sacred] books
> and [for] the performance of the mystical words.
> In its center the God-fearing hymnists [*hymnopoloi*] of Christ,
> by whose voice [*phōnē*] of immaculate breath, the divine sound [*omphē*]
> that proclaimed the human birth of Christ, came among men.[86]

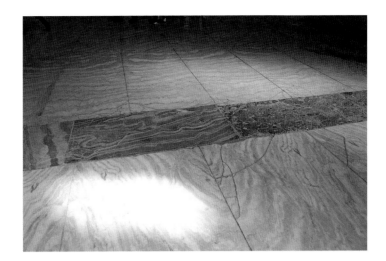

FIG. 83

Carian marble (*cippollino rosso*) as a floor panel in the pavement of Hagia Sophia.

The ambo is inspirited with the mixture of *omphē* and *phōnē*. As the *psaltai* sing, the divine *omphē* becomes reified in the human echoes. Thus chant produces the incarnation of Christ as "sonic emanation" in the luminous void of the *kallichoros* traversed by the *poloi* (simultaneously signifying both crosses and voices) of the *psaltai*.[87]

A similar mirroring synergy between human *phōnē* and *ēchos* and divine *omphē* is audible in the melodic contour of the *koinōnikon* for Pentecost (see fig. 50). Here Pneuma leads and human breath follows. The rise in the melody at *Kyrie* forms a model emulated in the singing of the aspiratory *ha ha,* which, like a sonic manifestation of the imperfect human breath, aspires to and eventually reaches the high pitch (high D), mirroring the height attained at *Kyrie.*

The same dynamic of *omphē* and human *ēcho* is imagined in the way the prophets become conduits of the Lord's word. In Paul the Silentiary's ekphrasis, David, divinely inspired by *omphē,* reproduces the divine voice as a human *ēchos.* The body of the prophet reflects divine speech, thereby giving it materiality. In the same way, Justin Martyr in the second century C.E., in his *Dialogue with Trypho,* VII, 1, speaks of the prophets as men who reiterated only what they heard and saw when inspirited by Holy Pneuma. The prophet functions as an ideal sonic mirror, echoing the divine utterance.[88]

The resonant acoustics of the Late Antique churches only enhanced this aural *esoptron,* while Hagia Sophia gave it further plastic embodiment in the *enōpion* view toward the dome. The *psaltai* as *hymnopoloi,* or celestial axes, make explicit how this arrangement functioned visually and aurally in the Great Church. As shown in the miniature from the Cosmas Indicopleustes manuscript, the choirs are vessels of the *musica mundana* (fig. 7).[89] The singers' voices come to be metonymically linked to the antipodes: voices and axes become interchangeable. Set in a ceaseless rotation, these *choroi* produce the sound of praise continuously sung by the spinning celestial bodies. Lingas, in his analysis of the *teleutaion* antiphon for Pentecost, has argued that the elaborate *allēlouïa* refrains exemplify the embodiment of this inaudible cosmic praise brought into the audible by the human chant of the *psaltai.*[90]

Henōsis as the Dissolution of Form

As the earlier chapters have demonstrated, chant as the emptying of breath in the space under the dome offers an invisible sonic aggregation that gives a sensorial presence to the metaphysical.[91] Further, the chanted intercalations allow the voice to break free from the semantics of the human register of speech.[92] The stretching of semantic chains leads to the dissolution of meaning, which in turn, I argue, is evocative of the power of water to polish and dissolve form.[93] Water relates to poetic creation as it smooths different voices in one enchanting "murmur" or *marmar-*. Gaston Bachelard evocatively correlates this power of water with poetic language: "*liquidity* is the very desire of language. Language needs to flow." Bachelard, of course, was not concerned with Byzantine architecture or liturgy, but his observation invites consideration of the affinity between the liquid behavior of sound in Hagia Sophia and the liquescent materiality of its decor.[94] The poetics of water in Paul the Silentiary and the psalmody (for instance, Psalms 62, 92) uncover a perception of divinity as a disembodied and liquescent voice, an *acousmêtre* reflected in the *ēchos* of human chant while simultaneously visualized in the wave pattern of Hagia Sophia's marmoreal interior.

The Late Antique faithful, exposed to the "earcon" of monodic singing in reverberant interiors, was primed to identify wet sound with the divine *omphē*. The writings of Ambrose, the bishop of Milan (373–397), present compelling evidence that this association of water with the Lord was shared across the Mediterranean. Ambrose spoke and wrote in Latin, but he knew and translated from Greek and in his own writings made extensive use of the ideas of the Eastern church fathers Basil of Caesarea and Gregory of Nazianzus. The impact of his thought on Saint Augustine is significant, and this makes Ambrose an important conduit of Eastern theological thought into the West.[95] In the following passage Ambrose approaches the notion of tranquillity through the image of the shimmering sea: "or even when under a balmy breeze it [the sea] shimmers, often in this case presenting itself to the beholder from afar in colors of purple, suggesting serene tranquillity. Such is the aspect of the sea when it does not beat the nearby shores with the onrush of its waves, but when the waters greet it in a fond embrace of peace. How gentle the sound, how pleasing the splash of water, how pleasant and rhythmic the wave-beats!"[96]

The rhythmic splash of waves and the gleaming depth (*porphyreos*) of the sea slowly transmute into an aural memory of psalmody chanted in monophony by the faithful. The Ambrosian ekphrasis uses the image of the shimmering sea in order to address the experience of chant.[97] The psalmody makes present the sound of the lapping sea. The rhythm of this murmuring movement ensures the establishment of harmony and produces an overall harmonizing and purifying effect:

> The sea, then, is a hiding-place for the temperate, an abode for those who wish to practice continency. . . . Moreover, it provides an incentive to devout living for the faithful, so that they may rival the gentle sound of lapping waters with the songs

of the psalms. Thus, the islands voice their approval with their tranquil chorus of blessed waters and with the singing of pious hymns resound.

How is it possible for me to comprehend all the beauty of the sea—a beauty beheld by the Creator? Why say more? What else is that melodic sound of the waves if not the melody of the people? Hence, the sea is often well compared to a church which "disgorges a tide" through all its vestibules at the first array of the approaching congregation; then, as the whole people unite in prayer, there is a hiss of receding waves; the echo of the psalms when sung in [responsorial] harmony by men and women, maidens and children is like the sound of breaking waves. Wherefore, what need I say of this water other than it washes away sin and that the salutary breath of the Holy Spirit is found in it?[98]

The image of the sea waves characterizes both the onrush of crowds into the church and the congregational singing. Perceiving the aural, chant, through the phenomenon of water sustains the belief in the manifestation of the divine in the liquescent. Shimmering and murmuring, this sound of the crowds and their rhythmical singing performs the liveliness of the sea: a *marmairousa* inspirited matter.

More abstractly, the "sound of many waters" can be brought into relation to the power of the reverberant acoustics to smooth out the cacophonous sounds of the congregational singing. Bachelard's contemplation on water is helpful in articulating this harmonizing effect of Hagia Sophia's "wet" interior: "water is the mistress of liquid language that softens rhythm and gives uniform substance to differing rhythms," he writes, and again, "a poeticized ear brings unity to discordant voices when it submits to the song of the water as its fundamental sound."[99] Bachelard recognizes the affinity between the power of poetic language to smooth out discordancy and the force of water to polish rough surfaces. In acoustic terms, the "sound of many waters" emerges as the effect of the reverberant acoustics of the Great Church, harmonizing the many voices into one loud and bright *ēchos* reflecting the divine *omphē* in its slow and majestic tempo.

6.

The Horizontal Mirror and the Poetics of the Imaginary

So far this study has traced how the material fabric of Hagia Sophia and its liturgical ritual created the conditions to perceive divine nearness in the synergy between light, voice, and space. Mirroring, manifested as optical and aural reflections, occurs naturally when a sound wave or a light ray propagates, bouncing off the polished marble surfaces in the interior of the Great Church. Focusing on these optical and aural reflections, this chapter returns to the Heideggerian notion of the horizontal mirror, analyzed in the first chapter. The *esoptron* dynamic ingathers, as Heidegger states, the fourfold into the one-fold: sky and earth, divine and human. Together, they become simultaneously present, like floating images on the reflective surface of water. Optical and nontactile presences, these ephemeral visions can easily vanish with the gentlest ripple. This horizontal-mirror dynamic, I argue, allows the imaginary to enter the sensorial without losing its ineffable nature. In a similar way, the poetic imagination sets images in one's conscious-ness; these visions, elicited by words and prosody, create constellations and synergies through which the boundaries of space and time dissolve, giving birth to the *metaxu*.

The mirror as an object or metaphor in medieval culture has been the subject of extensive research.[1] Building on this foundation, but introducing a new direction, this analysis uncovers a Byzantine conceptualization of the mirror as a performance and figural dynamic that enables divine nearness to appear in the sensorial. As such, the horizontal mirror as an aural and optical phenomenon becomes a medium for the metaphysical. This chapter explores how the *esoptron* dynamic structures a religious and poetic mode of being in Byzantium. It opens with Paul the Silentiary, continues with the mirroring of the Trisagion in the melodic contour of the Cheroubikon, the *esoptron* effect in the singing of psalmody and in the Eucharist liturgy evoked in Romanos Melodos's *kontakia,* and finishes with the reflective surfaces of liturgical objects aimed at ingathering human and divine. The horizontal-mirror phenomenon emerging in the optical and aural realms of sensation allows, I argue, for the distant to become close, and by destabilizing what is up and down, it engenders disorientation, which in turn can lead to transcendence.

Placing One's Steps on the Vault of Heaven

The mirroring dynamic produces the metaphysical in the sensorial; it has many different instantiations—call and response, voice and reverberation, *enōpion* and *katōpion* views. Paul the Silentiary introduces the horizontal-mirror dynamic at the moment of crossing the threshold of the Great Church. The sky's dawn chases night's shadows and ushers in the new day, while on earth the priests steer the assembled worshippers through the gates of the Great Church, leading them into the domed interior (see figs. 2, 19). The marble space beckons with its reverberant luminosity and encourages the worshipper to envision on its polished surface a *metaxu,* in between heaven and earth:

> But when, upon drawing back the veil of shadows,
> resplendent rose-fingered Dawn stepped upon the celestial vaults,
> then the congregation gathered and all the leaders of the thrones[2]
> who were subjects to the orders of the powerful emperor;
> [together they] carried their thanksgiving gifts to Christ the ruler,
> singing out loud God-fearing hymns with beseeching lips
> and offering silver-shining candles in their untiring hands.
> Following them was the priest and leader of the sacred choir,
> the much-hymned patriarch, whom the scepter-bearer of the Ausonians
>   [the Byzantine emperor] found worthy of the temple. In the whole of Rome
>   [Constantinople] even the broad street was becoming narrow, heading
>   toward the divine temple.
> The entire people, repeatedly uttering thanksgivings, believed to have set their
>   steps on the arches of the immaculate heavens.[3]

This excerpt starts with the shadows of night pulled back like a curtain only to reveal the splendors of heaven. This action, performed by Dawn in the celestial realm, is slowly beginning to be mirrored on earth. The congregation has assembled, led by the ecclesiastical elite and the patriarch, and they advance toward Hagia Sophia, overflowing the well-proportioned, colonnaded streets. The procession has so crowded the avenues that now these urban arteries are all but clogged. As the faithful process, they sing hymns in thanksgiving to God and carry candles radiant like silver. When they reach the temple, led by the patriarch, they gain the impression of stepping into the imagined celestial world. At first glance the verses seem to take poetic license in reversing floor and ceiling.

But looked at closely, it becomes clear that the words describe an inverted parallelism in the interior of the church: the ceiling appears as a mirror reflection on the polished surface of the marble floor. This *esoptron* phenomenon leads to the collapsing of distances; what is far appears paradoxically close, brought near by means of the immaterial reflection on the polished surface of the marble floor. This reflected heaven cannot be touched and held, yet it activates the imagination to dwell in the mirroring image of the celestial courts.

If, at the beginning of this passage, Dawn treads on the arches of heaven, at the end it is the congregation that imagines planting their feet on the celestial vault. Celestial and terrestrial are engaged in a mirroring dynamic. The phenomenal *esoptron* lures the congregation into accepting the phantasmal for the real. Indicated by the verb *dokeō*, meaning "to seem," "to appear," the poetry asks its listeners to imagine the shifting appearances of the polished marble pavement and accept its polymorphy as isomorphic with the celestial. The poetry invites the beholder to experience the text, not in a mimetic relationship to the space, but in a phenomenal one—that is, not for what it is essentially, but for what it appears to be chameleonically.

In its insistence on the imaginary, Paul's ekphrasis represents a Greek equivalent of a practice attested in medieval Arabic poetry. In her analysis of the way the first-person *prosopopeia* functions in the fourteenth-century Nasrid inscriptions written on the walls of the Alhambra, Olga Bush has recognized how these epigrams self-consciously eschew the reading of the text in a mimetic relationship to the actual surfaces of the walls on which they are inscribed.[4] Instead, the epigrams alert the viewer/reader to the *poikilia* of the visual and its deceptive isomorphism. These Arabic poems subtly conjure up in the mind of the reader connections with the appearance of other material substances not present on the walls. Consequently the polymorphy of this illusory isomorphism—which pertains, for instance, when painted and gilded stucco appears radiant like crystal and suggestive of the astral realm—engenders a new intimacy and nearness between materials that are otherwise incompatible.[5]

Paul, in his ekphrasis, builds a similar nearness between the luminous celestial vaults and the reflective surface of marble. The poetry subtly allows a shift from the solid materiality of the polished pavement to the immaterial dome of heaven. This connection emerges out of the phenomenal *poikilia*: the ephemeral light reflections off the marble surface cause the polymorphy of the stone to appear with the deceptive isotropy of the imagined celestial vault. The poetry steers the reader and listener to the phenomenal, framing the perceptual experience of polished marble as an imagined entry into a vitreous heaven.

The call to imagine in Paul the Silentiary further elicits the memory of intense sense perceptions. The ekphrasis self-consciously builds on close-ups: light as resplendent candle-burning, sound as hymn singing, and smell and touch as the proximity of densely packed bodies. These sensory markers activate the memory of the liturgy in general and the Eucharist in particular. In thus triggering memory, Paul taps into the way the religious ritual has trained his audience's imagination to recognize divine nearness in the phenomenal traces it leaves in the sensorial.

The Sonic Mirroring in the Cheroubikon

The entire liturgy in Hagia Sophia, with its sensual saturation, targets this multisensory experience of divine nearness that draws on mirroring (mimesis) as performance and embodiment rather than representation. Paul's call to imagine draws attention to the paradox of the distant appearing close. The singing of the Cheroubikon offers a model for this divine nearness that emerges in the visual and aural dimensions of the performance. The Cheroubikon originates in the Justinianic period; it is the hymn that accompanies the Great Entrance with the gifts processing toward the altar.[6] The text draws attention to a mirroring process: "We who mystically represent [*eikonizontes*] the Cherubim and sing [*prosadontes*] the thrice-holy hymn to the life-giving Trinity, let us now lay aside all worldly care [Luke 21:34] to receive the King of All escorted unseen by the angelic corps, Allēlouïa, allēlouïa, allēlouïa."[7] The Cheroubikon hymn charts two parallel actions of mirroring, a visual one and an aural one: a synaesthesis sustained by the two present participles of "representing" (*eikonizontes*) and "singing" (*prosadontes*). The first verse establishes the matrix of terrestrial-celestial mirroring; the priestly procession reflects the angelic. This spatial icon is designated with the verb "to icon" (*eikonizō*) as an enactment through which the invisible enters the visible and material, thereby creating a proleptic parallel to the Eucharistic incarnation that will take place at the altar.

The visual mirroring, expressed in *eikonizontes* of the Cheroubikon, is further recognized in the exegesis of the Constantinopolitan liturgy written by Patriarch Germanus in the early eighth century. His *Ekklēsiastikē historia* describes how, in procession, "the fans [*rhipidia*] and the deacons are in likeness of the six-winged Seraphim and the many-eyed Cherubim, for in this way earthly things imitate the heavenly."[8] The Great Entrance cortege thus harmonizes human action, transforming matter into a mirroring surface immaterially figuring the angelic cortege of the celestial liturgy.

While the ecclesiastical procession constitutes the visible and performative dimension signaled by *eikonizontes,* the action of singing marked by *prosadontes* identifies the sonic aspect of this ritual mirroring. The song, accompanying the procession to the altar, articulates an acoustic *esoptron*. In it the angelic *musica mundana* is reified as the *musica humana*. At the same time, the self-referentiality of "singing the Trisagion hymn to the Trinity," essentially singing about singing, opens a mise en abyme of aural mirrors.

The Trisagion in the Cheroubikon is a reference to a hymn that has been chanted since the fifth century onward in the anaphora of the Byzantine liturgy. The Trisagion performs the Old Testament prophetic visions of the Lord, surrounded by the worshipping angelic host (Isa. 6:3, Ezek. 1:24, Rev. 4:8).[9] The majestic power of their voices emerged in the chant of the *psaltai,* who traditionally sang the Trisagion from the ambo of the Great Church.[10]

Dimitri Conomos, in his analysis of the two hymns recorded in fourteenth- and fifteenth-century compositions, has indicated how the musical design of the Cheroubikon in general shares modal conformity with most of the Trisagion settings, which in turn are centered around pitches E and G. These seventeen Late Byzantine melodic

A typical 14th-century Trisagion

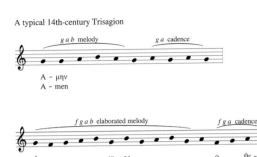

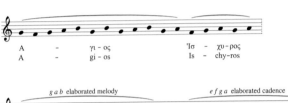

FIG. 84

A typical Trisagion

melody, based on the

fourteenth-century sources

transcribed by Dimitri

Conomos, adapted by

Laura Steenberge. © Laura

Steenberge.

settings of the Cheroubikon reflect the later kalophonic style of the Neo-Sabaïtic rite.[11] Engaging with these transcribed musical settings, the composer Laura Steenberge has convincingly shown how motivic fragments of the Trisagion appear in the melodic contour of the Cheroubikon.[12]

The Trisagion comprises the following: an "Amen" melody followed by two other melodies, of which the first is repeated twice, followed by the second. The "Amen" melody only has pitches G, a, b. The first melody expands the range to F, G, a, b. The second melody expands further to E, F, G, a, b (fig. 84).[13] Contours of motivic fragments of the Trisagion's "Amen" and "first" melodies appear in the earliest setting of the Cheroubikon recorded in a diastematic notation.[14] This Cheroubikon setting is identified as *palaion*, or "old," and sometimes ascribed to John of Damascus.[15] In it the melodic fragments to which the word *eikonizontes* is set mirror two segments of the Trisagion: the "Amen" (G a b) melody, on *eiko-*, and the first Trisagion melody (F G a b), on *-zōn* (fig. 85). Similar mirroring is evident in the arrangement of the Cheroubikon's phrase *triadi ton trisagion*, using the recognizable melodic formulas of the Trisagion's "Amen" and "first" melodies (fig. 86).[16] In singing these Trisagion-recognizable melodic fragments on *eikonizontes* and *triadi ton trisagion*, the human performers of the Cheroubikon double as the angelic choir, leaving an aural and visual trace of the celestial through the sonic imprint of their pneuma in space. This aural presence of the invisible celestial is so compelling in this context because the angels have no material bodies. They are energy that can only be made humanly perceptible in the imprint it leaves in matter; this *typos* and *sphragis* of the angelic in the material constitutes a form of horizontal mirroring and sonic energy reverberating in the *kallichoros*.[17]

Fragments of the Trisagion melody appear, rearranged

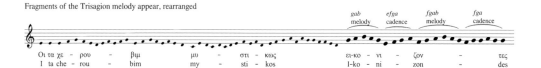

| | gab melody | efga cadence | fgab melody | fga cadence |

Οι τα χε – ρου – βιμ   μυ – στι – κως   ει-κο – νι – ζον – τες
I ta che – rou – bim   my – sti – kos   I-ko – ni – zon – des

The aural mirror draws attention to the power of the breath and voice to reify the divine. It is not surprising that when the patriarch prays to the Lord before the Great Entrance, his words activate this process: "give us the Logos (Word)

FIG. 85

Quotations from the Trisagion melody in the Cheroubikon attributed to John of Damascus, based on Dimitri Conomos's transcriptions, adapted by Laura Steenberge. © Laura Steenberge.

by means of opening our mouths for the invocation of the grace of the Holy Spirit."[18] Mystical power operates in the voice and in the parting of the lips that brings about the sensorial presence of Pneuma.[19] When the elite clergy processes down the northern aisle and into the nave carrying the gifts to the altar, they chant the Cheroubikon, and in the melody exhaled by their voices the faithful recognize the sound of the angels singing the Trisagion. The sight and sound of their performance becomes a material mirror in which the angelic liturgy acquires a temporal and spatial dimension on earth; it becomes what Maximus the Confessor expressed as *perigraphē,* bounding the unbounded: the macrocosm in the microcosm, the celestial in the terrestrial. To this end, a patriarchal prayer states: "Master and Lord our God, who has set down the regiments and armies of the angels and archangels in heavens for the [performance] of the liturgy in Your honor, make it so that with our entry the angels make an entry too, co-celebrating with us and co-praising with us your goodness."[20] The patriarchal prayer beseeches God to intervene, to manifest his energies through the angelic hosts, so that this celestial corps can enter together with the terrestrial procession and become co-celebrants in the rite. The plea is to gather mortal and angelic voices, so that the divine will become visually and aurally reflected in the performative mirror of the earthly liturgy.

Since the *esoptron* dynamic is aimed at bringing the celestial into the sensorial and terrestrial, how exactly does this horizontal mirror function? The euchologion Barberini 336 speaks of the faithful's having gathered before God *enōpion* (from *en-,* "in front of," and *ōps,* "face"), while God looks down on them *katōpion* (from *kata-,* "down," and *ōps,* "face") (see figs. 3, 7–9).[21] The two sides are set in mirroring reciprocity. The fact that the bishop's prayer evokes this mirroring dynamic reveals a process through which the spoken words shape human consciousness spatially to discern the horizontal *esoptron.*

As explored in chapter 1, this *enōpion-katōpion* dynamic inside the Justinianic Hagia Sophia is both architectonically direct and iconographically aniconic. The golden dome articulates a clear anagogical axis, and this view upward toward the cupola represents a dynamic that none of the typical basilicas' wooden roofs, topping box-shaped interiors, could elicit. At the same time, the Justinianic dome that met the gaze of the faithful in Hagia Sophia offered a circular field of gold with an enormous mosaic cross set inside.

Quotations of the Trisagion in the John of Damascus Cheroubikon

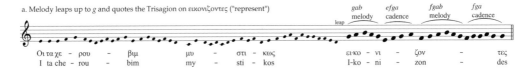

a. Melody leaps up to *g* and quotes the Trisagion on εικονιζοντες ("represent")

Οι τα χε - ρου - βιμ μυ - στι - κως ει-κο - νι - ζον - τες
I ta che - rou - bim my - sti - kos I-ko - ni - zon - des

b. On τριαδι τον τρισαγιον ("Trisagion to the Trinity"), melody and phrase structure resemble Trisagion hymn

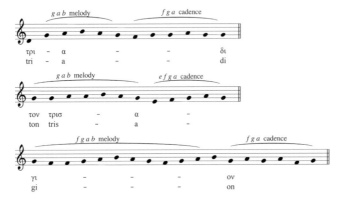

τρι - α - - δι
tri - a - - di

τον τρισ - α -
ton tris - a -

γι - - - ον
gi - - - on

FIG. 86

Melody of the phrase τριάδι τῶν τρισαγίων that shows phrasing from the Trisagion, based on Dimitri Conomos's transcriptions, adapted by Laura Steenberge. © Laura Steenberge.

This aniconic composition displayed the canonical shape of the *typos*—a cross in a circle—that constituted the Byzantine formula for *empsychōsis* (see figs. 15, 17–18, 39, 42–43, 46). It is only as a consequence of the Iconoclast controversy (726–843) that an anthropomorphic figuration showing Christ Pantokrator took over the *typos* in the cupola of newly constructed churches across the empire.[22] Thus the place for the aniconic cross in Justinian's Great Church became the canonical place for the image of Christ in the Middle and Late Byzantine domes.

The *typos* in Hagia Sophia's dome offers a symbolic representation of the divine; this restraint in the visual must have directed the worshipper's attention to seek the divine even more closely in the aural. Such a sonic *esoptron* occurs in Pseudo-Dionysius, who also depicts mirroring as the energy structuring the cosmos.[23] The importance of this specular synergy between terrestrial and celestial is further indicated in the presentation of the daily execution of imperial ceremony. The *Book of Ceremonies,* a tenth-century compilation of texts recording the rituals in the palace, sustains the view that public ceremony is a mirror figuring the celestial *taxis*:

> . . . and as if we were setting up in the middle of the palace a radiant and newly cleaned mirror in which are seen what befits the imperial rule and what is worthy of the senatorial body, so that the reins of power will be managed with order and beauty. So that the text will be clear and easily understood, we have used both ordinary and quite simple language and the same words and names applied and

used for each thing from of old. Through this the imperial power will have measure and order, reflecting the harmony and movement of the Creator in relation to the whole, and it will appear to those subject to it to be more dignified and for this reason both sweeter and more wonderful.[24]

This passage relies on the mirror to express that the entire project of assembling the instructional manual is aimed at preserving an order (*taxis*) that can be perfectly embodied in the rhythm of each of its subsequent temporal instantiations. The terrestrial imperial *taxis* in turn mirrors the universal *taxis*. The prescriptive nature of the manual shows clearly how the *esoptron* is a phenomenon, rather than an object or a metaphor. The mirror as a phenomenon emerges in the ceremony unfolding in time and space.

The Sonic Mirroring in the Psalmody

In much the same way, the psalmody, which formed the backbone of the cathedral liturgy, was perceived as engendering a mirroring process. The psalms were seen as an acoustic *esoptron* in which the faithful could see themselves and, by studying their reflection, correct their faults and imperfections. This was true in the singing of the fixed Psalm 140 (141) at vespers; the melodic contour of each line of the *stichologia* mirrors the one before, and the refrain sung by the congregation copies the model melody performed first by the *domestikos*.[25]

Saint Athanasius of Alexandria (d. 373), in his *Letter to Marcellinus*, confirms this perception of the psalmody as a mirroring dynamic that can lead to transformation. He first states that the psalms reflect the movements of one's soul:

[But even so, the Book of Psalms thus has a certain grace of its own, and a distinctive exactitude of expression. For in addition to the other things in which it enjoys an affinity and fellowship with the other books, it possesses, beyond that, this marvel of its own—namely,] that within it are represented and portrayed in all their great variety the movements of the human soul. It is like a picture in which you see yourself portrayed, and seeing, may understand and consequently form yourself upon the pattern given. . . . But in the Psalter, besides all these things, you learn about yourself. You find depicted in it all the movements of your soul, all its changes, its ups and downs, its failures and recoveries.[26]

This specular dynamic inherent in the psalms allows one to comprehend the poetry as a mirror tracing the desires and fears of one's soul. Seeing his or her reflection in the text, a person could correct and adjust the image and thus return to a harmonious state.

The mirror dynamic arises from the ability of the psalms to be embodied by all who approach and perform them. Saint Athanasius explains further how, from all Scripture, only the psalms offer language that can easily be appropriated as one's own by any reader or singer:

it is as though it were one's own words that one read; . . . the reader takes all its words upon his lips as though they were his own, and each one sings the Psalms as though they had been written for his special benefit, and takes them and recites them, not as though someone else were speaking or another person's feelings being described, but as himself speaking of himself, offering the words to God as his own heart's utterance. . . . it is his own doings that the Psalms describe; every one is bound to find his very self in them, and be he faithful soul or be he sinner, each [perceives] in them descriptions of himself.[27]

Saint Athanasius records the perception of the psalms as a poetic skin that can easily be slipped on by anybody and activated by any person coming and lending his or her breath to the recitation or singing. In a like fashion, the audience also shares this ease of inhabiting the poetry. The process initiated by the mirror results in a chain reaction in which the one pronouncing the poetry not only discovers himself but triggers a similar reflexive process in his audience: "It seems to me, moreover, that because the Psalms thus serve him who sings them as a mirror, wherein he sees himself and his own soul, he cannot help but render them in such a manner that their words go home with equal force to those who hear him sing, and stir them also to a like reaction."[28] The psalms establish a synergy between singer and listener, allowing each to recognize his or her own specular reflection in the performed poetry. Aspects of this mirroring process emerge in Cappella Romana's reconstruction of the singing of Psalm 140. The *domestikos* chants the refrain, which is echoed by the congregation at the end of each hemistich performed by the choir. Saint Athanasius allows us to understand that the sonic mirror of the psalmody established through the call-and-response model between soloist and congregation, soloist and choir, and choir and congregation gives rise to empathy; through it, creation comes back to the Creator, fusing with something larger than itself.

Learning how to become a Christian is also a specular process: the student becomes a mirror of his teacher. The *katēchoumenoi* constitute such an acoustic performative mirror. They are not just instructed in the religion, from *kata-ēcheō* (*kata-*, "down," and *ēcheō*, "sound"/"resound"), but they "re-sound," reverberate the teaching projected onto them.[29] Their ultimate goal is to become Christians, and thus spotless mirrors reflecting the divine word.

The Visual Mirror in the Vessels of the Eucharist

In the Cheroubikon and the psalmody, the sonic *esoptron* activates an empathetic response, which enables the faithful to experience the reification of the celestial in the terrestrial. The power of the mirror phenomenon grows from its capacity to activate multiple sensory modes. The acoustic one harmonizes with the visual, and together they bring to the fore associations with Isaiah's vision of the Lord (Isa. 6:6–7). The figural dynamics of the horizontal mirror are recognizable in the material conditions of a series of liturgical objects used in the Eucharistic rite. The Riha paten, today at Dumbarton Oaks, employs mirroring both iconographically and materially/phenomenally (fig. 87).[30] The plate, dated to 565–78, carries a narrative scene of the Last Supper, in which is depicted Christ administering the bread and wine to the apostles.[31] The rendition is liturgically implicated; it places the scene in the sanctuary of a church, indicated by the scallop shell marking the apse and the cornice identifying a sanctuary barrier. Two large oil lamps stand at the points where the strigilated columns meet the entablature. The altar at the center commands all the attention. No barrier separates the viewer from this table, and this arrangement conveys the sense of open access to and communion with the divine. We can imagine that as the bread is slowly distributed from this plate, the iconographic composition gradually emerges, giving the faithful visual access to the historical significance of the ritual act they are participating in.

Christ doubles in a mirror reflection across the vertical axis as he bends to distribute the bread and wine to the apostles. This specular doubling establishes a spatial dimension in which the grouping of the apostles can be read as two processions unfolding clockwise and counterclockwise, both issuing from Christ. The arrangement also allows the viewer to stand *enōpion,* or in front of, Christ and thus be integrated within the ring of the apostles.

The composition multiplies the reflective processes. The anthropomorphic doubling of Christ constitutes a replication of form in which the circular shape of the paten is refigured in the *choros* of the apostles, the tautologous depiction of the Eucharist on a vessel for the Eucharist, and the reenactment of the Last Supper in the liturgical rite. The object and its iconographic program constitute a mise en abyme.

The representational mirror, which I identify with the doubling of the figure of Christ, emerges along a vertical axis; the ritual mirror, which unfolds the contiguity between the narrative scene and the ritual act, is situated on the horizontal axis. The viewer becomes a participant, seeing his or her own image reflected in the empty space formed by the doubling of Christ. This mirroring continues as the faithful imitates the apostles in coming to receive the Eucharist.

Since it is the priest who offers the bread from the paten, the viewer never places his or her hands on the rim; the faithful is made a user outside of his- or herself, and this constitutes a new relational dynamic that releases the object from the subject's control. Similarly, the depicted altar table, with its reflective surface, reinforces this horizontal-mirror reflection, which in turn reproduces the appearance of a typical Byzantine silver-revetted altar (fig. 88).[32]

The Liquid Mirror in the Chalice

The same visual mirror dynamic is present in the Riha chalice; it is dated to 542 on the basis of its silver stamps and forms, along with the Riha paten, part of the Kaper Koraon hoard (fig. 89).[33] The object has a hemispherical body supported on a flaring foot with

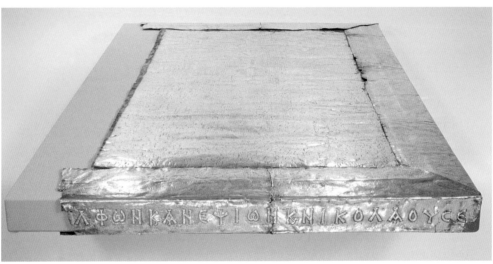

FIG. 87 (*top*)

Riha paten, 565–78, silver. Dumbarton Oaks Museum,
BZ.1924.5.

FIG. 88 (*bottom*)

Silver-revetted altar table, second half of the sixth century.
Dumbarton Oaks Museum, BZ.1963.36.11.

a knob and a short stem. Niello letters framed in gold record the words spoken by the bishop as he commemorates the sacrifice and Anastasis of Christ: "Your things from your own, we present to you, O Lord."[34] These words are pronounced before the *epiklēsis* with which the Holy Spirit is invoked to descend onto the gifts. The reflexivity of the phrase "your things from your own" is visually reciprocated in the reflective surface of the chalice. Executed in chased silver, its shiny surfaces have a mirroring capacity, which is brought to a near miraculous completion when wine is poured in. The surface of the liquid can reflect what exists in the field of vision above the chalice. In fact, the wine can gather the mirrored reflections of the ceiling as well as the face of the person who has approached and touched the rim with his or her lips. If the Attarouthi chalice served as a microcosmic mirror inversion of the dome (see

FIG. 89

Riha chalice, 542, silver, gold. Dumbarton Oaks Museum, BZ.1955.18.

figs. 16–17), the *perigraphē* of the micro- and macrocosms was accomplished through the liquid medium of the wine poured into the chalice in the course of the liturgy.

We can imagine how, during the distribution of the Eucharist, the priest holds the cup to the lips of the congregant. The latter cannot grasp the object by hand but only communes through his or her mouth, thus again transforming into a user outside his or herself.[35] It is this gathering capacity of the chalice, operating through the mirroring principle, that engenders the nearness of the divine. Christ, as "the one who brings near," in Greek *rusamenos* (from *ruomai-,* "to bring near"), has the capacity to gather the faithful near him.

When the priest tilts the chalice to the lips of the Christian, the communicant can see the reflection of the ceiling/sky above imbricated with a reflection of his or her own visage. Mortal and divine are gathered in an immaterial way as fleeting reflections of self and world on the surface of the liquid. The mirror's figural dynamic produces what the prayers consistently request: "admit us that we come close to your holy altar."[36] At this juncture rises the most potent conceptualization of medieval materiality: matter is a medium through which the Spirit becomes manifest in the world;[37] the surface of the wine is one such material medium enabling an evanescent oneness of the faithful with the divine to emerge.

This dissolution of the self into a larger whole corresponds to Jaś Elsner's definition of mystic vision in Late Antiquity: "Mystic viewing is predicated upon the

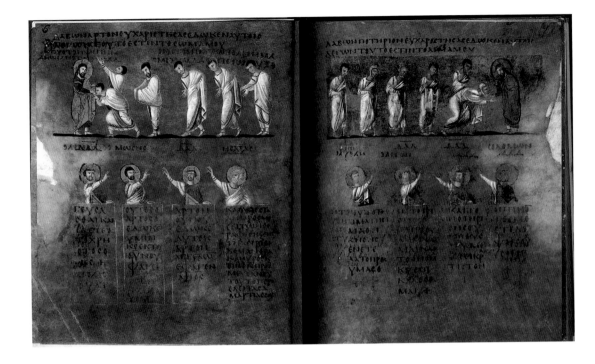

FIG. 90

Rossano Gospel book, Biblioteca arcivescovile, MS gr. 042, sixth century, parchment, tempera, and gold, fols. 3v–4r, showing the communion of the apostles.

assumption that in mystic experience the dualism of subject and object can be transcended into a unity that is neither subject nor object and yet is simultaneously both."[38] Elsner speaks of transcendence superseding a dichotomy of separation.

My analysis suggests that the ambiguity of subject and object triggered in the mystic vision is in fact characteristic of the collective experience of the Divine Liturgy and that the transcendence of self into the divine is built on the mirroring dynamic—visual and sonic—embedded in the rite.

The Chiasm in the Mirror: The Rossano Gospels

The sixth-century Rossano Gospel book shows how a figural composition, evocative of the Riha paten, further articulates the figural dynamic of the horizontal mirror by embedding it in the shape of the cross.[39] The historic Last Supper unfolds as a liturgical action and runs across the verso and recto of the two facing folios 3v–4r (fig. 90). The purple-dyed parchment, silver letters, and gold accents demonstrate the Gospel's luxury edition and possible provenance connected to the city of Constantinople. The rich materials and painting provide a glimpse into the splendor of the cathedral rite.[40] Occupying the upper register of each folio, the narrative images form a preface. The

Communion with the bread and wine is identified with biblical excerpts written in silver letters: Luke 22:19 on folio 3v and Matthew 26:27 on folio 4.

Below each narrative scene, four bust figures represent prophets, each raising one hand in indication of speech and the other holding a scroll recording his words. These texts tie the narrative representations more closely to the liturgical reality of the Eucharist celebration. The series starts with David extending a scroll with Psalm 33 (34): 8, the very verses with which the Eucharist is distributed to the faithful: "Taste and see that the Lord is [sweet]."[41] Then the Rossano shows two more quotes that recognize the celestial nature of Eucharist bread; Moses presents a quote from Exodus 16:15, "This bread given to us to eat is from heaven,"[42] while David holds a quote from Psalm 77 (78): 24–25: "and gave them the bread of heaven. Man ate angels' bread."[43] The Rossano Gospels completes the series of biblical quotes with Isaiah 6:6–7: "And there was sent to me one of the seraphs, and he had in his hand a coal [of fire] . . . and said, '[this] will take away thine iniquities and will purge off thy sins!'"[44] which serves as the model for the entire Eucharistic rite itself.

The selection of biblical quotes in the Rossano folios draws an arc beginning with Psalm 33:8, pronounced in the liturgy, and ending with the heavenly model in Isaiah 6:6–7, thereby creating a mirror in which the terrestrial liturgy reflects the celestial realm as the two prophets and their unfurled scrolls specularly reflect each other across a vertical axis on folio 3v. This visual and textual mirroring corresponds to the Cheroubikon's sonic mirroring of the melodic contour of the angels' singing the Trisagion.

The facing folio, 4r, offers another manifestation of the circular dynamic created by the prophetic quotes. Moses speaks through Exodus 24:8, but the actual quote is from Hebrews 9:20: "This is the blood of the testament which God hath enjoined unto you" (KJV).[45] David follows with an excerpt from Psalm 115:13: "I will take the cup of salvation, and call upon the name of the Lord."[46] David appears again, with a second quote, from Psalm 22 (23): 5: "thy cup cheers me."[47] And the prophetic line culminates with Solomon pronouncing from Wisdom of Sirach 24:21: "They that drink me shall yet be thirsty."[48] This collection of quotes starts by identifying the liquid as blood and recognizing in it the energy of the Holy Spirit, which has descended into matter through the act of calling (*epiklēsis*) the name of God. Drinking is offered in abundance; the cup spills over; but it never gives satiety, instead leaving the imbiber continually thirsty and desiring to return to the beginning, to the cup of wine. Similarly, the reflexivity of the ritual with the wine and the bread expressed in the processions of the two facing folios draws a circular perimeter, clockwise and counterclockwise, that locates in its center the power of the Holy Spirit.

The cross marks this chiastic position where Pneuma overshadows matter in its descent. The *stauros* emerges when looking at the two facing folios: the central margin shapes the stem, while the row of prophets indicates the crossarm. The chiastic structure of the composition on folios 3v–4r responds to the content of what is pictured on the parchment: the Eucharist ritual through which matter is inspirited and transformed into the body and blood of Christ.[49] The structure of this spatial figure is that of a cross

FIG. 91

Hagia Sophia, 532–37 and 562, carved vine cornice set
between the marble revetment and the gold mosaic in the
narthex.

in a circle, which this analysis has linked
to *typos, polos,* and *empsychōsis* and recognized in the design of the mosaics of
Justinian's dome, the *omphaloi* in the spandrels, the ambo, the Carian-marble fountain basin in the atrium, and the *sphragis* of
the Eucharist bread (see figs. 5, 7, 15, 39, 82). The composition, with its visual and textual
mirroring, suggests that the *esoptron* dynamic engenders the process of inspiriting.

Anthropomorphic and Aniconic Modes in Hagia Sophia

The liturgical objects such as the Riha paten and chalice allow the viewer to imagine the
Eucharist in the mirror of the figural representation. Yet the visual program of Hagia
Sophia used anthropomorphic imagery very sparingly. Such figural representations
concentrated exclusively at the templon barrier and altar. Paul the Silentiary speaks of
a woven cloth with gold and silver files displaying the enthroned Christ flanked by the
apostles Peter and Paul. His description seeks animation in this icon in the speaking
gesture of the Son of God as well as the *poikilia* of the *lampas* weave: "The whole robe
shines with gold, for on it gold leaf has been wrapped round thread after the manner
of a pipe or a reed, and so it projects above the lovely cloth, firmly bound with silken

thread by sharp needles."[50] The description insists on how the metallic threads of gold and silver create a texture that suffuses the work with shimmer. This phenomenal *poikilia* can imbue the figures with life.

FIG. 92

Hagia Sophia, 532–37 and 562, carved vine cornice above the marble revetment in the north aisle.

Yet in contrast to anthropomorphic figuration on the portable silk cloths and liturgical vessels in the altar area, the monumental program decorating Hagia Sophia's Justinianic interior was aniconic, eschewing the human figure (see figs. 2–3, 15, 69–70, 91). The mosaics employ just vegetal and geometric designs (figs. 70, 91). The mosaic's strict geometries contrast with the naturalistic vine rinceaux of the carved marble cornice (figs. 92–93). Together, the aniconic mosaic and stone carvings draw the eyes of the faithful to the mirroring structures of the book-matched marble revetments. Overall, the aesthetic experience in Hagia Sophia contrasts with the extensive narrative cycles in other major urban centers, especially Rome, where the naves of the Old St. Peter's, the Lateran, and St. Paul Outside the Walls displayed the stories from Genesis to the Second Coming.[51] Hagia Sophia's aniconic program thus created the conditions to seek the divine beyond the realm of narrative and mimetic representation. Instead, the aniconic interior decor brought into prominence nonfigural phenomena such as glitter, mirroring symmetries, fragrance, and reverberant sound. These phenomena performed rather than represented the metaphysical.

FIG. 93

Hagia Sophia, 532–37 and 562, carved vine cornice above the marble revetment in the south aisle.

The experience of the divine in Justinian's Hagia Sophia issued from reverberant sound and glittering light, both propagating in a space eschewing an anthropomorphic decor. The aural and optical—chanted words that are at the same time audible but not intelligible, and light phenomena such as glitter and shadow that are visual but not visible and lead to the optical dissolution of form—thus brought divine nearness through sonic emanation and visual aura.

Imagining the Eucharist: Romanos Melodos's *Kontakion* on the Prodigal Son

Romanos Melodos's *kontakion* of the Prodigal Son gives a compelling record of how the Eucharist was experienced in this space of mirroring surfaces, of the aural but not intelligible and the visual that is not visible.[52] I argue that the sung sermon invited worshippers to mirror the repentant behavior of the Prodigal Son and thus taste the paradise he experienced.[53] Sound, and more specifically singing tunefully, offered the most direct link to the mystical feast.

The introduction of the *kontakion* as a sung sermon coincided with the building of the Justinianic Hagia Sophia. Thus the genre, brought to prominence by Romanos Melodos in Constantinople, spoke directly to the architectural and urban setting in which it was performed.[54] We do not know for sure when the original *kontakion* on the Prodigal Son was sung; we have only Middle Byzantine sources, linked to Jerusalemite practices, which place the parable in the vigil of the second Sunday of Lent, after the reading from the Gospels.[55] Before the ninth century, the *kontakia* were most likely performed during lay occasional vigils on the eves of great feasts. This context may suggest a link with Hagia Sophia. The *kontakion* on the Prodigal Son was among Romanos Melodos's hymnography likely performed at such vigils in the *kallichoros* of the Great Church.[56] The elite choirs perhaps chanted this hymn with refrains, intoned by the congregation, meant to unfold in the acoustically resonant and visually aniconic interior of the Great Church. So what does it mean to imagine this poetry sung from the ambo?

The *kontakion's* two *prooimia* first invite worshippers to fall on their knees in repentance, mirroring the actions of the Prodigal Son. The faithful pray to be admitted at the mystic table and to receive the Eucharist. And while the elite choir sings the narrative content, the congregation responds with the refrain: "Lord and Master of the Ages."[57] As these words resonate in the space, they both beseech and invoke the Lord, making his invisible presence sensory in the resonant sound of this interior during the nightly vigil. A darkness like the sea must have enveloped this space with its flickering shimmer of myriad *polykandēlia*. Paul the Silentiary gives another glimpse into Hagia Sophia's lamplit void at night:

> But one would see silver ships lifting up
> their trade cargo of luminosity; suspended,
> they sail the illuminated air as if the sea
> trembles neither before the north wind
> nor when Boötes constellation goes down late.[58]

The ekphrasis self-consciously directs the listener's imagination to the experience of the sea at night; it emerges as an oneiric vision of ships flickering like specks of light on the immeasurable surface of water. This perceptual encounter of infinity shapes a socially shared imagination of divine presence in Byzantium. As the refrain of the *kontakion* on the Prodigal Son directs attention to God, "Lord and Master of the Ages," a resonant seascape of darkness and bobbing lights must have conditioned this perception of divine nearness. This sense of envelopment is enhanced by the first stanza of the *kontakion*, which speaks of the embrace:[59] the father has received his son. In a similar way, the congregation was enfolded by the visual darkness and sonic envelopment of a resonant sound field activated by the singing of the *kontakion*.

The third stanza takes up the image of a banquet and develops it by showing how mortal and divine have come together, evocative of Maximus the Confessor's *perigraphē*. Each of the first few lines starts with a hemistich about the human followed by a hemistich showing the mortal partaking in the divine. These first hemistiches declare: "let us hurry," "if we have been deemed worthy," "let us be fellow banqueters." They stretch out to connect to the respective finishing hemistiches: "to share in the feast," "to rejoice with the Father," "to partake in the Emperor of Ages." These first few lines display the human desire to intertwine with the divine. Then the Eucharist gifts of bread and wine are introduced, followed by the *taxis* of the celestial court. The Prodigal Son is included in the feast, revealing to repentant humanity a model communion with the divine. The *kontakion* invites the worshippers to see themselves in the mirror of the Prodigal Son in order to achieve a chiasm with the divine, which only the Eucharist can offer.

The following stanzas, 4 through 7, urge the angelic hosts to come and dress the Prodigal Son in the garments of incorruption one has first received at baptism, then to beautify this *eikōn tou Theou* that has lost its pulchritude, to sandal his feet, and to give him a ring with the *sphragis* of divine protection against the enemies of God. Stanza 8 urges that the sacrifice of the calf be performed in order for the feast to begin. Between this innocent calf and Christ emerges an elision, which signals the approach of the Eucharist. In stanza 9 the calf becomes the innocent lamb sacrificed for the feast. The flesh of this immaculate creature, conceived without blemish, is offered to the symposiasts together with the blood and water streaming from the lamb's side: an allusion to the Crucifixion. In stanza 10 the complexity of allusions increases; like superimposed reflections on a mirroring surface, these images conjure the Last Supper, the liturgical reality of Communion, and the Gospel narrative of the Prodigal Son. Of these three reflections, the Eucharist emerges suggestively with an almost exact quote from Psalm 33 (34): 8, with which the Eucharist is offered liturgically: "Taste and see that the Lord is [sweet]"; but *chrēstos*, for "sweet/enjoyable food" in the psalms, is replaced in the *kontakion* by the near homonym *Christos*, meaning "Christ." The sung sermon thus says: "Taste and see that the Lord is Christ."[60] Being an aural performance, the words stimulate the imagination of the performers to see Christ in the sensorial, which avoids the anthropomorphic—darkness submerging the interior of the Great Church at night and the gustatory memory of the Eucharist.

At this point the *kontakion* self-reflexively starts to describe the chants that rise in thanksgiving. In stanza 11 the angels serving at the feast, hearing the human songs, are enticed to reciprocate, imitating the terrestrial chants in their angelic voices. It is then that the *esoptron*'s dynamic fuses human and angelic in the sonic emanation of the hymns: "The angels serving at the banquet saw those / rejoicing and singing in harmony, / and eager to emulate them, they began to sing."[61] The human chant inspires the angels to sing. If in Pseudo-Dionysius the genealogy of chant follows the exact opposite trajectory, from the celestial to the terrestrial, in the *kontakion* on the Prodigal Son, like everything else in it, the *taxis* is completely reversed. This paradox and reversal only strengthens the message of forgiveness. The mercy of God is so strong that it is able to overcome the tremendous distance sinful humanity has put between itself and the Lord. By emphasizing the reversals, the *kontakion* establishes a belief in the ultimate acceptance of repentant humanity at the feast of the Lord.

The words of the angelic hymn are those of the Trisagion, eliciting in the mind of the worshippers the prophetic vision of standing in God's presence. Romanos invites the performers of his poetry, in their singing, to reproduce and thus hear the traces of the angelic chant. Once again, it is only in performance that the metaphysical becomes sensorial for the faithful. More specifically, in stanza 11 the sound of the Trisagion enters the sonic *esoptron* of the *kontakion*.

It is again sound that strikes the ears of the good son, who upon hearing the symphonic melody recognizes that a great and mystical feast is taking place. The stanzas from 12 through 17 recount his astonishment upon learning that his father has forgiven the prodigal brother. The father then exhorts the good son to have pity on his fallen sibling, for unlike him, he had always been at his parent's side. The good son eventually learns to submit to his father's decision and accepts the invitation to join the feast and the song of the angels in stanza 21. The last stanza implores the Lord to follow the example of the father and forgive fallen but repentant humanity.

From the surface of the polished marble floors figuring the reflected vision of heaven to the Cheroubikon echoing the song of the angels, to the psalmody and Eucharist vessels, fallen humanity had a series of *esoptra* in Hagia Sophia that enabled the faithful to see their faces reflected and, by seeing them, restore them to the ideal *eikōn tou Theou* of their birth and innocence. The mirroring dynamic, both sonic and visual, inside Hagia Sophia structured the religious experience, bringing about a sense of renewal. The spatial and sonic mirroring established the conditions for chiasm and *methexis* (partaking) in the Eucharist, which enabled humanity to become *empsychos* and to return, albeit ephemerally, to a state of being true images of God: performative *eikones tou Theou*. By not having a monumental figural program, the interior of Hagia Sophia subconsciously drew attention to the mirroring geometries that formed the infrastructure—visual and aural—of the process of renewal in the divine.

7.

Empathy and the Making of Art in Byzantium

If there were not in nature's voices such redoublings of onomatopoeia, if falling water did not re-echo the notes of the singing blackbird, it seems that we could not understand natural voices poetically. Art needs to learn from reflections, and music from echoes. [It is] by imitating that we invent.
—Gaston Bachelard, *Water and Dreams*

What does it mean to create by imitation or to invent by echoing voices? Bachelard's words quoted in the epigraph above suggest that imitation is by no means passive but in fact targets the source of artistic drive: the ability to feel empathy. This chapter traces the moments of empathy that allow the pagan conceptualizations of inspiration and animation to inform the Christian liturgical practice in Hagia Sophia. Here I focus on the Late Antique collection of symposiac Anacreontic verse and study it in connection with the ekphrasis and erotic poetry of Paul the Silentiary. Together, these texts are transmitted by a single Byzantine manuscript, dated to 930–40, today divided between two librar- ies: the Universitätsbibliothek Heidelberg (Palatinus MS gr. 23) and the Bibliothèque nationale de France, Paris (MS Suppl. gr. 384) (figs. 94–95).[1] This material is expanded by the Anacreontea of John of Gaza, another contemporary of the Justinianic Hagia Sophia (Vatican City, BAV, MS gr. Barb. 310).[2] I argue that the Anacreontic corpus and Paul's ekphrasis of the Great Church exhibit a shared notion of creativity as mirroring and inspiriting processes, implicating imitation, which is itself defined as a reflection and echo, rather than an original invention. This conceptualization of art making as imitation and inspiriting adds a new layer to the spiritual operations of mirroring and *empsychōsis* that this study has been tracing. In both the liturgical and the symposiac contexts, the *esoptron* gathers the metaphysical in the material. And through the *poiēsis* of matter, the inspirited artist replicates the creative act of the Demiurge. In the end, this chapter addresses the role of empathy in the practice of art history and engages Aby Warburg's concept of *Pathosformel*.

In the Mirror of Love and Drink

Palatinus 23 attests to a continual synergy between erotic sensuality and Christian piety in Byzantium. In both the horizontal mirror appears in moments of transcendence from the real to the imagined, and this elevation is aided by the cup of wine, inebriating the participants, making them forget their earthly worries. In the manuscript the Christian and the pagan resonate in their engagement with the metaphysical in the *poiēsis* of matter. The manuscript starts with the *Paraphrase of the Gospel of John,* composed by the fifth-century poet Nonnus of Panopolis, and follows with Paul the Silentiary's sixth-century ekphrasis of Hagia Sophia; contemporary epigrams for works of art; the collection of Hellenistic and later poetry known as the Palatine Anthology, among whose numbers are Paul's erotic poems; another sixth-century ekphrasis, but of a secular building, written by John of Gaza; the Anacreontic poetry; and finally the works by Gregory of Nazianzus (fig. 94).[3] The assembly suggests that the compiler, whom Alan Cameron has convincingly identified as the tenth-century poet Constantine of Rhodes, and the Byzantine patron for whom this manuscript was produced recognized a certain affinity in this mixture of Christian and pagan poetry.[4] It thus presents a redoubling of empathy: first the sixth-century resonance Paul finds in the fifth-century Nonnian Homeric epic hexameter and erotic verse and then the tenth-century appreciation of this empathy continuously sustained in the elite circles of Byzantium.

Art history has yet to address this cultural production, whose aesthetic sensibilities emerged out of mixed forms and modalities of Christian and paganizing literature, characterizing the poetry of Nonnus of Panopolis but also present in Palatinus 23.[5] My entry into this material is guided by a specific research question: rather than ask *what* explains this duality of Christian and pagan in the poetry produced in the fifth and sixth centuries, a question that dominates the work of philologists, I ask *how* the presence of this duality, a poetics of both Pneuma and Zephyr, can deepen our engagement with the function of Byzantine religious spaces and objects.

Paul's capacity to write Christian ekphrasis in Homeric hexameter and double as a poet of erotica is indicative of the larger transformation of the classical heritage in Byzantium.[6] The poetry of his fifth-century precursor Nonnus of Panopolis served as Paul's inspiration and exemplified this movement.[7] The Nonnian hexametric poetry and its public performance at *theatra* fostered this mingling of mythic, erotic, and sympotic with Christian subjects.[8] Nonnus's two major compositions, the epic *Dionysiaca* and the *Paraphrase of the Gospel of John,* bear witness to this syncretism.[9] Modern scholars studying Nonnus's oeuvre have been quite divided. The French school, led by Pierre Chuvin, has focused exclusively on the pagan output, the *Dionysiaca*, while the Italian

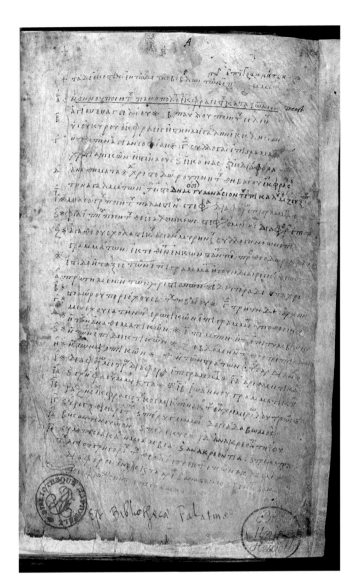

FIG. 94

Heidelberg, Universitäts-
bibliothek, Palatinus MS
gr. 23, 930–40 C.E., fol.
Ar, showing the list of contents written by scribe G,
identified as Constantine
the Rhodian.

school, represented by Domenico Accorinti and Gianfranco Agosti, among others, has focused its effort on Nonnus's Christian output, the *Paraphrase of the Gospel of John*.[10] Agosti and Accorinti, however, have also attempted to bridge the gap, to reconcile this paradoxical duality of the Christian and pagan facets of the Nonnian poetry.[11] In addition to Nonnian poetics, Neoplatonic exegesis of Homer, which developed in Late Antiquity, fostered this Christian return to and appropriation of Homeric epics.[12] "Borrowing," "mingling," and "syncretism" are some of the terms used to define this cultural dynamic; by contrast, I view and analyze it as an expression of empathy.

As seen in the previous chapter, Paul uses the oneiric image reflected on the polished marble floor in his ekphrasis of Hagia Sophia in order to indicate the worshipper's

FIG. 95
Paris, BnF, MS Suppl.
gr. 384, fol. 31r, begin-
ning of the Anacreontic
collection.

encounter with the celestial upon entering the church. The horizontal mirror emerges
also in his erotic poetry, but here it produces an obsession with the phantasmal:

> They say a man bitten by a mad dog
> sees the brute's image in the water.
> I ask myself: "Did [Eros] go rabid,
> and fix his bitter fangs in me,
> and lay my heart waste with madness?"
> For thy beloved image meets my eyes in the sea
> and in the eddying stream and in the wine-cup.[13]

The epigram addresses the madness of love, first comparing it to the bite of a rabid dog. The pain of this experience continually assails the sufferer as he sees the image of the dog in the reflective pool of water. In a similar way, rabid Eros has sunk his fangs into the lover, and the latter now sees the image of his beloved reflected in the sea, in the river, and in the wine of his chalice. By selecting water and wine as the two reflective pools, Paul builds the concept of the inescapability and persistence of the madness of love. At the same time, the reference to the wine and wine cup sets it parallel to the sympotic inebriation. Love dominates this world, destabilizing it by making love's subject obsessed with the object of his or her desire. The mirror has reversed the power relations, dispossessing the subject of control.

Both the dynamics of the horizontal mirror and inspiriting appear in the Anacreontic verses (fig. 95). Written and performed in such eastern Mediterranean centers as Gaza and concurrent with the development of the ostentatious liturgy in the Justinianic Hagia Sophia, these Anacreontic poems in the anthology of Palatinus 23 address light subjects such as love and drinking, consciously steering away from grief, war, suffering, and death.[14] This poetry embraces intoxication and severance from earthly worries in order to plunge its audience into a carefree dream space where time and death are suspended.

Mirroring defines the creative process through which this feeling of intoxication is elicited. The writer effaces his own persona, entering the shell/mask of Anacreon, thereby animating the old poetic form with a new breath.[15] The poems valorize the anonymous writer who is eager to reflect and echo the poetic output of Anacreon, to put on the wreath of Anacreon, and then to pass it on to the next composer. The first and the last poems in this collection open with the possibility for an incessant Anacreontic output, similar to the visualized eternal return to the Eucharist in the circular compositions of the Riha paten and the Rossano miniatures (see figs. 87, 90).[16]

> Anacreon caught sight of me
> that melodious man from Teos
> (I am relating a dream) and he spoke,
> and I, running towards him,
> threw my arms around him, kissed him.
>
> . . . .
>
> Taking off from his head a wreath,
> he gave it to me
> and it reeked of Anacreon himself.
> But I, foolish one, picked it up
> and bound it around my head,
> and from that time even up till now,
> I have never ceased to love.[17]

The chance encounter between the old poet and his young counterpart results in an embrace, kiss, and the passing of the wreath to the new head. The wreath symbolizes the identity of Anacreon, taken on by the new poet as he starts composing like his model, never ceasing to love. The unrequited love becomes a metaphor and a fountain of inspiration. Similarly, the wreath functions metaphorically as the sympotic occasion, the prize from an athletic competition, and, most importantly, the garland/collection of poems. What has passed on from the first word of the poem, which announces the name Anacreon, to the last is a desire to love, to compose without temporal bounds.

The circle/garland remains unbroken to the last poem (no. 60) in the collection, which exhorts its audience to "imitate Anacreon" and "drink a cup . . . a lovely cup of words."[18] The extended hand offering the nectar of words to the next in line ensures that the garland of Anacreontic poetry will continue on in perpetuity. The ring structure of the collection, as well as the impetus to imitate and take on the identity of Anacreon, constitutes the horizontal mirror of poetic inspiration. As the new poet approaches the reflective surface, he merges with Anacreon. Imitation, here conceived of as perfect reflectivity rather than individual originality, is presented as an ideal, the essence of the creative process.

In like fashion, the use of anaphora, tautology, chiastic structures, and refrain enrich the self-reflexivity of the Anacreontic output. The second poem in the collection exhibits a chiastic form, which in shape presents horizontal-mirror symmetry: the top and bottom lines mirror each other across a central horizon line:

A   1. Give me the lyre of Homer

  B   2. without its bloody chord;

    C   3. bring to me cups of lawfulness,

      D   4. bring them to me, blending the rules,

          5. ⊗ so that I will dance, drunk,

          6. ⊗ and under the influence of sensible madness,

     D'   7. singing along with the strings,

   C'   8. I will shout out the drinking song.

  A'   9. Give me the lyre of Homer

B'   10. without its bloody chord.[19]

The poem starts with a frame, AB (vv. 1–2), asking for the lyre of Homer from which the subjects of war and violence have been excised.[20] Then the poet requests a cup of wine, C (v. 3), blended like melodic strands, D (v. 4). At the chiastic center (vv. 5–6), the poet has transcended his normal condition; now drunk, he dances under the intoxication in a state of oxymoronic "sensible madness" of creation. He is now ready to reciprocate the gift of the wine cup by producing a new melody, D' (v. 7), once he has imbibed the liquid contents of the cup, C' (v. 8). The poem closes with the repetition of AB in A' B'. The chiastic composition contains the horizontal mirror, whose self-reflexivity becomes a metaphor for the creative act understood as imitation.

Poem no. 2 further synthesizes the Anacreontic goals: "Homer without the gore, wine without discord, and madness without violence," which is reminiscent of the Cheroubikon hymn's invitation to forget one's earthly worries.[21] This halcyon realm lulls trouble to sleep.[22] Caught in the reflective act of imitating Anacreon, the poet indulges in a dream world. The horizontal mirror destabilizes what is up and what is down, and this process releases the poet from the restraints of gravity.

In addition to chiasm, the mirroring dynamic is conveyed through the use of refrain and ring compositions. Poem no. 9 offers an apposite example of the Anacreontic use of refrain; its continual reiteration induces the very state of sensible madness that the poem aims to achieve: "Allow me, by the gods, I ask you, / to drink, to drink without stopping for breath. / I want, I want to be mad."[23] Here "to drink" and "I want" are each repeated, creating a sense of urgency and willingness to give oneself over to trouble-free intoxication. Then the core of the poem, in verses 4–6, 10–15, addresses the negative madness driving Alcmaeon, Orestes, Heracles, and Ajax in the past to acts of killing the audience would know from their familiarity with Greek tragedy. The Anacreontic refrain rejects this violence and gore in order to reverse the meaning of "madness," returning it to a joyous state of revelry in the middle of the poem, verses 7–9, and again at the end, lines 16–19:[24]

> But I, holding my wine-cup
> and this garland in my hair,
> {no bow, no sword,}
> I want, I want to be mad.[25]

The ring composition conveys a desire for perpetuity of this state of trouble-free enchantment. By repeating the refusal, "no bow, no sword," the poet indicates that his inspiration in past forms—epic and tragedy—is only in the form, but not in the content. Instead, his poetic madness pours in light subjects in this form: carefree love and drinking. The process of Anacreontic creation unfolds as a rediscovery and breathing-in of a new life into an old shell.

The circular shape of this Anacreontic poem recalls the singing of psalmody, during which a ring composition emerges in the completion of each verse by the refrain. This form focuses the creative energy on the repetition. The refrain further stretches the semantic chains of the psalms, creating a semantic disorientation that is then enhanced by the acoustic mirror of the reverberation. Another example is offered by the refrain of the *kontakion*. Human creativity unfolds as an imitation and an echo.

The Garland

The ring composition presents in poetry the equivalent of the horizontal-mirror phenomenon. Its shape also conjures up the image of the garland. The wreath in Anacreontic poetry carries a multiplicity of meanings: it is a marker of Anacreon, identifying the sympotic poet; a metaphor for the collection of verses; and an indicator of the sympotic setting, free of death, disease, and suffering, in which the poetry is performed and enjoyed. The image of the garland, I argue, furthers the slippage between Christian and pagan realms. For instance, the sixth poem in the Anacreontic collection alludes to baptism and the Eucharist while its subject engages in the "innocent" activity of plaiting a garland:

> While plaiting a garland once I found
> among the roses Eros.
> And picking him up by the wings
> I dipped him in the wine,
> raised the cup, and drank him down.
> And now inside my limbs
> he tickles me with his wings.[26]

The poem opens with the weaving of the garland and the serendipitous discovery of Eros, fluttering his wings among the roses. The poet captures and "baptizes" him in the cup of wine. But once he drinks Eros up, this mixture comes alive in his body, continually tickling him to compose carefree songs of love without consummation, madness without violence, and Homer without the bloodshed.

This alternative baptism in wine evokes two Christian ritual contexts—baptism and the Eucharist—both central to the creation of Christian identity. Though the exact date of this Anacreontic composition is unknown, it is legitimate to engage a Christian response, because this text was read by a Byzantine audience. The playfulness of the Anacreontic "baptism" lightly teases the seriousness of the Christian rite. Through the baptism in water, the catechumen earns the right to participate in the Eucharist and take a sip of the wine (see figs. 17, 89). And in consuming it together with the bread, the faithful achieves a temporal union with Christ. Albeit circumscribed in time, this *henōsis* offers a taste of life without earthly worries, in this respect reciprocal to the desired dream world of Anacreontea: a state unscathed by death, violence, or disease.

The decor of Hagia Sophia displays carved marble garlands in a similar strategy to circumscribe a territory removed from earthly worries. I argue that these carved cornices paradigmatically stimulate concepts from the poetics of both Pneuma and Zephyr. While it is easy to turn just to the Christian meaning of these visual elements, I insist on the lingering sympotic significance elicited by this decor. Marble vine encompasses the interior perimeter of the nave and narthex of the Great Church (see figs. 91–93). Carved in a low relief but forming a billowing shape, the cornice projects from the revetment at the border between stone and mosaic, literally in a space between matter (stone) and light (gold mosaic), earth and heaven. Harmonized with the Homeric language of Paul the Silentiary, this garland evokes sympotic notions of poetic creation, of dance, song, and unconsummated love leading to a "sensible madness."

This juxtaposition of Christian space and ritual to Anacreontic poetics and sympotic practices is borne out by the evidence of Palatinus 23. Some of the Anacreontic poems were produced contemporaneously with the construction of the Justinianic Hagia Sophia. They were performed before sympotic audiences capable of responding to both contexts. In another example of such a juxtaposition, this time with reverse dynamics, Romanos Melodos's *kontakion* on the Nativity was performed in front of symposiasts at the imperial banquet in the palace on Christmas.[27] And this empathy between sympotic and Christian *poiēsis* is sustained further in the tenth century as evidenced by the decision of Constantine of Rhodes to gather Paul's ekphrasis of the Great Church with the Anacreontea and other pagan poetic anthologies.

Inspiriting in the Anacreontic Poetry of John of Gaza

In both Christian and Anacreontic contexts, the call to sing centers on the creative energies of breath and exhalation. In performance the voice is embodied in space, making the act of inspiriting sonically perceptible.[28] As both the performer and his audience consume this sonic energy through their bodies, they become *empsychoi*.[29] The Anacreontic verses of John of Gaza (ca. 465–528), a contemporary of Paul the Silentiary, whose ekphrasis was also transmitted in the Codex Palatinus 23, offer further insights into this process of inspiriting.[30] His poems are recorded in a late tenth-century compilation (Vatican City, BAV, MS gr. Barb. 310).[31] This manuscript attests to the continuing Byzantine interest in Anacreontea beyond Palatinus 23. John's poems view poetic inspiration as stirred by Apollo and the Muses. In the opening hexameter canto of the first poem, John appeals to a Muse, asking her to arm him with the tortoise shell, alluding to Apollo's lyre. But instead of war, he would take on light subjects, thus accepting in a typical Anacreontic fashion the Homeric meter but breathing new, carefree content into it:[32]

> My friends, indeed, it is my lot; I myself rejoice, gazing
> at the iridescent Pieridan [Pierides = Muses] scale.
> The Muse of the far-shooter [Apollo] arms me with a breastplate, not against the
>   blood of battle
> or against a hostile snowstorm of enemies, because I know your expectations as a
>   far-seer's [Apollonian] target, and keeping an eye on that,
> I know that I can succeed in that [the poetry performance] only if Apollo con-
>   cedes me this honor.[33]

The Homeric hexameter draws attention to the request for divine inspiration. The poet seeks this *empsychōsis* while anxious at the possibility of failure. Only if Apollo agrees to help him will he succeed. John then turns to address the crowd as he disembarks onto his new Helicon, understood in this context as the city of Gaza. The meter changes to anaclastic ionic dimeter, characteristic of Anacreontics:

> What is this *choros*,
> issuing forth from a wise bee?
> Without knowing, my feet
> brought me inebriated
> to the middle of Mt. Helicon.
>
> The Lord of words, Apollo,
> and the Heliconian Muses,

bringing along the swift-rolling Hermes,
come to judge my dare.
What would happen to me, my friends, what should I do?

My heart, flee from the panic,
entering in allegiance, have courage!
[Like] those who breathe of loving Muse
and masters of ineffable discourses,
so too you will gain ineffable discourses.

This beautiful elder, the swan,
at the blowing of Zephyr, knows
how to modulate a clear song.
Now the crowd is here,
pouring out sweet dew.

All the cranes run to gather
the strewn seed;
I have come to sing
of the pleasure-loving seed of Gaza,
and the crowd has gathered.

Give me the lyre and I will rouse it,
as if the beautifully voiced Orpheus
sang with me this song.
Hey, the crowd has gathered,
and the sweet Muse gushes forth.

Phoebus ["the radiant" Apollo], enveloping me with his breath,
has started to strum his lyre,
modulating it with a wise hand,
and here the crowd is Phoebus,
laden [with nectar] of an ineffable bee.[34]

As John arrives at his Gazan Mt. Helicon, the crowds surround him, avidly awaiting his song. They are not static bystanders but rotate around him. This *choros* motion, as explained earlier, leads to the manifestation of *sophia*.[35] The poet assuages his stage fright by drawing on the examples of natural song inspired by the wind: the swan, once filled with the breeze of Zephyr, pours out a beautiful and clear song. The poet asks for the lyre of Orpheus, which he rouses with his hand, producing a song that distills in it the voice of Orpheus. Finally, as Apollo inspires the poet, the latter transforms into this deity for the duration of the poetic performance. His experienced hand makes the lyre vibrate. The crowd too morphs into this Apollo, filled with the enchanting nectar of poetry.[36] *Empsychōsis* brings about the metamorphosis of both poet and audience, who, just for the duration of the song, become Apollo himself.

A similar phenomenon has unfolded in Hagia Sophia. The song of the elite choir, sung from the ambo in the space under the dome, reverberates and becomes a divine *acousmêtre,* which feeds with its sonic energy the faithful assembled in the nave. This partaking in the sound of chant allows human and divine to become linked. The same dynamic can be expressed through the horizontal-mirror phenomenon; the mortal can see in his or her reflection on the luminous surface an ephemeral return to being an *eikōn tou Theou.*

The creation of poetry is linked to wind and water. Zephyr causes matter to vibrate and produce sound. These mellifluous voices liquefy words into a murmuring stream. The liquid sound of this poetic process in the penultimate stanza above is suggested in the Greek *rheō-*, "to flow," describing the action of the Muse, and *doneō-*, likening the action of the poet to the activity of the wind, which shakes, agitates, and stirs the branches of a tree. The murmuring sounds flow, connecting the voice of Orpheus to the Muse's liquid sound.

Bachelard, who wrote about the material base of poetic imagination in modern thought, reached conclusions that can be brought to bear on the Anacreontic conceptualization of poetic language. The image and sound of a flowing stream resonate with the power of poetic language: "*liquidity* is the very desire of language. Language needs to flow." While not addressing Byzantium, Bachelard illuminates the significance of the Byzantine characterization of poetic language as water: "Water is the mistress of liquid language, of smooth flowing language, of continued and continuing language, of language that softens rhythm and gives uniform substance to differing rhythms."[37] Why water? Because it polishes the surfaces of rocks, creating glistening surfaces in its wake. Thus created, these reflective mirrors can reify the celestial. Water also serves as the metaphor for the poetic creativity merging rhythms in a mellifluous song. John of Gaza similarly mixes hexameter with ionic dimeter, creating a new song for an audience like a swarm of bees, eager to feast on the nectar of his poetic flow.

The imaginative, poetic connection between the flow of water and the stream of words indicates yet another process of mirroring. Drawing on Tristan Tzara, Bachelard remarks how, "of all the elements, water is the most faithful mirror of voices."[38] It softens and harmonizes sounds. Its reflective surface becomes a metaphor for the artistic creation understood as perfect imitation. And in this sense the *esoptron* of water reproduces the Anacreontic process whereby a new song dissolves in its stream the voices of past poets. As the old shell becomes inspirited with a new desire, it produces a modulated sound that expresses and sustains the ancient model.

The Erotic Body

The inspiriting of the poet mirrors the inspiriting of nature. The image of Aphrodite rising from the foam of the sea, which again features an image of water and reflective surfaces, expresses this awakening. Her allure—here identified as *charis*, which marks the metamorphosis of matter infused by Pneuma—slips into the Christian realm. Paul the Silentiary draws on the sensual model when confronting the altar table of Hagia Sophia. In his Homeric vocabulary, the altar becomes a glistening virginal body, nude and attractive:

> Where am I brought, where has my unbridled speech led me?
> Restrain yourself, my bold voice, at the closing of my lips,
> refrain from denuding what is not licit for the eyes to gaze upon.
> You who perform the mystic rites [the priests] as the law mandates,
> spreading with your hand the veil dyed in purple by the Sidonian shells [murex],
>   cover the surface of the altar table.
> Stretching out on its four corners fluttering veils of silver,
> [you priests] show to the infinite people the golden sea and radiant works of art
>   made by an inspired hand.[39]

The poet, propelled by the winds of the sea, has lost orientation. His words convey the sense of being surrounded by an infinite mass of water. Without specifically naming it, he finds himself in a horizontal mirror. This spatial confusion paves the way for an epiphany. The poet sees the sacred—a glistening shape of gold—revealing through its radiance the source of divine energy invested in matter. Paul pleads with the priests to have these mysteries covered with the purple cloth and thus protected from the profane gaze. Yet rather than conceal, Paul's words encourage the haptic, profane, and desirous gaze by recalling the memory of the sensuous shape of Aphrodite emerging from the sea. Moreover, this appeal to touch is further supported by the word choice *phaidra daidalmata*, or "radiant works of art," conjuring up sculpted forms that invite the hand to feel the material glistening surfaces. The precious metal revetment thus transmutes into the haptic memory of a sensuous body.

This allusion to an anthropomorphic shape covered by a clinging drapery enhances the seductive process of paradoxically denuding by covering. Just as the ancient statuary presented bodies whose sensuous curves were made perceptible by the suggestive wrap and flow of the drapery, so too Paul invites his audience to contemplate the same process within the ecclesiastical space. In his ekphrasis, the revetment whose glitter dissolves form suddenly recuperates a sensuous shape in the folds of the cloth embracing it. Thus, as the priests cover the altar, they paradoxically reveal its sensuality.

Paul's ekphrasis, with its lingering image of Aphrodite, was received by an elite audience, which seems to have welcomed these erotic notes. Again, the contemporary Anacreontea give evidence for the production and public performance of such poetry of the sensuous. John of Gaza's verses speak of how nature awakens with desire at the touch of Aphrodite in spring:

> On the soft breezes born by the breath of Zephyr,
> I observe [Eros], the scion of the Graces.

All the groves are laden
with the rose-strewn loose tresses of Paphia [Aphrodite].

Eros, with a divinely inspired dart,
conjoins creature with creature,
preventing the abyss of oblivion
from separating tribe from tribe.

Pleasure-loving songs
exhale [chant] with the ineffable Muses
in the seasons of Dionysius,
when the spring comes again.

Perched on the lush green trees,
a bird sings a song;
all nature, roused with murmur,
dances in honor of spring.

Luminous Apollo, the lord of wisdom,
irradiates an aura;
seated [in the chariot pulled by] foals,
he gives rise to pleasing light.

Give me a rose from Kythera [reference to Aphrodite],
swarm of the wise bee,
let Kythera smile
when I modulate a song about the rose.[40]

Zephyr brings nature to life: the trees sprout leaves and blossoms, while pleasure-loving sounds fill the air. As the bird sings and Apollo brings the radiance of dawn, the poet modulates his human speech to match the alluring sounds of nature. All species, thrust into this intoxicated world, are overpowered by desire. While present only through her attributes of roses intertwined in the loose tresses of the Muses, or through her smile, Aphrodite emerges most palpably in Eros-desire attracting male to female.

John of Gaza never fully personifies Aphrodite; instead, he channels her presence in such aspects as roses or radiant smile. His restraint sustains the allure. Yet all forms are touched by Aphrodite's presence insofar as their substance responds, shifting appearance, becoming polymorphic, blossoming, and sprouting. The poem captures a protean world in a moment of transformation, triggered by a vital inbreathing. The *poikiloi* surfaces of marble and gold covering the interior of the Great Church must have offered a similar world made *empnous* and *empsychos* by Pneuma. Yet both the sympotic poetry and the aniconic interior of Hagia Sophia eschewed the mimetic representation of the sensual body. The latter emerged only in the attributes of roses and garlands or in accidents of appearance such as glitter, translucence, and shadow.

The Return of the Figure: From Byzantium to Botticelli

Byzantium in the Justinianic age produced poetics that straddled Christian mysticism and pagan eroticism without the need to exteriorize them in mimetic anthropomorphic figuration. By contrast, when the West rediscovered the sensuality of Latin poetry (Ovid and Claudian) in the fifteenth century, it responded with a pictorial production that was mimetic and focused on the human figure. Botticelli's *Primavera* anchors this conclusion (fig. 96).[41] While the subject matter it depicts recalls what John of Gaza treats in his Anacreontic poems, the painting anthropomorphizes this awakening of nature at spring. The three Graces interlock in a ring dance. Mercury dispels the clouds with his caduceus. His presence indicates that protean matter stands at the verge of a metamorphosis. Other figures in the panel reveal how this transfiguration operates. Zephyr's inseminating breath has caused pregnant Flora to exude a sprouting bough. Spring as a young maiden strews blossoms from the folds of her flower-bedecked dress. At the center, Aphrodite rules this enchanted world. The painter is known to have found inspiration for this panel in the poetry of Poliziano.[42] But it is yet to be explored if this Western production of both poetry and visual arts had access to Byzantine verse in manuscripts such as the Barberini 310.

Botticelli's painting anthropomorphizes the world evoked in the Hellenistic and Late Antique poetry and echoed in Poliziano's verse. His *Birth of Venus* offers another

FIG. 96

Sandro Botticelli, *Primavera*, ca. 1481, tempera on wood.
Uffizi, Florence.

example (fig. 97).[43] The surface of the sea, riffled by wind, dissolves the horizontal mirror. A breeze pushes toward the coast a shell in which Aphrodite stands, her hair sailing in the winds, her body rising from the foam of lapping waves. The verisimilar figuration of Botticelli's painting contrasts with the nonmimetic way in which Paul the Silentiary uses the erotic image of Aphrodite to express the mysticism of the liturgical ritual.

Botticelli's *Birth of Venus* responds both to the poetics of Poliziano's *La Giostra* and to the visual models of ancient statuary.[44] The painter's return to Graeco-Roman sculpture and relief was inspired by empathy, seeing a living form in the mimetic anthropomorphism of ancient art. Thus, Botticelli gives an example of how animation in fifteenth-century Florence was understood as lifelikeness, achieved through the mimetic representation of the human figure. The painter appropriated this form and enlivened it with accessories of movement such as wind-swept hair and drapery, aspects developed further in the poetry of Poliziano. The concept of *empsychōsis* has thus transformed from the Byzantine one, understood as liveliness and manifested in the phenomenology of visual glitter and shadow, into the Renaissance treatment of animation as lifelikeness, expressed in the successful rendering of pictorial naturalism focused on the human figure.

The Art Historian's Role: *Pathosformel* and Inspiration

Botticelli exemplifies how fifteenth-century Florentine artists found empathy with ancient sculptural forms and saw animation in their mimetic rendition of the human body. Aby Warburg called this empathetic response to the shell of past artistic traditions *Pathosformel*. The term refers to form that evokes emotion in the artist and viewer; it stirs the subject—the artist, his audience, the art historian—to discover expressive analogies between periods and cultures far removed from each other. For a painter like Botticelli, the ancient statues and reliefs transmitted *Pathosformeln* that were resonant with the current poetic and artistic sensitivity of fifteenth-century Florentine culture. The flotsam of antiquity thereby acquired new life, enlivened by a new spirit.

The Warburgian model presents a compelling example of how the art historian can cultivate the power of empathy to resuscitate the past. This role is not far from that of the Late Antique poet who takes the wreath, cup, and lyre of Anacreon in order to pour new spirit/voice into them. His empathy with the Anacreontic *Pathosformel* enables him to blow a new breath into the empty shell of pagan antiquity. A step further in this empathetic response is the capacity of the same sixth-century poet, such as Paul the Silentiary, to invest his Christian ekphrasis with the sensuality of sympotic poetry—with the result that both he and his audience could now view the interior of Hagia Sophia as a sensuous body that comes to life with the sound of chanting exhaled in this resonant chamber or with the shifting light of sunrise and sunset animating the mosaics and marble.

By bringing evidence that three of the major figures connected with the construction of Hagia Sophia were representatives of a pagan faction, Anthony Kaldellis has questioned

FIG. 97

Sandro Botticelli, *Birth of Venus*, ca. 1484, tempera on canvas. Uffizi, Florence.

whether Justinian's elite was uniformly Christian. Phokas, who was the praetorian prefect and the chief magistrate responsible for the initial gathering and disbursement of funds for the building of the Great Church in 532 was threatened twice with accusations of paganism, and in order to avoid the second trial, in 545, he committed suicide. He is likely the figure who invited the architects, Anthemius of Tralles and Isidore of Miletus, who appear in turn to have belonged to the circle of the pagan Ammonius Hermiae of Alexandria.[45] Ammonius, as Proclus's pupil, and the mathematician Eutocius transmitted the Neoplatonic ideas that geometry and by extension architecture express the transition from the multiplicity of creation to the unity of the One and thus serve as a medium for the contemplation of the higher reality that structures the cosmos. Exposure to the circle of Ammonius and Eutocius allowed Anthemius and Isidore to channel this Neoplatonic thinking and plastically express it in the construction of the Justinianic Hagia Sophia.[46] The ekphraseis of Procopius and of Paul the Silentiary betray further sympathies with these Neoplatonic ideas. Sympotic poetry adds another layer embedded in earlier non-Christian traditions. The Justinianic Hagia Sophia thus emerges as a magnet of changing appearances, *aiolomorphos* in its performance of Christian, Neoplatonic, and sympotic notions of *choros, sophia,* mirroring (*esoptron*), and *empsychōsis,* which collectively lead to the experience of a temporal divinization.

Conclusion

This inquiry into the aural and visual aspects of nonrepresentational iconicity manifested in glitter, mirroring, reverberation, stretching of semantic chains, and aspiratory sound brings to the fore the following question: can we transcend the usual way we approach and experience medieval art? Instead of only identifying "image" with a static object, say a painting set in front of us, could we approach iconicity as a performance in which we become implicated in the making of the work of art? In this way, are we not fulfilling the words of Saint Basil quoted earlier (chapter 3): "For regarding a portrait, you do not praise the image itself but marvel at the painter who produced it. As opposed to the object of praise being I and not someone else, I have let myself become a likeness of God. In *eikōn* I have the rational essence, and in likeness I become Christian."[1] We do not need to read these words only in terms of Christian religion: Is not the reading of the Qur'ān a similar process of performative iconicity, voicing the divine through one's body?

I see a poignant example of this performative iconicity in a spontaneous performance of chant in the shell of an abandoned Armenian church (church of the Holy Cross on the island of Aght'amar in Lake Van, eastern Turkey).[2] The singer, whose physical beauty is only transcended by the power of her voice, enchants. Her soaring voice, the steam of her breath, visible before the camera, activate the *esoptron* and *empsychōsis* dynamics. She exhales her breath in the *kallichoros* and in the process activates the resonant acoustics in response, inspiriting both the material structure and the visitors, who stop in their tracks, arrested by the first notes. We are all implicated in this performance as we consume the energy of pneuma offered to and sustained in the void.

At the same time, this performative iconicity, transforming participants into *eikones tou Theou*, emerges parallel to the representational iconicity covering the surfaces of the walls. Both types of *eikōnes* existed in Byzantium. It so happens that art history as a discipline has just focused on the images as representation, neglecting the performer/worshipper who becomes an *eikōn tou Theou* in the course of the liturgical performance.

If the contemporary Armenian example emerged as a spontaneous affair, the Justinianic Hagia Sophia was meticulously planned in all its elaborate detail, mobilizing the forces of an empire to sustain the most intense level of enchantment. Nourished by vast resources, its space embraced thousands of people and overwhelmed them with its liturgy, serviced by an immense state-supported staff. Both singing and listening to Byzantine chant in such a space was transformative for choristers and the faithful. Turning to digital technology and to the aesthetic act of performance has allowed the voice of this building to awaken and some of its reverberant energy to elicit amazement, giving rise to a new empathy for the past.

What this book has set out to uncover is a complex understanding of the medieval image as a synergy between participant and building as instrument of the human voice. Hagia Sophia's domed and double-shelled structure shapes a luminous void. This *kalli-choros* is imbued with light. When singing is exhaled in it, it can produce a synaesthetic radiance that both activates the cupola and "rains" down on the faithful below. The *kalli-choros* gives plastic, optical, and sonic expression to a long tradition of Christianizing Neoplatonic ideas about deification expressed in terms such as *sophia* and *choros*. As the first chapter reveals, this theurgic process is established on the horizontal-mirroring phenomenon: an *esoptron,* identifying the dome, the ambo, the altar, and the Eucharist vessels. These collectively ingather divine and human (expressed as the simultaneity of the *katōpion* and *enōpion* views).

Hagia Sophia's Justinianic decor, free of narrative and mimetic discursive modes, opens landscapes of the imagination, which connect to the experience of resonant sound. Chapters 2 to 4 have led into the reverberant interior. This *kallichoros* transforms the human voice into an emanation, no longer focused on the intelligibility of words but on their sensual valence. Using melismas and intercalations, the elite choir of the *psaltai* enhanced these acoustic effects, stretching the semantic chains and blurring the meaning. The resulting enveloping and sensually rich sound field defied the rational and syntagmatic register of human speech, opening access to the imagined celestial sound of the angelic choirs.

Hagia Sophia's reverberant and enveloping sound field places the faithful standing in the *naos* at the center of an air mass continuously ingathering the reflecting and refract-ing sonic energy. This aural phenomenon articulates through the tactility of acoustics what Psalm 50 (51) does through the chiasm: inspirits the faithful through God's vital Pneuma. Hagia Sophia's enveloping sound field injects energy into the people gathered in this reverberant chamber. The Great Church's sound field also eschews flatness and frontality, producing an immersive sonic environment of divine presence.

Viewed as a system, the synergy between Hagia Sophia's acoustics and melismatic chant in an aniconic and reflective interior renders the divine sensorial in synaesthetic brightness and visual polymorphy yet always beyond visible anthropomorphic figura-tion. This study has identified mirroring (chapters 1, 3, and 6) and inspiriting (chap-ter 2) as the main dynamics through which divine presence emerges in the interior of the Great Church. They are present in both the visual and the audible modalities, including the mirroring symmetries of the book-matched marbles, the patterns and shapes of the architectural decor, and the structure of the psalms and the performed chants.

Christian aesthetics are too often treated in a framework of biblical exegesis and imperial ideology. Yet this study opens alternative venues. It has been a surprise for this researcher to discover mirroring and inspiriting also in fifth- and sixth-century paganizing literature (chapter 7). The erotic and sympotic corpus of poetry of the Late Antique period reveals an equally potent investment in questions about *empsychōsis* and artistic creation understood as a complete abandonment of the self and merging with a fictional Anacreon. Thus the Christian space, ritual, and texts performed in Hagia Sophia's interior find resonance with a much larger envelope of social practices, including the wine-drinking and poetry-reciting symposia. Rather than a monolith of Christian piety, the Justinianic Hagia Sophia resonates with complex artistic practices. It also reveals an elite with multifarious identities that synergistically nourish serious and playful drives, some directed toward the sought-after life in Christ, others toward the delicious pleasures of poetry, wine, and drinking.

How do these urges sit with Justinian's thirty years of war, with the horrors of the pandemic plague of 541–42 and of his unrelenting campaigns to purge the elite? Perhaps in its very hedonism and abandonment, the Anacreontic corpus synchronizes with the Cheroubikon's call to forget all earthly worries and with Hagia Sophia's aesthetically rich liturgy. Both sympotic poetry and the Eucharistic rite appealed to a desire for transcendence achievable through sensually saturated phenomenon.

Hagia Sophia constitutes an aesthetic totality—optical and acoustic—that reenacts in its architectural fiction the perceptual experience of polymorphy linked in the Byzantine imagination to coruscating water. The medieval worshipper would have been immersed in a visual and aural field of *marmaron* and *marmarygma,* whose material flux and long reverberation evoked water and linked to the poetics identifying the divinity with the "sound of many waters."

The live auralization of Byzantine chant at Bing Hall offered modern audiences access to the wet sound of the Great Church (chapter 4).[3] This concert, combining voice with digital technology, established a new approach to the practice of cultural heritage and historic preservation through the aesthetic act. Yet, at the same time, its digitally produced signal lacked the material and visual correlates that the Byzantine faithful would have encountered in the marble-clad interior of Hagia Sophia. The modern audience was thus denied access not only to a vast marmoreal interior but also to a tradition of poetics, including Paul the Silentiary's ekphrasis, that shaped the experience of wet sound as divine *omphē.*

We think with buildings and through buildings. This study has consistently drawn attention to the poetics elicited by Hagia Sophia—the visual and audible. The analysis has focused frequently on the phenomenal and imagined rather than the real and represented.[4] Goethe once stated that architecture is petrified music.[5] This study has unraveled the opposite dynamic—the Late Antique architecture of marble and gold liquifying stone and sound. The polymorphy of the *marmaron* and the *marmarygma* of the gold mosaic, together with the acoustics of the voice as emanation, produce the effect of liquescence. This *aiolomorphos* presence unfolds in time; it is both ephemeral and uncontainable in the visible and intelligible.

I find a connection between this liquid behavior of sound in the Late Antique architecture of Hagia Sophia and the contemporary discussions of the concept of cyberspace. Lev Manovich has coined the term "augmented space" to define the phenomenon produced by the continuous feed of digital information layered over the physical embeddedness of the user in his or her own time and space.[6] Users inside such an augmented space interact with this bi- or multispatiality and the bi- or multitemporality, and their interaction with objects becomes multidimensional and also, I will add, multisensorial.

Hagia Sophia's architecture in the flow of the liturgy can be compared to the contemporary architecture of the cybersurface. The latter is a space whose shapes are inherently mutable and whose soft contours act as a metaphor of variability: the key quality of the computer-driven representations and systems. Hagia Sophia's changing, chameleonic appearances of marble and gold, combined with the reverberation of chant, transform the flow of information into a dense and enveloping sound field. The visual polymorphy of *marmarygma* and the blurring of the semantic register have the capacity to produce an augmented space; here human and divine, real and imagined, ingather in the fleeting reflection on the surface of the horizontal mirror. In some sense, perhaps, in the church dedicated to Holy Wisdom, the blurring of boundaries—structural, material, and aural—suggests that the unknowable can be known only in obscurity.

NOTES

Introduction

1. This vision of beauty would continuously have jostled with elements of chaos, cacophony, and malodorous smells. Yet the medieval ekphrasis and liturgical exegesis consistently dwell only on the visible beauty of the immersive sensual spectacle of the Great Church.

2. See the video available at https://hagiasophia.stanford.edu.

3. Robert G. Ousterhout, "The Sanctity of Place vs. the Sanctity of Building: Jerusalem vs. Constantinople," in *Architecture of the Sacred: Space, Ritual, and Experience from Classical Greece to Byzantium,* ed. Bonna D. Wescoat and Robert G. Ousterhout (Cambridge: Cambridge University Press, 2012), 281–306.

4. "Pentarchy," from the Greek *pentarchia,* means "power of five" and in this context refers to the five patriarchs, each residing in one of these five major cities: Jerusalem, Rome, Constantinople, Alexandria, and Antioch.

5. Rowland J. Mainstone, *Hagia Sophia: Architecture, Structure, and Liturgy of Justinian's Great Church* (London: Thames & Hudson, 1988), 145–83; Richard Krautheimer, *Early Christian and Byzantine Architecture,* 4th ed., revised by Richard Krautheimer and Slobodan Ćurčić, Pelican History of Art (New Haven: Yale University Press, 1986), 230–57; Robert G. Ousterhout, "Holy Space: Architecture and the Liturgy," in *Heaven on Earth: Art and the Church in Byzantium,* ed. Linda Safran (University Park: Pennsylvania State University Press, 1998), 81–120, esp. 87–92.

6. The dome suspended on a golden chain is a Homeric image (Homer, *Iliad* 8.18–27); Procopius employed it in his description of Hagia Sophia (*De aedificiis,* bk. 1, chap. 1, sect. 46). For further analysis of this verse, see Wolfgang Christian Schneider, "Sorgefrei und im Tanz der Weisheit: Philosophie und Theologie im Kuppelraum der Hagia Sophia Justinians," *Castrum Peregrini: Zeitschrift für Literatur, Kunst- und Geistesgeschichte* 271–72 (2006): 52–90, esp. 66–68, and Anthony Kaldellis, "The Making of Hagia Sophia and the Last Pagans of New Rome," *Journal of Late Antiquity* 6, no. 2 (2013): 347–66, esp. 365–66.

7. William L. MacDonald, "Roman Experimental Design and the Great Church," in *Hagia Sophia from the Age of Justinian to the Present,* ed. Robert Mark and Ahmet Ş. Çakmak (Cambridge: Cambridge University Press, 1992), 3–15; Slobodan Ćurčić, "Design and Structural Innovation in Byzantine Architecture Before Hagia Sophia," in ibid., 16–38.

8. Krautheimer, *Early Christian and Byzantine Architecture,* 206–9; Wolfgang Müller-Wiener, *Bildlexikon zur Topographie Istanbuls: Byzantion, Konstantinupolis, Istanbul bis zum Beginn d. 17. Jh.* (Tübingen: Wasmuth, 1977), 84–96; Robert L. Van Nice, *Saint Sophia in Istanbul: An Architectural Survey* (Washington, D.C., Dumbarton Oaks Center for Byzantine Studies, 1965).

9. Müller-Wiener, *Bildlexikon zur Topographie Istanbuls,* 90, and Helge Svenshon and Rudolf H. W. Stichel, "'System of Monads' as Design Principle in the Hagia Sophia: Neo-Platonic Mathematics in the Architecture of Late Antiquity," in *Nexus VI, Architecture and Mathematics,* ed. Sylvie Duvernoy and Orietta Pedemonte (Turin: Kim Williams Books, 2006), 111–20.

10. Hans Buchwald, "Saint Sophia, Turning Point in the Development of Byzantine Architecture?" in *Die Hagia Sophia in Istanbul: Bilder aus sechs Jahrhunderten und Gaspare Fossatis Restaurierung der Jahre 1847 bis 1849,* exh. cat., ed. Volker Hoffmann (Bern: Peter Lang, 1999), 29–58.

11. Christopher A. Weitze et al., "The Acoustical History of Hagia Sophia Revived Through Computer Simulation," http://www.odeon.dk/pdf/ForumAcousticum2002.pdf, accessed November 24, 2015; Patrizio Fausti, Roberto Pompoli, and Nicola Prodi, "Comparing the Acoustics of Mosques and Byzantine Churches," paper for the CAHRISMA Project (EU Contract ICA3-CT-1999-00007, Conservation of the Acoustical Heritage and Revival of Sinan's Mosques Acoustics, CAHRISMA, 2000–2003); Zerhan Karabiber, "The Conservation

of Acoustical Heritage," Workshop 4, CAHRISMA, Fifth Framework INCO-MED Programme of the European Commission, http://www.cyfronet.krakow.pl/~ncbratas/pdf/full_karabiber.pdf, accessed January 29, 2013.

12. Attested in a *Novella* of Justinian, Nov. 3.1, in *Novellae,* ed. Rudolf Schoell, vol. 3 of *Corpus iuris civilis,* ed. Paul Krueger et al. (Berlin: Weidmann, 1928), 20–21; Johannes Konidaris, "Die Novellen des Kaisers Herakleios," in *Fontes Minores,* ed. Dieter Simon, vol. 5, Forschungen zur byzantinischen Rechtsgeschichte 8 (Frankfurt: Klostermann, 1982), 62–72, 94–100.

13. Samuel Hazzard Cross and Olgerd P. Sherbowitz-Wetzor, eds. and trans., *The Russian Primary Chronicle: Laurentian Text* (Cambridge: Harvard University Press, 1973), 110–11.

14. Maximus the Confessor (b. ca. 580, d. 662), as a member of the Constantinopolitan aristocracy and imperial administration, provides access through his exegetical writings to some of the most insightful and sophisticated perceptions of the liturgy in the Great Church. Nicholas Constas, introduction to *On Difficulties in the Church Fathers: The Ambigua,* by Maximus the Confessor, ed. and trans. Nicholas Constas, vol. 1, Dumbarton Oaks Medieval Library 28 (Cambridge: Harvard University Press, 2014), vii–xxxii; Andrew Louth, *Maximus the Confessor* (London: Routledge, 1996). Research on the two Maximus vitae—a Greek one (BHG³ 1234) dated to the mid-tenth century, which places him in the Constantinopolitan elite, and a Syriac one from the seventh century, which locates him in an impoverished village in Palestine—has securely confirmed his aristocratic upbringing in the Byzantine capital and his early career at the top levels of the imperial administration. The Syriac life, while much closer to the lifetime of Maximus, is a lampoon on Maximus's childhood, subverting his aristocratic origins. See Luis Salés, "Maximos of Constantinople: A Political-Circumstantial Assessment of the *Greek* and *Syriac Lives of Maximus the Confessor*" (Byzantine Studies Conference, New York, October 22–25, 2015), abstracts, 83, http://www.bsana.net/conference/archives/byabstracts.html. I thank Salés for sharing his work and bibliography on Maximus the Confessor. On the Greek life, see S. L. Epifanovič, ed., *Materialy k izučeniju žizni i tvorenii prepodobnago Maksima Ispovednika* (Kiev: Tipografija Universiteta Sv. Vladimira, 1917); Wolfgang Lackner, "Der Amtstitel Maximos des Bekenners," *Jahrbuch der österreichischen Byzantinistik* 20 (1971): 63–65; and idem, "Zu Quellen und Datierung der Maximosvita (BHG³ 1234)," *Analecta Bollandiana* 85 (1967): 285–316. On the Syriac life, see Sebastian P. Brock, "An Early Syriac Life of Maximus the Confessor," *Analecta Bollandiana* 91 (1973): 299–345.

15. Maximus the Confessor, *On the Cosmic Mystery of Jesus Christ: Selected Writings from St. Maximus the Confessor,* trans. Paul Blowers and Robert Louis Wilken (Crestwood, N.Y.: St. Vladimir's Seminary Press), 116. Original: ὁμοιώσας ἑαυτῷ τὸν ἄνθρωπον καὶ ὑπεράνω πάντων τῶν οὐρανῶν ἀναβιβάσας, ἔνθα τὸ τῆς χάριτος φύσει μέγεθος ὑπάρχον προσκαλεῖται διὰ τὴν ἀπειρίαν τῆς ἀγαθότητος τὸν κάτω κείμενον ἄνθρωπον. Idem, *Ad Thalassium* 22, in PG 90, col. 320, and *Maximi Confessoris Qvaestiones ad Thalassium,* ed. Carl Laga and Carlos Steel, Corpus Christianorum, Series Graeca 7 (Turnhout: Brepols, 1980), 139. On the question of deification of humanity, see Jean-Claude Larchet, "The Mode of Deification," in *The Oxford Handbook of Maximus Confessor,* ed. Pauline Allen and Neil Bronwen (Oxford: Oxford University Press, 2015), 341–59, and Thomas Cattoi, "Liturgy as Cosmic Transformation," in ibid., 414–38.

16. Torstein Tollefsen, *Activity and Participation in Late Antique and Early Christian Thought* (Oxford: Oxford University Press, 2012), 159–83.

17. A short film on the aesthetics of Hagia Sophia, including samples of Byzantine chant digitally imprinted with the acoustics of the Great Church, is presented as an integral component of this research; it offers the reader a chance to transcend the limits of textual analysis and experience the temporal dimension of this Byzantine inspiriting of the inert. See https://hagiasophia.stanford.edu.

18. Sally M. Promey, ed., *Sensational Religion: Sensory Cultures in Material Practice* (New Haven: Yale University Press, 2014); David Howes, ed., *The Varieties of Sensory Experience: A Sourcebook in the Anthropology of the Senses* (Toronto: University of Toronto Press, 1991); Constance Classen, ed., *Worlds of Sense: Exploring the Senses in History Across Cultures* (London: Routledge, 1993); Constance Classen, David Howes, and Anthony Synnott, *Aroma: The Cultural History of Smell* (London: Routledge, 1994); Constance Classen, *The Color of Angels: Cosmology, Gender, and the Aesthetic Imagination* (London: Routledge, 1998); David Howes, ed., *Empire of the Senses: The Sensual Culture Reader* (Oxford: Berg, 2005); Constance Classen, ed., *The Book of*

Touch (Oxford: Berg, 2005); Susan Ashbrook Harvey, *Scenting Salvation: Ancient Christianity and the Olfactory Imagination* (Berkeley: University of California Press, 2006); Patricia Cox Miller, *The Corporeal Imagination: Signifying the Holy in Late Ancient Christianity* (Philadelphia: University of Pennsylvania Press, 2009). The Sensory Studies website is helpful in gathering the expanding bibliography, http://www.sensorystudies.org, accessed December 18, 2014.

19. Liz James, "Senses and Sensibility in Byzantium," *Art History* 27, no. 4 (2004): 523–37; Nadine Schibille, *Hagia Sophia and the Byzantine Aesthetic Experience* (Farham: Ashgate, 2014); Nicoletta Isar, *Chorós: The Dance of Adam; The Making of Byzantine Chorography, the Anthropology of the Choir of Dance in Byzantium* (Leiden: Alexandros Press, 2011); idem, "Chorography (*Chora, Choros*)—a Performative Paradigm of Creation of Sacred Space in Byzantium," in *Hierotopy: The Creation of Sacred Spaces in Byzantium and Medieval Russia,* ed. Alexei Lidov (Moscow: Indrik, 2006), 59–90; idem, "*Choros:* Dancing into the Sacred Space of Chora," *Byzantion* 75 (2005): 199–224; idem, "*Choros* of Light: Vision of the Sacred in Paulus the Silentiary's Poem *Descriptio S. Sophiae,*" *Byzantinische Forschungen* 28 (2004): 215–42; idem, "The Dance of Adam: Reconstructing the Byzantine *Choros,*" *Byzantinoslavica* 61 (2003): 79–204.

20. Διττὴν γὰρ οἶδε τὴν τῶν θείων γνῶσιν ὁ λόγος· τὴν μὲν σχετικήν, ὡς ἐν λόγῳ μόνῳ κειμένην καὶ νοήμασιν, καὶ τὴν κατ᾽ ἐνέργειαν τοῦ γνωσθέντος διὰ πείρας οὐκ ἔχουσαν αἴσθησιν, δι᾽ ἧς κατὰ τὴν παροῦσαν ζωὴν οἰκονομούμεθα, τὴν δὲ κυρίως ἀληθινὴν ἐν μόνῃ τῇ πείρᾳ κατ᾽ ἐνέργειαν δίχα λόγου καὶ νοημάτων ὅλην τοῦ γνωσθέντος κατὰ χάριν μεθέξει παρεχομένην τὴν αἴσθησιν, δι᾽ ἧς κατὰ τὴν μέλλουσαν λῆξιν τὴν ὑπὲρ φύσιν ὑποδεχόμεθα θέωσιν ἀπαύστως ἐνεργουμένην. Maximus the Confessor, *Ad Thalassium* 60, in PG 90, col. 622D. English translation in Blowers and Wilken, *On the Cosmic Mystery of Jesus Christ,* 126.

21. On the way the Eastern Orthodox liturgy foregrounded experience invested in the senses, see Robert F. Taft, *Through Their Own Eyes: Liturgy as the Byzantines Saw It,* Paul G. Manolis Distinguished Lectures (Berkeley: InterOrthodox Press, 2006).

22. Ibid., 133–60.

23. While the literature on architecture and ritual in Byzantium is significant, no study per se focuses on both the cathedral rite and its multisensory dimension. Thomas F. Mathews, *The Early Churches of Constantinople: Architecture and Liturgy* (University Park: Pennsylvania State University Press, 1971); Wescoat and Ousterhout, *Architecture of the Sacred*; Vasileios Marinis, *Architecture and Ritual in the Churches of Constantinople: Ninth to the Fifteenth Centuries* (Cambridge: Cambridge University Press, 2014).

24. This study draws on the ninth-century Khludov (Moscow, State Historical Museum, MS gr. 129), Pantokrator (Mt. Athos, Pantokrator MS gr. 61), and Paris (Paris, BnF, MS gr. 20) marginal Psalters and the eleventh-century Theodore Psalter (London, BL, MS gr. Add. 19352). Maria Evangelatou, "Liturgy and the Illustration of the Ninth-Century Marginal Psalters," *Dumbarton Oaks Papers* 63 (2009): 59–116, esp. 65–70, 97–98; Kathleen Anne Corrigan, *Visual Polemics in the Ninth-Century Byzantine Psalters* (Cambridge: Cambridge University Press, 1992), 104–34; W. Oliver Strunk, "The Byzantine Office at Hagia Sophia," *Dumbarton Oaks Papers* 9–10 (1956): 175–202; Nancy Patterson Ševčenko, "Illuminating the Liturgy: Illustrated Service Books in Byzantium," in Safran, *Heaven on Earth,* 186–228; George Galavaris, "Manuscripts and the Liturgy," in *Illuminated Greek Manuscripts from American Collections: An Exhibition in Honor of Kurt Weitzmann,* exh. cat., ed. Gary Vikan (Princeton: Princeton University Art Museum, distributed by Princeton University Press, 1973), 20–23.

25. For explication of the terms, I have used the liturgical index in Juan Mateos, ed., *Le Typicon de la Grande Église: Ms. Saint-Croix no. 40, xe siècle* (Rome: Pont. Institutum Orientalium Studiorum, 1963), 2:279–329.

26. Fabio Barry, "Walking on Water: Cosmic Floors in Antiquity and the Middle Ages," *Art Bulletin* 89, no. 4 (2007): 627–56; Bissera V. Pentcheva, "Hagia Sophia and Multisensory Aesthetics," *Gesta* 50, no. 2 (2011): 93–111; both inspired by the discussion of *marmar* in Erkinger Schwarzenberg, "Colour, Light, and Transparency in the Greek World," in *Medieval Mosaics: Light, Color, Materials,* ed. Eve Borsook, Fiorella Gioffredi Superbi, and Giovanni Pagliarulo, Villa I Tatti, the Harvard University Center for Italian Renaissance Studies 17 (Milan: Silvana, 2000), 15–34.

27. Jo Day, "Introduction: Making Senses of the Past," in *Making Senses of the Past: Toward a Sensory Archaeology,* ed. Jo Day (Carbondale: Southern Illinois University Press, 2013), 1–31. In the same volume, see also Heather

Hunter-Crawley, "Embodying the Divine: The Sensational Experience of the Sixth-Century Eucharist," 160–76.

28. Martin Heidegger, "The Thing," in *Poetry, Language, Thought,* trans. Albert Hofstadter (New York: Harper & Row, 1971), 177 and 174. Byzantinists have begun to draw on Heidegger's ideas, an approach beautifully exemplified in the study of how portable "things" functioned in Byzantine culture. See Glenn Peers, "Byzantine Things in the World," in *Byzantine Things in the World,* ed. Glenn Peers (Houston: Menil Collection, 2014), 41–86, and Charles Barber, "Thingliness," in ibid., 99–108. See also Roland Betancourt and Maria Taroutina, eds., *Byzantium/Modernism: The Byzantine as Method in Modernity* (Leiden: Brill, 2014).

29. Patricia Fumerton and Simon Hunt, eds., *Renaissance Culture and the Everyday* (Philadelphia: University of Pennsylvania Press, 1999); Margreta de Grazia, Maureen Quilligan, and Peter Stallybrass, eds., *Subject and Object in Renaissance Culture* (Cambridge: Cambridge University Press, 1996); Ann Rosalind Jones and Peter Stallybrass, *Renaissance Clothing and the Materials of Memory* (Cambridge: Cambridge University Press, 2000); Bill Brown, "Thing Theory," *Critical Inquiry* 28, no. 1 (2001): 1–22.

30. Aden Kumler and Christopher R. Lakey, "The Material Sense of Things in the Middle Ages," *Gesta* 51, no. 1 (2012): 1–17; Barber, "Thingliness."

31. Marc Richir, " Commentaire de Phénoménologie de la conscience esthétique de Husserl," *Revue d'esthétique* 36, *Esthétique et phénoménologie* (1999): 15–27.

32. Maurice Merleau-Ponty, "Eye and Mind," in *The Merleau-Ponty Reader,* ed. Ted Toadvine and Leonard Lawlor (Evanston: Northwestern University Press, 2007), 355, and idem, "The Intertwining—The Chiasm," in *The Visible and the Invisible,* edited by Claude Lefort, translated by Alphonso Lingis (Evanston: Northwestern University Press, 1968), 130–55.

33. In the melismatic style of singing, a single syllable can be stretched over several notes.

34. Day, "Introduction: Making Senses of the Past."

35. Bissera V. Pentcheva, *The Sensual Icon: Space, Ritual, and the Senses in Byzantium* (University Park: Pennsylvania State University Press, 2010); for the video, see www.thesensualicon.com.

36. See https://hagiasophia.stanford.edu, http://iconsofsound.stanford.edu/aesthetics.html, and https://www.youtube.com/watch?v=rsLgLNgA-_Q.

37. Wiesław Woszczyk, "Acoustics of Hagia Sophia: A Scientific Approach to Humanities and Sacred Space," in *Aural Architecture in Byzantium: Music, Acoustics, and Ritual,* ed. Bissera V. Pentcheva (Aldershot: Ashgate, 2017), draft manuscript accessible at http://auralarchitecture.stanford.edu.

38. Barry Blesser and Linda-Ruth Salter, *Spaces Speak, Are You Listening? Experiencing Aural Architecture* (Cambridge: MIT Press, 2007), 5.

39. Iconsofsound.stanford.edu and www.youtube.com/watch?v=uKLkJJ3ftIw and https://www.youtube.com/watch?v=bHpOiX2sO-s.

40. Blesser and Salter, *Spaces Speak,* 185–91, and Angelo Farina and Regev Ayalon, "Recording Concert Hall Acoustics for Posterity" (paper presented at the 24th AES [Audio-Engineering Studies] Conference on Multichannel Audio, Banff, Alberta, June 26–28, 2003), http://www.ramsete.com/Public/AES-24/183-AES24.PDF, accessed May 16, 2010.

41. See http://newsroom.ucla.edu/stories/measuring-the-sound-of-angels-singing, accessed October 14, 2015.

42. On the value of auralizations, see Farina and Ayalon, "Recording Concert Hall Acoustics for Posterity."

43. Deborah Howard and Laura Moretti, *Sound and Space in Renaissance Venice: Architecture, Music, Acoustics* (New Haven: Yale University Press, 2009); also see Vasco Zara, "Musica e architettura tra Medio Evo ed età moderna: Storia critica di un'idea," *Acta musicologica* 77 (2005): 1–26.

44. Carolyn Abbate, "Music—Drastic or Gnostic?" *Critical Inquiry* 30, no. 3 (2004): 505–36. See also Hans Ulrich Gumbrecht, *Production of Presence: What Meaning Cannot Convey* (Stanford: Stanford University Press, 2004).

45. Michael Bull and Les Bach, eds., *The Auditory Culture Reader* (Oxford: Berg, 2003); Mark M. Smith, ed., *Hearing History: A Reader* (Athens: University of Georgia Press, 2004); Ros Bandt, Michelle Duffy, and Dolly MacKinnon, eds., *Hearing Places: Sound, Place, Time, and Culture* (Newcastle upon Tyne: Cambridge Scholars, 2009); Jonathan Sterne, ed., *The Sound Studies Reader* (New York: Routledge, 2012).

46. Jonathan Sterne, "Sonic Imaginations," in Sterne, *Sound Studies Reader,* 1–17. Sterne employs an interdisciplinary method in his work. Idem, *The Audible Past: Cultural Origins of Sound Reproduction* (Durham: Duke University Press, 2003), and idem, *MP3: The Meaning of a Format* (Durham: Duke University Press, 2012).

47. R. Murray Schafer, *The New Soundscape: A Handbook for the Modern Music Teacher* (Scarborough, Ont.: Berandol Music; New York: Associated Music Publishers, 1969), and idem, *The Soundscape: Our Sonic Environment and the Tuning of the World* (New York: Knopf, 1977; repr., Rochester, Vt.: Destiny Books, 1994), 7–10, 131.

48. Schafer, *Soundscape,* 4, 10–11, 237–52.

49. Emily Thompson, *The Soundscape of Modernity: Architectural Acoustics and the Culture of Listening in America, 1900–1933* (2002; repr., Cambridge: MIT Press, 2004), 1–2.

50. Soundscape becomes an expression of territorialization, a concept developed in Gilles Deleuze and Félix Guattari, "On the Refrain," in *A Thousand Plateaus: Capitalism and Schizophrenia,* trans. Brian Massumi (Minneapolis: University of Minnesota Press, 1987), 310–50, esp. 316–17.

51. Alexander Lingas, "From Earth to Heaven: The Changing Musical Soundscape of Byzantine Liturgy," in *Experiencing Byzantium,* ed. Claire Nesbitt and Mark Jackson (Farnham: Ashgate, 2013), 311–58.

52. Jonathan Sterne, "Space Within Space: Artificial Reverb and the Detachable Echo." *Gray Room* 60 (2015): 110–131, doi:10.1162/GREY_a_00177.

53. See the Cappella Romana video at https://hagiasophia.stanford.edu.

54. Strunk, "Byzantine Office at Hagia Sophia," and Evangelatou, "Liturgy and the Illustration."

Chapter 1

1. Jonathan Z. Smith, *To Take Place: Toward Theory in Ritual* (Chicago: University of Chicago Press, 1987), written in critique of Mircea Eliade, *The Sacred and the Profane: The Nature of Religion,* trans. Willard R. Task (New York: Harcourt, 1987; original French, 1957).

2. Ousterhout, "Sanctity of Place." And in more general terms, Lidov, *Hierotopy.*

3. Michele Bacci, "Santidad localizada: Percepciones de los *loca sancta* de Palestina en la Edad Media," *Codex aquilarensis: Revista de arte medieval* 30 (2014): 109–32; Bruno Reudenbach, "*Loca sancta:* Zur materiellen Übertragung der heiligen Stätten," in *Jerusalem, du Schöne: Vorstellungen und Bilder einer heiligen Stadt,* ed. Bruno Reudenbach (Bern: Lang, 2008), 9–32; idem, "Holy Places and Their Relics," in *Visual Constructs of Jerusalem,* ed. Bianca Kühnel, Galit Noga-Banai, and Hanna Vorholt (Turnhout: Brepols, 2014), 197–206; Smith, *To Take Place,* 74–117, esp. 104. This relationship between the soil of the Holy Land and the sacred is well exemplified by the content and images of the Vatican reliquary box. On this subject, see Herbert L. Kessler, "*Arca Arcarum:* Nested Boxes and the Dynamics of Sacred Experience," *Codex aquilarensis: Revista de arte medieval* 30 (2014): 83–107; Beate Fricke, "Tales from Stones, Travels Through Time: Narrative and Vision in the Casket from the Vatican," *West 86th: A Journal of Decorative Arts, Design History, and Material Culture* 21, no. 2 (2014): 230–50; Derek Krueger, "Liturgical Time and Holy Land Reliquaries in Early Byzantium," in *Saints and Sacred Matter: The Cult of Relics in Byzantium and Beyond,* ed. Cynthia J. Hahn and Holger Klein (Washington, D.C.: Dumbarton Oaks Research Library and Collection, 2015), 11–31.

4. Paul the Silentiary, *Descriptio S. Sophiae,* vv. 546, 902.

5. Schibille, *Hagia Sophia.* Isar, *Chorós: The Dance of Adam.*

6. Ousterhout, "Sanctity of Place."

7. See Brown, "Thing Theory," and Bruno Latour, *We Have Never Been Modern,* trans. Catherine Porter (Cambridge: Harvard University Press, 1993), as well as Kumler and Lakey, "Material Sense of Things," for the way these studies are read by historians of medieval art.

8. Isar, "*Choros* of Light"; idem, "Chorography"; idem, "*Chōra:* Tracing the Presence," *Review of European Studies* 1, no. 1 (2009): 39–55; and idem, *Chorós: The Dance of Adam.*

9. Isar, "Chorography," 81. Jaś Elsner develops a similar interpretation of mystical vision in *Art and the Roman Viewer: The Transformation of Art from the Pagan World to Christianity* (Cambridge: Cambridge University Press, 1995), 88–124.

10. James L. Miller, *Measures of Wisdom: The Cosmic Dance in Classical and Christian Antiquity* (Toronto: University of Toronto Press, 1986).

11. A search for χώρα in the online TLG database on these writers shows that they consistently use this term only to signify place, space, land, position, and rank. Only the Akathistos hymn uses *chōra* to identify the vesseling power of the Virgin as a container of the uncontained: θεοῦ ἀχωρήτου χώρα (stanza 15, v. 6).

12. *A Greek-English Lexicon,* comp. Henry George Liddell and Robert Scott, with a revised supplement (Oxford: Clarendon Press, 1996); G. W. H. Lampe, *A Patristic Greek Lexicon* (Oxford: Clarendon Press, 1961); Pierre Chantraine, *Dictionnaire étymologique de la langue grecque: Histoire des mots* (Paris, Klincksieck, 1980), 4:1269–82.

13. Her work (primarily *Chorós: The Dance of Adam,* 100–106) draws on the analysis of John Sallis, *Chorology: On Beginning in Plato's "Timaeus"* (Bloomington: Indiana University Press, 1999), 91–145. What triggers the modern attraction to *chōra* is the fact that Timaeus specifies that it can be reached and contemplated outside the rational, accessed through the bastard logic of the dream. Jacques Derrida, "*Khōra,*" in *On the Name,* ed. Thomas Dutoit, trans. David Wood, John P. Leavey Jr., and Ian McLeod (Stanford: Stanford University Press, 1995), 89–127, 146–50, and idem, "Platos' Pharmacy," in *Dissemination,* trans. Barbara Johnson (Chicago: University of Chicago Press, 1981), 61–171.

14. Sallis, *Chorology,* 91–128; Isar, *Chorós: The Dance of Adam,* 77, 90–96, 100–13.

15. Gregory Shaw, "The *Chōra* of the *Timaeus* and the Iamblichean Theurgy," *Horizons* 3, no. 2 (2012): 103–29.

16. ὁ δὲ πάντα τε ἱλεωσάμενος καὶ ἑκάστῳ τὰ κεχαρισμένα καὶ κατὰ δύναμιν ὁμοιότατα γέρα προσενεγκών, ἀσφαλὴς καὶ ἄπταιστος ἀεὶ διαμένει, τέλεον καὶ ὁλόκληρον τὴν ὑποδοχὴν τοῦ θείου χοροῦ καλῶς ἀποπληρώσας. Iamblichus, *De mysteriis,* bk. 5, sect. 21; English translation in Shaw, "The *Chōra* of the *Timaeus,*" 121.

17. Shaw, "The *Chōra* of the *Timaeus.*"

18. According to Liddell and Scott, *Greek-English Lexicon, chōros* is not a cognate of *choros:* the former designates "land" and "place"; the latter, "dance"/"dance floor," "choir"/"choir floor." Procopius, *De aedificiis,* bk 1, chap. 1, sect. 44 (*chōra* for the dome); Paul the Silentiary, *Descriptio S. Sophiae,* vv. 419 (*chōros* for the dome), 446 (*chōros* for the space under the dome), 505 (*chōros* for the dome), 582 (*chōros* for the eastern apse), 736 (*chōros* for the top of the ciborium); idem, *Descriptio ambonis,* vv. 28, 48, 56–57, 132, 210, 233, 240 (*chōros* for the ambo).

19. Isar maintains that *chōra* functioned more like a noun than a verb. Isar, "Chorography," 81. Yet this reading applies better to the Greek term *choros,* which identifies both movement and space, an insight developed in Isar, *Chorós: The Dance of Adam,* 6–48.

20. Paul Friedländer, ed., *Johannes von Gaza, Paulus Silentiarius und Prokopios von Gaza; Kunstbeschreibungen justinianischer Zeit* (Leipzig: Teubner, 1912; repr., Hildesheim: Olms, 1969); English translation in Cyril Mango, *The Art of the Byzantine Empire, 312–1453: Sources and Documents* (Englewood Cliffs, N.J.: Prentice-Hall, 1972; repr., Toronto: University of Toronto Press, 1986), 80–96, and Peter N. Bell, *Three Political Voices from the Age of Justinian: Agapetus, "Advice to the Emperor"; "Dialogue on Political Science"; Paul the Silentiary, "Description of Hagia Sophia"* (Liverpool: Liverpool University Press, 2009), 189–212; French translation Marie-Christine Fayant and Pierre Chuvin, *Description de Sainte-Sophie de Constantinople* (Die: A. Die, 1997); Italian translation Maria Luigia Fobelli, *Un tempio per Giustiniano: Santa Sofia di Costantinopoli e la "Descrizione" di Paolo Silenziario* (Rome: Viella, 2005), 34–117.

21. Mango, *Sources and Documents,* 76. Original: ὁπηνίκα δέ τις εὐξόμενος ἐς αὐτὸ ἴοι, ξυνίησι μὲν εὐθὺς ὡς οὐκ ἀνθρωπείᾳ δυνάμει ἢ τέχνῃ, ἀλλὰ θεοῦ ῥοπῇ τὸ ἔργον τοῦτο ἀποτετόρνευται· ὁ νοῦς δέ οἱ πρὸς τὸν θεὸν ἐπαιρόμενος ἀεροβατεῖ, οὐ μακράν που ἡγούμενος αὐτὸν εἶναι, ἀλλ᾽ ἐμφιλοχωρεῖν μάλιστα οἷς αὐτὸς εἵλετο. Procopius, *De aedificiis,* bk. 1, chap. 1, sect. 60.

22. ἐγρομένη δ᾽ ἐφύπερθεν ἐς ἄπλετον ἠέρα πήληξ / πάντοθι μὲν σφαιρηδὸν ἑλίσσεται, οἷα δὲ φαιδρὸς / οὐρανὸς ἀμφιβέβηκε δόμου σκέπας. Paul the Silentiary, *Descriptio S. Sophiae,* vv. 489–91.

23. Procopius, *De aedificiis,* bk. 1, chap. 1, sect. 35.

24. *Choros* = *kyklos* and *stefanos,* according to Hesychius of Alexandria, as cited by Liddell and Scott, *Greek-English Lexicon,* s.v. χορός. Procopius, *De aedificiis,* bk. 1, chap. 1, sect. 44. The same is also true in Paul; that is, he uses only *kyklos* to describe the dome. Paul the Silentiary, *Descriptio S. Sophiae,* vv. 362–68 (*synthronon* shaped in a

kyklos with an ever-expanding circumference, a process designated by the verb *elissō*), 481–86 (dome, shaping a *kyklos*).

25. Paul the Silentiary, *Descriptio S. Sophiae*, vv. 546, 902.

26. Ibid., vv. 818, 831, discussed by Isar, "*Choros* of Light."

27. Paul the Silentiary, *Descriptio S. Sophiae*, vv. 155 (*choreia* as the honey-voiced ekphrasis), 288 (*choreia* as the dance of the stars in the dome), 333 and 344 (*choreia* as chanting hymns); idem, *Descriptio ambonis*, v. 47 (*choreia* as the chanting of the elite choir).

28. Paul the Silentiary, *Descriptio ambonis*, v. 46 (*choros* as the elite choir of the *psaltai* at the ambo).

29. While *choros* identifying the circular configuration of the *polykandēlia* has been studied perceptively by Isar, *choros* as chant has not received scholarly attention. Isar, "*Choros* of Light"; idem, *Chorós: The Dance of Adam*, 128–33.

30. Claude Calame, *Choruses of Young Women in Ancient Greece: Their Morphology, Religious Role, and Social Function*, trans. Derek Collins and Janice Orion (Lanham, Md.: Rowman & Littlefield, 1997; original French, Rome: Edizioni dell'Ateneo & Bizzarri, 1977); Herbert Golder, preface to *Arion: A Journal of Humanities and the Classics* 3, no. 1 (1994–95): 1–5; Helen H. Bacon, "The Chorus in Greek Life and Drama," in ibid., 6–24; Steven H. Lonsdale, "'Homeric Hymn to Apollo': Prototype and Paradigm of Choral Performance," in ibid., 25–40; Albert Henrichs, "'Why Should I Dance?': Choral Self-referentiality in Greek Tragedy," in ibid., 56–111; Claude Calame, "From Choral Poetry to Tragic Stasimon: The Enactment of Women's Song," in ibid., 136–54; Leslie Kurke, "Visualizing the Choral: Epichoric Poetry, Ritual, and Elite Negotiation in Fifth-Century Thebes," in *Visualizing the Tragic: Drama, Myth, and Ritual in Greek Art and Literature; Essays in Honour of Froma Zeitlin*, ed. Chris Kraus et al. (Oxford: Oxford University Press, 2007), 63–101; Isar, "*Choros* of Light"; idem, *Chorós: The Dance of Adam*, 6–96, 113–55; Pentcheva, *Sensual Icon*, 46–56, 149–82.

31. What follows is not an exhaustive list; it is only meant to show the important place of χορός in patristic writings: Clement of Alexandria, *Protrepticus*, chap. 1, sect. 1, subsection 3; chap. 1, sect. 8, subsection 2; chap. 8, sect. 79, subsection 2; chap. 12, sect. 119, subsection 1; Basil of Caesarea, *De Spiritu Sancto*, chap. 16, sect. 38 (on Isaiah 6:3); idem, *In Hexaemeron*, homily 4, sect. 5; idem, *In quadraginta martyres Sebastenses*, in PG 31, cols. 509, 521, 524; Gregory of Nyssa, *In sanctum et salutare pascha*, in *Gregorii Nysseni Opera*, 9:311; idem, *De instituto Christiano*, in ibid., vol. 8, pt. 1, 68–69, 78; idem, *In inscriptiones Psalmorum*, in ibid., 5:66, 68, 68, 74, 86–87 (both chant and circular motility), 299; idem, *Contra Eunomium*, bk. 2, chap. 1, sect. 101; idem, *Epistula 6*, sect. 10; idem, *Vita sanctae Macrinae*, sect. 33 (on the psalmody); idem, *De virginitate*, chap. 19, sect. 1; chap. 23, sect. 6; idem, *Encomium in sanctum Stephanum protomartyrem, II*, in PG 46, col. 728 (*choros* of the stars); idem, *De sancto Theodoro*, in PG 46, col. 748; idem, *In laudem SS. Quadraginta Martyrum*, in PG 46, cols. 753, 760; idem, *Vita atque encomium Sancti Patris Nostri Ephraem Syriae*, 848; Gregory of Nazianzus, *Epistulae 10*, sect. 10; 238, sect. 1; 246, sect. 6; idem, *Funebris oratio in laudem Basilii Magni*, chap. 79, sect. 1; idem, *De theologia*, sect. 29 (sun and stars); idem, *In Machabaeorum laudem*, in PG 35, cols. 920, 928; idem, *In novam Dominicam*, in PG 36, col. 617 (moon, stars). For a discussion of these texts, see Miller, *Measures of Wisdom*, 344–413, 483–522, on Gregory of Nazianzus and Pseudo-Dionysius respectively.

32. Gregory Shaw, *Theurgy and the Soul: The Neoplatonism of Iamblichus* (University Park: Pennsylvania State University Press, 1995); John Finamore, "Plotinus and Iamblichus on Magic and Theurgy," *Dionysius* 17 (1999): 83–94; Miller, *Measures of Wisdom*, 344–482.

33. Pseudo-Dionysius, *De ecclesiastica hierarchia*, chap. 6, sect. 5; chap. 7, sect. 2. Sarah Klitenic Wear and John Dillon, *Dionysius the Areopagite and the Neoplatonist Tradition: Despoiling the Hellenes* (Aldershot: Ashgate, 2007); Andrew Louth, *Denys the Areopagite* (London: Continuum, 2002); Rosemary Griffith, "Neo-Platonism and Christianity: Pseudo-Dionysius and Damascius," *Studia patristica* 29 (1997): 238–43; Alexander Golitzin, *Et introibo ad altare dei: The Mystagogy of Dionysius Areopagita; With Special Reference to Its Predecessors in the Eastern Christian Tradition* (Thessaloniki: Patriarchikon Idruma Paterikōn Meletōn, 1994); Miller, *Measures of Wisdom*, 483–521.

34. Αὕτη μὲν οὖν ἐστιν ὡς κατ' ἐμὴν ἐπιστήμην ἡ πρώτη τῶν οὐρανίων οὐσιῶν διακόσμησις ἡ «Κύκλῳ θεοῦ» καὶ περὶ θεὸν ἀμέσως ἑστηκυῖα καὶ ἁπλῶς καὶ ἀκαταλήκτως περιχορεύουσα τὴν αἰώνιον αὐτοῦ γνῶσιν κατὰ τὴν ὑπερτάτην ὡς ἐν ἀγγέλοις ἀεικίνητον ἵδρυσιν, πολλὰς μὲν καὶ μακαρίας ὁρῶσα καθαρῶς θεωρίας, ἁπλᾶς δὲ καὶ

ἀμέσους μαρμαρυγὰς ἐλλαμπομένη, καὶ θείας τροφῆς ἀποπληρουμένη πολλῆς μὲν τῇ πρωτοδότῳ χύσει μιᾶς δὲ τῇ ἀποικίλτῳ καὶ ἑνοποιῷ τῆς θεαρχικῆς ἑστιάσεως ἑνότητι, . . . Διὸ καὶ ὕμνους αὐτῆς ἡ θεολογία τοῖς ἐπὶ γῆς παραδέδωκεν ἐν οἷς ἱερῶς ἀναφαίνεται τὸ τῆς ὑπερτάτης αὐτῆς ἐλλάμψεως ὑπερέχον. Οἱ μὲν γὰρ αὐτῆς αἰσθητῶς εἰπεῖν «Ὡς φωνὴ ὑδάτων» ἀναβοῶσιν «Εὐλογημένη ἡ δόξα κυρίου ἐκ τοῦ τόπου αὐτοῦ». Pseudo-Dionysius, *De coelesti hierarchia,* chap. 7, sect. 4. My translation, based on *Pseudo-Dionysius: The Complete Works,* trans. Colm Luibheid (London: SPCK, 1987), 165.

35. See the relevant entries in Liddell and Scott, *Greek-English Lexicon,* and Lampe, *Patristic Greek Lexicon.*

36. On the Neoplatonic tradition of this idea, see Christian Schäfer, "Μονή, πρόοδος, und ἐπιστροφή in der Philosophie des Proklos und des Areopagiten Dionysius," in *Proklos: Methode, Seelenlehre, Metaphysik; Akten der Konferenz in Jena am 18.–20. September 2003,* ed. Matthias Perkams and Rosa Maria Piccone (Leiden: Brill, 2006), 340–62; A. H. Armstrong, "'Emanation' in Plotinus," *Mind* 46 (1937), 61–66; idem, "Beauty and the Discovery of Divinity in the Thought of Plotinus," in *Kephalaion: Studies in Greek Philosophy and Its Continuation Offered to Professor C. J. de Vogel,* ed. Jaap Mansfeld and Lambertus Marie de Rijk (Assen: Van Gorcum, 1975), 155–63; and Werner Beierwaltes, "Plotins Metaphysik des Lichtes," in *Die Philosophie des Neuplatonismus,* ed. Clemens Zintzen (Darmstadt: Wissenschaftliche Buchgesellschaft, 1977), 75–117.

37. Procopius uses *choros* as "dance." Procopius, *De aedificiis,* bk. 1, sect. 35. But Paul employs it to designate the circular shape and chant. Paul the Silentiary, *Descriptio ambonis,* vv. 46–49 (the choir chanting from the ambo). Gradually, in the ecclesiastical context, the meaning of *choros* shifts decisively from dance to chant, as evident, for instance, in the eleventh-century *Souda:* Χορός: τὸ σύστημα τῶν ἐν ταῖς ἐκκλησίαις ᾀδόντων. διῃρέθησαν δὲ οἱ χοροὶ τῶν ἐκκλησιῶν εἰς δύο μέρη ἐπὶ Κωνσταντίου τοῦ υἱοῦ Κωνσταντίνου τοῦ μεγάλου καὶ Φλαβιανοῦ, ἐπισκόπου Ἀντιοχείας, διχῇ τοὺς Δαυιτικοὺς ψαλμοὺς ᾀδόντες. ὅπερ ἐν Ἀντιοχείᾳ πρῶτον ἀρξάμενον εἰς πάντα περιῆλθε τῆς οἰκουμένης τὰ πέρατα. *Suidae lexicon,* ed. Ada Adler, Lexicographi Graeci 1 (1938; repr., Leipzig: Teubner, 1971), vol. 4, sect. 409, 815. I return to this rich passage—Pseudo-Dionysius, *De coelesti hierarchia,* chap. 7, sect. 4—in the later chapters of this book to unpack further layers of signification, such as the characterization of the celestial energy as the "sound of many waters" and the realization of its proleptic insight about reverberant sound in the acoustics of the Great Church.

38. Καὶ κινεῖσθαι μὲν οἱ θεῖοι λέγονται νόες κυκλικῶς μὲν ἑνούμενοι ταῖς ἀνάρχοις καὶ ἀτελευτήτοις ἐλλάμψεσι τοῦ καλοῦ καὶ ἀγαθοῦ, κατ᾽ εὐθεῖαν δέ, ὁπόταν προΐασιν εἰς τὴν τῶν ὑφειμένων πρόνοιαν εὐθείᾳ τὰ πάντα περαίνοντες, ἑλικοειδῶς δέ, ὅτι καὶ προνοοῦντες τῶν καταδεεστέρων ἀνεκφοιτήτως μένουσιν ἐν ταυτότητι περὶ τὸ τῆς ταυτότητος αἴτιον καλὸν καὶ ἀγαθὸν ἀκαταλήκτως περιχορεύοντες.

Ψυχῆς δὲ κίνησίς ἐστι κυκλικὴ μὲν ἡ εἰς ἑαυτὴν εἴσοδος ἀπὸ τῶν ἔξω καὶ τῶν νοερῶν αὐτῆς δυνάμεων ἡ ἑνοειδὴς συνέλιξις ὥσπερ ἔν τινι κύκλῳ τὸ ἀπλανὲς αὐτῇ δωρουμένη καὶ ἀπὸ τῶν πολλῶν τῶν ἔξωθεν αὐτὴν ἐπιστρέφουσα καὶ συνάγουσα πρῶτον εἰς ἑαυτήν, εἶτα ὡς ἑνοειδῆ γενομένην ἑνοῦσα ταῖς ἑνιαίως ἡνωμέναις δυνάμεσι καὶ οὕτως ἐπὶ τὸ καλὸν καὶ ἀγαθὸν χειραγωγοῦσα τὸ ὑπὲρ πάντα τὰ ὄντα καὶ ἓν καὶ ταὐτὸν καὶ ἄναρχον καὶ ἀτελεύτητον. Ἑλικοειδῶς δὲ ψυχὴ κινεῖται, καθ᾽ ὅσον οἰκείως ἑαυτῇ τὰς θείας ἐλλάμπεται γνώσεις, οὐ νοερῶς καὶ ἑνιαίως, ἀλλὰ λογικῶς καὶ διεξοδικῶς καὶ οἷον συμμίκτοις καὶ μεταβατικαῖς ἐνεργείαις. Τὴν κατ᾽ εὐθεῖαν δέ, ὅταν οὐκ εἰς ἑαυτὴν εἰσιοῦσα καὶ ἑνικῇ νοερότητι κινουμένη, τοῦτο γάρ, ὡς ἔφην, ἐστὶ τὸ κατὰ κύκλον, ἀλλὰ πρὸς τὰ περὶ ἑαυτὴν προϊοῦσα καὶ ἀπὸ τῶν ἔξωθεν ὥσπερ ἀπό τινων συμβόλων πεποικιλμένων καὶ πεπληθυσμένων ἐπὶ τὰς ἁπλᾶς καὶ ἡνωμένας ἀνάγεται θεωρίας. Pseudo-Dionysius, *De divinis nominibus,* chap. 4, sects. 8–9; English translation in Luibheid, *Pseudo-Dionysius,* 78.

39. Golitzin, *Et introibo ad altare dei,* 91–95, and Schäfer, "Μονή, πρόοδος, und ἐπιστροφή."

40. On the structure of the antiphon, see Robert F. Taft, "Christian Liturgical Psalmody: Origins, Development, Decomposition, Collapse," in *Psalms in Community: Jewish and Christian Textual, Liturgical, and Artistic Traditions,* ed. Harold W. Attridge and Margot E. Fassler (Atlanta: Society of Biblical Literature, 2003), 7–32.

41. On this particular *teleutaion* and its performance with genuflection (*gonyklisia*), see Dimitri E. Conomos, "Music for the Evening Office on Whitsunday," in *Actes de xve Congrès international d'études byzantines* (Athens: Association internationale des études byzantines, 1979), 453–69; Simon Harris, "The Byzantine Office of the Genuflexion," *Music and Letters* 77 (1996): 333–47; and Lingas, "From Earth to Heaven," 328–34.

42. This is a *Kontakarion* manuscript also known as *Psaltikon,* identifying the book for the precentor or soloist. See *Contacarium Ashburnhamense: Codex Bibl. Laurentianae Ashburnhamensis 64; Phototypice Depictus,*

ed. Carsten Høeg (Copenhagen: Munksgaard, 1956); Annalisa Doneda, "I manoscritti liturgico-musicali bizantini: Tipologie e organizzazione," in *El palimpsesto grecolatino como fenómeno librario y textual,* ed. Àngel Escobar, Collectión Actas, Filologia (Zaragoza: Institución "Fernando el Catolico," 2006), 103–110; and Christian Thodberg, *Der byzantinische Alleluiarionzyklus: Studien im kurzen Psaltikonstil,* Monumenta Musicae Byzantinae, Subsidia 8 (Copenhagen: E. Munksgaard, 1966), 9–31.

43. Doneda, "I manoscritti liturgico-musicali bizantini." For a detailed inventory of the liturgy these manuscripts transmit, see P. Bartolomeo Di Salvo, "Gli *Asmata* nella musica bizantina," *Bolletino della Badia Graeca di Grottaferrata* 13 (1959): 45–50, 127–45; 14 (1960): 145–78.

44. Cappella Romana, *Byzantium in Rome: Medieval Byzantine Chant from Grottaferrata,* ed. Ioannis Arvanitis and Alexander Lingas (Portland, Ore.: Cappella Romana, 2006), CD 2, tracks 5–7. Listen also to music sample 1 at https://hagiasophia.stanford.edu.

45. Τὴν οἰκουμέ-νε· νενενηγγην Ἀναγϊα. Lingas, "From Earth to Heaven," table III.

46. Ibid., 328–34.

47. Ibid., 334. For a definition of the anagogical character of Byzantine liturgy, see Kallistos Ware, bishop of Dioklea, "The Meaning of the Divine Liturgy for the Byzantine Worshipper," in *Church and People in Byzantium,* ed. Rosemary Morris, Society for the Promotion of Byzantine Studies Twentieth Spring Symposium of Byzantine Studies, Manchester, 1986 (Birmingham: Center for Byzantine, Ottoman, and Modern Greek Studies, 1990), 7–28, and Liz James and Ruth Webb, "'To Understand Ultimate Things and Enter Secret Places': Ekphrasis and Art in Byzantium," *Art History* 14, no. 1 (1991): 1–17.

48. Strunk, "Byzantine Office at Hagia Sophia," 200.

49. Miguel Arranz, *Molitvi i psalmopenie* (Rome: Opere religiose Russe, Russicum, 1997), and Strunk, "Byzantine Office at Hagia Sophia," 200.

50. Cosimo Stornajolo, ed., *Le miniature della Topografia cristiana di Cosma Indicopleuste, codice Vaticano greco 699* (Milan: Hoepli, 1908), 36–37, plate 26; Maja Kominko, *The World of Kosmas: Illustrated Byzantine Codices of the Christian Topography* (Cambridge: Cambridge University Press, 2013), 157–61; Doula Mouriki, "The Octateuch Miniatures of the Byzantine Manuscripts of Cosmas Indicopleustes" (Ph.D. diss., Princeton University, 1970). James Miller includes this image but does not explore it beyond the fact that it represents two types of movement: (1) the unbounded ancient dance and (2) the controlled and structured one of the ecclesiastical choirs. Miller, *Measures of Wisdom,* 392.

51. ἐκ Πνεύματος ἁγίου κινούμενος. Cosmas Indicopleustes, *Topographia Christiana,* bk. 5, sect. 116, in *Topographie chrétienne,* ed. Wanda Wolska-Conus, vol. 2, Sources chrétiennes 159 (Paris: Éditions du Cerf, 1970), 174–75.

52. ἐκ Πνεύματος ἁγίου κινούμενος. Ibid. The Middle Byzantine marginal Psalters depict this moment of Samuel's anointing David and render the act as parallel to the inspiriting of Holy Sion and to the Virgin's spermless conception and birth of Christ. See, e.g., Khludov Psalter, fol. 79, illustrating Ps. 77 (78): 68–69 (fig. 21).

53. Calame, *Choruses of Young Women;* idem, "From Choral Poetry to Tragic Stasimon"; Lonsdale, "'Homeric Hymn to Apollo'"; Kurke, "Visualizing the Choral."

54. By using an omega, the identifying inscription mixes two words that are not cognates but only a near phonetic pair: *chōros* ("place," from *chōra*) and *choros* ("choir"/"dance").

55. The singers are called *hymnopoloi,* a pun on *polos* as "axis," "pivot." Paul the Silentiary, *Descriptio ambonis,* v. 30.

56. Maximus the Confessor, *Ambigua,* bk. 7, Greek and English translation in Nicholas Constas, ed., *On Difficulties in the Church Fathers: The Ambigua,* vol. 1, Dumbarton Oaks Medieval Library, 28 (Cambridge: Harvard University Press, 2014), 75–141.

57. πάσης γὰρ κινήσεως κινητικώτερον σοφία, διήκει δὲ καὶ χωρεῖ διὰ πάντων διὰ τὴν καθαρότητα. Wisd. of Sol., 7:24. My translation.

58. Pseudo-Dionysius, *De coelesti hierarchia,* chap. 7, sect. 4.

59. John Meyendorff, "Wisdom—Sophia: Contrasting Approaches to a Complex Theme," *Dumbarton Oaks Papers* 41 (1987): 391–401, quote on 391; Zaga A. Gavrilović, "Divine Wisdom as Part of Byzantine Imperial Ideology: Research into the Artistic Interpretations of the Theme in Medieval Serbia; Narthex Programmes of Lesnovo and Sopoćani," *Zograf* 11 (1982): 45–53.

60. C. A. Trypanis, ed., *Fourteen Early Byzantine Cantica,* Wiener byzantinische Studien 5 (Vienna: Hermann Böhlaus, 1968), 139–47; English translation in Andrew Palmer, "The Inauguration Anthem of Hagia Sophia in Edessa: A New Edition and Translation with Historical and Architectural Notes and a Comparison with a Contemporary Constantinopolitan Kontakion," *Byzantine and Modern Greek Studies* 12 (1988): 117–67, esp. 140–44. See also Schibille, *Hagia Sophia,* 37–40.

61. ἡ σοφία γὰρ ἀληθῶς τοῦ πατρὸς ἀνῳκοδόμησεν ἑαυτῇ σαρκώσεως οἶκον, / καὶ ἐσκήνωσεν ἐν ἡμῖν ὑπὲρ νοῦν / ἡ πάντων ζωὴ καὶ ἀνάστασις. *Enkaineia kontakion of Hagia Sophia,* stanza 1, in Trypanis, *Fourteen Early Byzantine Cantica,* 142; English translation in Palmer, "Inauguration Anthem," 140 (refrain slightly altered).

62.   ἐν σαρκὶ ἐνοικήσας κατοικεῖν ἐν ναοῖς χειροτεύκτοις εὐδοκεῖ
      ἐνεργείᾳ τοῦ πνεύματος
      μυστικαῖς τελεταῖς τὴν αὐτοῦ παρουσίαν πιστούμενος,
      καὶ βροτοῖς χάριτι συνδιαιτᾶται
      ὁ τοῖς πᾶσι ἀχώρητος καὶ ἀπρόσιτος·
      καὶ οὐ μόνον ὁμόστεγος τοῖς ἐν γῇ ἐστιν οὐράνιος,
      ἀλλὰ δείκνυσι καὶ τραπέζης κοινοὺς καὶ τῆς σαρκὸς αὐτοῦ δεξιοῦται τῇ εὐωχίᾳ
      ἣν προτίθησι τοῖς πιστοῖς ὁ Χριστός

   Enkaineia kontakion of Hagia Sophia, stanza 4, in Trypanis, *Fourteen Early Byzantine Cantica,* 141. My translation. For an alternative English translation, see Palmer, "Inauguration Anthem," 140–41.

63. ἀπαύγασμα γάρ ἐστι φωτὸς ἀϊδίου καὶ ἔσοπτρον ἀκηλίδωτον τῆς τοῦ Θεοῦ ἐνεργείας καὶ εἰκὼν τῆς ἀγαθότητος αὐτοῦ. Wisd. of Sol., 7:26. My translation.

64. For light and vision in Plato, see Andrea Wilson Nightingale, *Spectacles of Truth in Classical Greek Philosophy: Theoria in Its Cultural Context* (Cambridge: Cambridge University Press, 2004). In Neoplatonism, see Sarah Iles Johnston, "*Fiat Lux, Fiat Ritus:* Divine Light and the Late Antique Defense of Ritual," in *The Presence of Light: Divine Radiance and Religious Experience,* ed. Matthew T. Kapstein (Chicago: University of Chicago Press, 2004), 5–24; Oiva Kuisma, *Art or Experience: A Study on Plotinus' Aesthetics,* Commentationes Humanarum Litterarum 120 (Helsinki: Societas Scientiarum Fennica, 2003); Shaw, *Theurgy and the Soul;* Pierre Hadot, *Plotinus, or The Simplicity of Vision,* trans. Michael Chase (Chicago: University of Chicago Press, 1993); A. H. Armstrong, "Platonic Mirrors," *Eranos Jahrbuch* 55 (1986): 147–81; and Beierwaltes, "Plotins Metaphysik des Lichtes." In Gregory of Nyssa, see Martin S. Laird, *Gregory of Nyssa and the Grasp of Faith: Union, Knowledge, and Divine Presence* (Oxford: Oxford University Press, 2004); Thomas Böhm, *Theoria, Unendlichkeit, Aufstieg: Philosophische Implikationen zu "De Vita Moysis" von Gregor von Nyssa* (Leiden: Brill, 1996); and Jean Daniélou, *L'être et le temps chez Grégoire de Nysse* (Leiden: Brill, 1970). In Pseudo-Dionysius, see William K. Riordan, *Divine Light: The Theology of Denys the Areopagite* (San Francisco: Ignatius Press, 2008); and Filip Ivanovic, *Symbol and Icon: Dionysius the Areopagite and the Iconoclastic Crisis* (Eugene, Ore.: Pickwick Publications, 2010). In Byzantine theology, see Meyendorff, "Wisdom—Sophia."

65. Schibille, *Hagia Sophia,* 37–41, 56–75, 97–197; John Elsner, "The Viewer and the Vision: The Case of the Sinai Apse," *Art History* 17 (1994): 81–102; Jaś Elsner, *Art and the Roman Viewer,* 88–124; Konrad Onasch, *Lichthöhle und Sternenhaus: Licht und Materie im spätantik-christlichen und frühbyzantinischen Sakralbau* (Dresden: Verlag der Kunst, 1993). On artificial light, see Laskarina Bouras and Maria G. Parani, *Lighting in Early Byzantium,* Dumbarton Oaks Byzantine Collection Publications 11 (Washington, D.C.: Dumbarton Oaks Research Library and Collection, distributed by Harvard University Press, 2008), and Lioba Theis, "Lampen, Leuchten, Licht," in *Byzanz, das Licht aus dem Osten: Kult und Alltag im Byzantinischen Reich vom 4. bis 15. Jahrhundert,* exh. cat., ed. Christoph Stiegemann (Mainz: Philipp von Zabern, 2001), 53–64.

66. W. Eugene Kleinbauer, "Antioch, Jerusalem, and Rome: The Patronage of Emperor Constantius II and Architectural Invention," *Gesta* 45 (2006): 125–45; Schibille, *Hagia Sophia,* 78–85; Friedrich Wilhelm Deichmann, "Das Oktogon von Antiocheia: Heroon-Martyrion, Palastkirche oder Kathedrale?" *Byzantinische Zeitschrift* 65 (1972): 40–56; Adalbert Birnbaum, "Die Oktogone von Antiochia, Nazianz und Nyssa: Rekonstruktionsversuche," *Repertorium für Kunstwissenschaft* 36 (1913): 181–209.

67. Schibille, *Hagia Sophia,* 43–62, 75–96. On the symbolic valence of the dome in Byzantium, see Kathleen E. McVey, "The Domed Church as a Microcosm: Literary Roots of an Architectural Symbol," *Dumbarton Oaks*

Papers 37 (1983): 91–121, and idem, "Spirit Embodied: The Emergence of Symbolic Interpretations of Early Christian and Byzantine Architecture," in *Architecture as Icon: Perception and Representation of Architecture in Byzantine Art,* ed. Slobodan Ćurčić and Evangelia Hadjitryphonos (Princeton: Princeton University Art Museum, distributed by Yale University Press, 2010), 39–71. For the symbolism of the dome, see Louis Hautecoeur, *Mystique et architecture: Symbolisme de cercle et de la coupole* (Paris: A. & J. Picard, 1954); Karl Lehmann, "The Dome of Heaven," *Art Bulletin* 27 (1945): 1–27; and Edmund Thomas, *Monumentality and the Roman Empire: Architecture in the Antonine Age* (Oxford: Oxford University Press, 2007), 53–69.

68. Nicoletta Isar, "The Iconic *Chōra*: A Space of Kenotic Presence and Void," *Transfiguration: Nordisk tidsskrift for kunst og kristendom* 2 (2000): 65–80; Schibille, *Hagia Sophia,* 84, 96.

69. Schibille, *Hagia Sophia,* 37–41, 47–96, 127–70, 194–97, 223–26; Lars O. Grobe, Oliver Hauck, and Andreas Noback, "Das Licht in der Hagia Sophia—eine Computersimulation," in *Byzanz—das Römerreich im Mittelalter,* Teil 2, 1, *Schauplätze,* ed. Falko Daim and Jörg Drauschke (Mainz: Römisch-Germanisches Zentralmuseum, 2010), 97–111.

70. Robert F. Taft, *The Great Entrance: A History of the Transfer of Gifts and Other Pre-anaphoral Rites,* Orientalia Christiana analecta 200, 2nd ed. (Rome: Pontificium Institutum Studiorum Orientalium, 1978); idem, "The Liturgy of the Great Church: An Initial Synthesis of Structure and Interpretation on the Eve of Iconoclasm," *Dumbarton Oaks Papers* 34–35 (1980–81): 45–76, esp. 47–48; Alexander Lingas, "Sunday Matins in the Byzantine Cathedral Rite: Music and Liturgy" (Ph.D. diss., University of British Columbia, 1996), 46; Ware, "Meaning of the Divine Liturgy," 7–28.

71. Suzy Dufrenne, *L'illustration des psautiers grecs du Moyen Âge,* vol. 1, *Pantocrator 61, Paris grec 20, British Museum 40731* (Paris: Klincksieck, 1966), 28, and Corrigan, *Visual Polemics,* 76–77 and fig. 83.

72. Golitzin, *Et introibo ad altare dei,* 119–167; Wear and Dillon, *Dionysius the Areopagite,* 51–73.

73. Σκοπὸς οὖν ἱεραρχίας ἐστὶν ἡ πρὸς θεὸν ὡς ἐφικτὸν ἀφομοίωσίς τε καὶ ἕνωσις αὐτὸν ἔχουσα πάσης ἱερᾶς ἐπιστήμης τε καὶ ἐνεργείας καθηγεμόνα καὶ πρὸς τὴν αὐτοῦ θειοτάτην εὐπρέπειαν ἀκλινῶς μὲν ὁρῶν ὡς δυνατὸν δὲ ἀποτυπούμενος καὶ τοὺς ἑαυτοῦ θιασώτας ἀγάλματα θεῖα τελῶν ἔσοπτρα διειδέστατα καὶ ἀκηλίδωτα, δεκτικὰ τῆς ἀρχιφώτου καὶ θεαρχικῆς ἀκτῖνος καὶ τῆς μὲν ἐνδιδομένης αἴγλης ἱερῶς ἀποπληρούμενα, ταύτην δὲ αὖθις ἀφθόνως εἰς τὰ ἑξῆς ἀναλάμποντα κατὰ τοὺς θεαρχικοὺς θεσμούς. Pseudo-Dionysius, *De coelesti hierarchia,* chap. 3, sect. 2, in *Corpus Dionysiacum,* vol. 2, ed. Günther Heil and Adolf Martin Ritter, Patristische Texte und Studien 36 (Berlin: De Gruyter, 1991), 18; English translation in Luibheid, *Pseudo-Dionysius,* 154.

74. Schibille, *Hagia Sophia,* 37–41, 47–96, 127–70, 194–97, 223–26.

75. On the acoustics of the dome, see Woszczyk, "Acoustics of Hagia Sophia," 4.

76. ἐν δὲ εἰσόδοις ὑμνεῖται; προΐεμαι ἐμὴν φωνὴν; ἐρῶ καὶ ἀνοίσω ἀπὸ χειλέων; ἀλήθειαν μελετήσει ὁ φάρυγξ μου; μετὰ δικαιοσύνης πάντα τὰ ῥήματα τοῦ στόματός μου. Prov. 8:1–8. My translations. For the Greek and English of the Septuagint and the Apocrypha, I have used throughout *The Septuagint with Apocrypha: Greek and English,* ed. Sir Lancelot C. L. Brenton (1851; repr., Peabody, Mass.: Hendrickson, 2003), unless otherwise indicated.

77. πάντα ἐνώπια τοῖς συνιοῦσι καὶ ὀρθὰ τοῖς εὑρίσκουσι γνῶσιν (They are all evident to those that understand, and right to those that find knowledge). Prov. 8:9.

78. ἀτμὶς γάρ ἐστι τῆς τοῦ Θεοῦ δυνάμεως καὶ ἀπόρροια τῆς τοῦ Παντοκράτορος δόξης εἰλικρινής. Wisd. of Sol. 7:25. My translation.

79.   Ὀφθαλμὸν τῆς καθόλου ὁρῶμεν   ἐκκλησίας τὸν πάνσεπτον τοῦτον ἀληθῶς καὶ πανεύφημον οἶκον
      πλησθησόμεθα οὖν   τοῖς αὐτοῦ ἀγαθοῖς, καθὼς γέγραπται,
      τῷ θεῷ ψάλλοντες·   "Ἅγιος ὄντως
      ὁ ναός σου, θαυμάσιος   [ἐν] δικαιότητι".
      τῆς τῶν ἄνω ἐκτύπωμα   λειτουργίας γνωριζόμενος
      † ἀγαλλιάσεως καὶ † σωτηρίας φωνὴν καὶ ἐν πνεύματι ἑορτάζοντων ἔνθα ἦχος·
      ὄν συνίστησιν ἐν ψυχαῖς ὁ θεός
      ἡ πάντων ζωὴ καὶ ἀνάστασις

Enkaineia kontakion of Hagia Sophia, stanza 17, in Trypanis, *Fourteen Early Byzantine Cantica,* 146–47; English translation in Palmer, "Inauguration Anthem," 143–44, with my emendations.

80. I return to this process of imprinting/sealing (*sphragis*) and explore it in relation to *empsychōsis* in the next two chapters of this book.

81. Πολλοὺς τῶν ἀνθρώπων κατιδὼν ὁ Θεὸς ῥαθυμοτέρους ὄντας, καὶ πρὸς τὴν τῶν πνευματικῶν ἀνάγνωσιν δυσχερῶς ἔχοντας, καὶ τὸν ἐκεῖθεν οὐχ ἡδέως ὑπομένοντας κάματον, ποθεινότερον ποιῆσαι τὸν πόντον βουλόμενος, καὶ τοῦ καμάτου τὴν αἴσθησιν ὑποτεμέσθαι, μελῳδίαν ἀνέμιξε τῇ προφητείᾳ, ἵνα τῷ ῥυθμῷ τοῦ μέλους ψυχαγωγούμενοι πάντες, μετὰ πολλῆς τῆς προθυμίας τοὺς ἱεροὺς ἀναπέμπωσιν αὐτῷ ὕμνους. Οὐδὲν γὰρ, οὐδὲν οὕτως ἀνίστησι ψυχήν, καὶ πτεροῖ, καὶ τῆς γῆς ἀπαλλάττει, καὶ τῶν τοῦ σώματος ἀπολύει δεσμῶν, καὶ φιλοσοφεῖν ποιεῖ, καὶ πάντων καταγελᾶν τῶν βιωτικῶν, ὡς μέλος συμφωνίας, καὶ ῥυθμῷ συγκείμενον θεῖον ᾆσμα. John Chrysostomos, *In Psalmum XLI*, in PG 55, col. 156; English translation in James W. McKinnon, ed., *Music in Early Christian Literature* (Cambridge: Cambridge University Press, 1987), no. 164, 79–80. See also Lingas, "Sunday Matins," 37.

82. ταῖς δὲ δυσὶν εἴτ᾽ οὖν πτέρυξι τῶν χειλέων τὸν ὕμνον βοῶντες. *St. Germanus of Constantinople: On the Divine Liturgy*, ed. Paul Meyendorff (Crestwood, N.Y.: St. Vladimir's Seminary Press, 1984), sect. 16.

83. Woszczyk, "Acoustics of Hagia Sophia," 183.

84. Ibid. Such acoustic rain has also been observed for the dome of San Vitale in Ravenna. David J. Knight, "The Archaeoacoustics of a Sixth-Century Christian Structure: San Vitale, Ravenna," in *Music and Ritual: Bridging Material and Living Cultures*, ed. Raquel Jiménez, Rupert Till, and Mark Howell (Berlin: Ēkhō Verlag, 2013), 133–46, esp. 136.

85. See note 79 above.

86. Only *primikērios* appears in the tenth-century Typikon of the Great Church. Mateos, *Le Typicon de la Grande Église*, 2:315. Neil Moran, *Singers in Late Byzantine and Slavonic Painting* (Leiden: Brill, 1986), 14–50.

87. Mateos, *Le Typicon de la Grande Église*, 2:283.

88. Sometimes the *anagnōstai* lined along the solea (*sōlaia*), an isthmus-like corridor connecting the ambo with the chancel barrier. Ibid., 2:283.

89. Gregor Maria Hanke, *Vesper und Orthros des Kathedralritus der Hagia Sophia zu Konstantinopel: Eine struktur-analytische und entwicklungsgeschichtliche Untersuchung unter besonderer Berücksichtigung der Psalmodie und der Formulare in den Euchologien* (Ph.D. diss., Philosopisch-Theologische Hochschule St. Georgen, Frankfurt am Mein, 2002), 1:263; Neil Moran, "The Choir of the Hagia Sophia," *Oriens Christianus* 89 (2005): 1–7; idem, *Singers in Late Byzantine and Slavonic Painting*, 14–50; Lingas, "Sunday Matins," 43–44.

90. Mateos, *Le Typicon de la Grande Église*, 2:289 (*ebdomas*).

91. Paul the Silentiary, *Descriptio ambonis*, vv. 50–60; Fobelli, *Un tempio per Giustiniano*, 168–76, figs. 35–36; Stephan G. Xydis, "The Chancel Barrier, Solea, and Ambo of Hagia Sophia," *Art Bulletin* 29 (1947): 1–24.

92. Paul the Silentiary, *Descriptio ambonis*, vv. 50–60; Rudolf H. W. Stichel, *Einblicke in den virtuellen Himmel: Neue und alte Bilder vom Inneren der Hagia Sophia in Istanbul*, exh. cat., ed. Helge Svenshon (Tübingen: Wasmuth, 2008), figs. 59–62, 64, 66.

93. Chapters 4 and 5 address how this platform is understood as *omphalos*, a place filled with divine grace, and how this inspiriting is also manifested in the onyx/alabaster used for the walls of the ambo.

94. Paul the Silentiary, *Descriptio ambonis*, vv. 110–15.

95. Moran, *Singers in Late Byzantine and Slavonic Painting*, 26–29. On the Mt. Athos lectionary, see Mary-Lyon Dolezal, "Illuminating the Liturgical Word: Text and Image in a Decorated Lectionary (Mount Athos, Dionysiou Monastery, cod. 587)," *Word and Image* 12 (1996): 23–60. A lectionary records the cathedral liturgy; more specifically, it records the Gospel readings arranged according to their order of appearance; it starts with a *synaxarion* section (listing moveable feasts, beginning with Easter Sunday) and follows with a *menologion* section (listing fixed feasts starting with the commencement of the liturgical year on September 1). See Mary-Lyon Dolezal, "The Middle Byzantine Lectionary: Textual and Pictorial Expression of Liturgical Ritual" (Ph.D. diss., University of Chicago, 1991), and John Lowden, *The Jaharis Gospel Lectionary: The Story of a Byzantine Book* (New Haven: Yale University Press; New York: Metropolitan Museum of Art, 2009).

96. Moran, *Singers in Late Byzantine and Slavonic Painting*, 34.

97. Paul the Silentiary, *Descriptio S. Sophiae*, vv. 374–75, 687. In the Palaiologan period further changes took place: the *psaltai* are recorded as standing along the left and right sides of the corridor known as the solea, while the

anagnōstai stood further east, at the end of the solea, and along the sanctuary barrier. See Moran, *Singers in Late Byzantine and Slavonic Painting,* 26–29.

98. George P. Majeska, "Notes on the Archaeology of St. Sophia at Constantinople: The Green Marble Bands on the Floor," *Dumbarton Oaks Papers* 32 (1978): 299–308.

99. Van Nice, *Saint Sophia in Istanbul,* plate 1.

100. Xydis, "Chancel Barrier, Solea, and Ambo"; Peter H. F. Jakobs, *Die frühchristlichen Ambone Griechenlands* (Bonn: Halbert, 1987); Fobelli, *Un tempio per Giustiniano,* 156–61, 168–76, figs. 35–36; Nino Zchomelidse, *Art, Ritual, and Civic Identity in Medieval Southern Italy* (University Park: Pennsylvania State University Press, 2014), 25–33, fig. 10.

101. Some evidence—from Titos Basilica in Gortyna, Crete, and Basilica B at Philippi—suggests a placement of the ambo nearer the center of the nave, under the dome. Jakobs, *Die frühchristlichen Ambone Griechenlands,* 44–50, 67–68, 96–110, 154–55, 266–67, 300–302, plates 49, 76–78.

102. Paul the Silentiary, *Descriptio ambonis,* vv. 50–60.

103. Germanus, *Ekklēsiastikē historia,* in PG 98, col. 392; English translation in Meyendorff, *On the Divine Liturgy,* sect. 10.

104. Paul the Silentiary, *Descriptio ambonis,* vv. 229–54.

105. Palmer, "Inauguration Anthem," 117–67; McVey, "Domed Church as a Microcosm."

106. Trans. Palmer, "Inauguration Anthem," 133.

107. Emma Loosley, *The Architecture and Liturgy of the Bema in Fourth- to Sixth-Century Syrian Churches* (Boston: Brill, 2012), 58–59, 68–70; Georges Tchalenko, *Églises syriennes à Bêma* (Paris: Geuthner, 1990); Palmer, "Inauguration Anthem," 163; McVey, "Domed Church as a Microcosm," 95, 103; Robert F. Taft, "Some Notes on the Bema in the East and West Syrian Traditions," *Orientalia christiana periodica* 34 (1968): 326–359; idem, "On the Use of the Bema in the East-Syrian Liturgy," *Eastern Churches Review* 3 (1970): 30–39.

108. Loosley, *Architecture and Liturgy of the Bema,* 59–58, 68–70.

109. Zchomelidse has already offered this excellent insight about the ambo in Hagia Sophia in Constantinople as a Holy Sion. Zchomelidse, *Art, Ritual, and Civic Identity,* 25–30.

110. Iamblichus, *De mysteriis,* bk. 8, sect. 3, v. 36, discussed further in Shaw, "The *Chōra* of the *Timaeus,*" 117; idem, *Theurgy and the Soul,* 110–20.

111. Γνωριζέσθω δὲ πλέον <ἁ>πάντων   τὸ θαυμάσιον τέμενος τοῦτο   τοῦ θεοῦ ἐνδιαίτημα πάνσεπτον
καὶ ἐν τῷ προφανεῖ   ἐνδεικνύμενον τὸ ἀξιόθεον,
τεχνικὴν ἅπασαν   ὑπερανέχον
ἐπιστήμην ἀνθρώπινον   ἐν τοῖς δώμασιν·
οὐρανός τις ἐπίγειος   καὶ ὁρᾶται καὶ κηρύσσεται
καὶ μορφώματι καὶ λατρείᾳ θεοῦ·   ὃν ἡρετίσατο ἑαυτῷ εἰς κατοικεσίαν,
ἐν πνεύματι ἐστήριξας αὐτόν,
ἡ πάντων ζωὴ καὶ ἀνάστασις.

Enkaineia kontakion of Hagia Sophia, stanza 5, Greek in Trypanis, 143; English translation in Palmer, "Inauguration Anthem," 141, with my emendations.

112. Paul the Silentiary, *Descriptio S. Sophiae,* vv. 489–92, 506–8, 738. See my further discussion of this cross in the great dome in chapter 3.

113. I return to this cross-in-a-circle design in chapter 3.

114. Chapter 6 explores how the liquid contained in the chalice engenders another example of mirroring as an unstable surface reflection.

115. Meyendorff, *On the Divine Liturgy,* sect. 38, 66–67. Original: Δίσκος ἐστὶν ἀντὶ τῶν χειρῶν Ἰωσὴφ καὶ Νικοδήμου τῶν κηδευσάντων τὸν Χριστόν. Ἑρμηνεύεται δὲ δίσκος καὶ ὅπερ ἐπιφέρεται ὁ Χριστὸς κύκλον οὐρανοῦ, ἐμφαίνων ἡμῖν ἐν μικρᾷ περιγραφῇ τὸν νοητὸν ἥλιον Χριστὸν χωρῶν ἐν τῷ ἄρτῳ καὶ ὁρώμενος.

116. See chapter 6.

117. *Poloi* also distinguish the crosses on the omophorion of the bishop. See Warren T. Woodfin, *The Embodied Icon: Liturgical Vestments and Sacramental Power in Byzantium* (Oxford: Oxford University Press, 2012), 20. The word *poloi* is also used for the elite singers in the ambo, thus identifying the singing platform as a revolving celestial sphere. Paul the Silentiary, *Descriptio ambonis,* v. 30.

118. Paul the Silentiary, *Descriptio ambonis,* vv. 30–32.

119. On *polos* and *hymnopolos,* see the relevant entries in Liddell and Scott, *Greek-English Lexicon.*

120. Mateos, *Le Typicon de la Grande Église,* 1:28–33, esp. 32–33.

121. Ὁ λόγος γὰρ ὁ τοῦ σταυροῦ τοῖς μὲν ἀπολλυμένοις μωρία ἐστί, τοῖς δὲ σῳζομένοις ἡμῖν δύναμις Θεοῦ ἐστι. γέγραπται γάρ· ἀπολῶ τὴν σοφίαν τῶν σοφῶν, καὶ τὴν σύνεσιν τῶν συνετῶν ἀθετήσω. ποῦ σοφός; ποῦ γραμματεύς; ποῦ συζητητὴς τοῦ αἰῶνος τούτου; οὐχὶ ἐμώρανεν ὁ Θεὸς τὴν σοφίαν τοῦ κόσμου τούτου; ἐπειδὴ γὰρ ἐν τῇ σοφίᾳ τοῦ Θεοῦ οὐκ ἔγνω ὁ κόσμος διὰ τῆς σοφίας τὸν Θεόν, εὐδόκησεν ὁ Θεὸς διὰ τῆς μωρίας τοῦ κηρύγματος σῶσαι τοὺς πιστεύοντας. ἐπειδὴ καὶ Ἰουδαῖοι σημεῖον αἰτοῦσι καὶ Ἕλληνες σοφίαν ζητοῦσιν, ἡμεῖς δὲ κηρύσσομεν Χριστὸν ἐσταυρωμένον, Ἰουδαίοις μὲν σκάνδαλον, Ἕλλησι δὲ μωρίαν, αὐτοῖς δὲ τοῖς κλητοῖς, Ἰουδαίοις τε καὶ Ἕλλησι, Χριστὸν Θεοῦ δύναμιν καὶ Θεοῦ σοφίαν. 1 Cor. 1:18–24 (from *Hē Kainē Diathēkē: Enkrisei tēs megalēs tō Christō ekklēsias* [Constantinople, 1904; repr., Athens: Stamoulē, 2004], hereafter the source for all quotes from the Greek New Testament).

122. Chapter 3 explores further how this sign of *sophia* as the *stauros*-inside-*choros* marks the process of inspiriting, or *empsychōsis.*

123. See in chapter 5 how this miniature depicting the rotating earth is also expressive of the *esoptron* of celestial and terrestrial music.

124. Paul the Silentiary, *Descriptio S. Sophiae,* vv. 489–91.

125. ἐξ αὐτοῦ γὰρ καὶ τὸ ἁπλῶς κινεῖσθαι ἡμᾶς, ὡς ἀρχῆς, καὶ τὸ πῶς κινεῖσθαι πρὸς αὐτὸν ὡς τέλος ἐστίν. εἰ δὲ κινεῖται ἀναλόγως ἑαυτῷ νοερῶς τὸ νοερόν, καὶ νοεῖ πάντως. εἰ δὲ νοεῖ, καὶ ἐρᾷ πάντως τοῦ νοηθέντος· εἰ δ᾽ ἐρᾷ, καὶ πάσχει πάντως τὴν πρὸς αὐτὸ ὡς ἐραστὸν ἔκστασιν· εἰ δὲ πάσχει, δηλονότι καὶ ἐπείγεται· εἰ δὲ ἐπείγεται, καὶ ἐπιτείνει πάντως τὸ σφοδρὸν τῆς κινήσεως· εἰ δ᾽ ἐπιτείνει σφοδρῶς τὴν κίνησιν, οὐχ ἵσταται μέχρις ἂν γένηται ὅλον ἐν ὅλῳ τῷ ἐραστῷ καὶ ὑφ᾽ ὅλου περιληφθῇ, ἑκουσίως ὅλον κατὰ προαίρεσιν τὴν σωτήριον περιγραφὴν δεχόμενον, ἵν᾽ ὅλον ὅλῳ ποιωθῇ τῷ περιγραφόντι, ὡς μηδ᾽ ὅλως λοιπὸν βούλεσθαι ἐξ ἑαυτοῦ αὐτὸ ἐκεῖνο ὅλον γνωρίζεσθαι δύνασθαι τὸ περιγραφόμενον, ἀλλ᾽ ἐκ τοῦ περιγράφοντος· ὡς ἀὴρ δι᾽ ὅλου πεφωτισμένος φωτὶ καὶ πυρὶ σίδηρος ὅλος ὅλῳ πεπυρακτωμένος ἢ εἴ τι ἄλλο τῶν τοιούτων ἐστίν. Maximus the Confessor, *Ambigua,* bk. 7, in Constas, *On Difficulties in the Church Fathers,* 1:86–87 (with both Greek and English).

126. Tollefsen, *Activity and Participation,* 159–83. On the *henōsis,* or union, in Pseudo-Dionysius, see Golitzin, *Et introibo ad altare dei,* 77–118; Wear and Dillon, *Dionysius the Areopagite,* 117–30; Ysabel de Andia, *Henosis: L'union à Dieu chez Denys l'Aréopagite* (Leiden: Brill, 1996); and Andrew Louth, "The Reception of Dionysius up to Maximus the Confessor," in *Re-thinking Dionysius the Areopagite,* ed. Sarah Coakley and Charles M. Stang (Chichester: Wiley-Blackwell, 2009), 43–53. On this concept in Gregory of Nyssa, see David L. Balás, *Metousia Theou: Man's Participation in God's Perfections According to Saint Gregory of Nyssa,* Studia Anselmiana philosophica theologica 55 (Rome: Herder, 1966).

Chapter 2

1. Stefano Parenti and Elena Velkovska, eds., *L'Eucologio Barberini gr. 336,* Ephemerides liturgicae, Subsidia 80 (Rome: C.L.V.-Edizioni liturgiche, 1995), prayer 150.20, 163–64. Vincenzo Ruggieri, "Consacrazione e dedicazione di chiesa secondo il *Barberinianus graecus 336,*" *Orientalia christiana periodica* 54 (1988): 79–118, esp. 85; alternative English translation in Vitalijs Permjakovs, "'Make This the Place Where Your Glory Dwells': Origins and Evolution of the Byzantine Rite for the Consecration of a Church" (Ph.D. diss., University of Notre Dame, 2012), 190.

2. Permjakovs, "'Make This the Place Where Your Glory Dwells,'" and Ruggieri, "Consacrazione e dedicazione di chiesa." The Greek sources can be accessed in Parenti and Velkovska, *Eucologio Barberini gr. 336,* and Jacques Goar, *Euchologion sive rituale graecorum* (Venice: Ex typographia Bartholomaei Javarina, 1730; repr., Graz: Akademische Druck- und Verlagsanstalt, 1960), 653–70. On the Armenian rite, see Michael Daniel Findikyan, "The Armenian Ritual of the Dedication of a Church: A Textual and Comparative Analysis of Three Early Sources," *Orientalia christiana periodica* 64 (1998): 75–121; idem, "Armenian Hymns of the Holy Cross and the Jerusalem Encaenia," *Revue des études arméniennes* 32 (2010): 25–58; and F. C. Conybeare, ed., *Rituale*

Armenorum: Being the Administration of the Sacraments and Breviary Rites of the Armenian Church (Oxford: Clarendon Press, 1905). On the Georgian rite, see Kornelis S. Kekelidze, *Drevne-gruzinskij Archieratikon: Gruzinskij tekst* (Tbilisi: Losaberidze, 1912), 135–41; English translation in F. C. Conybeare and Oliver Wardrop, "The Georgian Version of the Liturgy of St. James," *Revue de l'Orient chrétien* 18 (1913): 396–410, and 19 (1914): 155–73, esp. 172–73. On the Syro-Palestinian liturgy of Antioch, see Kathleen E. McVey, "The Sogitha on the Church of Edessa in the Context of Other Early Greek and Syriac Hymns for the Consecration of Church Buildings," *ARAM* 5 (1993): 329–70. On the Coptic rite, see René-Georges Coquin, ed., *Livre de la consécration du sanctuaire de Benjamin: Introduction, édition, traduction et annotations* (Cairo: Institut français d'archéologie oriental du Caire, 1975).

3. Permjakovs, "'Make This the Place Where Your Glory Dwells,'" 451–592; Ruggieri, "Consacrazione e dedicazione di chiesa."

4. Christina Maranci, "The Great Outdoors: Liturgical Encounters with the Early Medieval Armenian Church," in Pentcheva, *Aural Architecture,* draft manuscript accessible at http://auralarchitecture.stanford.edu, and idem, "'Holiness Befits Your House' (Ps. 92 [93]: 5): A Preliminary Report on the Apse Inscription at Mren," *Revue des études arméniennes* 36 (2014–15): 243–63. I thank the author for sharing her manuscripts with me.

5. Parenti and Velkovska, *Eucologio Barberini gr. 336.*

6. Hans Robert Jauss, *Toward an Aesthetic of Reception,* trans. Timothy Bahti (Minneapolis: University of Minnesota Press, 1982), 3–45.

7. On the development and interaction of the cathedral and monastic rites, see Lingas, "From Earth to Heaven"; Robert F. Taft, *The Byzantine Rite: A Short History* (Collegeville, Minn.: Liturgical Press, 1992); and idem, "Liturgy of the Great Church." A Late Byzantine synthesis of the mystagogical tradition is offered by Saint Symeon of Thessaloniki in his *Treatise on Prayer,* trans. H. L. N. Simmons (Brookline, Mass.: Hellenic College Press, 1984), and *Liturgical Commentaries,* ed. and trans. Steven Hawkes-Teeples (Toronto: Pontifical Institute of Mediaeval Studies, 2011). On the monastic rite, see Thomas Pott, *Byzantine Liturgical Reform: A Study of Liturgical Change in the Byzantine Tradition,* trans. Paul Metendorff (Crestwood, N.Y.: St. Vladimir's Orthodox Seminary Press, 2010).

8. Kathleen Anne Corrigan has argued for the importance of the monastic angle in the Khludov. Corrigan, *Visual Polemics,* 104–34. Yet Maria Evangelatou has offered strong counterarguments showing that all three ninth-century marginal Psalters and their audiences were well versed in the cathedral rite. Evangelatou, "Liturgy and the Illustration," 65–70, 97–98. This argument is supported by the earlier work of Oliver Strunk, who used these manuscripts to reconstruct the cathedral liturgy of the hours. Strunk, "Byzantine Office at Hagia Sophia."

9. Sirarpie Der Nersessian, *L'illustration des psautiers grecs du Moyen Âge,* vol. 2, *Londres Add. 19.352,* Bibliothèque des cahiers archéologiques 5 (Paris: Klincksieck, 1970); Charles Barber, ed., *The Theodore Psalter: Electronic Facsimile* (Champaign: University of Illinois Press in association with the British Library, 2000).

10. Paul the Silentiary, *Descriptio S. Sophiae* and *Descriptio ambonis.* For the *Enkaineia kontakion of Hagia Sophia,* see Trypanis, *Fourteen Early Byzantine Cantica,* 139–147. *Narratio de S. Sophia* [*Diēgēsis peri tēs Hagias Sophias*], in *Scriptores originum Constantinopolitanarum,* ed. Theodor Preger (Leipzig: Teubner, 1901), 1:74–108. The *Narratio* gives information for the nonliturgical part of the ceremony; on this, see also Ekaterina Kovaltchuk, "The Encaenia of St. Sophia: Animal Sacrifice in a Christian Context," *Scrinium* 4 (2008): 161–203, and idem, "The Holy Sepulchre of Jerusalem and St. Sophia of Constantinople: An Attempt at Discovering a Hagiographic Expression of the Byzantine Encaenia Feast," *Scrinium* 6 (2010): 263–338.

11. Parenti and Velkovska, *Eucologio Barberini gr. 336,* xxiii.

12. Permjakovs, "'Make This the Place Where Your Glory Dwells,'" 179–82, 202, 576–77, 595, 598–614. Marie-France Auzepy, "Les Isauriens et l'espace sacré: L'église et les reliques," in *Le sacré et son inscription dans l'espace à Byzance et en Occident,* ed. Michel Kaplan, Byzantina Sorbonensia 18 (Paris: Publications de la Sorbonne, 2001), 13–24.

13. For reconstruction of the sequence, see Permjakovs, "'Make This the Place Where Your Glory Dwells,'" 186–97.

14. Greek in Parenti and Velkovska, *Eucologio Barberini gr. 336,* prayer 150, 161–62; Ruggieri, "Consacrazione e dedicazione di chiesa," 84–85. My translation. For an alternative English translation, see Permjakovs, "'Make This the Place Where Your Glory Dwells,'" 189.

15. Καὶ κατάπεμψον τὸ πανάγιόν σου καὶ προσκυνητὸν καὶ πανταδύναμον πνεῦμα, καὶ ἁγίασον τὸν οἶκον τοῦτον. Πλήρωσον αὐτὸν φωτὸς ἀϊδίου, αἱρέτισαι αὐτὸν εἰς κατοικίαν σήν, ποίησον αὐτὸν τόπον σκηνώματος δόξης σου. Permjakovs, "'Make This the Place Where Your Glory Dwells,'" 190 (with both Greek and English).

16. Bissera V. Pentcheva, "The Aesthetics of Landscape and Icon at Sinai," *Res: Anthropology and Aesthetics* 65–66 (2015): 194–211.

17. Permjakovs draws this parallel with 3 Kings 8:29. Permjakovs, "'Make This the Place Where Your Glory Dwells,'" 561.

18. ἐν τῷ εἶναι ὀφθαλμοὺς σου ἀνεωγμένους ἐπ᾽ αὐτὸν ἡμέρας καὶ νυκτός, καὶ ὦτα σου προσέχοντα εἰς δέησιν τῶν ἐν φόβῳ σου. Permjakovs, "'Make This the Place Where Your Glory Dwells,'" 190 (with both Greek and English).

19. Φύλαξον αὐτὸν ἕως τῆς συντελείας τοῦ αἰῶνος ἀσάλευτον, καὶ τὸ ἐν αὐτῷ θυσιαστήριον ἅγιον ἁγίων ἀνάδειξον τῇ δυνάμει καὶ ἐνεργείᾳ τοῦ παναγίου σου πνεύματος· δόξασον αὐτὸν ὑπὲρ τὸ κατὰ νόμον ἱλαστήριον, ὥστε τὰς ἐν αὐτῷ τελουμένας ἱερουργίας εἰς τὸ ἅγιον καὶ ὑπερουράνιον καὶ νοερόν σου θυσιαστήριον καταντᾷν, καὶ τὴν χάριν ἡμῖν τοῦ ἀχράντου κατακομίζειν ἐπισκιάσεως. Parenti and Velkovska, *Eucologio Barberini gr. 336*, prayer 150, 163–64; Ruggieri, "Consacrazione e dedicazione di chiesa," 85. My translation. For an alternative English translation, see Permjakovs, "'Make This the Place Where Your Glory Dwells,'" 190.

20. ὑπὲρ τοῦ ἁγιασθῆναι τὸν οἶκον τοῦτον καὶ τὸ ἐν αὐτῷ θυσιαστηρίου τῇ ἐπιφοιτήσει καὶ δυνάμει καὶ ἐνεργείᾳ τοῦ ἁγίου πνεύματος, δεηθῶμεν. Parenti and Velkovska, *Eucologio Barberini gr. 336*, prayer 150, 160; Ruggieri, "Consacrazione e dedicazione di chiesa," 83. My translation. For an alternative English translation, see Permjakovs, "'Make This the Place Where Your Glory Dwells,'" 188.

21. Corrigan, *Visual Polemics*, 76–73 and fig. 83.

22. All Eastern liturgies of consecration present elements that draw parallels with Jerusalem. Findikyan, "Armenian Ritual"; idem, "Armenian Hymns"; Permjakovs, "'Make This the Place Where Your Glory Dwells,'" 77–116, 233–450.

23. Permjakovs, "'Make This the Place Where Your Glory Dwells,'" 248, on the altar at Golgotha; 119, 321–330, on Holy Sion.

24. Ibid., 119, 249, 322–24.

25. The Georgian *iadgari* Tbilisi A86 is discussed in ibid., 303–75.

26. Ibid., 324.

27. Ibid.

28. Ibid., 191. Greek in Parenti and Velkovska, *Eucologio Barberini gr. 336*, prayer 150, 164–65; Ruggieri, "Consacrazione e dedicazione di chiesa," 86.

29. Permjakovs has explained the connection between the *kathierōsis* of the altar in Barberini 336 and the anointing of the waters of the baptismal font with oil. Permjakovs, "'Make This the Place Where Your Glory Dwells,'" 375–81, 418–27.

30. ΩΣ ΑΓΑΠΗΤΑ τὰ σκηνώματά σου, Κύριε τῶν δυνάμεων. ἐπιποθεῖ καὶ ἐκλείπει ἡ ψυχή μου εἰς τὰς αὐλὰς τοῦ Κυρίου, ἡ καρδία μου καὶ ἡ σάρξ μου ἠγαλλιάσαντο ἐπὶ Θεὸν ζῶντα. καὶ γὰρ στρουθίον εὗρεν ἑαυτῷ οἰκίαν καὶ τρυγὼν νοσσιὰν ἑαυτῇ, οὗ θήσει τὰ νοσσία ἑαυτῆς, τὰ θυσιαστήριά σου, Κύριε τῶν δυνάμεων, ὁ Βασιλεύς μου καὶ ὁ Θεός μου. Ps. 83 (84): 1–3.

31. ραντιεῖς με ὑσσώπῳ, καὶ καθαρισθήσομαι, πλυνεῖς με, καὶ ὑπὲρ χιόνα λευκανθήσομαι. ἀκουτιεῖς μοι ἀγαλλίασιν καὶ εὐφροσύνην, ἀγαλλιάσονται ὀστέα τεταπεινωμένα. Ps. 50 (51): 7–8. Parenti and Velkovska, *Eucologio Barberini gr. 336*, prayer 152, 166. The Khludov Psalter illustrates these verses with Christ washing the feet of the apostles.

32. John Jebb, *Sacred Literature; Comprising a Review of the Principles of Composition Laid Down by the Late Robert Lowth . . . in His Praelections and Isaiah: And an Application of the Principles So Reviewed, to the Illustration of the New Testament; in a Series of Critical Observations on the Style and Structure of That Sacred Volume* (London: Cadell & Davies; Edinburgh: W. Blackwood, 1820), 53–74; Thomas Boys, *Tactica Sacra: An Attempt to Develope, and to Exhibit to the Eye by Tabular Arrangements, a General Rule of Composition Prevailing in the Holy Scriptures* (London: Hamilton, 1824); John Forbes, *The Symmetrical Structure of Scripture, or the Principles of Scripture Parallelism Exemplified in an Analysis of the Decalogue, the Sermon on the Mount, and Other Passages of the Sacred Writings* (Edinburgh: T. & T. Clark, 1854), 35–46; idem, *Studies on the Book of Psalms: The Structural Connection of the Book of Psalms, Both in Single Psalms and in the Psalter as an Organic Whole*, ed. James Forrest

(Edinburgh: T. & T. Clark, 1888). New studies were initiated by Nils W. Lund; see, by Lund, "The Presence of Chiasmus in the New Testament," *Journal of Religion* 10, no. 1 (1930): 74–93, and "Chiasmus in the Psalms," *American Journal of Semitic Languages and Literatures* 49, no. 4 (1933): 281–312. Lund's approach was critically assessed by Thomas W. Manson, "Review of *Chiasmus in the New Testament,* by Nils W. Lund," *Journal of Theological Studies* 45 (1944): 81–84. Studies of chiasm continue to be developed. See John W. Welch, ed., *Chiasmus in Antiquity: Structures, Analyses, Exegesis* (Hildesheim: Gerstenberg, 1981); John Breck, *The Shape of Biblical Language: Chiasmus in the Scriptures and Beyond* (Crestwood, N.Y.: St. Vladimir's Seminary Press, 1994); John W. Welch and Daniel B. McKinlay, eds., *Chiasmus Bibliography* (Provo, Utah: Research Press, 1999); and Ellie Assis, "Chiasmus in Biblical Narrative: Rhetoric of Characterization," *Prooftexts* 22 (2002): 273–304.

33. Breck, *Shape of Biblical Language,* 25–26, 53. See also my discussion in chapter 3, 85–87.

34.   8 Thou shalt cause me to hear gladness and joy: the afflicted bones shall rejoice.
          9 Turn away thy face from my sins, and blot out all mine iniquities.
             10 Create in me a clean heart, O God; and renew a right spirit in my inward parts.
                11 Cast me not away from thy presence; and remove not thy holy Spirit from me.
             12 Restore to me the joy of thy salvation: establish me with thy directing Spirit.
          13 [Then] will I teach transgressors thy ways; and ungodly men shall turn to thee.
       14 Deliver me from blood-guiltiness, O God, the God of my salvation: [and] my tongue shall joyfully declare thy righteousness.

35. In fact, on December 22, a day before the annual commemoration of the inauguration of Hagia Sophia, in the early morning, while the church was still closed for the congregation and before the public procession to the Forum of Constantine, the *psaltai* mounted the ambo and sang Psalm 50. Mateos, *Le Typicon de la Grande Église,* 1:144.

36. Ibid., 1:146–49.

37. Ibid., 2:309–10 (*orthros*); Lingas, "Sunday Matins," 68, 88–95; Miguel Arranz, "L'office de l'Asmatikos Orthros ('matines chantées') de l'ancien Euchologe byzantin," *Orientalia christiana periodica* 47 (1981): 122–57; Hanke, *Vesper und Orthros,* 2:287, 304, 314, 320, 342, 344, 351, 367, 372–73, 378–79, 381–85, 504, 506–516, 524, 589, .pdf available at http://www.mgh.de/bibliothek/opac/?wa72ci_url=/cgi-bin/mgh/regsrchindex.pl?wert=vesper+und+orthros+des+kathedralritus+der+hagia+sophia+zu+konstantinopel&recnums=338621&index=1&db=opac, accessed November 15, 2013.

38. ὡς ὤμοσε τῷ Κυρίῳ, ηὔξατο τῷ Θεῷ ᾿Ιακώβ· εἰ εἰσελεύσομαι εἰς σκήνωμα οἴκου μου, εἰ ἀναβήσομαι ἐπὶ κλίνης στρωμνῆς μου, εἰ δώσω ὕπνον τοῖς ὀφθαλμοῖς μου καὶ τοῖς βλεφάροις μου νυσταγμὸν καὶ ἀνάπαυσιν τοῖς κροτάφοις μου, ἕως οὗ εὕρω τόπον τῷ Κυρίῳ, σκήνωμα τῷ Θεῷ ᾿Ιακώβ. ἰδοὺ ἠκούσαμεν αὐτὴν ἐν ᾿Εφραθᾷ, εὕρομεν αὐτὴν ἐν τοῖς πεδίοις τοῦ δρυμοῦ· εἰσελευσόμεθα εἰς τὰ σκηνώματα αὐτοῦ, προσκυνήσομεν εἰς τὸν τόπον, οὗ ἔστησαν οἱ πόδες αὐτοῦ. ἀνάστηθι, Κύριε, εἰς τὴν ἀνάπαυσίν σου, σὺ καὶ ἡ κιβωτὸς τοῦ ἁγιάσματός σου. Ps 131 (132): 2–8.

39. ὤμοσε Κύριος τῷ Δαυΐδ ἀλήθειαν καὶ οὐ μὴ ἀθετήσει αὐτήν· ἐκ καρποῦ τῆς κοιλίας σου θήσομαι ἐπὶ τοῦ θρόνου σου. Ps. 131 (132): 11.

40. ἕνεκεν Δαυΐδ τοῦ δούλου σου <u>μὴ ἀποστρέψῃς τὸ πρόσωπον</u> τοῦ χριστοῦ σου. Ps. 131 (132): 10. Compare to <u>μὴ ἀπορρίψῃς με ἀπὸ τοῦ προσώπου σου</u> καὶ τὸ πνεῦμά σου τὸ ἅγιον μὴ ἀντανέλῃς ἀπ᾿ ἐμοῦ. Ps. 50 (51): 11.

41. Parenti and Velkovska, *Eucologio Barberini gr. 336,* prayer 152.4, 166–67. Another occasion on which the sign of the cross is made is the inspiriting of the neophyte during baptism; see ibid., prayer 112.2, 96; prayer 114, 98; prayer 118.3, 105; prayer 122.3, 112; prayer 123.4, 114–15; prayer 124.5, 116. On the cross, blessing, sealing, and inspiriting, see Pentcheva, *Sensual Icon,* 28–36.

42. Permjakovs, "'Make This the Place Where Your Glory Dwells,'" 375–81, 418–27. On the Antioch transplant of *myron* in the *kathierōsis* rites, see ibid., 471–74, 492.

43. ΙΔΟΥ δὴ τί καλὸν ἢ τί τερπνόν, ἀλλ᾿ ἢ τὸ κατοικεῖν ἀδελφοὺς ἐπὶ τὸ αὐτό; ὡς μύρον ἐπὶ κεφαλῆς τὸ καταβαῖνον ἐπὶ πώγωνα, τὸν πώγωνα τοῦ ᾿Ααρών, τὸ καταβαῖνον ἐπὶ τὴν ᾤαν τοῦ ἐνδύματος αὐτοῦ· ὡς δρόσος ᾿Αερμὼν ἡ καταβαίνουσα ἐπὶ τὰ ὄρη Σιών· ὅτι ἐκεῖ ἐνετείλατο Κύριος τὴν εὐλογίαν, ζωὴν ἕως τοῦ αἰῶνος. Ps. 132 (133): 1–3.

44. Harvey, *Scenting Salvation,* 65–89, 125–47, 169–85, 222–40. Pentcheva, *Sensual Icon,* 36–45, 54–55.

45. The text survives in two recensions: *Severus ibn al-Muqaffaʿ: Alexandrinische Patriarchengeschichte von S. Marcus bis Michael I, 61–767; Nach ältesten 1266 geschriebenen Hamburger Handschrift im arabischen Urtext,*

ed. Christian Friedrich Seybold (Hamburg: L. Gräfe, 1912), 104–112; and *History of the Patriarchs of the Coptic Church of Alexandria*, ed. Basil Evetts (Paris: Firmin-Didot, 1907), 2:503–18. Coquin, *Livre de la consécration du sanctuaire de Benjamin*.

46. Permjakovs, "'Make This the Place Where Your Glory Dwells,'" 493–506.

47. Coquin, *Livre de la consécration du sanctuaire de Benjamin*, 131–41. English translation in Permjakovs, "'Make This the Place Where Your Glory Dwells,'" 497–98.

48. J.-M. Vosté, *Pontificale iuxta ritum ecclesiae Syrorum occidentalium id est Antiochiae: Versio Latina* (Vatican City: Congregazione Pro Ecclesia orientali, 1941), pt. 1, prayer 4, 78; Permjakovs, "'Make This the Place Where Your Glory Dwells,'" 534 and 548–49 (a thirteenth-century record, in the Nomocanon of Bar Hebraeus [1225/26–1286], of the anointment of a whole church through the tracing of a cross-shaped choreography).

49. Germanus, *Historia mystica ecclesiae catholicae*, in Meyendorff, *On the Divine Liturgy*, sect. 1; Permjakovs, "'Make This the Place Where Your Glory Dwells,'" 574–77.

50. Ὁ Κύριος ἐβασίλευσεν, εὐπρέπειαν ἐνεδύσατο, ἐνεδύσατο Κύριος δύναμιν καὶ περιεζώσατο· καὶ γὰρ ἐστερέωσε τὴν οἰκουμένην, ἥτις οὐ σαλευθήσεται. ἕτοιμος ὁ θρόνος σου ἀπὸ τότε, ἀπὸ τοῦ αἰῶνος σὺ εἶ. ἐπῆραν οἱ ποταμοί, Κύριε, ἐπῆραν οἱ ποταμοὶ φωνὰς αὐτῶν· ἀροῦσιν οἱ ποταμοὶ ἐπιτρίψεις αὐτῶν. ἀπὸ φωνῶν ὑδάτων πολλῶν θαυμαστοὶ οἱ μετεωρισμοὶ τῆς θαλάσσης, θαυμαστὸς ἐν ὑψηλοῖς ὁ Κύριος. τὰ μαρτύριά σου ἐπιστώθησαν σφόδρα· τῷ οἴκῳ σου πρέπει ἁγίασμα, Κύριε, εἰς μακρότητα ἡμερῶν. Ps. 92 (93): 1–5.

51. Parenti and Velkovska, *Eucologio Barberini gr. 336*, prayer 150, 163–64; Ruggieri, "Consacrazione e dedicazione di chiesa," 85. For an alternative English translation, see Permjakovs, "'Make This the Place Where Your Glory Dwells,'" 190.

52. Parenti and Velkovska, *Eucologio Barberini gr. 336*, prayer 152.6–7, 167.

53. νίψομαι ἐν ἀθῴοις τὰς χεῖράς μου καὶ κυκλώσω τὸ θυσιαστήριόν σου, Κύριε, τοῦ ἀκοῦσαί με φωνῆς αἰνέσεώς σου καὶ διηγήσασθαι πάντα τὰ θαυμάσιά σου. Κύριε, ἠγάπησα εὐπρέπειαν οἴκου σου καὶ τόπον σκηνώματος δόξης σου. Ps. 25 (26): 6–8.

54. Ἐν δὲ τῷ θυμιᾶν τὸν πατριάρχην, εἷς τῶν συμπαρόντων αὐτῷ ἐπισκόπων, βαστάζων τὸ ἀγγεῖον τοῦ μύρου, ἀκολουθεῖ ὄπισθεν αὐτοῦ, καὶ ποιεῖ σταυροὺς ἐκ τοῦ μύρου εἰς ἕκαστον κίονα καὶ πισσὸν τοῦ αὐτοῦ τοῦ ναοῦ. Permjakovs, "'Make This the Place Where Your Glory Dwells,'" 194 (with both Greek and English).

55. The tenth-century codex Tbilisi A86 (a euchologion) is published by Kekelidze, *Drevne-gruzinskij Archieratikon*, 135–41; for an English translation, see Conybeare and Wardrop, "Georgian Version of the Liturgy," esp. 172–73.

56. Permjakovs, "'Make This the Place Where Your Glory Dwells,'" 403.

57. For the text, see Coquin, *Livre de la consécration du sanctuaire de Benjamin*, 131–41; Permjakovs, "'Make This the Place Where Your Glory Dwells,'" 498.

58. Κύριε τοῦ οὐρανοῦ καὶ τῆς γῆς, ὁ τὴν ἁγίαν σου ἐκκλησίαν ἀρρήτῳ σοφίᾳ θεμελιώσας, καὶ ἀντίτυπον τῆς ἀγγελικῆς ἐν οὐρανῷ λειτουργίας τὴν τῆς ἱερωσύνης τάξιν ἐπὶ τῆς γῆς συστησάμενος. Parenti and Velkovska, *Eucologio Barberini gr. 336*, prayer 152, 168; Ruggieri, "Consacrazione e dedicazione di chiesa," 89; English translation in Permjakovs, "'Make This the Place Where Your Glory Dwells,'" 194–95.

59. Permjakovs, "'Make This the Place Where Your Glory Dwells,'" 195.

60. Ibid. 3 Kings 8:11: καὶ οὐκ ἠδύναντο οἱ ἱερεῖς στήκειν λειτουργεῖν ἀπὸ προσώπου τῆς νεφέλης, ὅτι ἔπλησε δόξα Κυρίου τὸν οἶκον.

61. Permjakovs, "'Make This the Place Where Your Glory Dwells,'" 196.

62. The hymn is sung at *orthros* in conjunction with Psalm 50 on the third day of the Armenian octave celebrating the *enkaineia* of the Holy Sepulchre at Jerusalem. Findikyan, "Armenian Hymns," 46, 88.

63. Thodberg, *Der byzantinische Alleluiarionzyklus*, 11–12, 32; idem, "Alleluia," *Grove Music Online*, accessed September 17, 2014; Permjakovs, "'Make This the Place Where Your Glory Dwells,'" 335–39; James W. McKinnon, *The Advent Project: The Later-Seventh-Century Creation of the Roman Mass Proper* (Berkeley: University of California Press, 2000), 249–79.

64. Τὸ δὲ ἀλληλούϊα τῇ ἑβραΐδι διαλέκτῳ ἐστὶν τὸ ΑΛ ἔρχεται, ἐφάνη· τὸ ΗΛ ὁ Θεός, τὸ δὲ ΟΥΙΑ αἰνεῖτε, ὑμνεῖτε, τὸν ζῶντα Θεόν. Quoted in Germanus, *Ekklesiastikē historia*, sect. 29, attributed to Basil of Caesaraea. F. E. Brightman, "The Historia Mystagogica and Other Greek Commentaries on the Byzantine Liturgy," *Journal of*

Theological Studies 9, no. 34 (1908): 248–67, and no. 35 (1908): 387–97, esp. 387, sect. 41. Athanasius of Alexandria, *Expositiones in Psalmos*, Pss. 104 and 134, in PG 27, cols. 441C and 525A; Justin Martyr, *Quaestiones et responsiones*, 50, in PG 6, col. 1296A.

65. Thodberg, *Der byzantinische Alleluiarionzyklus*, 11, 40.

66. Müller-Wiener, *Bildlexikon zur Topographie Istanbuls*, 112–17.

67. Thodberg, *Der byzantinische Alleluiarionzyklus*, 80, 94, 122, 145, 199, 228.

68. Ibid., 41–44.

69. Ibid., 24, 40–41.

70. McKinnon, *Advent Project*, 249–79. See also Thodberg, "Alleluia."

71. James W. McKinnon, "Vaticana Latina 5319 as a Witness to the Eighth-Century Roman Proper of the Mass," in *Cantus Planus: Papers Read at the Seventh Meeting, Sopron, Hungary, 1995*, ed. László Dobszay (Budapest: Hungarian Academy of Sciences, 1998), 403–14; Bruno Stäblein and Margareta Landwehr-Melnicki, eds., *Die Gesänge des altrömischen Graduale: Vat. lat. 5319*, Monumenta Monodica Medii Aevi 2 (Kassel: Bärenreiter, 1970). Marcel Pérès and the Ensemble Organum, *Chants de l'Église de Rome: Periode byzantine* (Harmonia Mundi, 1998), compact disc.

72. Pérès and the Ensemble Organum, *Chants de l'Église de Rome*.

73. ἀκολουθία τῆς γονυκλισίας· μετὰ τὴν ἐκτενὴν ἀναβαίνει ὁ δομέστικος ἐν τῷ ἄμβωνι καὶ ἄρχεται οὕτως. Ashburnhamensis 64, fol. 258r.

74. On the challenge of transcribing and performing Byzantine chant as it has survived in Middle Byzantine manuscripts, see Alexander Lingas, "Performance Practice and the Politics of Transcribing Byzantine Chant," *Acta Musicae Byzantinae* 6 (2003): 56–76. On Middle Byzantine diastematic notation, see Christian Troelsgård, *Byzantine Neumes: A New Introduction to the Middle Byzantine Musical Notation* (Copenhagen: Museum Tuscilanum Press, 2011).

75. Lingas, "From Earth to Heaven," 328–34. Listen to music sample 1 at https://hagiasophia.stanford.edu.

76. Germanus, *Ekklesiastikē historia*, sect. 29.

77. Listen to music sample 1 at https://hagiasophia.stanford.edu.

78. Weitze et al., "Acoustical History of Hagia Sophia"; Woszczyk, "Acoustics of Hagia Sophia," 4; Pentcheva, "Hagia Sophia and Multisensory Aesthetics," 101–6.

79. On the terms "wet" and "dry" as descriptors of sound and their origins in the usage of modern recording engineers, see Sterne, "Space Within Space," esp. 129. My subsequent chapters explore the link between water and mystical experience, more specifically how the image of the glittering sea operates in the interior of Hagia Sophia and how it expresses the animation of the inert.

80. Guglielmo Cavallo, Jean Gribomont, and William C. Loerke, *Codex purpureus Rossanensis, Museo dell'Arcivescovado, Rossano calabro: Commentarium* (Rome: Salerno editrice; Graz: Akademische Druck- und Verlagsanstalt, 1987). John Lowden, "The Beginning of Biblical Illustration," in *Imaging the Early Medieval Bible*, ed. John Williams (University Park: Pennsylvania State University Press, 1999), 18–21.

81. Permjakovs, "'Make This the Place Where Your Glory Dwells,'" 191. Greek in Parenti and Velkovska, *Eucologio Barberini gr. 336*, prayer 150, 164–65; Ruggieri, "Consacrazione e dedicazione di chiesa," 86.

82. The identification of the altar with *hagiasma* and water is one of the reasons why the lines of Psalm 92:5 are frequently set in the arch of the bema of Byzantine churches. For an overview of the Armenian and Byzantine churches displaying Psalm 92:5 in the apse, see Maranci, "'Holiness Befits Your House.'"

83. Weitze et al., "Acoustical History of Hagia Sophia"; Woszczyk, "Acoustics of Hagia Sophia," 4; Pentcheva, "Hagia Sophia and Multisensory Aesthetics," 101–6.

84. I thank Laura Steenberge, who first pointed out this connection to me.

Chapter 3

1. J. L. Austin, *How to Do Things with Words* (Oxford: Clarendon Press, 1962), and Judith Butler, *Gender Trouble: Feminism and the Subversion of Identity* (New York: Routledge, 1999).

2. Slobodan Ćurčić, "Architecture as Icon," in Ćurčić and Hadjitryphonos, *Architecture as Icon,* 3–37, and K. McVey, "Spirit Embodied: The Emergence of Symbolic Interpretations of Early Christian and Byzantine Architecture," in ibid., 39–71.

3. Byzantine Iconoclasm is a richly researched field, yet none of the existing studies recognizes the existence of performative iconicity and the role it played in shaping this crisis. These major studies have only engaged the representational model of what an image is: Hans Belting, *Likeness and Presence: A History of the Image Before the Era of Art,* trans. Edmund Jephcott (Chicago: University of Chicago Press, 1994); Charles Barber, *Figure and Likeness: On the Limits of Representation in Byzantine Iconoclasm* (Princeton: Princeton University Press, 2002); Leslie Brubaker and John Haldon, *Byzantium in the Iconoclast Era (ca. 680–850): The Sources, an Annotated Survey* (Aldershot: Ashgate, 2001); idem, *Byzantium in the Iconoclast Era, c. 680–850: A History* (Cambridge: Cambridge University Press, 2011); Leslie Brubaker, *Inventing Byzantine Iconoclasm* (London: Bristol Classical Press, 2012); Thomas F. X. Noble, *Images, Iconoclasm, and the Carolingians* (Philadelphia: University of Pennsylvania Press, 2009); Jaś Elsner, "Iconoclasm as Discourse: From Antiquity to Byzantium," *Art Bulletin* 94, no. 3 (2012): 368–94.

4. Pentcheva, *Sensual Icon,* 57–96.

5. Maximus the Confessor, *Ambigua,* bk. 7, in Constas, *On Difficulties in the Church Fathers,* 1:86–87 (with Greek and English).

6. In developing this subject, I draw on Anca Vasiliu, *Eikōn: L'image dans le discours des trois Cappadociens* (Paris: Presses universitaires de France, 2010).

7. καὶ εἶπεν ὁ θεός Ποιήσωμεν ἄνθρωπον κατ᾽ εἰκόνα ἡμετέραν καὶ καθ᾽ ὁμοίωσιν, καὶ ἐποίησεν ὁ θεὸς τὸν ἄνθρωπον, κατ᾽ εἰκόνα θεοῦ ἐποίησεν αὐτόν, ἄρσεν καὶ θῆλυ ἐποίησεν αὐτούς. καὶ ηὐλόγησεν αὐτοὺς ὁ θεὸς λέγων. Gen. 1:26–28, from *Septuaginta,* ed. Alfred Rahlfs (1935; repr., Stuttgart: Württembergische Bibelanstalt, 1975).

8. καὶ ἔπλασεν ὁ θεὸς τὸν ἄνθρωπον χοῦν ἀπὸ τῆς γῆς καὶ ἐνεφύσησεν εἰς τὸ πρόσωπον αὐτοῦ πνοὴν ζωῆς, καὶ ἐγένετο ὁ ἄνθρωπος εἰς ψυχὴν ζῶσαν. Gen. 2:7.

9. Blessing occurs at the cleansing of the new altar (see no. 1 under "Ritual Actions and the Singing of Psalms" in chapter 2), Parenti and Velkovska, *Eucologio Barberini gr. 336,* prayer 150, 164–65; three times when making the sign of cross at the wine libation (no. 3), ibid., prayer 152, 166; at the chrismation (no. 6), ibid., prayer 152.4, 166–67; and finally at the incensing (no. 8), ibid., prayer 152.6–7, 167.

10. Luke 20:24.

11. καὶ βαπτισθεὶς ὁ Ἰησοῦς ἀνέβη εὐθὺς ἀπὸ τοῦ ὕδατος· καὶ ἰδοὺ ἀνεῴχθησαν αὐτῷ οἱ οὐρανοί, καὶ εἶδε τὸ Πνεῦμα τοῦ Θεοῦ καταβαῖνον ὡσεὶ περιστερὰν καὶ ἐρχόμενον ἐπ᾽ αὐτόν· καὶ ἰδοὺ φωνὴ ἐκ τῶν οὐρανῶν λέγουσα· οὗτός ἐστιν ὁ υἱός μου ὁ ἀγαπητός, ἐν ᾧ εὐδόκησα. Matt. 3:16–17, as well as Mark 1:9–11 and Luke 3:21–22.

12. ἔτι αὐτοῦ λαλοῦντος ἰδοὺ νεφέλη φωτεινὴ ἐπεσκίασεν αὐτούς, καὶ ἰδοὺ φωνὴ ἐκ τῆς νεφέλης λέγουσα· οὗτός ἐστιν ὁ υἱός μου ὁ ἀγαπητός, ἐν ᾧ εὐδόκησα· αὐτοῦ ἀκούετε. Matt. 17:5. Mark 9:7, Luke 9:34–35. On *episkiazō,* see also Miller, *Corporeal Imagination,* 142.

13. Mark 6:41, Luke 9:16 (feeding the multitude), Matt. 26:26, Mark 14:22, Luke 24:30, 1 Cor. 10:16 (Last Supper).

14. ὃς ἐρρύσατο ἡμᾶς ἐκ τῆς ἐξουσίας τοῦ σκότους καὶ μετέστησεν εἰς τὴν βασιλείαν τοῦ υἱοῦ τῆς ἀγάπης αὐτοῦ, ἐν ᾧ ἔχομεν τὴν ἀπολύτρωσιν, τὴν ἄφεσιν τῶν ἁμαρτιῶν· ὅς ἐστιν εἰκὼν τοῦ Θεοῦ τοῦ ἀοράτου, πρωτότοκος πάσης κτίσεως. Col. 1:13–15.

15. ὅτι οὓς προέγνω, καὶ προώρισε συμμόρφους τῆς εἰκόνος τοῦ υἱοῦ αὐτοῦ, εἰς τὸ εἶναι αὐτὸν πρωτότοκον ἐν πολλοῖς ἀδελφοῖς. Rom. 8:29.

16. My analysis here relies on Vasiliu, *Eikōn,* 11–298.

17. Ibid., 115–28.

18. Gregory of Nyssa, *De hominis opificio,* bk. 16, sects. 7 and 17, in PG 44, cols. 180, 185.

19. "Ποιήσωμεν ἄνθρωπον κατ᾽ εἰκόνα ἡμετέραν καὶ καθ᾽ ὁμοίωσιν." Τὸ μὲν τῇ κτίσει ἔχομεν· τὸ δὲ ἐκπροαιρέσεως κατορθοῦμεν. Ἐν τῇ πρώτῃ κατασκευῇ συνυπάρχει ἡμῖν τὸ κατ᾽ εἰκόνα γεγενῆσθαι Θεοῦ· ἐκ προαιρέσεως ἡμῖν κατορθοῦται τὸ καθ᾽ ὁμοίωσιν εἶναι Θεοῦ. Τοῦτο δὲ τὸ κατὰ προαίρεσιν, δυνάμει ἡμῖν ἐνυπάρχει· ἐνεργείᾳ δὲ ἑαυτοῖς ἐπάγομεν. Εἰ μὴ προλαβὼν εἶπεν ὁ Κύριος ποιῶν ἡμᾶς· «Ποιήσωμεν» καὶ «καθ᾽ ὁμοίωσιν,» εἰ μὴ τὴν τοῦ γενέσθαι καθ᾽ ὁμοίωσιν δύναμιν ἡμῖν ἐχαρίσατο, οὐκ ἂν τῇ ἑαυτῶν ἐξουσίᾳ τὴν πρὸς Θεὸν ὁμοίωσιν ἐδεξάμεθα. Νῦν μέντοι δυνάμει ἡμᾶς ἐποίησεν ὁμοιωτικοὺς Θεῷ. Δύναμιν δὲ δοὺς πρὸς τὸ ὁμοιοῦσθαι Θεῷ, ἀφῆκεν ἡμᾶς ἐργάτας εἶναι τῆς πρὸς Θεὸν ὁμοιώσεως, ἵνα ἡμέτερος ᾖ τῆς ἐργασίας ὁ μισθός, ἵνα μὴ ὥσπερ παρὰ

ζωγράφου γενόμεναι, εἰκῇ κείμεναι, ἵνα μὴ τὰ τῆς ἡμετέρας ὁμοιώσεως ἄλλῳ ἔπαινον φέρῃ. Ὅταν γὰρ τὴν εἰκόνα ἴδῃς ἀκριβῶς μεμορφωμένην πρὸς τὸ πρωτότυπον, οὐ τὴν εἰκόνα ἐπαινεῖς, ἀλλὰ τὸν ζωγράφον θαυμάζεις. Ἵνα τοίνυν τὸ θαῦμα ἐμὸν γένηται καὶ μὴ ἀλλότριον, ἐμοὶ κατέλιπε τὸ καθ᾽ ὁμοίωσιν Θεοῦ γενέσθαι. Κατ᾽ εἰκόνα γὰρ ἔχω τὸ λογικὸς εἶναι, καθ᾽ ὁμοίωσιν δὲ γίνομαι ἐν τῷ Χριστιανὸς γενέσθαι. Basil of Caesarea, *De creatione hominis,* bk. 1, sect. 16, vv. 1–20, in *Sur l'origine de l'homme: Hom. x et xi de l'Hexhaemeron,* intro. and trans. Alexis Smets and Michel van Esbroeck (Paris: Éditions du Cerf, 1970), 206–9, with my emendations.

20. Ἡ γὰρ εἰκών, εἰ μὲν ἔχει τὴν πρὸς τὸ πρωτότυπον ὁμοιότητα, κυρίως τοῦτο κατονομάζεται. Εἰ δὲ παρενεχθείη τοῦ προκειμένου ἡ μίμησις, ἄλλο τι, καὶ οὐκ εἰκὼν ἐκείνου τὸ τοιοῦτον ἐστι. Gregory of Nyssa, *De hominis opificio,* bk. 16, sect. 3, in PG 44, col. 180B; French translation in Grégoire de Nysse, *La creation de l'homme,* trans. Jean Laplace, Sources chrétiennes 6 (1943; repr., Paris: Éditions du Cerf, 2002); English translation in *On the Making of Man,* in *Gregory of Nyssa: Dogmatic Treatises, Etc.,* A Select Library of Nicene and Post-Nicene Fathers of the Christian Church, 2nd ser., vol. 5 (Oxford: Parker; New York: Christian Literature, 1893), 404.

21. ὥσπερ δε ἔφαμεν τῇ ὁμοιώσει τοῦ πρωτοτύπου καλλοῦς καθακοσμεῖσθαι τὸν νοῦν, οἷον τι κατόπτρον τῷ χαρακτῆρι τοῦ ἐμφαινομένου μορφούμενον· κατὰ τὴν αὐτὴν ἀναλογίαν, καὶ τὴν οἰκονομουμένην ὑπ᾽ αὐτοῦ φύσιν ἔχεσθαι τοῦ νοῦ λογιζόμεθα, καὶ τῷ παρακειμένῳ κάλλει καὶ αὐτὴν κοσμεῖσθαι, οἷον τι κατόπτρου κάτοπτρον γινομένη, . . .

καὶ οὗτος ἐπ᾽ αὐτὸν τὸν νοῦν τοῦ κατὰ τὴν ὕλην αἴσχους διὰ τῆς φύσεως ἡ διάδοσις γίνεται, ὡς μηκωετι τοῦ θεοῦ εἰκόνα ἐν τῷ χαρακτῆρι καθορᾶσθαι τοῦ πλάσματος. οἷον γὰρ τι κάτοπτρον κατὰ νώτου τὴν τῶν ἀγαθῶν ἰδέαν ὁ νοῦς ποιησάμενος, ἐκβάλλει μὲν τῆς ἐκλάμψεως τοῦ ἀγαθοῦ τὰς ἐμφάσεις, τῆς δὲ ὕλης τὴν ἀμορφίαν εἰς ἑαυτὸν ἀναμάσσεται. Gregory of Nyssa, *De hominis opificio,* bk. 12, in PG 44, cols. 161C, 164A. The French translation renders *nous* as "spirit" and "soul": Grégoire de Nysse, *La creation de l'homme,* 131; my translation, based on Philip Schaff, *On the Making of Man,* in *A Select Library of Nicene and Post-Nicene Fathers of the Christian Church,* vol. 5. For analysis, see Vasiliu, *Eikōn,* 128–33.

22. Maximus the Confessor, *Ambigua,* bk. 7, in Constas, *On Difficulties in the Church Fathers,* 1:86–87.

23. Parenti and Velkovska, *Eucologio Barberini gr. 336,* prayer 150, 163–64; Ruggieri, "Consacrazione e dedicazione di chiesa," 85. My translation. For an alternative English translation, see Permjakovs, "'Make This the Place Where Your Glory Dwells,'" 190.

24. ὅταν δὲ συνίωσιν, οὐκ εἰκόνα ἄψυχον, οὐδὲ εἰκόνα τινὸς τῶν ἐπὶ γῆς, ἀλλ᾽ αὐτοῦ ποιοῦντες τοῦ Θεοῦ. John Chrysostomos, *In Epistolam ad Colossenses,* in PG 62, cols. 299–392, esp. col. 387C. My translation.

25. Pseudo-Dionysius, *De ecclesiastica hierarchia,* chap. 2, sect. 7 (on baptism); chap. 3, intro.; and chap. 3, sect. 7 (on the Eucharist); English translation in Luibheid, *Pseudo-Dionysius,* 203, 209–11, 216–18. Taft, "Liturgy of the Great Church," and Pentcheva, *Sensual Icon,* 17–44.

26. Constantine V, *Peuseis,* recorded in Patriarch Nikephoros, *Antirrheticus II adversus Constantinum Copronymum,* in PG 100, col. 337B; repr. in *Textus Byzantinos ad iconomachiam pertinentes,* ed. Herman Hennephof (Leiden: Brill, 1969), 55 n. 167. My translation. On the *Peuseis,* see Stephen Gero, *Byzantine Iconoclasm During the Reign of Constantine V* (Louvain: Secrétariat du Corpus SCO, 1977), 37–52, and Pentcheva, *Sensual Icon,* 57–96.

27. On *typōsis,* see Pentcheva, *Sensual Icon,* 28–36, 57–96.

28. *The Oxford Dictionary of Byzantium,* ed. Alexander Kazhdan et al. (Oxford: Oxford University Press, 1991), s.v. "stylite"; Harvey, *Scenting Salvation,* 186–222; Peter Brown, "The Rise and Function of the Holy Man in Late Antiquity," *Journal of Roman Studies* 61 (1971): 80–101.

29. On the architectural complex and vita of Saint Symeon the Stylite the Younger (d. 592), see Jacqueline Lafontaine-Dosogne, *Itinéraires archéologiques dans la région d'Antioche: Recherches sur le monastère et sur l'iconographie de S. Syméon Stylite le Jeune* (Brussels: Éditions de Byzantion, 1967). For the hagiography, see *La vie ancienne de S. Syméon Stylite le Jeune (521–592),* ed. and trans. Paul van den Ven, 2 vols., Subsidia Hagiographica 32 (Brussels: Société des Bollandistes, 1962–70).

30. Pentcheva, *Sensual Icon,* 17–44.

31. *Vita S. Symeonis Stylitae Junioris,* chaps. 32, 34, 37, and 250. My translation.

32. Paul Speck, "Γραφαῖς ἢ γλυφαῖς: Zu dem Fragment des Hypatios von Ephesos über die Bilder mit einem Anhang zu dem Dialog mit einem Juden des Leontios von Neapolis," in *Varia 1,* Poikila Byzantina 4 (Bonn: R. Habelt, 1984), 211–72, esp. 242–49.

33. My translation. For the Greek, see Hans Georg Thümmel, *Die Frühgeschichte der ostkirchlichen Bilderlehre: Texte und Untersuchungen zur Zeit vor dem Bilderstreit,* Texte und Untersuchungen zur Geschichte der altkirchlichen Literatur 139 (Berlin: Akademie Verlag, 1992), 347.

34. René Bornert, *Les commentaires byzantins de la Divine Liturgie du VIIe au XVe siècle* (Paris: Institut français d'études byzantines, 1966); Taft, "Liturgy of the Great Church"; Hans-Joachim Schulz, *The Byzantine Liturgy: Symbolic Structure and Faith Expression* (New York: Pueblo, 1986).

35. Maximus the Confessor, *Mystagogia,* chaps. 1–5, in PG 91, cols. 664–84; English translation in *The Church, the Liturgy, and the Soul of Man: The Mystagogia of St. Maximus the Confessor,* trans. Dom Julian Stead, O.S.B. (Still River, Mass.: St. Bede's Publications, 1982), 65–82, and Blowers and Wilken, *On the Cosmic Mystery of Jesus Christ,* 13, 19. On the way Maximus legitimized the views of Origen and Pseudo-Dionysius, see Lars Thunberg, *Man and the Cosmos: The Vision of St. Maximus the Confessor* (Crestwood, N.Y.: St. Vladimir's Seminary Press, 1985).

36. Τὴν τοίνυν ἁγίαν Ἐκκλησίαν κατὰ πρώτην θεωρίας ἐπιβολὴν, τύπον καὶ εἰκόνα Θεοῦ φέρειν, ἔλεγεν ὁ μακάριος γέρων ἐκεῖνος, ὡς τὴν αὐτὴν αὐτῷ κατὰ μίμησιν καὶ τύπον ἐνέργειαν ἔχουσαν. Maximus the Confessor, *Mystagogia,* chap. 1, in PG 91, col. 664D. My translation. For an alternative English translation see Stead, *The Church, The Liturgy, and the Soul of Man,* 65.

37. Pentcheva, *Sensual Icon,* 28–36, and Nicoletta Isar, "Undoing Forgetfulness: Chiasmus of Poetical Mind—a Cultura Paradigm of Archetypal Imagination," *Europe's Journal of Psychology* 1, no. 3 (2005), http://ejop.psychopen.eu/article/view/370/html.

38. Lund, "Chiasmus in the Psalms"; idem, "Presence of Chiasmus in the New Testament"; Assis, "Chiasmus in Biblical Narrative"; Welch, *Chiasmus in Antiquity*; Breck, *Shape of Biblical Language.*

39. Lund, "Chiasmus in the Psalms."

40. Ibid., 289–91.

41. Breck, *Shape of Biblical Language.*

42. The corresponding arrangement in Greek is as follows:

   A. v. 1 Κύριε ὁ κύριος ἡμῶν, ὡς θαυμαστὸν τὸ ὄνομά σου ἐν πάσῃ τῇ γῇ,

      B. v. 2 ὅτι ἐπήρθη ἡ μεγαλοπρέπειά σου ὑπεράνω τῶν οὐρανῶν ἐκ στόματος νηπίων καὶ θηλαζόντων κατηρτίσω αἶνον

         C. v. 3 ἕνεκα τῶν ἐχθρῶν σου τοῦ καταλῦσαι ἐχθρὸν καὶ ἐκδικητήν

            D. v. 4 ὅτι ὄψομαι τοὺς οὐρανούς, ἔργα τῶν δακτύλων σου, σελήνην καὶ ἀστέρας, ἃ σὺ ἐθεμελίωσας.

              ⊗ **E. v. 5 τί ἐστιν ἄνθρωπος, ὅτι μιμνήσκῃ αὐτοῦ, ἢ υἱὸς ἀνθρώπου, ὅτι ἐπισκέπτῃ αὐτόν;**

              ⊗ **E. v. 6 ἠλάττωσας αὐτὸν βραχύ τι παρ' ἀγγέλους, δόξῃ καὶ τιμῇ ἐστεφάνωσας αὐτόν·**

            D'. v. 7 καὶ κατέστησας αὐτὸν ἐπὶ τὰ ἔργα τῶν χειρῶν σου, πάντα ὑπέταξας ὑποκάτω τῶν ποδῶν αὐτοῦ,

         C'. v. 8 πρόβατα καὶ βόας πάσας, ἔτι δὲ καὶ τὰ κτήνη τοῦ πεδίου,

      B' v. 9 τὰ πετεινὰ τοῦ οὐρανοῦ καὶ τοὺς ἰχθύας τῆς θαλάσσης, τὰ διαπορευόμενα τρίβους θαλασσῶν.

   A' v. 10 κύριε ὁ κύριος ἡμῶν, ὡς θαυμαστὸν τὸ ὄνομά σου ἐν πάσῃ τῇ γῇ.

43. A. Frolow, *La relique de la Vraie Croix: Recherches sur le développement d'un culte,* Archives de l'Orient chrétien 7 (Paris: Institut français d'études byzantines, 1961), no. 34, 180–81; Anne L. McClanan, *Representations of Early Byzantine Empresses: Image and Empire* (New York: Palgrave Macmillan, 2002), 166; Cynthia J. Hahn, *Strange Beauty: Issues in the Making and Meaning of Reliquaries, 400–Circa 1204* (University Park: Pennsylvania State University Press, 2012), 73–74.

44. Inscription: "ligno quo Christus humanum subdidit hostem dat Romae Justinus opem et socia decorum" (By means of the wood with which Christ conquered man's enemy, Justin gives help to Rome, and his wife offers decoration to it).

45. Theban *ostraka* (potsherds) from the second century C.E. attest the chiastic system used for children learning the alphabet. J. Grafton Milne, "Relics of Graeco-Egyptian Schools," *Journal of Hellenic Studies* 28 (1908): 121–22 (no. 1). For further evidence on the chiastic system of learning the alphabet, see Quintilian, *Institutio*

oratoria bk. 1, chap. 1, 25; Henri Irénée Marrou, *A History of Education in Antiquity,* trans. George Lamb (New York: Sheed & Ward, 1956), 151, 269–70; Augustine Stock, "Chiastic Awareness and Education in Antiquity," *Biblical Theology Bulletin* 14, no. 1 (1984): 23–27; and Breck, *Shape of Biblical Language,* 29–30.

46. On the Justinianic mosaics, see Alessandra Guiglia Guidobaldi, "I mosaici aniconici della Santa Sofia di Costantinopoli nell'età di Giustiniano," in *La mosaïque gréco-romaine VII: Actes du VIIème colloque international pour l'étude de la mosaïque antique, Tunis, 3–7 octobre 1994* (Tunis: Institut national du patrimoine, 1999), 2:691–702. Schibille, *Hagia Sophia,* 109–14.

47. Nadine Schibille has discussed the cross in the Justinianic mosaics as a *symbolon* of Holy Wisdom, salvation, and divine illumination. Schibille, *Hagia Sophia,* 129–39. By contrast, my analysis uncovers the Byzantine understanding of the theurgic powers of the cross, especially its power to bring about *empsychōsis*.

48. Paul the Silentiary, *Descriptio S. Sophiae,* vv. 492, 506, 738, 828, 882.

49.   ἐγρομένη δ' ἐφύπερθεν ἐς ἄπλετον ἠέρα πήληξ
      πάντοθι μὲν σφαιρηδὸν ἑλίσσεται, οἷα δὲ φαιδρὸς
      οὐρανὸς ἀμφιβέβηκε δόμου σκέπας· ἀκροτάτης δὲ
      σταυρὸν ὑπὲρ κορυφῆς ἐρυσίπτολιν ἔγραφε τέχνη.

      . . . .

      ἔ[νθα] τύπος σταυροῖο μεσόμ[φα]λος ἔνδοθι κύκ[λου]
      [λ]επταλέηι ψηφῖδι χαράσσεται, ὄφρα σαώσηι
      νηὸν ἀειφρούρητον ὅλου κόσμοιο σαωτήρ.

      Paul the Silentiary, *Descriptio S. Sophiae,* vv. 489–92, 506–8. My translation.

50. Homer, *Iliad,* bk. 6, v. 305.

51. Paul the Silentiary, *Descriptio S. Sophiae,* v. 738. On the symbol of the cross as expressive of divine illumination, see Schibille, *Hagia Sophia,* 129–39.

52.   ἀλλὰ καὶ ὑψιλόφοις ἐπὶ κίοσιν, ἔνθοδι πέζης
      λαϊνέης προβλῆτος, ἕλιξ πολύκεστος ἀκάνθης
      ὑγρὰ διερπύζων ἀνελίσσετο, δεσμὸς ἀλήτης,
      χρύσεος, ἱμερόεις, ἀκίδα τρηχεῖαν ἑλίσσων·
      μάρμαρα δ' ὀμφαλόεντα περιστέφει εἴκελα δίσκοις
      πορφυρέοις, στίλβοντα χάριν θελξίφρονα πέτρης

      Paul the Silentiary, *Descriptio S. Sophiae,* vv. 658–63. My translation.

53. A "fixed" psalm was performed daily; the rest of the psalms were sung according to their schedule as units in the weekly rotation of singing the entire corpus of psalms. Strunk, "Byzantine Office at Hagia Sophia." Arranz, "L'office de l'Asmatikos Orthros."

54. Lingas, "Sunday Matins," 68, 88–95. Hanke, *Vesper und Orthros,* 2:287, 304, 314, 320, 342, 344, 351, 367, 372–73, 378–79, 381–85, 504, 506–16, 524, 589, http://www.mgh.de/bibliothek/opac/?wa72ci_url=/cgi-bin/mgh /regsrchindex.pl?wert=vesper+und+orthros+des+kathedralritus+der+hagia+sophia+zu+konstantinopel& recnums=338621&index=1&db=opac.

55. Weitze et al., "Acoustical History of Hagia Sophia"; Woszczyk, "Acoustics of Hagia Sophia"; Pentcheva, "Hagia Sophia and Multisensory Aesthetics," 101–6.

56. Maximus the Confessor, *Mystagogia,* chap. 1, in PG 91, col. 664D.

57. Dimitri E. Conomos, *The Late Byzantine and Slavonic Communion Cycle: Liturgy and Music* (Washington, D.C.: Dumbarton Oaks Research Library and Collection, 1985), 53–54.

58. A total of five Greek *asmatika* survive: three in Grottaferrata, one at Mt. Athos, and one in Macedonia; all use Middle Byzantine musical notation, which dates them after 1200. Yet based on the evidence of three Russian manuscripts that preserve the old paleoslavonic notation, it is now accepted that the Byzantine *asmatika* date back to 800–1050 C.E. Scholars consider the musical settings recorded in the *asmatika* to be complete, as opposed to those in compilations of other types of chants, such as the *psaltika,* made for the soloists, which are missing the settings for the choral refrains. Simon Harris, ed., *The Communion Chants of the Thirteenth-Century Byzantine Asmatikon* (Amsterdam: Hardwood Academic Publishers, 1999), ix–x. Conomos, *Late Byzantine and Slavonic Communion Cycle,* 53, 56. Lingas, "Sunday Matins," 19–25, 53–66, 190–91.

59. This particular *koinōnikon* is considered the "second" and thus more recent version in the Typikon of the Great Church: Jerusalem, Stavros 40, dated to ca. 950–970 C.E. See Mateos, *Le Typicon de la Grande Église,* 2:138–39, vv. 20–21; Harris, *Communion Chants,* ix–x, 34–35, 117, 134, no. 17; Conomos, *Late Byzantine and Slavonic Communion Cycle,* 22, 46–51, 53–66, 190–91.

60. Harris, *Communion Chants,* ix–x, and Conomos, *Late Byzantine and Slavonic Communion Cycle,* 19–25, 53–66, 190–91.

61. Harris, *Communion Chants,* xi, 2–115; Conomos, *Late Byzantine and Slavonic Communion Cycle,* 60–61.

62. I thank Laura Steenberge, who first pointed out this connection to me. Listen to music sample 2 at https://hagiasophia.stanford.edu.

63. Troelsgård, *Byzantine Neumes,* 60–69.

64. I have marked grace notes in gray.

65. Cappella Romana, *Byzantium in Rome,* CD 2, track 4.

66. Listen to music sample 2 at https://hagiasophia.stanford.edu.

67. The recording took place on February 6, 2013, in the recording room of CCRMA, Stanford University. On transcribing Byzantine music and the need to take into account in this process the inherited performance tradition, see Lingas, "Performance Practice."

68. Listen to music sample 3 at https://hagiasophia.stanford.edu.

69. Listen to music sample 4 at https://hagiasophia.stanford.edu.

Chapter 4

1. Lingas, "From Earth to Heaven."

2. Sterne, "Space Within Space," 124–27.

3. Blesser and Salter, *Spaces Speak,* 5.

4. For the auralization of the no-longer-extant Ospedale degli Incurabili in Venice, see http://www.srcf.ucam .org/~djh1000/soundandspace/index2.php?building=Incurabili, accessed January 21, 2016. This audio project was linked to the print publication by Howard and Moretti, *Sound and Space in Renaissance Venice.*

5. Schafer, *Soundscape,* 130.

6. Thompson, *Soundscape of Modernity,* 3. Blesser and Salter, *Spaces Speak,* 133–34, 139, 143, 246.

7. R. S. Shankland and H. K. Shankland, "Acoustics of St. Peter's and Patriarchal Basilicas in Rome," *Journal of the Acoustical Society of America* 50, no. 2 (1971): 389–96. Ettore Cirillo and Francesco Martellota, *Worship, Acoustics, and Architecture* (Brentwood, Essex: Multi-Science Publishing, 2006), 9–16, 51–60. Iégor Reznikoff, "The Evidence of the Use of Sound Resonance from Paleolithic to Medieval Times," in *Archaeoacoustics,* ed. Chris Scarre and Graeme Lawson (Cambridge: McDonald Institute for Archaeological Research, 2006), 77–84.

8. Sterne, "Space Within Space." On reverberation, see also Blesser and Salter, *Spaces Speak,* 237–38, 273.

9. Blesser and Salter, *Spaces Speak,* 246; and see Sterne, "Space Within Space," 118, addressing this passage.

10. Blesser and Salter, *Spaces Speak,* 247.

11. Weitze et al., "Acoustical History of Hagia Sophia."

12. Jonathan S. Abel et al., "Estimating Room Impulse Responses from Recorded Balloon Pops," in *Audio Engineering Society 129th Convention* (November 2010), http://www.aes.org/e-lib/browse.cfm?elib=15594.

13. Woszczyk, "Acoustics of Hagia Sophia."

14. Turgut Ercetin and Jonathan Abel, "Exploring the Acoustics of Hagia Sophia," https:// soundmaterialimagination.stanford.edu, accessed January 19, 2016.

15. Anders Gade, "Acoustics in Halls for Speech and Music," in *Springer Handbook of Acoustics,* ed. Thomas D. Rossing (New York: Springer, 2007), 301–50, esp. 303, 307–9.

16. Howard and Moretti, *Sound and Space in Renaissance Venice,* 219, http://www.winmls.com/2004/help /reverbtimesrt60.htm, site visited June 3, 2010.

17. Blesser and Salter, *Spaces Speak,* 1–9, and Thompson, *Soundscape of Modernity,* 2–3.

18. Weitze et al., "Acoustical History of Hagia Sophia."

19. Ibid. Eugène Michel Antoniadi remarked on a special place in the solea where the reverberation was particularly prolonged. Antoniadi, *Ekphrasis tes Hagias Sophias, etoi melete synthetike kai analytike hypo epopsin architektoniken, archaiologiken kai historiken tou polythryletou temenous Konstantinoupoleos* (Leipzig: Teubner, 1907), 1:108. Shankland and Shankland, "Acoustics of St. Peter's," 392, 395.

20. For a sound source in the apse, see the measurements released at http://www.odeon.dk/acoustics-ancient -church-hagia-sofia, accessed April 26, 2010. For a sound source in the space under the dome (*kallichoros*), see Weitze et al., "Acoustical History of Hagia Sophia."

21. Woszczyk, "Acoustics of Hagia Sophia," 4.

22. Leo Beranek, *Concert Halls and Opera Houses. Music, Acoustics, and Architecture,* 2nd ed. (New York: Springer, 2004), 21, 29.

23. The speech transmission index, STI (0 = completely unintelligible, 1 = perfectly intelligible), is very low; a sound source set in the east end of the apse has poor intelligibility in the nave under the dome, STI 0.3–0.4, and is unintelligible in the aisles and galleries, where STI is below 0.2; similarly the high T values (Center Time, time of the center of gravity of the squared impulse response) measured indicate poor clarity. See http://www.odeon.dk/acoustics-ancient-church-hagia-sofia, site visited April 26, 2010.

24. San Vitale offers a good comparison with respect to acoustics suited for monody. See Knight, "Archaeoacoustics of a Sixth-Century Christian Structure."

25. Woszczyk, "Acoustics of Hagia Sophia," 4.

26. Ibid., and Moran, "Choir of the Hagia Sophia," 7. On the same acoustic effect produced by the dome of San Vitale, see Knight, "Archaeoacoustics of a Sixth-Century Christian Structure," 136. For a general discussion of the acoustics of domes, see H. Kuttruff, *Room Acoustics,* 5th ed. (London: Spoon Press, 2009), 117–20, fig. 4.13.

27. On the character of Hagia Sophia's acoustics, see Jonathan S. Abel et al., "Recreation of the Acoustics of Hagia Sophia in Stanford's Bing Concert Hall for the Concert Performance and Recording of Cappella Romana" (paper presented at the International Symposium on Room Acoustics, Toronto, Canada, June 9–11, 2013), ftp://s00279.cisti.nrc.ca/outgoing/CD_ISRA2013/Papers/P055.pdf, 2–3, accessed January 10, 2014, and Woszczyk, "Acoustics of Hagia Sophia," 4.

28. Woszczyk, "Acoustics of Hagia Sophia," 4.

29. In the present context the term "anechoic," which means "free from echoes and reverberations," should be understood relatively, signifying a performance conducted with close miking, which picks up minimal room acoustics.

30. Listen to music sample 7 at https://hagiasophia.stanford.edu.

31. John G. Neuhoff, "Ecological Psychoacoustics: Introduction and History," in *Ecological Psychoacoustics,* ed. John G. Neuhoff (Amsterdam: Elsevier Academic Press, 2004), 1–13. I thank Miriam Kolar for bringing this study to my attention. David M. Howard and Jamie A. S. Angus, *Acoustics and Psychoacoustics,* 4th ed. (Amsterdam: Focal, 2009). Eberhard Zwicker and Hugo Fastl, *Psychoacoustics: Facts and Models,* Springer Series in Information Sciences 22 (repr., Berlin: Springer, 2007). Reverberation is mostly studied in the context of the modern period. For the psychoacoustic effects of reverb in the recording of popular music, see Peter Doyle, *Echo and Reverb: Fabricating Space in Popular Music Recording, 1900–1960* (Middletown: Wesleyan University Press, 2005), 64–234.

32. Blesser and Salter, *Spaces Speak,* 260–72. Vesa Välimäki et al., "Fifty Years of Artificial Reverberation," *IEEE Transactions on Audio, Speech, and Language Processing* 20 (2012): 1421–48.

33. Blesser and Salter, *Spaces Speak,* 122–23.

34. Sterne, "Space Within Space," 120–27.

35. Doyle, *Echo and Reverb,* 14. Sterne, "Space Within Space," 124–27.

36. Blesser and Salter, *Spaces Speak,* 266–67, 273.

37. Ibid., 239–46.

38. Ibid., 244.

39. The name of the software is Odeon®.

40. See http://www.odeon.dk/byzantine-hymns-churches-constantinople, accessed April 20, 2011.

41. Balloons are among the sound sources recommended. See Francesco Martellotta et al., "Guidelines for Acoustical Measurements in Churches," *Applied Acoustics* 70, no. 2 (2009): 378–88, esp. 386.

42. Abel et al., "Estimating Room Impulse Responses."

43. Ibid. For this recording the Greek Byzantine Choir of Lycourgos Angelopoulos sang the Cheroubikon in the refectory of Fontevraud Abbey. *The Divine Liturgy of St. John Chrysostom* (Paris: Opus 111, 1993), compact disc, OPS 30–78. The version of the Cheroubikon hymn performed was originally composed by Gregorios Protopsaltes (1778–1821). On Protopsaltes, see Alexander Lingas, "Gregorios the Protopsaltes." *Grove Music Online*, accessed March 12, 2010.

44. Listen to music sample 6 at https://hagiasophia.stanford.edu.

45. See http://www.cappellaromana.org, site visited December 5, 2014.

46. See http://iconsofsound.stanford.edu/auralization.html.

47. Abel and Kurt Werner. "Live Auralization of Cappella Romana." See https://ccrma.stanford.edu/~njb /research/AES129_Balloon_Slides.pdf, site visited September 2, 2015.

48. Abel and Kurt Werner. "Live Auralization of Cappella Romana." Abel et al., "Recreation of the Acoustics of Hagia Sophia"; Fernando Lopez-Lezcano et al., "Byzantium in Bing: Live Virtual Acoustics Employing Free Software," https://ccrma.stanford.edu/~nando/publications/hagia_sophia_lac2013.pdf, accessed July 10, 2013; Jonathan S. Abel et al., "Prokeimenon for the Feast of St. Basil (12th Century)," from the concert *Transitions 2011, Night 1: Acousmatic Soundscapes Under the stars*, Center for Computer Research in Music and Acoustics, Stanford University, September 28, 2011.

49. For VAT, see http://sites.music.mcgill.ca/vat, and for CIRMMT (Centre for Interdisciplinary Research in Music Media and Technology), http://www.cirmmit.org. Wiesław Woszczyk, "Active Acoustics in Concert Halls—A New Approach," *Archives of Acoustics* 36, no. 2 (2011): 1–14. Wiesław Woszczyk, Doyuen Ko, and Brett Leonard, "Virtual Acoustics at the Service of Music Performance and Recording," *Archives of Acoustics* 37, no. 1 (2012): 109–13. Idem, "Virtual Stage Acoustics: A Flexible Tool for Providing Useful Sounds for Musicians," *Proceedings of the International Symposium on Room Acoustics*, ISRA, August 29–31, 2010, Melbourne, Australia, 1–8, http://www.acoustics.asn.au/conference_proceedings/ICA2010/cdrom-ISRA2010/Papers /01e.pdf, accessed September 15, 2015. For the recordings done using VAT at CIRMMT, see Tom Beghin, Martha de Francisco, and Wiesław Woszczyk, *The Virtual Haydn: Complete Works for Solo Keyboard* (Hong Kong: Naxos Blu-Ray Audio, 2009).

50. Abel and Kurt Werner. "Live Auralization of Cappella Romana"; Abel et al., "Recreation of the acoustics of Hagia Sophia"; Lopez-Lezcano et al., "Byzantium in Bing"; Abel et al., "Prokeimenon for the Feast of St. Basil."

51. Abel and Kurt Werner. "Live Auralization of Cappella Romana." Abel et al., "Recreation of the Acoustics of Hagia Sophia," 6.

52. Each chorister was wired with a microphone transmitting his or her voice on an independent channel. To reduce the chance of feedback, each device, pointing downward, was taped onto the forehead of the singer, so that it caught minimum interfering sound from the room and from nearby singers. The microphone signals were sent to wireless receivers in a technical room beside the hall. From there the signals were routed to the hall's main mixer for level control and signal equalization and on to an audio workstation for mixing, processing, and projection into the hall. For technical details, see Abel et al., "Recreation of the Acoustics of Hagia Sophia," 8–9. On the rigging system of Bing Hall, see Randi Minetor, "J. R. Clancy Provides Custom Rigging Solutions for Bing Concert Hall at Stanford University," *LiveDesign*, February 11, 2013, at http://livedesignonline .com/blog/j-r-clancy-provides-custom-rigging-solutions-bing-concert-hall-stanford-university.

53. Abel and Kurt Werner. "Live Auralization of Cappelle Romana." Abel et al., "Recreation of the Acoustics of Hagia Sophia," 9, and for the concert, see video at http://hagiasophia.stanford.edu.

54. For the Icons of Sound engineering experiment with live auralization using Cappella Romana's concert of Byzantine chant at Stanford's Bing Hall, see https://hagiasophia.stanford.edu, video 2; see also www.youtube .com/watch?v=uKLkJJ3ftIw and www.youtube.com/watch?v=bHpOiX2sO-s. For a review of the event, http://www.sfcv.org/reviews/stanford-live/cappella-romana-time-travel-to-constantinople and http://live .stanford.edu/programnotes/cap2Feature.pdf.

55. Stephen Hinton, "A Note on the Vineyard Style," *Stanford Live*, January 2013, 11–12, and Cynthia Haven, "Finely Tuned," *Stanford Magazine*, January/February 2013, 46–53. Olcott's design is inspired by Hans Scharoun and Edgar Wisniewski's Berlin Philharmonic Hall, 1960–63. Edgar Wisniewski, *Die Berliner Philharmonie und ihr Kammermusiksaal: Der Konzertsaal als Zentralraum* (Berlin: Gebrüder Mann, 1993).

56. Lev Manovich, "The Poetics of Augmented Space," *Visual Communication* 5, no. 2 (2006): 219–40. Sterne, "Space Within Space," 120.

57. Manovich, "Poetics of Augmented Space," 220–21, 224–25, 229.

58. Ibid., 226.

59. Thompson, *Soundscape of Modernity,* 1–293.

60. Ibid., 33–45.

61. Henry L. Bottomley, "The Story of St. Thomas' Church," *Architectural Record* 35 (1914): 101–31.

62. Thompson, *Soundscape of Modernity,* 180–90. On the Gustavino vaulting and new artificial stone, see George R. Collins, "The Transfer of Thin Masonry Vaulting from Spain to America," *Journal of the Society of Architectural Historians* 27, no. 3 (1968): 176–201.

63. Richard Pounds, Daniel Raichel, and Martin Weaver, "The Unseen World of Guastavino Acoustical Tile Construction: History, Development, Production," *APT Bulletin* 30 (1999): 33–39. In the late twentieth century, sealer was applied to the Akoustolith tiles in order to increase the reverberation in the space and thus make it more suitable for sacred music. See James G. Ferguson Jr. and Robert B. Newman, "Gothic Sound for the Neo-Gothic Chapel of Duke University," *Journal of the Acoustical Society of America* 66, no. 1 (1979): S26.

64. David Lloyd Klepper, "The Acoustics of St. Thomas Church, Fifth Avenue," *Journal of the Audio Engineering Society* 43, nos. 7–8 (1995): 599–601.

65. Thompson, *Soundscape of Modernity,* 3.

66. Ibid., 3, 7, 171–72, 243.

67. Ibid., 229–35.

68. Ibid., 233; Blesser and Salter, *Spaces Speak,* 109–11.

69. Blesser and Salter, *Spaces Speak,* 109–116.

70. Thompson, *Soundscape of Modernity,* 243.

71. Gade, "Acoustics in Halls for Speech and Music," 313–14.

72. Thompson, *Soundscape of Modernity,* 248–53.

73. Blesser and Salter, *Spaces Speak,* 62–63.

74. Ibid., 145.

75. Yolande Harris, "The Building as Instrument," in Bandt, Duffy, and MacKinnon, *Hearing Places,* 404–11.

76. Ibid., 405.

77. See the video at https://hagiasophia.stanford.edu.

78. Ibid., 409.

79. Michel Chion, "Wasted Words," in *Sound Theory / Sound Practice,* ed. Rick Altman (New York: Routledge), 104–110.

80. Michel Chion, *The Voice in Cinema,* trans. Claudia Gorbman (New York: Columbia University Press, 1999), 16–29.

81. Kaldellis, "Making of Hagia Sophia"; Nadine Schibille, "The Profession of the Architect in Late Antique Byzantium," *Byzantion* 79 (2009): 360–79; George Leonard Huxley, *Anthemius of Tralles: A Study of Later Greek Geometry,* Greek, Roman, and Byzantine Monographs 1 (Cambridge, Mass.: Eaton Press, 1959), 6–19; Glanville Downey, "Byzantine Architects: Their Training and Methods," *Byzantion* 18 (1948): 99–118, esp. 112–14; Alan Cameron, "Isidore of Miletus and Hypatia: On the Editing of Mathematical Texts," *Greek, Roman, and Byzantine Studies* 31 (1990): 103–27.

82. Judith McKenzie, *The Architecture of Alexandria and Egypt, c. 300 B.C. to A.D. 700* (New Haven: Yale University Press, 2007), 134–35, 322–50; S. Cuomo, *Technology and Culture in Greek and Roman Antiquity* (Cambridge: Cambridge University Press, 2007), 131–64; Kaldellis, "Making of Hagia Sophia." On the transmission of Hellenistic science in Alexandria, see Lucio Russo, *The Forgotten Revolution: How Science Was Born in 300 BC and Why It Had to Be Reborn* (Berlin: Springer, 2004), 329–97.

83. McKenzie, *Architecture of Alexandria and Egypt,* 134–35, 234–35, 251, 282, 324–50. Judith McKenzie, *The Architecture of Petra* (Oxford: Oxford University Press, 1990, repr., Oxford: Oxbow Press, 2005), 51, 138, figs. 75, 76b. Jürgen J. Rasch, "Die Kuppel in der römischen Architektur: Entwicklung, Formgebung, Konstruktion," *Architectura* 15 (1985): 117–139.

84. The treatises of Heron of Alexandria (active around 62 C.E.) on stereometry and optics were part of the curriculum for *mechanikoi*. McKenzie, *Architecture of Alexandria and Egypt*, 322–28.

85. On Anthemius's engineering of special effects such as the sound of thunder or the earthquake, see Agathias, *Histories* 5.6.7–5.8.5; discussed in Ernst Darmstädter, "Anthemios und sein 'künstliches Erdbeben' in Byzanz," *Philologus* 88 (1933): 477–82, and Kaldellis, "Making of Hagia Sophia." The following studies engage only the architectural form and engineering of the dome in Hagia Sophia and do not address the acoustics: Shiro Kato et al., "Finite-Element Modeling of the First and Second Domes of Hagia Sophia," in Mark and Çakmak, *Hagia Sophia from the Age of Justinian to the Present*, 103–19; Rabun Taylor, "A Literary and Structural Analysis of the First Dome on Justinian's Hagia Sophia, Constantinople," *Journal of the Society of Architectural Historians* 55 (1996): 66–78.

86. Nadine Schibille, "Astronomical and Optical Principles in the Architecture of Hagia Sophia in Constantinople," *Science in Context* 22 (2009): 27–46; Iakovos Potamianos and Wassim Jabi, "Interactive Parametric Design and the Role of Light in Byzantine Churches," in *Communicating Space(s): Proceedings of the 24th Conference on Education in Computer Aided Design in Europe, 6.–9.9.2006*, ed. Vassilis Bourdakis and Dimitris Charitos (Volos: University of Thessaly, 2006), 798–803; Wassim Jabi and Iakovos Potamianos, "Geometry, Light, and Cosmology in the Church of Hagia Sophia," *International Journal of Architectural Computing* 5, no. 2 (2007): 303–19; and Iakovos Potamianos, "The Mathematics of the Ideal Dome," in *Aesthetics and Architectural Composition: Proceedings of the Dresden International Symposium of Architecture 2004*, ed. Ralf Weber and Matthias Albrecht Amann (Mammendorf: Pro Literatur Verlag, 2005), 66–72.

87. Isidore was a professor of geometry and mechanics and was allegedly responsible for the design of a special compass for drawing parabolas. Schibille, "Astronomical and Optical Principles," 40; Robert G. Ousterhout, *Master Builders of Byzantium* (Princeton: Princeton University Press, 1999), 44; Alan Cameron, "Isidore of Miletus and Hypatia."

88. On Anthemius's interest in optics, see Schibille, "Astronomical and Optical Principles," 40; Alan Cameron, "Isidore of Miletus and Hypatia." Huxley, *Anthemius of Tralles*, 1–43; Downey, "Byzantine Architects," 112–14.

89. Agathias, *Histories*, 5.6.7–5.8.5, and Darmstädter, "Anthemius und sein 'künstliches Erdbeben.'"

90. Kaldellis, "Making of Hagia Sophia."

91. Alan Cameron, "Isidore of Miletus and Hypatia," 122; Anthony Cutler, "Structure and Aesthetic at Hagia Sophia in Constantinople," *Journal of Aesthetics and Art Criticism* 25 (1966): 27–35.

92. Mainstone, *Hagia Sophia*, 149–217; Müller-Wiener, *Bildlexikon zur Topographie Istanbuls*, 112–17 (Hagia Eirēnē), 177–83 (Sts. Sergius and Bacchus); Jonathan Badrill, "The Church of Sts. Sergius and Bacchus in Constantinople and the Monophysite Refugees," *Dumbarton Oaks Papers* 54 (2000): 1–11; Helge Svenshon and Rudolf H. W. Stichel, "Neue Beobachtungen an der ehemaligen Kirche der Heiligen Sergios und Bakchos (Küçük Ayasofya Camisi) in Istanbul," *Istanbuler Mitteilungen* 50 (2000): 389–409; Tassos Papacostas, "The Medieval Progeny of the Holy Apostles: Trails of Architectural Imitation Across the Mediterranean," in *The Byzantine World*, ed. Paul Stephenson (New York: Routledge, 2010), 386–405; Andreas Thiel, *Die Johanneskirche in Ephesos* (Wiesbaden: Reichert, 2005), 37–48; Joseph D. Alchermes, "Art and Architecture in the Age of Justinian," in *The Cambridge Companion to the Age of Justinian*, ed. Michael Maas (Cambridge: Cambridge University Press, 2005), 343–75. The church of St. Polyeuktos might be included in this group, although there is an ongoing debate whether the building had a dome. R. M. Harrison, *Excavations at Saraçhane in Istanbul* (Princeton: Princeton University Press; Washington, D.C.: Dumbarton Oaks Research Library and Collection, 1986), 1:406–11; Jonathan Badrill, "A New Temple for Byzantium: Anicia Juliana, King Solomon, and the Gilded Ceiling of the Church of St. Polyeuktos in Constantinople," in *Social and Political Life In Late Antiquity*, ed. William Bowden, Adam Gutteridge, and Carlos Machado, Late Antique Archaeology 3.1 (Leiden: Brill, 2006), 339–70.

93. Ćurčić, "Design and Structural Innovation."

94. Chris Scarre, "Sound, Place, and Space: Towards an Archaeology of Acoustics," in Scarre and Lawson, *Archaeoacoustics*, 1–10.

95. On average the RT increases by two seconds. This conclusion can be gleaned from the objective parameters measured and recorded in a select group of Early Christian and Romanesque basilicas in Cirillo and Martellotta, *Worship, Acoustics, and Architecture,* 52–94, 201, 206.

96. Scarre, "Sound, Place, and Space," 8–9.

97. Kenneth John Conant, *Carolingian and Romanesque Architecture, 800 to 1200* (Harmondsworth: Penguin Books, 1974), 187, discussed in Scarre, "Sound, Place, and Space," 8–9.

98. Cirillo and Martellotta, *Worship, Acoustics, and Architecture,* 5: "In fact, the idea that a space must fit a specific kind of music (or sound experience) is relatively new and basically derives from functionalism according to which form follows function."

99. Software such as CATT® or Odeon®. Gade, "Acoustics in Halls for Speech and Music," 302–3, 316–46.

100. Blesser and Salter, *Spaces Speak,* 5; see also 68, 86, 89, 90, 93. The Greek theater buildings exhibit acoustics that foster the transmission of human speech with great clarity, but no textual records attest that the design decision to use such dry acoustics was based on consideration of function. Eleonora Rocconi, "Theatres and Theatre Design in the Graeco-Roman World: Theoretical and Empirical Approaches," in Scarre and Lawson, *Archaeoacoustics,* 71–76.

101. J. B. Ward-Perkins, "Constantine and the Origins of the Christian Basilica," *Papers of the British School at Rome* 22 (1954): 69–90; Richard Krautheimer, "The Constantinian Basilica," *Dumbarton Oaks Papers* 21 (1967): 115–40; Gregory T. Armstrong, "Constantine's Churches: Symbol and Structure," *Journal of the Society of Architectural Historians* 33, no. 1 (1974): 5–16. Krautheimer, *Early Christian and Byzantine Architecture,* 39–199.

102. Claudia Barsanti, "L'esportazione di marmi dal Proconneso nelle regioni pontiche durante il IV–VI secolo," *Rivista dell'Istituto nazionale d'archeologia e storia dell'arte* 12 (1989): 91–220; Nuşin Asgari, "The Proconnesian Production of Architectural Elements in Late Antiquity, Based on Evidence from the Marble Quarries," in *Constantinople and Its Hinterland: Papers from the Twenty-Seventh Spring Symposium of Byzantine Studies, Oxford, April 1993,* ed. Cyril Mango and Gilbert Dagron (Aldershot: Ashgate, 1995), 263–88; Jean-Pierre Sodini, "Marble and Stoneworking in Byzantium: Seventh–Fifteenth Centuries," in *The Economic History of Byzantium: From the Seventh Through the Fifteenth Century,* ed. Angeliki E. Laiou (Washington, D.C.: Dumbarton Oaks Research Library and Collection, 2002), 1:129–46; Patrizio Pensabene, "Le principali cave di marmo bianco," in *I marmi colorati della Roma imperiale,* ed. Marilda De Nuccio and Lucrezia Ungaro (Venice: Marsilio, 2002), 203–5; Yuri Alessandro Marano, *Il commercio del marmo nell'Adriatico tardoantico (IV–VI secolo d.C.): Scambi, maestranze, committenze* (Ph.D. diss., University of Padua, 2008); Michael Greenhalgh, *Marble Past, Monumental Present: Building with Antiquities in the Mediaeval Mediterranean,* The Medieval Mediterranean 80 (Leiden: Brill, 2009), 69–81, 99–100, 113, 133.

103. Shankland and Shankland, "Acoustics of St. Peter's"; Cirillo and Martellota, *Worship, Acoustics, and Architecture,* 9–16, 51–60.

104. Cirillo and Martellota, *Worship, Acoustics, and Architecture,* 9–16, 51–60.

105. William L. MacDonald, *The Pantheon: Design, Meaning, and Progeny* (London: Lane, 1976).

106. Laura Salah Nasrallah, "Empire and Apocalypse in Thessaloniki: Interpreting the Early Christian Rotunda," *Journal of Early Christian Studies* 13, no. 4 (2005): 465–508; I. G. Iliadis, "The Natural Lighting in the Dome of the Rotunda in Thessaloniki," *Lighting Research and Technology* 37 (2005): 183–97.

107. Emmanuel G. Tzekakis, "Reverberation Time of the Rotunda of Thessaloniki," *Journal of the Acoustical Society of America* 57, no. 5 (1975): 1207–9; Panagiotis Karampatzakes, "Akoustikes metrēseis se 11 byzantinous naous tēs Thessalonikēs" (unpublished manuscript). I thank the author for sharing his manuscript with me.

108. Blesser and Salter, *Spaces Speak,* 82–83.

109. Robert S. Nelson, ed., *Visuality Before and Beyond the Renaissance: Seeing as Others Saw* (New York: Cambridge University Press, 2000).

110. Mateos, *Le Typicon de la Grande Église,* 2:283 (*anagnōstēs* and *antiphōnon*), 328–29 (*psaltai*); Lingas, "Sunday Matins," 80–88; Taft, "Christian Liturgical Psalmody."

111. Blesser and Salter, *Spaces Speak*, 63.

112. Socrates, *Historia Ecclesiastica*, bk. 6, in PG 67, cols. 689C–691A, discussed in Moran, *Singers in Late Byzantine and Slavonic Painting*, 25.

113. John Francis Baldovin, *The Urban Character of Christian Worship: The Origins, Development, and Meaning of Stational Liturgy*, Orientalia Christiana analecta 228 (Rome: Pontificium Institutum Studiorum Orientalium, 1987).

114. Lingas, "Sunday Matins," 27–37; Taft, "Christian Liturgical Psalmody." Robert F. Taft, *Liturgy of the Hours in the East and West: The Origins of the Divine Office and Its Meaning for Today* (Collegeville, Minn.: Liturgical Press, 1993), 33–34, 42–48, 211–13, 273–91.

115. Psalm 140 as a fixed psalm for vespers was introduced into Constantinople from the cathedral liturgy of Antioch in the fourth century. Hanke, *Vesper und Orthros*, 1:167 and 2:287, 345–48; Alexander Lingas, "Festal Cathedral Vespers in Late Byzantium," *Orientalia christiana periodica* 63 (1997): 421–59; Miguel Arranz, "L'office de l'Asmatikos Hesperinos ('vêpres chantées') de l'ancien Euchologe byzantin," *Orientalia christiana periodica* 44 (1978): 107–30, 391–419.

116. Hanke, *Vesper und Orthros*, 2:631–34, nos. 8, 15; Parenti and Velkovska, *Eucologio Barberini gr. 336*, prayer 56, 52–53; prayer 63, 59–60.

117. Strunk, "Byzantine Office at Hagia Sophia"; Miguel Arranz, "La liturgie des heures selon l'ancien Euchologe byzantin," in *Eulogia: Miscellanea liturgica in onore di P. Burkhard Neunheuser O.S.B.*, Studia Anselmiana 68, Analecta liturgica 1 (1979): 1–19; Taft, *Liturgy of the Hours*; Lingas, "Sunday Matins"; Stefano Parenti, "The Cathedral Rite of Constantinople: Evolution of a Local Tradition," *Orientalia christiana periodica* 77 (2011): 449–69; Hanke, *Vesper und Orthros*.

118. Lingas, "From Earth to Heaven"; Hanke, *Vesper und Orthros*, 2:285, 295–300; on the attribution of the "distributed Psalter" to Patriarch Anthimos, as witnessed in the eleventh-century Vatican manuscript BAV gr. 342, see I. B. Pitra, ed., *Iuris Ecclesiastici Graecorum Historia et Monumenta Iussu Pii ix. Pont. Max.*, vol. 2 (Rome: Typis Collegii Urbani, 1868), 209.

119. Hanke, *Vesper und Orthros*, 2:390–91. Strunk, "Byzantine Office at Hagia Sophia," 200–202.

120. Hanke, *Vesper und Orthros*, 2:390–91. The Constantinopolitan office has fourteen odes; the Palestinian, nine.

121. Troelsgård, *Byzantine Neumes*, 76–78; the manuscripts include Paris, BnF, MS gr. 261, and Grottaferrata, MSS gr. E.α. 2, Γ.γ. 2, Γ.γ. 4, and Γ.γ. 7.

122. Athens, National Library, MSS gr. 2062 (late fourteenth century) and gr. 2061 (first quarter of the fifteenth century).

123. Listen to music sample 5 at https://hagiasophia.stanford.edu. Hanke, *Vesper und Orthros*, 2:342–49. Lingas, "Festal Cathedral Vespers in Late Byzantium." Alexander Lingas, with the Greek Byzantine Choir (dir. Lycourgos Angelopoulos), reconstructed a vespers service according to the cathedral rite of Hagia Sophia in the Chapel of St. Peter's College, Oxford, Saturday May 26, 2001.

124. Τὴν σωτήριόν σου ἔγερσιν δοξάζομεν, φιλάνθρωπε. Only a single manuscript (Athens, National Library, MS gr. 899, fols. 194v–195r, fifteenth century) records the melody of this *kekragarion*.

125. Lingas, "Festal Cathedral Vespers in Late Byzantium," 437, 443, 457.

126. Hanke, *Vesper und Orthros*, 2:631–35; Parenti and Velkovska, *Eucologio Barberini gr. 336*, 42–60, specifically prayers 47.5, 48.5, 53.2, 59.2, 63.2, 64.3.

127. Hans Ulrich Gumbrecht, "The Charm of Charms," in *A New History of German Literature*, ed. David E. Wellbery (Cambridge: Harvard University Press, 2005), 1–7.

128. Taft, *Liturgy of the Hours*, 55–56; Lingas, "Sunday Matins," 30, 32; Evangelia Spyrakou, *Singers' Choirs According to the Byzantine Tradition*, Institute of Byzantine Musicology Studies 14 (Athens: Institute of Byzantine Musicology, 2008), 407–9. I thank Christian Troelsgård for this last reference.

129. Maximus the Confessor, *Mystagogia*, chap. 5, in PG 91, col. 676B; English translation in Stead, *The Church, The Liturgy, and the Soul of Man*, 75.

130. καὶ ὡς διὰ θυσιαστηρίου τοῦ νοός, τὴν ἐν ἀδύτοις πολυύμνητον τῆς ἀφανοῦς καὶ ἀγνώστου μεγαλοφωνίας σιγὴν τῆς θεότητος δι᾽ ἄλλης λάλου τε καὶ πολυφθόγγου σιγῆς προσκαλούμενον. Maximus the Confessor, *Mystagogia*, chap. 4, in PG 91, col. 672C; English translation in Stead, *The Church, The Liturgy, and the Soul of Man*, 72.

131. Schafer, *Soundscape*, 15–21, 118, 170–71. Doyle, *Echo and Reverb*, 37.

Chapter 5

1. The original Greek for this chapter's epigraph:

Καὶ τίς ἐριγδούποισι χανὼν στομάτεσσιν Ὁμήρου
μαρμαρέους λειμῶνας ἀολλισθέντας ἀείσει
ἠλιβάτου νηοῖο κραταιπαγέας περὶ τοίχους
καὶ πέδον εὐρυθέμειλον;

The translation in the text is my own.

2. Michael John Roberts, *The Jeweled Style: Poetry and Poetics in Late Antiquity* (Ithaca: Cornell University Press, 1989); Gianfranco Agosti, "Niveaux de style, littérarité, poétiques: Pour une histoire du système de la poésie classicisante au vie siècle," in *"Doux remède . . .": Poésie et poétique à Byzance,* ed. Paolo Odorico, Panagiotis A. Agapitos, and Martin Hinterberger, Dossiers byzantins 9 (Paris: Centre d'études byzantines, néo-hélleniques et sud-est européenes, 2008), 99–119; idem, "Immagini e poesia nella tarda antichità: Per uno studio dell'estetica visuale della poesia greca fra iii e vi sec. d.C.," *Incontri triestini di filologia classica* 4 (2004–5): 351–74; Jaś Elsner, "Late Antique Art: The Problem of the Concept and the Cumulative Aesthetic," in *Approaching Late Antiquity,* ed. Simon Swain and Mark Edwards (Oxford: Oxford University Press, 2004), 271–309. On the aesthetic of glitter (*poikilia*) in Nonnus of Panopolis (mid- to late fifth century c.e.), whose poetry and style Paul the Silentiary emulates, see Martin String, *Untersuchungen zum Stil der Dionysiaka des Nonnos von Panopolis* (Ph.D. diss., University of Hamburg, 1966), 33–70, and Antoni Gonzalez-Senmartí, "La ποικιλία como principio estilistico de las *Dionisiacas* de Nono," *Anuari de filologia* 7 (1981): 101–7.

3. Roberts, *Jeweled Style,* 38–65. On *varietas,* see also Jaś Elsner, "From the Culture of Spolia to the Cult of Relics: The Arch of Constantine and the Genesis of Late Antique Forms," *Papers of the British School at Rome* 68 (2000): 149–84; on the perception of color in Byzantium as brilliance rather than hue, Liz James, *Light and Colour in Byzantine Art* (Oxford: Clarendon Press, 1996).

4. Roberts, *Jeweled Style,* 55.

5. Agosti, "Niveaux de style, littérarité, poétiques," and idem, "Immagini e poesia nella tarda antichità."

6. Fobelli, *Un tempio per Giustiniano,* 15–31; Mary Whitby, "The Occasion of Paul the Silentiary's Ekphrasis of S. Sophia," *Classical Quarterly* 35, no. 1 (1985): 215–28; Ruth Macrides and Paul Magdalino, "The Architecture of Ekphrasis: Construction and Context of Paul the Silentiary's Poem on Hagia Sophia," *Byzantine and Modern Greek Studies* 12 (1988), 47–82; Kenneth Rainsbury Dark and Jan Kostenec, "A New Archaeological Study of Hagia Sophia, Istanbul," in *Proceedings of the 22nd International Congress of Byzantine Studies, Sofia, 22–27 August 2011,* vol. 1, ed. Iliya Iliev (Sofia: Bulgarian Historical Heritage Foundation, 2011), 213–37. Schibille, *Hagia Sophia,* 97–127.

7. Schibille, *Hagia Sophia,* 43–171; Pentcheva, "Hagia Sophia and Multisensory Aesthetics."

8. It is this spiritual aspect that my work adds to the now extensive bibliography of ekphrasis in premodern Greek and Latin literature: Andrew Sprague Becker, *The Shield of Achilles and the Poetics of Ekphrasis* (London: Rowman & Littlefield, 1995); James A. W. Heffernan, *Museum of Words: The Poetics of Ekphrasis from Homer to Ashbery* (Chicago: University of Chicago Press, 1993); W. J. T. Mitchell, *Picture Theory: Essays on Verbal and Visual Representation* (Chicago: University of Chicago Press, 1994); Simon Goldhill and Robin Osborne, eds., *Art and Text in Ancient Greek Culture* (Cambridge: Cambridge University Press, 1994); Jaś Elsner, ed., *Art and Text in Roman Culture* (Cambridge: Cambridge University Press, 1996); James Elkins, *On Pictures and the Words That Fail Them* (Cambridge: Cambridge University Press, 1998); the essays edited by Jaś Elsner in *Ramus* 31 (2002); Liz James, ed., *Art and Text in Byzantine Culture* (Cambridge: Cambridge University Press, 2006); Ruth Webb, *Ekphrasis, Imagination, and Persuasion in Ancient Rhetorical Theory and Practice* (Farnham: Ashgate, 2009); Michael Squire, *Image and Text in Graeco-Roman Antiquity* (Cambridge: Cambridge University Press, 2009); idem, "Making Myron's Cow Moo? Ekphrastic Epigram and the Poetics of Simulation," *American Journal of Philology* 131 (2010), 589–634; idem, "Reading a View: Poem and Picture in the Greek Anthology," *Ramus* 39 (2010), 73–103; Akiko Motoyoshi Sumi, *Description in Classical Arabic Poetry: Waṣf, Ekphrasis, and Interarts Theory* (Leiden: Brill, 2004).

9. Whitby, "Occasion of Paul the Silentiary's Ekphrasis," and Macrides and Magdalino, "Architecture of Ekphrasis."

10. κρίνει δὲ τούτους οὐ κυαμοτρῶξ Ἀττικός,
     ἀλλ' ἄνδρες εὐσεβεῖς τε καὶ συγγνώμονες,
     οἷς καὶ τὸ θεῖον καὶ βασιλεὺς ἐφήδεται,
     οἱ τὰς πόλεις τάττοντες, οἱ τὰς ἡνίας
     ὅλων ἔχοντες καὶ λόγων καὶ πραγμάτων.
     Paul the Silentiary, *Descriptio S. Sophiae*, vv. 125–29; English translation in Bell, *Three Political Voices*, 195.

11. Alan Cameron, "Poetry and Literary Culture in Late Antiquity," in *Approaching Late Antiquity: The Transformation from Early to Late Empire*, ed. Simon Swain and Mark Edwards (Oxford: Oxford University Press, 2004), 327–54.

12. Paul the Silentiary, *Descriptio S. Sophiae*, vv. 617–20. Agosti, "Niveaux de style, littérarité, poétiques"; Bell, *Three Political Voices*, 16; Fobelli, *Un tempio per Giustiniano*, 9, 13 n. 2. Glanville Downey, *Constantinople in the Age of Justinian* (Norman: University of Oklahoma Press, 1960), 147–64, esp. 159.

13. James W. Halporn, Martin Oswald, and Thomas G. Rosenmeyer, *The Meters of Greek and Latin Poetry* (London: Methuen, 1963), 10, 14. M. L. West, *Greek Metre* (Oxford: Clarendon Press, 1982), 35, 39–40.

14. Jaś Elsner, "The Rhetoric of Buildings in the *De Aedificiis* of Procopius," in James, *Art and Text in Byzantine Culture*, 33–57, and Macrides and Magdalino, "Architecture of Ekphrasis."

15. Alessandra Guiglia Guidobaldi and Claudia Barsanti, eds., *Santa Sofia di Costantinopoli: L'arredo marmoreo della grande chiesa giustinianea*, Studi di antichità cristiana 60 (Vatican City: Pontificio istituto di archeologia Cristiana, 2004); Alessandra Guiglia Guidobaldi, "I marmi di Giustiniano: Sectilia parietali nella Santa Sofia di Costantinopoli," in *Medioevo mediterraneo: L'Occidente, Bisanzio e l'Islam; Atti del Convegno internazionale di studi, Parma, 21–25 settembre 2004*, ed. Arturo Carlo Quintavalle, I convegni di Parma 7 (Milan: Mondadori Electa, 2007), 160–174.

16. Eugenio Russo, *Le decorazioni di Isidoro il Giovane per S. Sofia di Costantinopoli* (Rome: Viella, 2011).

17. Bente Kiilerich, "The Aesthetic Viewing of Marble in Byzantium: From Global Impression to Focal Attention," *Arte medievale*, 4th ser., 2 (2012): 9–28.

18. Barry, "Walking on Water."

19. Majeska, "Notes on the Archaeology of St. Sophia."

20. MacDonald, *Pantheon*, 35. Federico Guidobaldi and Alessandra Guiglia Guidobaldi, *Pavimenti marmorei di Roma dal IV al IX secolo*, Studi di antichità cristiana 36 (Vatican City: Pontificio istituto di archeologia cristiana, 1983). See also the fourth-century floor of a patrician house in Rome, in Fulvia Bianchi, Matthias Bruno, and Marilda De Nuccio, "La Domus Sopra le Sette Sale: La decorazione pavimentale e parietale dell'aula absidata," in De Nuccio and Ungaro, *I marmi colorati della Roma imperiale*, 161–69.

21. Barry, "Walking on Water," 627–32, and W. R. Lethaby, "Pavements like the Sea," in *Architecture, Mysticism, and Myth*, 2nd ed. (London: Percival, 1892; repr., Mineola, N.Y.: Dover, 2004), 201–20.

22. Theophrastus, *De lapidibus*, ed. and trans. D. E. Eichholz (Oxford: Clarendon Press, 1965), and Robert Halleux, *Le problème des métaux dans la science antique* (Paris: Société d'édition Les belles lettres, 1974); Barry, "Walking on Water," 631–32.

23. Barry, "Walking on Water," 632–34.

24. Barsanti, "L'esportazione di marmi dal Proconneso"; Asgari, "Proconnesian Production of Architectural Elements"; Sodini, "Marble and Stoneworking in Byzantium"; Pensabene, "Le principali cave di marmo bianco," 203–5; Marano, *Il commercio del marmo*; Greenhalgh, *Marble Past, Monumental Present*, 69–81, 99–100, 113, 133.

25. See, by J. B. Ward-Perkins, "Materials, Quarries, and Transportation," "The Roman System in Operation," "The Trade in Sarcophagi," and "Nicomedia and the Marble Trade," all in *Marble in Antiquity: Collected Papers of J. B. Ward-Perkins*, ed. Hazel Dodge and Bryan Ward-Perkins, Archaeological Monographs of the British School at Rome 6 (London: British School at Rome, 1992), 13–22, 23–30, 31–38, 61–105, and Dario Monna and Patrizio Pensabene, *Marmi dell'Asia Minore* (Rome: Consiglio nazionale delle ricerche, 1977), 147–74.

26. Asgari, "Proconnesian Production of Architectural Elements"; Barsanti, "L'esportazione di marmi dal Proconneso."

27. Barsanti, "L'esportazione di marmi dal Proconneso," 102–10. Ward-Perkins, "Trade in Sarcophagi"; Sodini, "Marble and Stoneworking in Byzantium," 134–35. Friedrich Wilhelm Deichmann, *Ravenna, Hauptstadt des spätantiken Abendlandes* (Wiesbaden: F. Steiner, 1976), 2:206–30; Claudia Barsanti, Alessandra Guiglia

Guidobaldi, and Jean-Pierre Sodini, "La sculpture architecturale en marbre au VIe siècle à Constantinople et dans les régions sous influence constantinopolitaine," in *Acta XIII Congressus internationalis archaeologiae christianae, Split-Poreč, 1994,* ed. Nenad Cambi and Emilio Marin (Split: Archeološki muzej; Rome: Pontificio istituto di archeologia cristiana, 1998), 301–76; Gerhard Kapitän, "The Church Wreck off Marzamemi," *Archaeology* 22, no. 2 (1969): 122–33; idem, "Elementi architettonici per una basilica dal relitto navale del VI secolo di Marzamemi (Siracusa)," in *XXVII corso di cultura sull'arte ravennate e bizantina* (Ravenna: Edizioni del Girasole, 1980), 71–136; Justin Leidwanger and Sebastiano Tusa, "Marzamemi II 'Church Wreck' Excavation: 2014 Field Season," *Archaeologia Maritima Mediterranea* 12 (2015): 103–15; M. Fischer, "Marble from Pentelicon, Paros, Thasos, and Proconnesus in Ancient Israel: An Attempt at a Chronological Distinction," in *ASMOSIA VII: Actes du VIIe Colloque international de l'ASMOSIA, Thasos, 15–20 septembre, 2003,* Bulletin de correspondance hellénique, supplément 51 (Athens: École française d'Athènes, 2009), 399–412.

28. Asgari, "Proconnesian Production of Architectural Elements," shows the difference between the second-century Roman imperial and fifth-century Late Antique procedures in carving Corinthian capitals. See also Sodini, "Marble and Stoneworking in Byzantium," 129–31.

29. Schwarzenberg, "Colour, Light, and Transparency"; Barry, "Walking on Water," 631–32.

30. Since the publication of my *Sensual Icon,* 2010, a spurt of exciting new research in Byzantine materiality has taken place. See Peers, "Byzantine Things in the World"; Barber, "Thingliness"; Roland Betancourt, "Introduction: The Slash as Method," in Betancourt and Taroutina, *Byzantium/Modernism,* 179–94; Rico Franses, "Lacan and Byzantine Art: In the Beginning Was the Image," in ibid., 311–29; and Charles Barber, "Beyond Representation/The Gift of Sight," in ibid., 330–48.

31. See the video at https://hagiasophia.stanford.edu.

32. Pentcheva, "Hagia Sophia and Multisensory Aesthetics." On agency in Byzantine art, see Peers, "Byzantine Things in the World." Oustide Byzantine art, my work has resonance with the study of animation in Islamic art. See Matthew D. Saba, "Abbasid Lusterware and the Aesthetics of *'Ajab,*" *Muqarnas* 29 (2012): 187–212; Finbarr Barry Flood, "Notes from the Field: Anthropomorphism," *Art Bulletin* 94, no. 1 (2012): 18–20; idem, "Presentation, (Re)animation, and the Enchantments of Technology," *Res: Anthropology and Aesthetics* 61–62 (2012): 229–36; idem, "Bodies and Becoming: Mimesis, Mediation, and the Ingestion of the Sacred in Christianity and Islam," in Promey, *Sensational Religion,* 459–93; idem, "From Icon to Coin: Potlatch, Piety, and Idolatry in Medieval Islam," in *Ritual, Images, and Daily Life: The Medieval Perspective,* ed. Gerhard Jaritz (Vienna: LIT, 2012), 163–72.

33. Paul the Silentiary, *Descriptio S. Sophiae,* vv. 605–8 and 664–67.

34.   πᾶν δὲ πέδον στορέσασα Προκοννήσοιο κολώνη
       ἀσπασίως ὑπέθηκε βιαρκεῖ νῶτον ἀνάσσηι·
       ἠρέμα δὲ φρίσσουσα διέπρεπε Βοσπορὶς αἴγλη
       ἀκροκελαινιόωντος ἐπ' ἀργεννοῖο μετάλλου.

Paul the Silentiary, *Descriptio S. Sophiae,* vv. 664–67. My translation.

35. *Akrokelainiōs* is a rare Homeric term. Homer, *Iliad,* bk. 21, v. 249; Liddell and Scott, *Greek-English Lexicon,* 56; Richard John Cunliffe, *A Lexicon of the Homeric Dialect,* new ed. (Norman: University of Oklahoma Press, 1977); also in Nonnus of Panopolis, *Dionysiaca,* bk. 18, v. 156.

36. On *poikilia* in Homer, see Gregory Nagy, *Homer the Preclassic,* Sather Classical Lectures 67 (Berkeley: University of California Press, 2010), 273–310; in Late Antiquity and Byzantium, Roberts, *Jeweled Style,* 44–65, and Agosti, "Immagini e poesia nella tarda antichità"; specifically in art, Bissera V. Pentcheva, "The Performative Icon," *Art Bulletin* 88, no. 4 (2006): 631–55, esp. 644–48, and idem, *Sensual Icon,* 139–43.

37. I observed these changes in the appearance of the Proconnesian marble at sunrise on December 5, 2010, when I was given permission to take pictures in Hagia Sophia during the early hours of the day before the building had opened to tourists.

38. Schwarzenberg, "Colour, Light, and Transparency"; Barry, "Walking on Water," 631–32.

39. Homer, *Iliad,* bk. 14, v. 273 (the shimmering sea); bk. 12, v. 195 (armor); bk. 13, v. 22 (golden palaces), v. 801 (bronze); bk. 16, v. 279 (armor), v. 664 (harness), v. 735 (stone); bk. 17, v. 594 (bronze); bk. 18, v. 480 (the rim of the shield), v. 617 (armor); bk. 23, v. 27 (harnesses of bronze). Homer, *Odyssey,* bk. 8, v. 265 (twinkling of

dancing feet); bk. 9, v. 499 (rock). On *marmar-* and *porphyry*, see Nagy, *Homer the Preclassic*, 273–310, and Richard T. Neer, *The Emergence of the Classical Style in Greek Sculpture* (Chicago: University of Chicago Press, 2010), 76–77.

40. Nonnus of Panopolis, *Dionysiaca*, bk. 1, vv. 255, 304, 320; bk. 2, v. 199; bk. 6, v. 333; bk. 27, v. 232; bk. 45, v. 336; bk. 47, v. 253 (lightning, fire, rays); bk. 1, v. 4; bk. 2, v. 259; bk. 12, v. 14; bk. 15, v. 332; bk. 22, v. 157; bk. 28, v. 269; bk. 36, v. 43; bk. 38, vv. 302, 426 (arm, armor, hooves, fingers); bk. 4, v. 21; bk. 11, v. 309; bk. 18, v. 71; bk. 20, v. 19; bk. 22, v. 153; bk. 25, v. 386; bk. 40, v. 355 (architecture, works of art, cloth); bk. 4, v. 380; bk. 5, v. 182; bk. 10, v. 167 (water); bk. 7, v. 303; bk. 9, v. 4; bk. 34, v. 42; bk. 35, v. 123 (moon); bk. 34, v. 174; bk. 35, v. 369; bk. 40, v. 278 (pearl); bk. 38, vv. 102, 151, 249 (tears); bk. 44, v. 221 (dew). R. Shorrock, *The Challenge of Epic: Allusive Engagement in the "Dionysiaca" of Nonnus* (Leiden: Brill, 2001); Gennaro D'Ippolito, *Studi nonniani: L'epillio nelle Dionisiache*, Quaderni dell'Istituto di filologia greca della Università di Palermo 3 (Palermo: Presso l'Accademia, 1964). On the popularity of Nonnus in sixth-century Constantinople, see Alan Cameron, *The Greek Anthology: From Meleager to Planudes* (Oxford: Clarendon Press; New York: Oxford University Press, 1993), 46.

41. Χρυσεοκολλήτους δὲ τέγος ψηφῖδας ἔέργει,
     ὧν ἄπο μαρμαίρουσα χύδην χρυσόρρυτος ἀκτὶς
     ἀνδρομέοις ἄτλητος ἐπεσκίρτησε προσώποις.

     Paul the Silentiary, *Descriptio S. Sophiae*, vv. 668–70. My translation.

42. Procopius of Caesarea, *Santa Sofia di Costantinopoli: Un tempio di luce (De aedificiis I 1,1–78)*, ed. and trans. Paolo Cesaretti and Maria Luigia Fobelli (Milan: Jaca, 2011), 120–22, 127–31.

43. See the video at https://hagiasophia.stanford.edu.

44. Jane Bennett, *Vibrant Matter: A Political Ecology of Things* (Durham: Duke University Press, 2010).

45. Nonnus of Panopolis, *Dionysiaca*, bk. 4, vv. 137, 380; bk. 8, v. 342; bk. 9, v. 104; bk. 27, v. 235; bk. 28, v. 227; bk. 30, v. 255; bk. 33, v. 24; bk. 35, v. 41; bk. 40, v. 414; bk. 42, vv. 351, 452.

46. 224 Ὡς δὲ θαλασσαίοισιν ἐν οἴδμασι νῆσος ἀνίσχει,

     .   .   .   .

     229 οὕτω ἀπειρεσίοιο κατ' ἔνδια μέσσα μελάθρου
     230 λάεσι πυργωθεὶς ἀναφαίνεται ὄρθιος ἄμβων,

     .   .   .   .

     247 ἔνθεν ὑποτροπάδην χρυσέην εὐάγγελος ἀνὴρ
     248 βίβλον ἀερτάζων διανίσσεται. ἱεμένης δὲ
     249 πληθύος, ἀχράντοιο θεοῦ κατὰ μύστιδα τιμήν,
     250 χείλεα καὶ παλάμας ἱερὴν περὶ βίβλον ἐρεῖσαι,
     251 κύματα κινυμένων περιάγνυται ἄσπετα δήμων.

     Paul the Silentiary, *Descriptio ambonis*, vv. 224, 229–30, 247–51. My translation.

47. Marcia K. Johnson, "Reflection, Reality Monitoring, and the Self," in *Mental Imagery*, ed. Robert Kunzendorf (New York: Plenum Press, 1991), 3–16; Ronald A. Finke, *Principles of Mental Imagery* (Cambridge: MIT Press, 1989); George Lakoff, *Women, Fire, and Dangerous Things: What Categories Reveal About the Mind* (Chicago: University of Chicago Press, 1987); Ronald W. Langacker, *Foundations of Cognitive Grammar*, 2 vols. (Stanford: Stanford University Press, 1987–91).

48. Alfred Gell, *Art and Agency: An Anthropological Theory* (Oxford: Clarendon Press, 1998), 116–22.

49. Paul's image of the spiritually inspired crowd transforming into waves breaking at the shores of an island resembles Merleau-Ponty's chiasm and more specifically his quote of Paul Klee. The artist explains the interdigitation of painter and nature as follows: "In a forest, I have felt many times over that it was not I who looked at the forest. Some days I felt that the trees were looking at me, were speaking to me. . . . I was there, listening. . . . I think that the painter must be penetrated by the universe and not want to penetrate it. . . . I expect to be inwardly submerged, buried. Perhaps I paint to break out." Quoted in Georges Charbonnier, *Le monologue du peintre* (Paris: Imprimerie Chantenay, 1959), 143–45, as translated in Maurice Merleau-Ponty, "Eye and Mind," 351–78, quote on 358.

50. For *aiolomorphos*, see Liddell and Scott, *Greek-English Lexicon*, 40; Paul the Silentiary, *Descriptio S. Sophiae*, v. 884; and idem, *Descriptio ambonis*, v. 80.

51. καὶ φύσιν αἰολόμορφον ἔχων ποικίλλεται αἴγλῃ.
    τοῦ μὲν ἔπι τροχάουσι διαμπερὲς οἶά τε δῖναι,
    πῆι μὲν ἴσαι κύκλοισιν ἀτέρμοσι, πῆι δέ γε κύκλων
    βαιὸν ἀποπλαγχθέντας ὑπεκτανύουσιν ἑλιγμούς.
    ἔστι δὲ πῆι μὲν ἔρευθος ἰδεῖν κεκερασμένον ὤχρωι,
    πῆι δὲ καλὸν βροτέοισι σέλας στονύχεσσιν ὁμοῖον.
    ἄλλοθι δ᾽ ὁρμηθεῖσα πρὸς ἀργεννὸν σέλας αἴγλη,
    ἠρέμα μιμνάζουσα, χάριν μιμήσατο πύξου
    ἠὲ μελισσήεντος ἐπήρατον εἰκόνα κηροῦ,
    ὃν καθαραῖς προχοῇσι βροτοὶ νίζοντες ἐρίπναις
    πολλάκι τερσαίνουσιν ὑπ᾽ ἠελιώτιδας αὐγάς·
    ὃς δὲ μεταΐσσει μὲν ἐς ἄργυφον, εἰσέτι δ᾽ οὔπω
    τρέψεν ὅλην χροιὴν ἔτι λείψανα χρύσεα φαίνων.
    Paul the Silentiary, *Descriptio ambonis*, vv. 80–92. My translation.

52. On *ochros*, see James, *Light and Colour in Byzantine Art*, 51.

53. On how ekphrasis draws on perceptual mimesis, see Webb, *Ekphrasis, Imagination, and Persuasion*, 107–30; idem, "Accomplishing the Picture: Ekphrasis, Mimesis, and Martyrdom in Asterios of Amaseia," in James, *Art and Text in Byzantine Culture*, 13–32; and Verity Platt "Viewing, Desiring, Believing: Confronting the Divine in a Pompeian House," *Art History* 25, no. 1 (2002): 87–112.

54. Webb, *Ekphrasis, Imagination, and Persuasion*, 107–30, esp. 127–28, relying on Elaine Scarry, *Dreaming by the Book* (New York: Farrar, Straus, Giroux, 1999), 6; idem, "The Aesthetics of Sacred Space: Narrative, Metaphor, and Motion in *Ekphraseis* of Church Buildings," *Dumbarton Oaks Papers* 53 (1999): 59–74, esp. 64. On the active role of the listener in the creation of meaning, see Wolfgang Iser, "The Reading Process: A Phenomenological Approach," in *Reader-Response Criticism: From Formalism to Post-Structuralism*, ed. Jane P. Tompkins (Baltimore: Johns Hopkins University Press, 1980), 50–69.

55. On *choros* and circular movement, see Isar, *Chorós: The Dance of Adam*, 97–208. Barbara E. Bowe, "Dancing into the Divine: The Hymn of the Dance in the *Acts of John*," *Journal of Early Christian Studies* 7, no. 1 (1999): 83–104.

56. τὴν δὲ κυρίως ἀληθινὴν ἐν μόνῃ τῇ πείρᾳ κατ᾽ ἐνέργειαν δίχα λόγου καὶ νοημάτων ὅλην τοῦ γνωσθέντος κατὰ χάριν μεθέξει παρεχομένην τὴν αἴσθησιν, δι᾽ ἧς κατὰ τὴν μέλλουσαν λῆξιν τὴν ὑπὲρ φύσιν ὑποδεχόμεθα θέωσιν ἀπαύστως ἐνεργουμένην. Maximus the Confessor, *Ad Thalassium*, chap. 60; English translation in Blowers and Wilken, *On the Cosmic Mystery of Jesus Christ*, 126.

57. On the splendor marking mystical union, see Elsner, *Art and the Roman Viewer*, 88–124; Johnston, "*Fiat Lux, Fiat Ritus*"; Rico Franses, "When All That Is Gold Does Not Glitter: On the Strange History of Looking at Byzantine Art," in *Icon and Word: The Power of Images in Byzantium; Studies Presented to Robin Cormack*, ed. Antony Eastmond and Liz James (Aldershot: Ashgate, 2003), 13–24.

58. τοὺς δὲ χαμαιπαγέες πίσυρες μεγάλοισι [κα]ρήνοις
    κίονες ὀχλίζουσιν ὑπ᾽ ἀστυφέλικτον ἀνάγκην
    χρυσόκομοι χαρίτεσσι κατήορο[ι,]ται
    Θεσσαλίδος πέτρης ἀμαρύγματα· μέσσα δὲ νηοῦ
    ἔνδια καλλιχόροιο διακρίνουσιν ἐδέθλων
    γείτονος αἰθούσης περιμήκεος. οὔ ποτε τοίους
    κίονας ἐτμήξαντο Μολοσσίδος ἔνδοθι γαίης,
    ὑψιλόφους, χαρίεντας, ἐΰχλοας ἄλσεσι[
    ἄνθεσι δαιδαλέοισι τεθηλότας.
    Paul the Silentiary, *Descriptio S. Sophiae*, vv. 542–50. My translation.

59. On the gilding of the carved capitals, see W. Eugene Kleinbauer, Antony White, and Henry Matthews, *Hagia Sophia* (London: Scala; Istanbul: Archaeology and Art Publications, 2004), 34.

60. Thomas F. Torrance, *The Doctrine of Grace in the Apostolic Fathers* (Edinburgh: Oliver & Boyd, 1948, repr., Grand Rapids, Mich.: Eerdmans, 1960), 139–41; Stephen Duffy, *The Dynamics of Grace: Perspectives in*

Theological Anthropology, New Theology Studies 3 (Collegeville, Minn.: Liturgical Press, 1993), 27–42; Kazhdan et al., *Oxford Dictionary of Byzantium* (Oxford: Clarendon Press, 1991), 1:863–64.

61. Schibille, *Hagia Sophia*, 99–109, 241–42. This evocation of a meadow in spring is characteristic of the literature of this period; see Roberts, *Jeweled Style*, 55.

62. Kiilerich, "Aesthetic Viewing of Marble in Byzantium." Guiglia Guidobaldi and Barsanti, *Santa Sofia di Costantinopoli*, 3–21. Annette Kleinert, *Die Inkrustation der Hagia Sophia: Zur Entwicklung der Inkrustationsschemata im römischen Kaiserreich* (Münster: University of Münster, 1979), 45–93.

63. Kiilerich, "Aesthetic Viewing of Marble in Byzantium," 9–18.

64. ὅσσα τ' Ὄνυξ ἀνέηκε διαυγάζοντι μετάλλῳ
    ὠχριόων ἐρίτιμα, καὶ Ἀτρακὶς ὁππόσα λευροῖς
    χθὼν πεδίοις ἐλόχευσε καὶ οὐχ ὑψαύχενι βήσσῃ,
    πῇ μὲν ἅλις χλοάοντα καὶ οὐ μάλα τῆλε μαράγδου,
    πῇ δὲ βαθυνομένου χλοεροῦ κυανώπιδι μορφῇ·
    ἣν δέ τι καὶ χιόνεσσιν ἀλίγκιον ἄγχι μελαίνης
    μαρμαρυγῆς, μικτὴ δὲ χάρις συνεγείρετο πέτρου.

    Paul the Silentiary, *Descriptio S. Sophiae*, vv. 640–46. My translation.

65. On the onyx/alabaster, see Kiilerich, "Aesthetic Viewing of Marble in Byzantium," 10.

66. Bente Kiilerich identifies the marble of Atrakis with *marmor Thessalicum* or *verde antico*. Kiilerich, "Aesthetic Viewing of Marble in Byzantium," 10. For further information on *verde antico*, see Lorenzo Lazzarini, *Poikiloi lithoi, versiculores maculae: I marmi colorati della Grecia antica* (Pisa: Fabrizio Serra Editore, 2007), 223–44; Raniero Gnoli, *Marmora Romana* (Rome: Edizioni dell'elefante, 1971), 162–65; and Monica T. Price, *Decorative Stone: The Complete Sourcebook* (London: Thames & Hudson, 2007), 186–87.

67. James, *Light and Colour in Byzantine Art*; idem, "Color and Meaning in Byzantium," *Journal of Early Christian Studies* 11, no. 2 (2003): 223–33; Franses, "When All That Is Gold Does Not Glitter"; Schwarzenberg, "Colour, Light, and Transparency in the Greek World"; Procopius of Caesarea, *Santa Sofia di Costantinopoli*, 122–26.

68. Franses, "When All That Is Gold Does Not Glitter."

69. John Onians, "Abstraction and Imagination in Late Antiquity," *Art History* 3 (1980): 1–23, and see also James Trilling, "The Image Not Made by Hands and the Byzantine Way of Seeing," in *The Holy Face and the Paradox of Representation*, ed. Herbert L. Kessler and Gerhard Wolf, Villa Spelman Colloquia 6 (Bologna: Nuova Alfa, 1998), 109–28. Kiilerich restates the same argument, seeking figuration in the abstract form created by the marble veining; see Kiilerich, "Aesthetic Viewing of Marble in Byzantium," 19–21.

70. Onians, "Abstraction and Imagination in Late Antiquity," 23.

71. λαότορον δ' ἀνὰ τοῖχον ἐὔγραφα δαίδαλα τέχνης
    πάντοθεν ἀστράπτουσιν. ἁλιστεφέος Προκονήσου
    ταῦτα φάραγξ ἐλόχευσε. πολυτμήτων δὲ μετάλλων
    ἁρμονίη γραφίδεσσιν ἰσάζεται· ἐν γὰρ ἐκείνῃ
    τετρατόμοις λάεσσι καὶ ὀκτατόμοισι νοήσεις
    ζευγνυμένας κατὰ κόσμον ὁμοῦ φλέβας· ἀγλαΐην δὲ
    ζωοτύπων λάϊγγες ἐμιμήσαντο δεθεῖσαι.

    Paul the Silentiary, *Descriptio S. Sophiae*, vv. 607–11. My translation.

72. Gregory of Nyssa, *De hominis opificio*, bk. 12, in PG 44, cols. 161C, 164A; Maximus the Confessor, *Mystagogia*, chaps. 1 and 2, in PG 91, cols. 664D and 669D.

73. Onians, "Abstraction and Imagination in Late Antiquity," 23; Trilling, "The Image Not Made by Hands," 117–27. Kiilerich takes a different position, arguing that Paul's passage exemplifies the reverse relation, in which nature imitates art; see Kiilerich, "Aesthetic Viewing of Marble in Byzantium," 19–20.

74. Georges Didi-Huberman, *Fra Angelico: Dissemblance and Figuration*, trans. Jane Marie Todd (Chicago: University of Chicago Press, 1995), 22–101, and Elkins, *On Pictures and the Words That Fail Them*, 241–66.

75. On repetition and infinity, see Zainab Bahrani, *The Infinite Image: Art, Time, and Aesthetic Dimension in Antiquity* (London: Reaktion, 2014), 115–44.

76. Ἐπῆραν οἱ ποταμοί, Κύριε, ἐπῆραν οἱ ποταμοὶ φωνὰς αὐτῶν, ἀπὸ φωνῶν ὑδάτων πολλῶν· θαυμαστοὶ οἱ μετεωρισμοὶ τῆς θαλάσσης· θαυμαστὸς ἐν ὑψηλοῖς ὁ Κύριος. Τὰ μαρτύριά σου ἐπιστώθησαν σφόδρα· τῷ οἴκῳ σου πρέπει ἁγίασμα, Κύριε, εἰς μακρότητα ἡμερῶν. Ps 92 (93): 3–5.

77. καὶ ἤκουν τὴν φωνὴν τῶν πτερύγων αὐτῶν ἐν τῷ πορεύεσθαι αὐτὰ ὡς φωνὴν ὕδατος πολλοῦ. Ezek. 1:24. καὶ ἤκουσα ὡς φωνὴν ἐκ τοῦ οὐρανοῦ ὡς φωνὴν ὑδάτων πολλῶν. Rev. 14:2. καὶ ἤκουσα ὡς φωνὴν ὄχλου πολλοῦ καὶ ὡς φωνὴν ὑδάτων πολλῶν. Rev. 19:6. Niketas of Remesiana, d. 414, repeats these two passages from Revelations, quoted in Calvin Stapert, *A New Song for an Old World: Musical Thought in the Early Church* (Grand Rapids, Mich.: William B. Eerdmans, 2007), 14.

78. Isar, *Chorós: The Dance of Adam,* 97–208.

79. 2 Sam. 6:14. I thank Herbert Kessler, who drew my attention to David's penitent dance; see also Allan Russell Juriansz, *King David's Naked Dance: The Dreams, Doctrines, and Dilemmas of the Hebrews* (Bloomington, Ind.: iUniverse, 2013).

80.   μηκεδανὸς δ' ἐπὶ τοῖσι πύλαις παραπέπ[ταται] αὐλῶν,
         δεχνύμενος προσιόντας ὑπ' εὐρ[υπ]όροισι θυρέτροις,
         μῆκος ἔχων ὅσον εὖρος ἀνάκτορα θέσκελα νηοῦ.
         χῶρος ὅδε Γραικοῖσι φατίζεται ἀνδράσι νάρθηξ.
         ἔνθα δέ τις κατὰ νύκτα διαμπερὲς ἦχος ἀνέρπων
         εὐκέλαδος Χριστοῖο βιαρκέος οὔατα θέλγει,
         ὁππόθι τιμήεντα θεουδέος ὄργια Δαυὶδ
         ἀντιπόροις ἰαχῇσιν ἀείδεται ἀνδράσι μύστης,
         Δαυὶδ πρηϋνόοιο, τὸν ᾔνεσε θέσκελος ὀμφή,
         φωτὸς ἀγακλήεντος, ὅθεν πολύυμνος ἀπορρὼξ
         γαστέρι δεξαμένη τὸν ἀμήτορα παῖδα θεοῖο
         Χριστὸν ἀνεβλάστησεν ἀπειρογάμοισι λοχείαις,
         μητρῴοις δ' ὑπέθηκε τὸν ἄσπορον υἱέα θεσμοῖς.
    Paul the Silentiary, *Descriptio S. Sophiae,* vv. 425–37. My translation.

81. On the Homeric *omphē* as divine voice and inspiration, see Cunliffe, *Lexicon of the Homeric Dialect,* 293. Paul also uses *omphē* as inspiration. Paul the Silentiary, *Descriptio S. Sophiae,* v. 997.

82. *Omphalos* appears in Paul the Silentiary, *Descriptio S. Sophia,* v. 506 (cross in the dome), v. 594 (fountain in the atrium), v. 662 (porphyry disks in the spandrels of the ground-level arcade), v. 715 (cross-shaped epigraphy recording the names of Justinian and Theodora incised in the capitals of the columns in the ground-level arcade); idem, *Descriptio ambonis,* v. 31 (about the ambo where the professional choir stands).

83. Stone quarried in Iasus of Caria, also known as *cipollino rosso,* is a red breccia with black and white veining; see Gnoli, *Marmora Romana,* 243–45, and Price, *Decorative Stone,* 120.

84.   μηκεδανῆς δ' ἐρίτιμον ἐς ὀμφαλὸν ἵσταται αὐλῆς
         εὐρυτάτη φιάλη τις, Ἰασσίδος ἔκτομος ἄκρης,
         ἔνθα ῥόος κελαδῶν ἀναπάλλεται ἠέρι πέμπειν
         ὁλκὸν ἀναθρώσκοντα βίῃ χαλκήρεος αὐλοῦ,
         ὁλκὸν ὅλων παθέων ἐλατήριον.
    Paul the Silentiary, *Descriptio S. Sophiae,* vv. 594–98. My translation.

85. Paul the Silentiary, *Descriptio S. Sophiae,* vv. 429–30.

86.   οὐκοῦν πρόσειμι τῷ σεβασμίῳ τόπῳ,
         ὃν ὁ βασιλεὺς ἔναγχος ἐξειργασμένος
         κάλλιστον εἶναι χωρίον τοῖς βιβλίοις
         τῶν μυσταγωγῶν ἱερούργηκεν λόγων.
         Ὑμνοπόλοι Χριστοῖο θεουδέες, ὧν ὑπὸ φωνῆς
         πνεύματος ἀχράντοιο μετ' ἀνέρας ἤλυθεν ὀμφή
         ἀνδρομέην Χριστοῖο διαγγέλλουσα λοχείην.
    Paul, *Descriptio ambonis,* vv. 26–32. My translation.

87. On the music of the spheres (*musica mundana*), see, from the first century c.e., *The Manual of Harmonics of Nicomachus the Pythagorean,* trans. Flora R. Levin (Grand Rapids, Mich.: Phanes Press, 1994), chap. 3, 45–60, and, from the fifth century, Macrobius, *Commentary on the Dream of Scipio,* trans. William Harris Stahl (New York: Columbia University Press, 1952), chaps. 3–4, 193–200.

88. Justin Martyr, *Dialogus cum Tryphone Judaeo,* VII, 1, in PG 6, col. 492B: ἀλλὰ μόνα ταῦτα εἰπόντες ἃ ἤκουσαν καὶ ἃ εἶδον ἁγίῳ πληρωθέντες πνεύματι (but being filled by the Holy Spirit, they spoke those things only which they heard or saw).

89. Vatican City, BAV, ms gr. 699, fol. 63v. See my discussion in chapter 1.

90. Lingas, "From Earth to Heaven," 334. Listen to music sample 1 at https://hagiasophia.stanford.edu.

91. Hans Ulrich Gumbrecht's argument about alliteration as the aggregation of matter is based on a pre-Christian charm from the Germanic monastery at Fulda (founded in 744). The charm summons the spirits to heal a horse through prosody. The use of alliteration creates a metaphysical presence. Gumbrecht, "The Charm of Charms," in *A New History of German Literature,* ed. David E. Wellbery (Cambridge: Harvard University Press, 2005), 1–7. Similarly, on refrain as aggregation, see Deleuze and Guattari, "On the Refrain," 323.

92. See chapter 2.

93. Gaston Bachelard, *Water and Dreams: An Essay on the Imagination of Matter,* trans. Edith R. Farrell (1983; repr., Dallas: Dallas Institute of Humanities and Culture, 2006), 84–85.

94. Bachelard, *Water and Dreams,* 187–95.

95. Boniface Ramsey, *Ambrose* (London: Routledge, 1997), 18, 51–54, 60. On the conduit of Greek ideas to Milan, see the letter from Basil the Great to Ambrose of 375 (letter no. 197), http://www.ccel.org/ccel/schaff /npnf208.ix.cxcviii.html, accessed October 15, 2015; Basil of Caesarea, *Letters and Selected Works,* ed. Philip Schaff and Henry Wace, *A Select Library of Nicene and Post-Nicene Fathers of the Christian Church,* vol. 8 (Edinburgh: T & T Clark; Grand Rapids, Mich.: Eerdmans, 1989), 234–35. Henry Maguire, *Earth and Ocean: The Terrestrial World in Early Byzantine Art* (University Park: Pennsylvania State University Press, 1987), 41–56.

96.   vel cum aequore crispanti, clementioribus auris, et blando serenae tranquilitatis purpurascentem praefert colorem, qui eminus spectantibus frequenter offunditur, quando non violentis fluctibus vicina tundit littora, sed vel pacificis ambit et salutat amplexibus, quam dulcis sonus, quam jucundus fragor, quam, grata et consona resutatio, ego tamen non oculis, aestimantum creaturae decorum arbitor: sed secundum rationem operationis judicio operatoris convenire, et congruere definitum.

Ambrose, *Hexameron,* bk. 3, chap. 5, sect. 21, in PL 14, col. 177C; English translation in Ambrose, *Hexameron, Paradise, and Cain and Abel,* trans. John J. Savage, The Fathers of the Church 42 (New York: Fathers of the Church, 1961), 83. Ambrose also speaks of the faithful as musical instruments, who in chanting the psalmody produce the harmonious Logos, in which the Holy Spirit operates. Ambrose, *Hexameron,* bk. 3, chap. 1, sects. 3–6; English translation in Savage, *Hexameron,* 68–70.

97. Stapert, *New Song for an Old World,* 107, and McKinnon, *Music in Early Christian Literature,* 130.

98.   Mare est ergo secretum temperantiae, exercitium continentiae, . . . tum fidelibus viris atque devotis incentivum devotionis, ut cum undarum leniter alluentium sono certent cantus psallentium, plaudant insulae tranquillo fluctuum sanctorum choro, hymnis sanctorum personent. Unde mihi ut omnem pelagi pulchritudinem comprehendam quam vidit operatur? Et quid plura? Quid aliud ille concentus undarum, nisi quidam concentus est plebis? Unde bene mari plerumque comparatur Ecclesia, quae primo ingredientis populi agmine totis vestibulis undas vomit: deinde in oratione totius plebis tanquam undis refluentibus stridet, cum responsoriis psalmorum, cantus virorum, mulierum, virginum, parvulo-rum, consonus undarum fragor resultat. Nam illud quid dicam, quod unda peccatum abluit, et sanctis Spiritus aura salutaris aspirat.

Ambrose, *Hexameron,* bk. 3, chap. 5, sect. 23, in PL 14, col. 178B–C; English translation in Savage, *Hexameron,* 84.

99. Bachelard, *Water and Dreams,* 187, 194.

Chapter 6

1. On the mirror in the context of the science of optics, see Katherine H. Tachau, *Vision and Certitude in the Age of Ockham: Optics, Epistemology, and the Foundations of Semantics, 1250–1345* (Leiden: Brill, 1988); Jeffrey Hamburger, "Speculations on Speculation: Vision and Perception in the Theory and Practice of Mystical Devotion," in *Deutsche Mystik im abendländischen Zusammenhang: Neu erschlossene Texte, neue methodische Ansätze, neue theoretische Konzepte,* ed. Walter Haug and Wolfram Schneider-Lastin (Tübingen: Max Niemeyer, 2000), 353–408; Gerhard Wolf, *Schleier und Spiegel: Traditionen des Christusbildes und die Bildkonzepte der Renaissance* (Munich: Fink, 2002); David Summers, *Vision, Reflection, and Desire in Western Painting* (Chapel Hill: University of North Carolina Press, 2007); Hans Belting, *Florenz und Bagdad: Eine westöstliche Geschichte des Blicks* (Munich: Beck, 2008); and Samuel Y. Edgerton, *The Mirror, the Window, and the Telescope: How Renaissance Linear Perspective Changed Our Vision of the Universe* (Ithaca: Cornell University Press, 2009). For a study specifically focusing on the actual object, the mirror, in Western medieval art, see Herbert L. Kessler, "Speculum," *Speculum* 86, no. 1 (2011): 1–41. On the mirror as metaphor, see Marcia L. Colish, *The Mirror of Language: A Study in the Medieval Theory of Knowledge,* rev. ed. (Lincoln: University of Nebraska Press, 1983).

2. The metonym of the thrones (*thoōkos*) refers to the ecclesiastical elite that sits on the *synthronon* or steps in the great apse.

3. ἀλλ' ὅτε δὴ σκιόεσσαν ἀναστείλασα καλύπτρην
   οὐρανίας ῥοδόπηχυς ὑπέδραμεν ἄντυγας αἴγλη,
   δὴ τότε λαὸς ἅπας συναγείρετο, πᾶς τε θοώκων
   ἀρχός, ὑποδρήσσων σθεναροῦ βασιλῆος ἐφετμαῖς
   καὶ Χριστῷ βασιλῆϊ χαρίσια δῶρα κομίζων,
   ἱκεσίοις στομάτεσσι θεουδέας ἤπυεν ὕμνους,
   ἄργυφον εὐκαμάτοις ὑπὸ χείρεσι κηρὸν ἀνάπτων.
   ἕσπετο δ' ἀρητήρ, ἱερῆς δ' ἐξῆρχε χορείης,
   ἀρητὴρ πολύυμνος, ὃν ἄξιον εὕρετο νηοῦ
   Αὐσονίων σκηπτοῦχος· ὅλης δ' ἐστείνετο Ῥώμης
   ἀτραπὸς εὐρυάγυια. μολὼν δ' ἐπὶ θέσπιδας αὐλὰς
   δῆμος ἅπας ἐπέβωσε χαρίσιον, οὐρανίας δὲ
   ἀχράντους ἐδόκησεν ἐς ἄντυγας ἴχνια θέσθαι.
   Paul the Silentiary, *Descriptio S. Sophiae,* vv. 337–50. My translation.

4. Olga Bush, "'When My Beholder Ponders': Poetic Epigraphy in the Alhambra," *Artibus Asiae* 66, no. 2 (2006): 55–67. The epigram, written on the right side at the entrance, appears in a frame around a stucco decoration that nonmimetically refers to a niche:
   1. All of art had offered me its beauty, giving me perfection and splendor.
   2. He who sees me imagines (*t-n-n*) me at all hours giving what the water jug seeks.
   3. When my beholder ponders my beauty, his visual perception causes his imagination to be deceived,
   4. Since so diaphanous I am, that he sees the moon; its halo happily settles in me.
   From the poet Ibn Zamrak, as translated in ibid., 55.

5. Bush, "'When My Beholder Ponders.'" On the mirror as an aesthetic principle in Islamic art, see Valérie Gonzalez, *Beauty and Islam: Aesthetics in Islamic Art and Architecture* (London: I. B. Tauris, 2001); idem, *Le piège de Salomon: La pensée de l'art dans le Coran* (Paris: Albin Michel, 2002); and Persis Berlekamp, *Wonder, Image, and Cosmos in Medieval Islam* (New Haven: Yale University Press, 2011), 91–97.

6. Taft, *Great Entrance,* 53–118.

7. Οἱ τὰ χερουβὶμ μυστικῶς εἰκονίζοντες καὶ τῇ ζωοποιῷ Τριάδι τὸν τρισάγιον ὕμνον προσάδοντες, πᾶσαν τὴν βιωτικὴν ἀποθώμεθα μέριμναν ὡς τὸν Βασιλέα τῶν ὅλων ὑποδειξόμενοι, ταῖς ἀγγελικαῖς ἀοράτως δορυφορουμένον τάξεσιν. Ἀλληλούϊα, ἀλληλούϊα, ἀλληλούϊα. Greek text in Taft, *Great Entrance,* 54, and Dimitri E. Conomos, *Byzantine Trisagia and Cheroubika of the Fourteenth and Fifteenth Centuries: A Study of*

the Late Byzantine Liturgical Chant (Thessaloniki: Patriarchal Institute for Patristic Studies, 1974), 31. English translation in Taft, *Great Entrance,* 54.

8. Germanus, *Historia mystica ecclesiae catholicae,* sect. 41. Greek and English in Meyendorff, *On the Divine Liturgy,* 94–95.

9. Juan Mateos, *La célébration de la parole dans la liturgie byzantine,* Orientalia Christiana analecta 191 (Rome: Pontificium Institutum Studiorum Orientalium, 1971), 91–118.

10. As reported by the monk Job in the sixth century, according to Photios's *Bibliotheca,* PG 103, col. 772A.

11. Conomos, *Byzantine Trisagia and Cheroubika,* 31–38, 121. On the Neo-Sabaïtic rite, see Miguel Arranz, "Les grandes étapes de la liturgie byzantine: Palestine—Byzance—Russie; Essai d'aperçu historique," in *Liturgie de l'Église particulière et liturgie de l'Église universelle: Conférences Saint-Serge, xxiie Semaine d'études liturgiques, Paris, 30 juin–3 juillet 1975* (Rome: Edizioni liturgiche, 1976), 43–72, and Taft, *Byzantine Rite.* On the mixture of Neo-Sabaïtic and cathedral rites in the liturgy of Hagia Sophia in Thessaloniki, see Symeon of Thessaloniki, *Treatise on Prayer.*

12. Laura Steenberge, "We Who Mystically Represent the Cherubim," in Pentcheva, *Aural Architecture.*

13. Ibid. and Conomos, *Byzantine Trisagia and Cheroubika,* 53–56, 65–66.

14. Steenberge, "We Who Mystically Represent the Cherubim."

15. Conomos, *Byzantine Trisagia and Cheroubika,* 145–46. The setting appears in Athens, National Library, MS gr. 2458, fol. 144r, dated to 1336.

16. Steenberge, "We Who Mystically Represent the Cherubim."

17. Glenn Peers, *Subtle Bodies: Representing Angels in Byzantium,* Transformation of the Classical Heritage 32 (Berkeley: University of California Press, 2001), 161–71, 177, 191. Idem, "Breathless, Speechless Images: On the Chalke Gate Epigram," *Cahiers des études anciennes* 34 (1998): 109–12.

18. καὶ δὸς ἡμῖν λόγον ἐν ἀνοίξει τοῦ στόματος ἡμῶν, εἰς τὸ ἐπικαλεῖσθαι τὴν χάριν τοῦ ἁγίου σου Πνεύματος. Velkovska and Parenti, *Eucologio Barberini gr. 336,* prayer 11, 8. My translation.

19. Daniel Galadza, "*Logikē Latreia* (Romans 12:1) as a Definition of the Liturgy," *Logos: A Journal of Eastern Christian Studies* 52, nos. 1–2 (2011): 109–24.

20. Δέσποτα Κύριε ὁ Θεός, ὁ καταστήσας ἐν οὐρανοῖς τάγματα καὶ στρατιὰς ἀγγέλων καὶ ἀρχαγγέλων πρὸς λειτουργίαν τῆς σῆς δόξης, ποίησον σὺν τῇ εἰσόδῳ ἡμῶν εἴσοδον ἁγίων ἀγγέλων γενέσθαι, συλλειτουργούντων ἡμῖν καὶ συνδοξολογούντων τὴν σὴν ἀγαθότητα. Velkovska and Parenti, *Eucologio Barberini gr. 336,* prayer 5, 3. My translation.

21. Parenti and Velkovska, *Eucologio Barberini gr. 336,* prayer 9, 6; prayer 11, 8.

22. The domed architecture of Hagia Sophia finds an echo in the later quincunx churches. On the origins of the quincunx church, see Robert G. Ousterhout, "The Architecture of Iconoclasm: Buildings," in Brubaker and Haldon, *Byzantium in the Iconoclast Era (ca. 680–850): The Sources,* 3–19. On the emergence of the tradition of placing the Christ Pantokrator in the dome, see Ravinder Binning, "Christ's All-Seeing Eye in the Dome," in Pentcheva, *Aural Architecture.*

23. Pseudo-Dionysius, *De coelesti hierarchia,* chap. 7, sect. 4, and chap. 3, sect. 2.

24. καὶ οἷόν τι κάτοπτρον διαυγὲς καὶ νεόσμηκτον ἐν μέσοις τοῖς ἀνακτόροις ἱδρύσασθαι, ἐν ᾧ καὶ τὰ τῇ βασιλείῳ ἀρχῇ πρέποντα καὶ τὰ τῷ συγκλητικῷ συστήματι ἄξια κατοπτευόμενα, ἐν τάξει καὶ κόσμῳ αἱ τοῦ κράτους ἡνίαι διεξάγοιντο. Ὡς ἂν δὲ σαφῆ καὶ εὐδιάγνωστα εἶεν τὰ γεγραμμένα, καὶ καθωμιλημένῃ καὶ ἁπλουστέρᾳ φράσει κεχρήμεθα καὶ λέξεσι ταῖς αὐταῖς καὶ ὀνόμασι τοῖς ἐφ' ἑκάστῳ πράγματι πάλαι προσαρμοσθεῖσι καὶ λεγομένοις, ὑφ' ὧν τοῦ βασιλείου κράτους ῥυθμῷ καὶ τάξει φερομένου, εἰκονίζοι μὲν τοῦ δημιουργοῦ τὴν περὶ τόδε τὸ πᾶν ἁρμονίαν καὶ κίνησιν, καθορῷτο δὲ καὶ τοῖς ὑπὸ χεῖρα σεμνοπρεπέστερον, καὶ διὰ τοῦτο ἡδύτερόν τε καὶ θαυμαστότερον. Constantine Porphyrogennetos, *De ceremoniis,* bk. 1, in *Le livre des cérémonies,* ed. Albert Vogt (Paris: Société d'édition *Les belles lettres,* 1967), 1:2; English translation in *Book of Ceremonies,* trans. Ann Moffatt and Maxeme Tall (Canberra: Australian Association for Byzantine Studies, 2012), 4–5.

25. Listen to music sample 5 at https://hagiasophia.stanford.edu.

26. Ἡ δέ γε βίβλος τῶν Ψαλμῶν καὶ οὕτως ἔχει τινὰ πάλιν χάριν ἰδίαν καὶ παρατήρησιν ἐξαίρετον· πρὸς γὰρ τοῖς ἄλλοις, ἐν οἷς πρὸς τὰς ἄλλας βίβλους ἔχει τὴν σχέσιν καὶ κοινωνίαν, λοιπὸν καὶ ἴδιον ἔχει τοῦτο θαῦμα, ὅτι καὶ τὰ ἑκάστης ψυχῆς κινήματα, τάς τε τούτων μεταβολὰς καὶ διορθώσεις ἔχει διαγεγραμμένας καὶ διατετυπωμένας

ἐν ἑαυτῇ· ὥστε τινὰ τὸν βουλόμενον ὡς ἄπειρον ἐξ αὐτῆς λαμβάνειν καὶ κατανοεῖν, οὕτω τὸ τυποῦν ἑαυτόν, ἐκεῖ γέγραπται . . . Ἐν δὲ τῇ βίβλῳ τῶν Ψαλμῶν, πρὸς τῷ ταῦτα μανθάνειν τὸν ἀκούοντα, ἔτι καὶ τὰ κινήματα τῆς ἑαυτοῦ ψυχῆς ἐν αὐτῇ κατανοεῖ καὶ διδάσκεται· καὶ λοιπὸν πρὸς ὃ πάσχει καὶ ἐν ᾧ συνέχεται, δύναται πάλιν ἐκ ταύτης ἔχεσθαι τὴν εἰκόνα τῶν λόγων. Athanasius of Alexandria, *Epistula ad Marcellinum*, in PG 27, col. 20; English translation in *The Life of Antony and The Letter to Marcellinus*, trans. Robert C. Gregg (New York: Paulist Press, 1980), 107–8, with emendations, from http://www.athanasius.com/psalms/aletterm.htm, accessed October 22, 2014.

27. ὡς ἰδίους ὄντας λόγους ἀναγινώσκει. . . . ὁ λέγων τὰ ἄλλα ὡς ἴδια ῥήματα λαλῶν ἐστι, καὶ ὡς περὶ αὐτοῦ γραφέντας αὐτοὺς ἕκαστος ψάλλει, καὶ οὐχ ὡς ἑτέρου λέγοντος ἢ περὶ ἑτέρου σημαίνοντος δέχεται, καὶ διεξέρχεται· ἀλλ' ὡς αὐτὸς περὶ αὐτοῦ λαλῶν διατίθεται· καὶ οἷά ἐστι τὰ λεγόμενα, ταῦτα ὡς αὐτὸς πράξας καὶ ἐξ ἑαυτοῦ λαλῶν ἀναφέρει τῷ Θεῷ, . . . τήν τε ἑκατέρου πρᾶξιν περιέχουσιν οἱ Ψαλμοί. Ἀνάγκη δὲ πάντα ἄνθρωπον ἐν τούτοις συνέχεσθαι, καὶ ἢ ὡς φυλάξαντα τὴν ἐντολὴν, ἢ ὡς παραβάντα ταύτην, λέγειν τοὺς περὶ ἑκάστου γεγραμμένους λόγους. Athanasius of Alexandria, *Epistula ad Marcellinum*, in PG 27, cols. 21 and 24; English translation in Gregg, *Letter to Marcellinus*, 109, http://www.athanasius.com/psalms/aletterm.htm.

28. Καί μοι δοκεῖ τῷ ψάλλοντι γίνεσθαι τούτους ὥσπερ εἴσοπτρον, εἰς τὸ κατανοεῖν καὶ αὐτὸν ἐν αὐτοῖς καὶ τὰ τῆς ἑαυτοῦ ψυχῆς κινήματα, καὶ οὕτως αἰσθόμενον ἀπαγγέλλειν αὐτούς. Καὶ γὰρ καὶ ὁ ἀκούων τοῦ ἀναγινώσκοντος ὡς περὶ αὐτοῦ λεγομένην τὴν ᾠδὴν καταδέχεται. Athanasius of Alexandria, *Epistula ad Marcellinum*, in PG 27, col. 24; English translation in Gregg, *Letter to Marcellinus*, 111, http://www.athanasius.com/psalms/aletterm.htm.

29. Parenti and Velkovska, *Eucologio Barberini gr. 336*, prayer 9, 6. On *ēcheō*, see Liddell and Scott, *Greek-English Lexicon*, 780.

30. Marlia Mundell Mango, *Silver from Early Byzantium: The Kaper Koraon and Related Treasures* (Baltimore: Walters Art Gallery, 1986) , no. 35, 165–70. Susan A. Boyd and Marlia Mundell Mango, eds., *Ecclesiastical Silver Plate in Sixth-Century Byzantium* (Washington, D.C.: Dumbarton Oaks Research Library and Collection, 1992). Hunter-Crawley, "Embodying the Divine." I would emphasize that I do not assume that these late sixth-century liturgical objects discovered in Syria and today displayed at Dumbarton Oaks were ever used in the Justinianic liturgy of Hagia Sophia. Yet, rather than put them aside because they do not come from the ritual context of the Great Church, I draw on this Syrian silver in order to explore general principles of the construction of mystical experience at the culmination of the Eucharistic rite.

31. The inscription asks for rest for (the souls of) Sergia, John, and Theodosios and for the salvation of Megalos, Nonnus, and their children: +ὑπὲρ ἀναπαύσεως Σεργίας Ἰωάννου, καὶ Θεοδοσίου καὶ σωτηρίας Μεγάλου καὶ Νοννοῦ καὶ τῶν αὐτῶν τέκνων.

32. Susan A. Boyd, "A 'Metropolitan' Treasure from a Church in the Provinces: An Introduction to the Study of the Sion Treasure," in Boyd and Mango, *Ecclesiastical Silver Plate in Sixth-Century Byzantium*, 5–38, esp. 32–34.

33. Mango, *Silver from Early Byzantium*, no. 30, 144–46. Boyd and Mango, *Ecclesiastical Silver Plate in Sixth-Century Byzantium*, 5–92. Hunter-Crawley, "Embodying the Divine."

34. ΤΑ ΣΑ ΕΚ ΤΩΝ ΣΩΝ ΣΟΙ ΠΡΟΣΦΕΡΟΜΕΝ Κ[υρι]Ε. From F. E. Brightman, ed., *Liturgies Eastern and Western* (Oxford: Clarendon Press, 1896), 386. Velkovska and Parenti, *Eucologio Barberini gr. 336*, prayer 34, 34. My translation.

35. On the Byzantine practice of distributing the bread and wine separately before the year 1000, see Robert F. Taft, "One Bread, One Body: Ritual Symbols of Ecclesial Communion in the Patristic Period," in *Nova Doctrina Vetusque: Essays on Early Christianity in Honor of Frederic W. Schlatter, S.J.*, ed. Douglas Kries and Catherine Brown Tkacz, American University Studies, ser. 7, Theology and Religion 207 (New York: Lang, 1999), 23–50.

36. πρόσδεξαι ἡμᾶς προσεγγίζοντας τῷ ἁγίῳ σου θυσιαστηρίῳ. From Parenti and Velkovska, *Eucologio Barberini gr. 336*, prayer 13, 10. My translation.

37. For my sustained critique of the modern misreading of Heidegger's Thing, see Bissera V. Pentcheva, "Cross, Tunic, Body: Theology Through the Phenomenology of Light," in *La stauroteca di Bessarione: Atti delle giornate internazionali di studio la stauroteca di Bessarione,* ed. Peter Schreiner and Valeria Poletto (Venice: Istituto veneto di scienze, lettere ed arti; Gallerie dell'Accademia; Istituto ellenico; Centro tedesco di studi veneziani, forthcoming).

38. Elsner, *Art and the Roman Viewer*, 88–124, quote on 90.

39. Guglielmo Cavallo, Jean Gribomont, and William C. Loerke, *Codex purpureus Rossanensis, Museo dell'Arcivescovado, Rossano calabro: Commentarium* (Rome: Salerno editrice; Graz: Akademische Druck- und Verlagsanstalt, 1987).

40. Lowden, "Beginning of Biblical Illustration," esp. 21. Lowden's attribution to Constantinople challenges Loerke's conclusion about Syria/Palestine as provenance. Cavallo, Gribomont, and Loerke, *Codex purpureus Rossanensis*, 6–11, 166.

41. γεύσασθε καὶ ἴδετε ὅτι χρηστὸς ὁ Κύριος. Ps. 33 (34): 8.

42. οὗτος ὁ ἄρτος, ὃν ἔδωκε Κύριος ὑμῖν φαγεῖν. Exod. 16:15. My translation.

43. ἄρτον οὐρανοῦ ἔδωκεν αὐτοῖς· / ἄρτον ἀγγέλων ἔφαγεν ἄνθρωπος. Ps. 77 (78): 24–25.

44. καὶ ἀπεστάλη πρός με ἓν τῶν Σεραφίμ, καὶ ἐν τῇ χειρὶ εἶχεν ἄνθρακα πύρος καὶ εἶπεν πρὸς με υἱέ ἀνθρώπου τοῦτο περιέλει τὰς ἁμαρτίας σου. Isa. 6:6–7.

45. ἰδοὺ τὸ αἷμα τῆς διαθήκης, ἧς διέθετο Κύριος πρὸς ὑμᾶς. Heb. 9:20 and Exod. 24:8.

46. ποτήριον σωτηρίου λήψομαι, καὶ τὸ ὄνομα Κυρίου ἐπικαλέσομαι. Ps. 115:13.

47. καὶ τὸ ποτήριόν σου μεθύσκον με. Ps. 22 (23): 5.

48. οἱ πίνοντές με ἔτι διψήσουσιν. Sir. 24:21.

49. For more on the cross as marking a chiasm of Spirit branding matter, see Pentcheva, *Sensual Icon*, 28–36, 72–96.

50.   ἐν γὰρ ἐκείνηι
τρητὸς λεπταλέος περὶ νήματα χρυσὸς ἑλιχθείς,
σχήμασιν ἢ σωλῆνος ὁμοίιος ἤ τινος αὐλοῦ,
δέσμιος ἱμερόεντος ἐρείδεται ὑψόθι πέπλου,
ὀξυτέραις ῥαφίδεσσι δεθεὶς καὶ νήμασι Σηρῶν.

Paul the Silentiary, *Descriptio S. Sophiae*, vv. 781–85; English translation in Mango, *Sources and Documents*, 89.

51. Rosamond McKitterick et al., eds. *Old St. Peter's, Rome* (Cambridge: Cambridge University Press, 2013); Herbert L. Kessler, *Old St. Peter's and Church Decoration in Medieval Italy* (Spoleto: Centro italiano di studi sull'alto Medioevo, 2002); Herbert L. Kessler and Johanna Zacharias, *Rome, 1300: On the Path of the Pilgrim* (New Haven: Yale University Press, 2000), 162–74, 195–206; Roberta Vicchi, *Die Patriarchalbasiliken Roms: Peterskirche, San Giovanni in Laterano, San Paolo fuori le Mura, Santa Maria Maggiore*, trans. Christiane Büchel (Antella: Scala, 1999); Marilyn Aronberg Lavin, *The Place of Narrative: Mural Decoration in Italian Churches, 431–1600* (Chicago: University of Chicago Press, 1990); William Tronzo, "The Prestige of St. Peter's: Observations on the Function of Monumental Narrative Cycles in Italy," in *Pictorial Narrative in Antiquity and the Middle Ages*, ed. Herbert L. Kessler and Marianna Shreve Simpson, Studies in Art History 16 (Washington, D.C.: National Gallery of Art, 1986), 93–112; Beat Brenk, *Die frühchristlichen Mosaiken in S. Maria Maggiore zu Rom* (Wiesbaden: Steiner, 1975). For more on the role of anthropomorphic figuration in papal programs, see Erik Thunø, *Image and Relic: Mediating the Sacred in Early Medieval Rome*, Analecta Romana Instituti Danici, Supplementum 32 (Rome: Erma di Bretschneider, 2002).

52. On the liturgical evocations in this *kontakion*, see Romanos Melodos, *Hymnes*, ed. José Grosdidier de Matons, vol. 3, Sources chrétiennes 114 (Paris: Éditions du Cerf, 1965), 227–61, esp. 228–29, and Krueger, "Liturgical Time and Holy Land Reliquaries." For the text, see *Sancti Romani Melodi Cantica*, ed. Paul Maas and C. A. Trypanis (Oxford: Clarendon Press, 1963–70; repr., London: Sandpiper Books, 1997), 1:420–30, and Romanos Melodos, *Hymnes*, 3:227–61. For the memory of the Eucharist in this *kontakion*, see Daniel Schriever, "Memory, Architecture, Performance: Romanos the Melodist *On the Prodigal Son*" (Byzantine Studies Conference, New York, October 22–25, 2015), abstracts, 86.

53. For the understanding of the mirroring as liturgically enacted by the faithful, see Derek Krueger's study of Theodore Stoudites's triodion, *Liturgical Subjects: Christian Ritual, Biblical Narrative, and the Formation of the Self in Byzantium* (Philadelphia: University of Pennsylvania Press, 2014), 164–200.

54. Romanos Melodos, *Hymnes*, 3:228. José Grosdidier de Matons, *Romanos le Mélode et les origines de la poésie religieuse à Byzance* (Paris: Beauchesne, 1977).

55. According to Patmos, MS gr. 213 (eleventh century); Athos, Vatopaedi, MS gr. 1041 (tenth–eleventh centuries); Romanos Melodos, *Hymnes*, 3:227; *Sancti Romani Melodi Cantica*, 1:420. By the Middle Byzantine period, the Parable of the Prodigal Son was part of Lent. Krueger, *Liturgical Subjects*, 3, 176–77.

56. Alexander Lingas, "The Liturgical Place of the Kontakion in Constantinople," in *Liturgy, Architecture, and Art in the Byzantine World: Papers of the XVIII International Byzantine Congress (Moscow, 8–15 August 1991) and Other Essays Dedicated to the Memory of Fr. John Meyendorff*, ed. C. C. Akentiev (St. Petersburg: Publications of the St. Petersburg Society for Byzantine and Slavic Studies, 1995), 50–57.

57. ὁ τῶν αἰώνων δεσπότης καὶ κύριος. Konkation no. 28, in Romanos Melodos, *Hymnes*, 3:234–61.

58. ἀλλὰ καὶ ἀργυρέας τις ἴδοι νέας· ἐμπορίης δὲ
φόρτον ἀερτάζουσι φαεσφόρον· ἐκκρεμέες δὲ
εὐφαέος πλώουσι κατ᾿ ἠέρος ἀντὶ θαλάσσης
οὐδὲ νότον τρομέουσι καὶ ὀψεδύοντα Βοώτην.

Paul the Silentiary, *Descriptio S. Sophiae*, vv. 851–54. My translation.

59. ὃν ἔλαβον   ἐν τοῖς σπλάγχνοις μου. From Romanos Melodos's *kontakion* on the Prodigal Son, stanza 1, v. 11, in *Hymnes*, 3:236–37.

60. Grosdidier de Matons makes the same observation in ibid., 247 n. 3.

61. Ἄγγελοι εἴδοσαν αὐτοὺς   οἱ ὑπουργοῦντες τῷ δείπνῳ
οὕτως εὐφραινομένους   καὶ συντόνως μελῳδοῦντας,
καὶ ζηλοῦσι τούτους   καὶ ἤρξαντο ὑμνῳδίας·.

From Romanos Melodos's *kontakion* on the Prodigal Son, stanza 11, vv. 1–3, in ibid., 248. My translation.

Chapter 7

1. Karl Preisendanz, *Anthologia palatina: Codex palatinus et Codex parisinus phototypice editi* (Leiden: A. W. Sijthoff, 1911); Cameron, *Greek Anthology*.

2. Federica Ciccolella, ed., *Cinque poeti bizantini: Anacreontee dal Barberiniano greco 310* (Alessandria: Edizioni dell'Orso, 2000), 117–73; Carlo Gallavotti, "Note su testi e scrittori di codici greci," *Rivista di studi bizantini e neoellenici*, n.s., 24 (1987): 29–83.

3. Alan Cameron, *Greek Anthology*, 298–307.

4. Ibid., 70, 99–116, 298–307.

5. Instead, it has been the philologists who have tried to address the syncretic Nonnian poetry in relation to the visual arts; see Gianfranco Agosti, "Contextualizing Nonnus's Visual World," in *Nonnus of Panopolis in Context: Poetry and Cultural Milieu in Late Antiquity*, ed. Konstantinos Spanoudakis (Berlin: De Gruyter, 2014), 141–74.

6. Pierre Chuvin, "Homère christianisé: Esthétique profane et symbolique chrétienne dans l'oeuvre de Paul le Silentiaire," *Cristianesimo nella storia* 30 (2009): 471–81.

7. Gianfranco Agosti and Fabrizio Gonnelli, "Materiali per la storia dell'esametro nei poeti cristiani greci," in *Struttura e storia dell'esametro greco*, ed. Marco Fantuzzi and Roberto Pretagostini (Rome: Gruppo editorial internazionale, 1995), 1:289–434; Agosti, "Niveaux de style, littérarité, poétiques"; Francis Vian, "Nonno ed Omero," *Koinonia* 15 (1991): 5–18; Neil Hopkinson, "Nonnus and Homer," in *Studies in the Dionysiaca of Nonnus*, ed. Neil Hopkinson (Cambridge: Cambridge Philosophical Society, 1994), 9–42.

8. Gianfranco Agosti, "Literariness and Levels of Style in Epigraphic Poetry of Late Antiquity," *Ramus* 37, nos. 1–2 (2008): 191–213, esp. 206–9; idem, "La voce dei libri: Dimensioni performative dell'epica greca tardo-antica," in *Approches de la troisième sophistique: Hommages à Jacques Schamp*, ed. Eugenio Amato, Alexandre Roduit, and Martin Steinrück, Collection Latomus 296 (Brussels: Latomus, 2006), 33–62; idem, "*Saxa loquuntur*? Epigrammi epigrafici e diffusione della *paideia* nell'Oriente tardoantico," *Antiquité tardive* 18 (2010):163–80; Peter Brown, *Power and Persuasion in Late Antiquity: Towards a Christian Empire* (Madison: University of Wisconsin Press, 1992), 35–71; Alan Cameron, "Poetry and Literary Culture in Late Antiquity," esp. 341–46; Mary Whitby, "Writing in Greek: Classicism and Compilation, Interaction and Transformation,"

in *Theodosius II: Rethinking the Roman Empire in Late Antiquity,* ed. Christopher Kelly (Cambridge: Cambridge University Press, 2013), 195–218.

9. Nonnus of Panopolis, *Les Dionysiaques,* ed. and trans. Francis Vian et al. (Paris: Société d'édition *Les belles lettres,* 1976–2006). Idem, *Parafrasi del Vangelo di San Giovanni: Canto B,* ed. and trans. Enrico Livrea (Bologna: EDB, 2000). Gianfranco Agosti and Domenico Accorinti have considered the pagan and Christian aspects of Nonnus's oeuvre and begun to outline a more comprehensive approach: Accorinti, "Hermes e Cristo in Nonno," *Prometheus* 21, no. 1 (1995): 23–32; idem, "Poésie et poétique dans l'oeuvre de Nonnos de Panopolis, in Odorico, Agapitos, and Hinterberger, *"Doux remède . . . ,"* 67–98; Agosti, "L'epica greca tardoantica tra oralità e scrittura," in *Atti del Convegno nazionale di studi "Arma virumque cano . . .": L'epica dei Greci e dei Romani, Torino, 23–24 april 2007,* ed. Renato Uglione (Turin: Edizione dell'Orso, 2008), 231–59, esp. 231–37; idem, *"Saxa loquuntur?"*; idem, "Cristianizzazione della poesia greca e dialogo interculturale," *Cristiansesimo nella storia* 31 (2009): 313–35.

10. Nonnus of Panopolis, *Les Dionysiaques,* vol. 2, *Chants III–V,* and vol. 3, *Chants VI–VIII,* ed. and trans. P. Chuvin (Paris: Société d'édition *Les belles lettres,* 1976 and 1992); Pierre Chuvin, *Mythologie et géographie dionysiaques: Recherches sur l'oeuvre de Nonnos de Panopolis* (Clermont-Ferrand [Puy-de-Dôme]: ADOSA, 1991); Nonnus of Panopolis, *Parafrasi del Vangelo di S. Giovanni: Canto xx,* ed. and trans. Domenico Accorinti (Pisa: Scuola normale superiore, 1996); idem, *Parafrasi del Vangelo di San Giovanni: Canto B;* idem, *Parafrasi del Vangelo di S. Giovanni: Canto I,* ed. and trans. Claudio De Stefani (Bologna: Pàtron, 2002); idem, *Parafrasi del Vangelo di San Giovanni: Canto quinto,* ed. and trans. Gianfranco Agosti (Florence: Università degli studi di Firenze, Dipartimento di scienze dell'antichità Giorgio Pasquali, 2003); idem, *Parafrasi del Vangelo di San Giovanni: Canto IV,* ed. and trans. Mariangela Caprara (Pisa: Edizioni della Normale, 2005); idem, *Parafrasi del Vangelo di S. Giovanni: Canto tredicesimo,* ed. and trans. Claudia Greco (Alessandria: Edizioni dell'Orso, 2004).

11. Accorinti, "Hermes e Cristo." Idem, "Poésie et poétique"; Agosti, "L'epica greca tardoantica." Idem, *"Saxa loquuntur?"*; idem, "Cristianizzazione della poesia greca"; and, more recently, Spanoudakis, *Nonnus of Panopolis in Context.*

12. Robert Lamberton, *Homer the Theologian: Neoplatonist Allegorical Reading and the Growth of the Epic Tradition* (Berkeley: University of California Press, 1986); idem, "The Neoplatonists and the Spiritualization of Homer," in *Homer's Ancient Readers: The Hermeneutics of Greek Epic's Earliest Exegetes,* ed. Robert Lamberton and John J. Keaney (Princeton: Princeton University Press, 1992), 115–33; Carine Van Liefferinge, "Homère erre-t-il loin de la science théologique? De la réhabilitation du 'divin' poète par Proclus," *Kernos: Revue internationale et pluridisciplinaire de religion grecque antique* 15 (2002): 199–210.

13.   ΠΑΥΛΟΥ ΣΙΛΕΝΤΙΑΡΙΟΥ

    Ἀνέρα λυσσητῆρι κυνὸς βεβολημένον ἰῷ
       ὕδασι θηρείην εἰκόνα φασὶ βλέπειν.
    λυσσώων τάχα πικρὸν Ἔρως ἐνέπηξεν ὀδόντα
       εἰς ἐμὲ καὶ μανίαις θυμὸν ἐληίσατο.
    σὴν γὰρ ἐμοὶ καὶ πόντος ἐπήρατον εἰκόνα φαίνει
       καὶ ποταμῶν δῖναι καὶ δέπας οἰνοχόον.

    Paul the Silentiary, poem 266, Greek and English translation in William Roger Paton, ed. and trans., *The Greek Anthology* (Cambridge: Harvard University Press, 1970), 1:266–67.

14. Patricia A. Rosenmeyer, *The Poetics of Imitation: Anacreon and the Anacreontic Tradition* (Cambridge: Cambridge University Press, 1992).

15. Ibid., 74–97; Martin L. West, ed., *Carmina Anacreontea* (Leipzig: Teubner, 1984); Manuel Baumbach and Nicola Dümmler, eds., *Imitate Anacreon! Mimesis, Poiesis, and the Poetic Inspiration in the Carmina Anacreontea* (Berlin: De Gruyter, 2014); Alexander Müller, *Die Carmina Anacreontea und Anakreon: Ein literarisches Generationenverhältnis* (Tübingen: Narr, 2010).

16. Rosenmeyer, *Poetics of Imitation,* 63–73.

17.   Ἀνακρέων ἰδών με
    ὁ Τήϊος μελωιδός
    (ὄναρ λέγω) προσεῖπεν·

ὃ δ᾽ ἐξελὼν καρήνου
ἐμοὶ στέφος δίδωσι·
τὸ δ᾽ ὠζ᾽ Ἀνακρέοντος.
ἐγὼ δ᾽ ὁ μωρὸς ἄρας
ἐδησάμην μετώπωι·
καὶ δῆθεν ἄχρι καὶ νῦν
ἔρωτος οὐ πέπαυμαι.

West, *Carmina Anacreontea*, no. 1, vv. 1–3, 11–17, p. 1; English translation in Rosenmeyer, *Poetics of Imitation*, 239.

18.   τὸν Ἀνακρέοντα μιμοῦ,
τὸν ἀοίδιμον μελιστήν.
φιάλην πρόπινε παισίν,
φιάλην λόγων ἐραννήν.

West, *Carmina Anacreontea*, no. 60, vv. 30–33, pp. 47–48; English translation in Rosenmeyer, *Poetics of Imitation*, 266. See also Glenn W. Most, "Τὸν Ἀνακρέοντα μιμοῦ: Imitation and Enactment in the *Anacreontics*," in Baumbach and Dümmler, *Imitate Anacreon*, 145–60.

19.   Δότε μοι λύρην Ὁμήρου
φονίης ἄνευθε χορδῆς·
φέρε μοι κύπελλα θεσμῶν,
φέρε μοι νόμους κεράσσας,
μεθύων ὅπως χορεύσω,
ὑπὸ σώφρονος δὲ λύσσης
μετὰ βαρβίτων ἀείδων
τὸ παροίνιον βοήσω·
δότε μοι λύρην Ὁμήρου
φονίης ἄνευθε χορδῆς.

West, *Carmina Anacreontea*, no. 2, 2; English translation in Rosenmeyer, *Poetics of Imitation*, 239–40.

20. On Anacreontic disarmament, see Rosenmeyer, *Poetics of Imitation*, 127–29.

21. Ibid., 129.

22. West, *Carmina Anacreontea*, no. 38, vv. 18, 25; no. 45 vv. 2, 10; no. 48, v. 2.

23.   Ἄφες με, τοὺς θεούς σοι,
πιεῖν, πιεῖν ἀμυστί·
θέλω, θέλω μανῆναι.

West, *Carmina Anacreontea*, no. 9, vv. 1–3, p. 6; English translation in Rosenmeyer, *Poetics of Imitation*, 242.

24. Rosenmeyer, *Poetics of Imitation*, 82–85.

25.   ἐγὼ δ᾽ ἔχων κύπελλον
καὶ στέμμα τοῦτο χαίτης
{οὐ τόξον, οὐ μάχαιραν,}
θέλω, θέλω μανῆναι.

West, *Carmina Anacreontea*, no. 9, vv. 16–19, p. 7; English translation in Rosenmeyer, *Poetics of Imitation*, 242.

26.   Στέφος πλέκων ποτ᾽ εὗρον
ἐν τοῖς ῥόδοις Ἔρωτα,
καὶ τῶν πτερῶν κατασχών
ἐβάπτισ᾽ εἰς τὸν οἶνον,
λαβὼν δ᾽ ἔπιον αὐτόν·
καὶ νῦν ἔσω μελῶν μου
πτεροῖσι γαργαλίζει.

West, *Carmina Anacreonta*, no. 6, 5; English translation in Rosenmeyer, *Poetics of Imitation*, 241.

27. Romanos Melodos, *Hymns*, 2:44.

28. Bissera V. Pentcheva, "Performing the Sacred in Byzantium: Image, Breath, and Sound," *Performance Research International* 19, no. 3 (2014): 120–28.

29. Pentcheva, "Hagia Sophia and Multisensory Aesthetics," 104–6.

30. John of Gaza's ekphrasis of a world map is in quarternions 41–42 of the Codex Palatinus 23, which is today part of Paris, BnF, Suppl. MS gr. 384; Cameron, *Greek Anthology*, 299.

31. Ciccolella, *Cinque poeti bizantini*, 117–73. Gallavotti, "Note su testi e scrittori di codici greci."

32. John evokes Homer without the gore of war also in his ekphrasis of the world map. Delphine Lauritzen, "La Muse d'Homère dans la *Description* de Jean de Gaza," *Il calamo della memoria* 5 (2012): 221–34.

33. Ὦ φίλοι, ἤτοι κλῆρος ἐμός, χαίρω δὲ καὶ αὐτὸς
Πιερικὴν πλάστιγγα πολύτροπον ὄμμασι λεύσσων·
Μοῦσά με νῦν θώρηξεν ἑκηβόλος, οὐδ' ἐπὶ χάρμην,
οὐκ ἐπὶ δυσμενέων νίφα βάρβαρον, ἀλλὰ μενοινὴν
ὑμετέρην σκοπὸν οἶδα τανύσκοπον, ἥν ῥα δοκεύων
εἴσομαι αἴ κε τύχωμι, πόρη δέ μοι εὖχος Ἀπόλλων.

John of Gaza, *epibatērios*, vv. 1–6, in Ciccolella, *Cinque poeti bizantini*, 128–29. My translation.

34. Ὁ χορὸς τίς ἐστιν οὗτος,
ὁ σοφῆς βρύων μελίσσης;
ἔλαθον πόδες με μᾶλλον
μεμεθυσμένον λαβόντες
Ἑλικῶνος εἰς τὸ μέσσον.

Ὁ δ' ἄναξ λόγων Ἀπόλλων
Ἑλικωνίδες τε Μοῦσαι
τροχαλὸν λαβόντες Ἑρμῆν
κρίσιν εἰσφέρουσι τόλμῃ·
τί πάθω, φίλοι, τί ῥέξω;

Κραδίη, φύγοις τὸ τάρβος,
ἔχε θάρσος εἰσδραμοῦσα,
φιλίης πνέουσι Μούσης,
νοερῶν λόγων κρατοῦσι,
νοεροὺς λόγους κομίζοις.

Ὁ καλὸς γέρων ὁ κύκνος,
Ζεφύρου πνέοντος, ἔγνω
λιγυρὸν μέλος τι μέλπειν
ὁ δὲ δῆμός ἐστιν οὗτος
γλυκερὴν χέων ἐέρσην.

Γέρανοι τρέχουσι πᾶσαι
σπόρον αὔλακος διώκειν·
φιλοτερπέος δὲ Γάζης
σπόρον ἤλυθον λιγαίνειν,
ὁ δὲ δῆμός ἐστιν οὗτος.

Δότε βάρβιτον, δονήσω,
ὁ δὲ καλλίμολπος Ὀρφεὺς
σὺν ἐμοὶ μέλος λιγαίνοι·
ὁ δὲ δῆμός ἐστιν οὗτος,
γλυκερὴ ῥέουσα Μοῦσα.

Περί με πνέων ὁ Φοῖβος
χέλυν ἤλυθεν τινάσσειν

παλάμῃ σοφῇ μελίζων·
ὁ δὲ δῆμός ἐστι Φοῖβος
νοερῆς γέμων μελίσσης.

John of Gaza, *epibatērios*, vv. 6–41, in Ciccolella, *Cinque poeti bizantini*, 130–33. My translation.

35. See chapter 1. Already in Hesiod (*Theogony* 1–21) the Muses perform the circular dance, to which the poets are drawn for inspiration. Miller, *Measures of Wisdom*, 28–29.

36. On the identification of the swarms of wise bees with the circle of contemporary sixth-century poets, see Federica Ciccolella, "'Swarms of the Wise Bee': Literati and Their Audience in Sixth-Century Gaza," in Amato, Roduit, and Steinrück, *Approches de la troisième sophistique*, 80–95.

37. Bachelard, *Water and Dreams*, 187.

38. Ibid., 193.

39.   Πῆι φέρομαι; πῆι μῦθος ἰὼν ἀχάλινος ὁδεύει;
ἴσχεο τολμήεσσα μεμυκότι χείλεϊ φωνή,
μηδ' ἔτι γυμνώσειας ἃ μὴ θέμις ὄμμασι λεύσσειν.
μυστιπόλοι δ' ὑπὸ χερσίν, ὅσοις τόδε θεσμὰ κελεύει,
Σιδονίης φοίνικι βεβαμμένον ἄνθεϊ κόχλου
φᾶρος ἐφαπλώσαντες ἐρέψατε νῶτα τραπέζης,
τέτρασι δ' ἀργυρέῃσιν ἐπὶ πλευρῇσι καλύπτρας
ὀρθοτενεῖς πετάσαντες ἀπείρονι δείξατε δήμωι
χρυσὸν ἅλις καὶ φαιδρὰ σοφῆς δαιδάλματα τέχνης.

Paul the Silentiary, *Descriptio S. Sophiae*, vv. 755–63.

40.   Ζεφύρου πνέοντος αὔραις
Χαρίτων θάλος δοκεύω·
ῥοδέης ἄπαντα χαίτης
Παφίης γέμουσιν ἄλση.

Ὁ δ' Ἔρως σοφῷ βελέμνῳ
φύσιν εἰς φύσιν συνάπτει,
ἵνα μὴ χανοῦσα λήθη
γένος ἐκ γένους καλύψῃ.

Φιλοτερπέες δὲ μολπαὶ
Διονυσίαις ἐν ὥραις
ἔαρος νέον φανέντος
νοεραῖς πνέουσι Μούσαις.

Χλοερῶν ὕπερθε δένδρων
μέλος ὄρνεον λιγαίνει,
δεδονημένη δὲ πᾶσα
φύσις εἰς ἔαρ χορεύει.

Σοφίης ἄναξ Ἀπόλλων
φαέθων ἔλαμψε φέγγος,
ὑπερήμενος δὲ πώλοις
γλυκερὸν φάος προσαύξει.

Δότε μοι ῥόδον Κυθήρης,
ἀγέλαι σοφῆς μελίττης,
ἵνα Κύπριδος γελώσης
μέλος εἰς ῥόδον τινάξω

John of Gaza, poem 4, in Ciccolella, *Cinque poeti bizantini*, 143–49. My translation.

41. Charles Dempsey, *The Portrayal of Love: Botticelli's "Primavera" and Humanist Culture at the Time of Lorenzo the Magnificent* (Princeton: Princeton University Press, 1992); Joanne Snow-Smith, *The "Primavera" of Sandro Botticelli: A Neoplatonic Interpretation* (New York: Lang, 1992).

42. Aby Warburg, "Sandro Botticelli's *Birth of Venus* and *Spring*: An Examination of Concepts of Antiquity in the Italian Early Renaissance" (1893), in *The Renewal of Pagan Antiquity: Contributions to the Cultural History of the European Renaissance,* intro. Kurt W. Forster, trans. David Britt (Los Angeles: Getty Research Institute, 1999), 88–156; Georges Didi-Huberman, "The Imaginary Breeze: Remarks on the Air of the Quattrocento," *Journal of Visual Culture* 2 (2003): 275–89.

43. Dempsey, *Portrayal of Love,* and Warburg, "Sandro Botticelli's *Birth of Venus.*"

44. Warburg, "Sandro Botticelli's *Birth of Venus,*" and Didi-Huberman, "Imaginary Breeze."

45. Kaldellis, "Making of Hagia Sophia." The strong Neoplatonic bias of the intellectual circle of Alexandria, from which the architects of Hagia Sophia came, speaks to the continual and strong presence of the pagan faction. This evidence gives further support to Kaldellis's argument that these pagan circles extended well into the sixth century, and it thus challenges Alan Cameron's thesis placing the last pagans in the closing of the fourth century. Cameron, *The Last Pagans of Rome* (Oxford: Oxford University Press, 2011). On Procopius, see Anthony Kaldellis, *Procopius of Caesarea: Tyranny, History, and Philosophy at the End of Antiquity* (Philadelphia: University of Pennsylvania Press, 2004), 51–60, 104–6.

46. Dominic J. O'Meara, "Geometry and the Divine in Proclus," in *Mathematics and the Divine: A Historical Study,* ed. T. Koetsier and L. Bergmans (Amsterdam: Elsevier, 2005), 135–45. This Neoplatonic perception of geometry is confirmed by the analysis of the mathematics of the plan. See Svenshon and Stichel, "'System of Monads.'" It is also confirmed by the study of light and its relationship to Neoplatonic ideas of beauty and the One. Schibille, *Hagia Sophia,* 171–240.

Conclusion

1. Basil of Caesarea, *De creatione hominis,* bk. 1, sect. 16.

2. Nelly Gasparyan, an Armenian woman, singing a prayer in an abandoned cathedral in eastern Turkey, http://www.chonday.com/Videos/armewsing3, last visited January 16, 2016.

3. See http://hagiasophia.stanford.edu for a video of the concert. Also https://www.youtube.com/watch?v=bHpOiX2sO-s.

4. I see an invitation to go in this direction in Hans Belting, *An Anthropology of Images: Picture, Medium, Body,* trans. Thomas Dunlap (Princeton: Princeton University Press, 2011), 1–36.

5. *Goethe's Literary Essays,* selected and arranged by Joel Elias Spingarn (New York: Harcourt, Brace, 1921), 267. The origin of this thought is in Schelling's *Philosophie der Kunst:* "Architecture is music in space, as it were, frozen music."

6. Manovich, "Poetics of Augmented Space," 229, and, particularly in the context of sound and artificial reverberation, Sterne, "Space Within Space."

BIBLIOGRAPHY

Abbreviations

BHG *Bibliotheca Hagiographica Graeca.* 3rd ed. Edited by François Halkin. 3 vols. Brussels: Société des Bollan-
distes, 1957.
PG *Patrologiae Cursus Completus: Series Graeca.* Edited by J.-P. Migne. 161 vols. Paris: Migne, 1857–66.
PL *Patrologiae Cursus Completus: Series Latina.* Edited by J.-P. Migne. 221 vols. Paris: Migne, 1844–64.

Dictionaries

Chantraine, Pierre. *Dictionnaire étymologique de la langue grecque: Histoire des mots.* 4 vols. Paris: Klincksieck,
1968–80.
Cunliffe, Richard John. *A Lexicon of the Homeric Dialect.* New ed. Norman: University of Oklahoma Press, 1977.
A Greek-English Lexicon. Compiled by Henry George Liddell and Robert Scott. With a revised supplement.
Oxford: Clarendon Press, 1996.
Lampe, G. W. H. *A Patristic Greek Lexicon.* Oxford: Clarendon Press, 1961.
The Oxford Dictionary of Byzantium. Edited by Alexander Kazhdan, Alice-Mary Talbot, Anthony Cutler, Timo-
thy E. Gregory, and Nancy P. Ševčenko. 3 vols. Oxford: Oxford University Press, 1991.

Primary Sources

Agathias
Historiarum Libri Quinque. Edited by Rudolf Keydell. Berlin: De Gruyter, 1967.
Ambrose
Hexameron. In PL 14, cols. 123–272.
English translation by John J. Savage in Ambrose, *Hexameron, Paradise, and Cain and Abel.* The Fathers of
the Church 42. New York: Fathers of the Church, 1961.
Anacreontic anthology
West, Martin L., ed. *Carmina Anacreontea.* Leipzig: Teubner, 1984.
English translation in Rosenmeyer, Patricia A. *The Poetics of Imitation: Anacreon and the Anacreontic Tradi-
tion.* Cambridge: Cambridge University Press, 1992.
Anthologia Graeca
Beckby, Hermann, ed. *Anthologia Graeca: Griechisch-Deutsch.* 2nd ed. 4 vols. Munich: Heimeran, 1965–68.
Paton, William Roger, ed. and trans. *The Greek Anthology.* 5 vols. Loeb Classical Library. Cambridge: Harvard
University Press, 1970.
Athanasius of Alexandria
Epistula ad Marcellinum de interpretatione Psalmorum. In PG 27, cols. 11–60.
English translation by Robert C. Gregg in *Athanasius: The Life of Antony and The Letter to Marcellinus.* New
York: Paulist Press, 1980.

Basil of Caesarea

De creatione hominis. In *Sur l'origine de l'homme.*

De Spiritu Sancto. In *Sur le Saint-Esprit,* edited by Benoît Pruche, with Greek and French, Sources chrétiennes 17bis. Paris: Éditions du Cerf, 1968.

In Hexaemeron. In *Homélies sur l'Hexaéméron,* edited by Stanislas Giet, with Greek and French, 2nd ed., rev. and enl., Sources chrétiennes 26bis. Paris: Éditions du Cerf, 1968.

In quadraginta martyres Sebastenses. In PG 31, cols. 508–25.

Letters and Selected Works. Edited by Philip Schaff and Henry Wace. A Select Library of Nicene and Post-Nicene Fathers of the Christian Church, vol. 8. Edinburgh: T. & T. Clark; Grand Rapids, Mich.: Eerdmans, 1989.

Lettres. Edited by Yves Courtonne. With Greek and French. 3 vols. Paris: Société d'édition *Les belles lettres,* 1957–66.

Sur l'origine de l'homme: Hom. X et XI de l'Hexhaemeron. Introduced and translated by Alexis Smets and Michel van Esbroeck. Paris: Éditions du Cerf, 1970.

Cedrenus, George

Compendium Historiarum. Edited by Immanuel Bekker. 2 vols. Corpus Scriptorum Historiae Byzantinae. Bonn: Weber, 1838–39.

Clement of Alexandria

Protrepticus. In PG 9, cols. 777–94.

Le Protreptique. Edited by Claude Mondésert. With Greek and French. Sources chrétiennes 2bis. Paris: Éditions du Cerf, 1949.

Stromata. In *Clemens Alexandrinus,* edited by Ludwig Früchtel, Otto Stählin, and Ursula Treu, Die griechischen christlichen Schriftsteller der ersten Jahrhunderte 52 (15), 17. Berlin: Akademie Verlag, 1960, 1970.

Consecration of the Sanctuary of Benjamin

Coptic in Coquin, *Livre de la consécration du sanctuaire de Benjamin.*

English translation in *History of the Patriarchs of the Coptic Church of Alexandria,* edited by Basil Evetts, 2:131–41. Paris: Firmin-Didot, 1907.

Constantine V, emperor

Peuseis [Inquiries]. Fragments in Patriarch Nikephoros, *Antirrheticus II adversus Constantinum Copronymum,* in PG 100, cols. 205–534.

Excerpts. In *Textus Byzantinos ad iconomachiam pertinentes,* edited by Herman Hennephof, 52–57. Leiden: Brill, 1969.

Excerpts. In Hans Georg Thümmel, *Die Frühgeschichte der ostkirchlichen Bilderlehre: Texte und Untersuchungen zur Zeit vor dem Bilderstreit,* Texte und Untersuchungen zur Geschichte der altkirchlichen Literatur 139. Berlin: Akademie Verlag, 1992.

English translation in Stephen Gero, *Byzantine Iconoclasm During the Reign of Constantine V,* 37–52. Louvain: Secrétariat du Corpus SCO, 1977.

Constantine Porphyrogennetos, *De ceremoniis*

Moffatt, Ann, and Maxeme Tall, trans. *Book of Ceremonies: With the Greek Edition of the Corpus Scriptorum Historiae Byzantinae (Bonn, 1829).* With Greek and English. 2 vols. Canberra: Australian Association for Byzantine Studies, 2012.

Reiske, Johann Jakob, ed. *De ceremoniis aulae Byzantinae.* 2 vols. Corpus Scriptorum Historiae Byzantinae, 9–10. Bonn: Weber, 1829.

Vogt, Albert, ed. *Le livre des cérémonies.* 2 vols. Paris: Société d'édition *Les belles lettres,* 1967.

Contacarium, see *Psaltikon*

Cosmas Indicopleustes, *Topographia Christiana*

Wolska-Conus, Wanda, ed. *Topographie chrétienne.* 3 vols. Sources chrétiennes 141, 159, 197. Paris: Éditions du Cerf, 1968–73.

Enkaineia kontakion of Hagia Sophia, composed 562 (in Constantinople) (537)

　　Greek in *Fourteen Early Byzantine Cantica,* edited by C. A. Trypanis, Wiener byzantinische Studien 5:139–47. Vienna: Hermann Böhlaus, 1968.

　　English translation in Andrew Palmer, "The Inauguration Anthem of Hagia Sophia in Edessa: A New Edition and Translation with Historical and Architectural Notes and a Comparison with a Contemporary Constantinopolitan Kontakion," *Byzantine and Modern Greek Studies* 12 (1988): 140–44.

Euchologion, Byzantine

　　In Jacques Goar, *Euchologion sive rituale graecorum.* Venice: Ex typographia Bartholomaei Javarina, 1730. Reprint, Graz: Akademische Druck- und Verlagsanstalt, 1960.

Euchologion Barberini

　　Parenti, Stefano, and Elena Velkovska, eds. *L'Eucologio Barberini gr. 336.* Ephemerides liturgicae, Subsidia 80. Rome: C.L.V.-Edizioni liturgiche, 1995.

George of Cyprus (or Leontios of Cyprus)

　　Adversos Judeos, bk. v. In Hans Georg Thümmel, *Die Frühgeschichte der ostkirchlichen Bilderlehre: Texte und Untersuchungen zur Zeit vor dem Bilderstreit,* Texte und Untersuchungen zur Geschichte der altkirchlichen Literatur 139:340–54, no. 70. Berlin: Akademie Verlag, 1992.

Germanus, patriarch of Constantinople

　　Historia mystica ecclesiae catholicae. In *St. Germanus of Constantinople: On the Divine Liturgy,* edited by Paul Meyendorff. Crestwood, N.Y.: St. Vladimir's Seminary Press, 1984.

Graduale Vat. lat. 5319 (Old Roman Gradual)

　　In Stäblein and Landwehr-Melnicki, *Die Gesänge des altrömischen Graduale.*

Gregory of Nazianzus

　　De theologia. In *Die fünf theologischen Reden,* edited by Joseph Barbel, with Greek and German. Düsseldorf: Patmos-Verlag, 1963.

　　Funebris oratio in laudem Basilii Magni. In *Discours funèbres en l'honneur de son frère Césaire et de Basile de Césarée,* with Greek and French. Paris: Picard, 1908.

　　Lettres théologiques. Edited by Paul Gallay. With Greek and French. Sources chrétiennes 208. Paris: Éditions du Cerf, 1974.

　　In Machabaeorum laudem. In PG 35, cols. 911–34.

　　In novam Dominicam. In PG 36, cols. 607–22.

Gregory of Nyssa

　　De hominis opificio. In PG 44, cols. 123–56.

　　　　French translation by Jean Laplace, *La creation de l'homme.* Sources chrétiennes 6. 1943. Reprint, Paris: Éditions du Cerf, 2002.

　　　　English translation by Philip Schaff, *On the Making of Man. A Select Library of Nicene and Post-Nicene Fathers of the Christian Church. Second series* (Edinburgh: T & T Clark; Grand Rapids, Mich.: Eerdmans, 1988–1991), vol. 5.

　　De sancto Theodoro. In PG 46, cols. 736–48.

　　De virginitate. In *Traité de la virginité,* edited by Michel Aubineau, Sources chrétiennes 119, with Greek and French. Paris: Éditions du Cerf, 1966.

　　Encomium in sanctum Stephanum protomartyrem. Edited by Otto Lendle. With Greek and German. Leiden: Brill, 1968.

　　Encomium in sanctum Stephanum protomartyrem, II. In PG 46, cols. 721–36.

　　Gregorii Nysseni Opera. Leiden: Brill, 1952–.

　　Gregorii Nysseni Opera: Supplementum. Edited by Hadwiga Hörner. Leiden: Brill, 1972.

　　In laudem SS. Quadraginta Martyrum. In PG 46, cols. 749–72.

　　Vita sanctae Macrinae. In *Vie de sainte Macrine,* edited by Pierre Marval, Sources chrétiennes 178, with Greek and French. Paris: Éditions du Cerf, 1971.

Hesiod

Theogony. Edited by M. L. West. Oxford: Clarendon Press, 1966.

Homer

Ilias. In *Homeri Opera,* edited by Thomas W. Allen. Oxford: Clarendon Press, 1919.

Iliad. Edited and translated by A. T. Murray. 2 vols. Loeb Classical Library. 1924. Reprint, Cambridge: Harvard University Press, 1995.

Iamblichus

De mysteriis. Edited by Edouard des Places. Paris: Société d'édition *Les belles lettres,* 1966.

On the Mysteries. Translated by Emma Clarke, John Dillon, and Jackson Hershbell. Altanta: Society of Biblical Literature, 2003.

John Chrysostomos

Divine Liturgy. In *Liturgies Eastern and Western,* edited by F. E. Brightman, 309–44. Oxford: Clarendon Press, 1896.

In Epistolam ad Colossenses. In PG 62, cols. 299–392.

In Psalmum XLI. In PG 55, cols. 35–498.

English translation in McKinnon, *Music in Early Christian Literature.*

John of Damascus

Contra imaginum calumniatores orationes tres. Vol. 3 of *Die Schriften des Johannes von Damaskos.* Edited by Bonifatius Kotter. Berlin: De Gruyter, 1975.

John of Gaza

Anacreontea, in Ciccolella, *Cinque poeti bizantini.*

Justin Martyr

Quaestiones et responsiones. In PG 6, cols. 1241–1400.

Justinian

Novellae. Edited by Rudolf Schoell. Vol. 3 of *Corpus iuris civilis,* edited by Paul Krueger et al. Berlin: Weidmann, 1928.

Kontakarion, see *Psaltikon*

Leontius of Neapolis, Pseudo-, see George of Cyprus

Macrobius

Commentarii in Somnium Scipionis. Edited by James Willis. Bibliotheca Scriptorum Graecorum et Romanorum Teubneriana. Leipzig: Teubner, 1963.

Commentary on the Dream of Scipio. Translated by William Harris Stahl. New York: Columbia University Press, 1952.

Maximus the Confessor

Ad Thalassium. In PG 90, cols. 241–786.

Laga, Carl, and Carlos Steel, eds. *Maximi Confessoris Quaestiones ad Thalassium.* With Greek and Latin. 2 vols. Corpus Christianorum, Series Graeca 7 and 22. Turnhout: Brepols, 1980–90.

English translation by Paul Blowers and Robert Louis Wilken in *On the Cosmic Mystery of Jesus Christ: Selected Writings from St. Maximus the Confessor.* Crestwood, N.Y.: St. Vladimir's Seminary Press, 2003.

English translation by Despina D. Prassas in *St. Maximus the Confessor's Questions and Doubts.* DeKalb: Northern Illinois University Press, 2010.

Ambigua

Constas, Nicholas, ed. and trans. *On Difficulties in the Church Fathers: The Ambigua.* With Greek and English. 2 vols. Dumbarton Oaks Medieval Library 28–29. Cambridge: Harvard University Press, 2014.

English translation by Paul Blowers and Robert Louis Wilken in *On the Cosmic Mystery of Jesus Christ: Selected Writings from St. Maximus the Confessor.* Crestwood, N.Y.: St. Vladimir's Seminary Press, 2003.

Mystagogia. In PG 91, cols. 658–718.

   English translation by Dom Julian Stead, O.S.B., *The Church, the Liturgy, and the Soul of Man: The Mystagogia of St. Maximus the Confessor.* Still River, Mass.: St. Bede's Publications, 1982.

Muqaffa, Severus ibn al-

   Severus ibn al-Muqaffa': Alexandrinische Patriarchengeschichte von S. Marcus bis Michael I, 61–767; Nach ältesten 1266 geschriebenen Hamburger Handschrift im arabischen Urtext. Edited by Christian Friedrich Seybold. Hamburg: L. Gräfe, 1912.

Mystagogical texts on the Byzantine liturgy

   Bornert, René, ed. *Les commentaires byzantins de la Divine Liturgie du VIIe au XVe siècle.* Paris: Institut français d'études byzantines, 1966.

Narratio de S. Sophia [*Diēgēsis peri tēs Hagias Sophias*]

   In *Scriptores originum Constantinopolitanarum,* edited by Theodor Preger, 1:74–108. Leipzig: Teubner, 1901.

Nicomachus the Pythagorean

   The Manual of Harmonics of Nicomachus the Pythagorean. Translated by Flora R. Levin. Grand Rapids, Mich.: Phanes Press, 1994.

Nonnus of Panopolis

   Dionysiaca

      Edited by Francis Vian, Pierre Chuvin, et al., as *Les Dionysiaques.* 19 vols. Paris: Société d'édition *Les belles lettres,* 1976–2006.

      English translation by W. H. D. Rouse, *Dionysiaca.* 3 vols. Loeb Classical Library. London: Heinemann, 1940.

   Paraphrase of the Gospel of John

      Parafrasi del Vangelo di S. Giovanni: Canto I. Edited and translated by Claudio De Stefani. Bologna: Pàtron, 2002.

      Parafrasi del Vangelo di San Giovanni: Canto B. Edited and translated by Enrico Livrea. Bologna: EDB, 2000.

      Parafrasi del Vangelo di San Giovanni: Canto IV. Edited and translated by Mariangela Caprara. Pisa: Edizioni della Normale, 2005.

      Parafrasi del Vangelo di San Giovanni: Canto quinto. Edited and translated by Gianfranco Agosti. Florence: Università degli studi di Firenze, Dipartimento di scienze dell'antichità Giorgio Pasquali, 2003.

      Parafrasi del Vangelo di S. Giovanni: Canto tredicesimo. Edited and translated by Claudia Greco. Alessandria: Edizioni dell'Orso, 2004.

      Parafrasi del Vangelo di S. Giovanni: Canto XX. Edited and translated by Domenico Accorinti. Pisa: Scuola normale superiore, 1996.

Paul the Silentiary, *Descriptio S. Sophiae et ambonis*

   Bauten. Vol. 5 of *Prokop: Werke.* Edited by Otto Veh. Munich: Heimeran, 1977.

   Description de Sainte-Sophie de Constantinople. Edited and translated by Marie-Christine Fayant and Pierre Chuvin. With Greek and French. Die: A. Die, 1997.

   Excerpts in English translation. In Cyril Mango, *The Art of the Byzantine Empire, 312–1453: Sources and Documents,* 80–96. Englewood Cliffs, N.J.: Prentice-Hall, 1972. Reprint, Toronto: University of Toronto Press, 1986.

   In *Johannes von Gaza, Paulus Silentiarius und Prokopios von Gaza; Kunstbeschreibungen justinianischer Zeit,* edited by Paul Friedländer. Leipzig: Teubner, 1912. Reprint, Hildesheim: Olms, 1969.

   Italian translation by Maria Luigia Fobelli, *Un tempio per Giustiniano: Santa Sofia di Costantinopoli e la "Descrizione" di Paolo Silenziario.* Rome: Viella, 2005.

   Two *prooimia* (introductions). In Peter N. Bell, *Three Political Voices from the Age of Justinian: Agapetus, "Advice to the Emperor"; "Dialogue on Political Science"; Paul the Silentiary, "Description of Hagia Sophia."* Liverpool: Liverpool University Press, 2009.

Photios

    Bibliotheca. PG 103.

Plato

    Timaeus. In *Platonis Opera,* vol. 4, edited by Johannes Burnet. 1902. Reprint, Oxford: Clarendon Press, 1968.

        English translation by H. D. P. Lee in *Timaeus and Critias.* Harmondsworth: Penguin Books, 1971.

Procopius of Caesarea, *De aedificiis*

    In *Procopii Caesariensis opera omnia,* edited by Jakob Haury, revised by Gerhard Wirth, vol. 4. Leipzig: Teubner, 1964.

    Italian translation by Paolo Cesaretti and Maria Luigia Fobelli, *Santa Sofia di Costantinopoli: Un tempio di luce (De aedificiis I 1,1–78).* Milan: Jaca, 2011.

    English translation by H. B. Dewing in *Procopius,* vol. 7. Cambridge: Harvard University Press, 1940.

Prudentius, *Liber Peristephanon*

    In *Prudentius,* edited by H. J. Thomson, vol. 2. Cambridge: Harvard University Press, 1953.

Psaltikon

    Contacarium Ashburnhamense: Codex Bibl. Laurentianae Ashburnhamensis 64; Phototypice Depictus. Edited by Carsten Høeg. Copenhagen: Munksgaard, 1956.

Pseudo-Dionysius

    Corpus Dionysiacum: Pseudo-Dionysius Areopagita. Vol. 1, edited by Beate Regina Suchla, and vol. 2, edited by Günther Heil and Adolf Martin Ritter. Patristische Texte und Studien 33 and 36. Berlin: De Gruyter, 1990–91.

    English translation by Colm Luibheid in *Pseudo-Dionysius: The Complete Works.* London: SPCK, 1987.

Quintilian, *Institutio oratoria*

    Winterbottom, Michael, ed. *Institutionis oratoriae libri duodecim.* 2 vols. Oxford: Clarendon Press, 1970.

    English translations from books 1, 2, and 10 in *Quintilian on the Teaching of Speaking and Writing,* edited by James J. Murphy. Carbondale: Southern Illinois University Press, 1987.

Romanos Melodos

    Hymnes. Edited and translated by José Grosdidier de Matons. 5 vols. Sources chrétiennes 99, 110, 114, 128, 283. Paris: Éditions du Cerf, 1964–81.

    Kontakia of Romanos, Byzantine Melodist. Translated by Marjorie Carpenter. 2 vols. Columbia: University of Missouri Press, 1970.

    Sancti Romani Melodi Cantica. Edited by Paul Maas and C. A. Trypanis. 2 vols. Oxford: Clarendon Press, 1963–70. Reprint, London: Sandpiper Books, 1997.

The Russian Primary Chronicle

    Cross, Samuel Hazzard, and Olgerd P. Sherbowitz-Wetzor, eds. and trans. *The Russian Primary Chronicle: Laurentian Text.* Cambridge: Harvard University Press, 1953.

Septuaginta

    Brenton, Lancelot C. L., ed. *The Septuagint with Apocrypha: Greek and English.* Peabody, Mass.: Hendrickson, 1986.

    Rahlfs, Alfred, ed. *Septuaginta.* 2 vols. 1935. Reprint, Stuttgart: Württembergische Bibelanstalt, 1975.

Skylitzes, John

    Synopsis Historiarum. Edited by Hans Thurn. Corpus Fontium Historiae Byzantinae 5. Berlin: De Gruyter, 1973.

Socrates, *Historia Ecclesiastica*

    In PG 67, cols. 30–842.

Symeon of Thessaloniki

    The Liturgical Commentaries. Edited and translated by Steven Hawkes-Teeples. Toronto: Pontifical Institute of Mediaeval Studies, 2011.

    Treatise on Prayer. Translated by H. L. N. Simmons. Brookline, Mass.: Hellenic College Press, 1984.

Symeon the Stylite

La vie ancienne de S. Syméon Stylite le Jeune (521–592). Edited and translated by Paul van den Ven. 2 vols. Subsidia Hagiographica 32. Brussels: Société des Bollandistes, 1962–70.

Vita S. Symeonis Stylitae Junioris. In BHG³ 1689–91.

Theophrastus

De lapidibus. Edited and translated by D. E. Eichholz. Oxford: Clarendon Press, 1965.

Typika (monastic foundation documents)

Dmitrievskij, Aleksej, ed. Opisanie liturgicheskih' rukopisei. 3 vols. Kiev: G. T. Korchak'-Novizkago, 1895–1917. Reprint, Hildesheim: G. Olms, 1965.

Typikon of the Great Church

Mateos, Juan, ed. Le Typicon de la Grande Église: Ms. Saint-Croix no. 40, xe siècle. 2 vols. Rome: Pont. Institutum Orientalium Studiorum, 1963.

Vita Maximi Confessoris

In BHG³ 1234.

Epifanovič, S. L., ed. Materialy k izučeniju žizni i tvorenii prepodobnago Maksima Ispovednika. Kiev: Tipografija Universiteta Sv. Vladimira, 1917.

Syriac in Sebastian P. Brock, "An Early Syriac Life of Maximus the Confessor." Analecta Bollandiana 91 (1973): 299–346.

Secondary Sources

Abbate, Carolyn. "Music—Drastic or Gnostic?" Critical Inquiry 30, no. 3 (2004): 505–36.

Abel, Jonathan S., Nicholas J. Bryan, Patty P. Huang, Miriam Kolar, and Bissera V. Pentcheva. "Estimating Room Impulse Responses from Recorded Balloon Pops." In Audio Engineering Society 129th Convention (November 2010), http://www.aes.org/e-lib/browse.cfm?elib=15594.

Abel, Jonathan S., and Miriam Kolar. "On the Acoustics of the Underground Galleries of Ancient Chavín de Huántar, Peru." Paper presented at the Acoustics '08 conference, Paris, France, 2008.

Abel, Jonathan S., Bissera V. Pentcheva, Miriam Kolar, Micheal J. Wilson, Nicholas J. Bryan, Patty P. Huang, Fernando Lopez-Lezcano, and Cappella Romana. "Prokeimenon for the Feast of St. Basil (12th Century)." From the concert Transitions 2011, Night 1: Acousmatic Soundscapes Under the Stars, Center for Computer Research in Music and Acoustics, Stanford University, September 28, 2011.

Abel, Jonathan S., and Kurt James Werner. "Live Auralization of Cappella Romana at the Bing Concert Hall, Stanford University." In Pentcheva, Aural Architecture, 198–223.

Abel, Jonathan S., Wiesław Woszczyk, Doyuen Ko, Scott Levine, Jonathan Hong, Travis Skare, Michael J. Wilson, Sean Coffin, and Fernando Lopez-Lezcano. "Recreation of the Acoustics of Hagia Sophia in Stanford's Bing Concert Hall for the Concert Performance and Recording of Cappella Romana." Paper presented at the International Symposium on Room Acoustics, Toronto, Canada, June 9–11, 2013, ftp://s00279.cisti.nrc.ca/outgoing/CD_ISRA2013/Papers/P055.pdf, accessed January 10, 2014.

Accorinti, Domenico. "Hermes e Cristo in Nonno." Prometheus 21, no. 1 (1995): 23–32.

———. "Poésie et poétique dans l'oeuvre de Nonnos de Panopolis." In Odorico, Agapitos, and Hinterberger, "Doux remède . . . ," 67–98.

Agosti, Gianfranco. "Contextualizing Nonnus's Visual World." In Spanoudakis, Nonnus of Panopolis in Context, 141–74.

———. "Cristianizzazione della poesia greca e dialogo interculturale." Cristianesimo nella storia 31 (2009): 313–35.

———. "L'epica greca tardoantica tra oralità e scrittura." In Uglione, Atti del Convegno nazionale di studi "Arma virumque cano . . . ," 231–59.

———. "Immagini e poesia nella tarda antichità: Per uno studio dell'estetica visuale della poesia greca fra III e IV sec. d.C." *Incontri triestini di filologia classica* 4 (2004–5): 351–74.

———. "Literariness and Levels of Style in Epigraphic Poetry of Late Antiquity." *Ramus* 37, nos. 1–2 (2008): 191–213.

———. "Niveaux de style, littérarité, poétiques: Pour une histoire du système de la poésie classicisante au VIe siècle." In Odorico, Agapitos, and Hinterberger, *"Doux remède . . . ,"* 99–119.

———. "*Saxa loquuntur?* Epigrammi epigrafici e diffusione della *paideia* nell'Oriente tardoantico." *Antiquité tardive* 18 (2010): 163–80.

———. "La voce dei libri: Dimensioni performative dell'epica greca tardoantica." In Amato, Roduit, and Steinrück, *Approches de la troisième sophistique,* 33–62.

Agosti, Gianfranco, and Fabrizio Gonnelli. "Materiali per la storia dell'esametro nei poeti cristiani greci." In Fantuzzi and Pretagostini, *Struttura e storia dell'esametro greco,* 1:289–434.

Akentiev, C. C., ed. *Liturgy, Architecture, and Art in the Byzantine World: Papers of the XVIII International Byzantine Congress (Moscow, 8–15 August 1991) and Other Essays Dedicated to the Memory of Fr. John Meyendorff.* St. Petersburg: Publications of the St. Petersburg Society for Byzantine and Slavic Studies, 1995.

Alchermes, Joseph D. "Art and Architecture in the Age of Justinian." In Maas, *Cambridge Companion to the Age of Justinian,* 343–75.

Altman, Rick, ed. *Sound Theory / Sound Practice.* New York: Routledge, 1992.

Altripp, Michael, and Claudia Nauerth, eds. *Architektur und Liturgie: Akten des Kolloquiums vom 25. bis 27. Juli 2003 in Greifswald.* Spätantike, frühes Christentum, Byzanz, Reihe B, Studien und Perspektiven, vol. 21. Wiesbaden: Reichert, 2006.

Amato, Eugenio, Alexandre Roduit, and Martin Steinrück, eds. *Approches de la troisième sophistique: Hommages à Jacques Schamp.* Collection Latomus 296. Brussels: Latomus, 2006.

Andia, Ysabel de. *Henosis: L'union à Dieu chez Denys l'Aréopagite.* Leiden: Brill, 1996.

Angelopoulos, Lycourgos, dir. *The Divine Liturgy of St. John Chrysostom.* The Greek Byzantine Choir. OPS 30–78. Paris: Opus 111, 1993. Compact disc.

Antoniadi, Eugène Michel. *Ekphrasis tes Hagias Sophias, etoi melete synthetike kai analytike hypo epopsin architektoniken, archaiologiken kai historiken tou polythryletou temenous Konstantinoupoleos.* 3 vols. Leipzig: Teubner, 1907–9.

Armstrong, A. H. "Beauty and the Discovery of Divinity in the Thought of Plotinus." In Mansfeld and Rijk, *Kephalaion,* 155–63.

———. "'Emanation' in Plotinus." *Mind* 46 (1937): 61–66.

———. "Platonic Mirrors." *Eranos Jahrbuch* 55 (1986): 147–81.

Armstrong, Gregory T. "Constantine's Churches: Symbol and Structure." *Journal of the Society of Architectural Historians* 33, no. 1 (1974): 5–16.

Arranz, Miguel, ed. *L'eucologio costantinopolitano agli inizi del secolo XI.* Rome: Pontifica Università Gregoriana, 1996.

———. "Les grandes étapes de la liturgie byzantine: Palestine—Byzance—Russie; Essai d'aperçu historique." In *Liturgie de l'Église particulière et liturgie de l'Église universelle,* 43–72.

———. "La liturgie des heures selon l'ancien Euchologe byzantin." In *Eulogia: Miscellanea liturgica in onore di P. Burkhard Neunheuser O.S.B.,* Studia Anselmiana 68, Analecta liturgica 1:1–19. Rome: Editrice Anselmiana, 1979.

———. *Molitvi i psalmopenie.* Rome: Opere religiose Russe, Russicum, 1997.

———. "L'office de l'Asmatikos Hesperinos ('vêpres chantées') de l'ancien Euchologe byzantin." *Orientalia christiana periodica* 44 (1978): 107–30, 391–419.

———. "L'office de l'Asmatikos Orthros ('matines chantées') de l'ancien Euchologe byzantin." *Orientalia christiana periodica* 47 (1981): 122–57.

Asgari, Nuşin. "The Proconnesian Production of Architectural Elements in Late Antiquity, Based on Evidence from the Marble Quarries." In *Constantinople and Its Hinterland: Papers from the Twenty-Seventh Spring*

Symposium of Byzantine Studies, Oxford, April 1993, edited by Cyril Mango and Gilbert Dagron, 263–88. Aldershot: Ashgate, 1995.

Assis, Ellie. "Chiasmus in Biblical Narrative: Rhetoric of Characterization." *Prooftexts* 22 (2002): 273–304.

Åström, Paul, and Mendel Kleiner. "The Brittle Sound of Ceramics—Can Vases Speak?" *Archaeology and Natural Science* 1 (1993): 66–72.

Attridge, Harold W., and Margot E. Fassler, eds. *Psalms in Community: Jewish and Christian Textual, Liturgical, and Artistic Traditions.* Atlanta: Society of Biblical Literature, 2003.

Austin, J. L. *How to Do Things with Words.* Oxford: Clarendon Press, 1962.

Auzépy, Marie-France. "Les Isauriens et l'espace sacré: L'église et les reliques." In Kaplan, *Le sacré et son inscription,* 13–24.

Bacci, Michele. "Santidad localizada: Percepciones de los *loca sancta* de Palestina en la Edad Media." *Codex aqvilarensis: Revista de arte medieval* 30 (2014): 109–32.

Bachelard, Gaston. *Water and Dreams: An Essay on the Imagination of Matter.* Translated by Edith R. Farrell. 1983. Reprint, Dallas: Dallas Institute of Humanities and Culture, 2006.

Bacon, Helen H. "The Chorus in Greek Life and Drama." *Arion: A Journal of Humanities and the Classics* 3, no. 1 (1994–95): 6–24.

Badrill, Jonathan. "The Church of Sts. Sergius and Bacchus in Constantinople and the Monophysite Refugees." *Dumbarton Oaks Papers* 54 (2000): 1–11.

———. "A New Temple for Byzantium: Anicia Juliana, King Solomon, and the Gilded Ceiling of the Church of St. Polyeuktos in Constantinople." In Bowden, Gutteridge, and Machado, *Social and Political Life in Late Antiquity,* 339–70.

Bahrani, Zainab. *The Infinite Image: Art, Time, and Aesthetic Dimension in Antiquity.* London: Reaktion, 2014.

Balás, David L. *Metousia Theou: Man's Participation in God's Perfections According to Saint Gregory of Nyssa.* Studia Anselmiana philosophica theologica 55. Rome: Herder, 1966.

Baldovin, John Francis. *The Urban Character of Christian Worship: The Origins, Development, and Meaning of Stational Liturgy.* Orientalia Christiana analecta 228. Rome: Pontificium Institutum Studiorum Orientalium, 1987.

Bandt, Ros, Michelle Duffy, and Dolly MacKinnon, eds. *Hearing Places: Sound, Place, Time, and Culture.* Newcastle upon Tyne: Cambridge Scholars, 2009.

Barber, Charles. "Beyond Representation/The Gift of Sight." In Betancourt and Taroutina, *Byzantium/Modernism,* 330–48.

———. *Figure and Likeness: On the Limits of Representation in Byzantine Iconoclasm.* Princeton: Princeton University Press, 2002.

———, ed. *The Theodore Psalter: Electronic Facsimile.* Champaign: University of Illinois Press in association with the British Library, 2000.

———. "Thingliness." In Peers, *Byzantine Things in the World,* 99–108.

Barrie, Thomas. *The Sacred In-Between: The Mediating Roles of Architecture.* London: Routledge, 2010.

Barry, Fabio. "Walking on Water: Cosmic Floors in Antiquity and the Middle Ages." *Art Bulletin* 89, no. 4 (2007): 627–56.

Barsanti, Claudia. "L'esportazione di marmi dal Proconneso nelle regioni pontiche durante il IV–VI secolo." *Rivista dell'Istituto nazionale d'archeologia e storia dell'arte* 12 (1989): 91–220.

Barsanti, Claudia, Alessandra Guiglia Guidobaldi, and Jean-Pierre Sodini. "La sculpture architecturale en marbre au VIe siècle à Constantinople et dans les régions sous influence constantinopolitaine." In Cambi and Marin, *Acta XIII Congressus internationalis archaeologiae christianae,* 301–76.

Baumbach, Manuel, and Nicola Dümmler, eds. *Imitate Anacreon! Mimesis, Poiesis, and the Poetic Inspiration in the Carmina Anacreontea.* Berlin: De Gruyter, 2014.

Becker, Andrew Sprague. *The Shield of Achilles and the Poetics of Ekphrasis.* London: Rowman & Littlefield, 1995.

Beghin, Tom, Martha de Francisco, and Wiesław Woszczyk. *The Virtual Haydn: Complete Works for Solo Keyboard.* Hong Kong: Naxos Blu-Ray Audio, 2009.

Beierwaltes, Werner. "Plotins Metaphysik des Lichtes." In Zintzen, *Die Philosophie des Neuplatonismus,* 75–117.

Belting, Hans. *An Anthropology of Images: Picture, Medium, Body.* Translated by Thomas Dunlap. Princeton: Princeton University Press, 2011.

———. *Florenz und Bagdad: Eine westöstliche Geschichte des Blicks.* Munich: Beck, 2008.

———. *Likeness and Presence: A History of the Image Before the Era of Art.* Translated by Edmund Jephcott. Chicago: University of Chicago Press, 1994.

Benjamin, Walter. "The Task of the Translator." Translated by James Hynd and E. M. Valk. In Weissbort and Eysteinsson, *Translation—Theory and Practice,* 298–307.

Bennett, Jane. *Vibrant Matter: A Political Ecology of Things.* Durham: Duke University Press, 2010.

Beranek, Leo. *Concert Halls and Opera Houses: Music, Acoustics, and Architecture.* 2nd ed. New York: Springer, 2004.

Berlekamp, Persis. *Wonder, Image, and Cosmos in Medieval Islam.* New Haven: Yale University Press, 2011.

Betancourt, Roland. "Introduction: The Slash as Method." In Betancourt and Taroutina, *Byzantium/Modernism,* 179–94.

Betancourt, Roland, and Maria Taroutina, eds. *Byzantium/Modernism: The Byzantine as Method in Modernity.* Leiden: Brill, 2014.

Bianchi, Fulvia, Matthias Bruno, and Marilda De Nuccio. "La Domus Sopra le Sette Sale: La decorazione pavimentale e parietale dell'aula absidata." In De Nuccio and Ungaro, *I marmi colorati della Roma imperiale,* 161–69.

Binning, Ravinder. "Christ's All-Seeing Eye in the Dome." In Pentcheva, *Aural Architecture.*

Birnbaum, Adalbert. "Die Oktogone von Antiochia, Nazianz und Nyssa: Rekonstruktionsversuche." *Repertorium für Kunstwissenschaft* 36 (1913): 181–209.

Blesser, Barry, and Linda-Ruth Salter. *Spaces Speak, Are You Listening? Experiencing Aural Architecture.* Cambridge: MIT Press, 2007.

Böhm, Thomas. *Theoria, Unendlichkeit, Aufstieg: Philosophische Implikationen zu "De vita Moysis" von Gregor von Nyssa.* Leiden: Brill, 1996.

Borsook, Eve, Fiorella Gioffredi Superbi, and Giovanni Pagliarulo, eds. *Medieval Mosaics: Light, Color, Materials.* Villa I Tatti, the Harvard University Center for Italian Renaissance Studies 17. Milan: Silvana, 2000.

Bornert, René. *Les commentaires byzantins de la Divine Liturgie du VIIe au XVe siècle.* Paris: Institut français d'études byzantines, 1966.

Bottomley, Henry L. "The Story of St. Thomas' Church." *Architectural Record* 35 (1914): 101–31.

Bouras, Laskarina, and Maria G. Parani. *Lighting in Early Byzantium.* Dumbarton Oaks Byzantine Collection Publications 11. Washington, D.C.: Dumbarton Oaks Research Library and Collection. Distributed by Harvard University Press, 2008.

Bourdakis, Vassilis, and Dimitris Charitos. *Communicating Space(s): Proceedings of the 24th Conference on Education in Computer Aided Design in Europe, 6.–9.9.2006.* Volos: University of Thessaly, 2006.

Bowden, William, Adam Gutteridge, and Carlos Machado, eds. *Social and Political Life in Late Antiquity.* Late Antique Archaeology 3.1. Leiden: Brill, 2006.

Bowe, Barbara E. "Dancing into the Divine: The Hymn of the Dance in the *Acts of John.*" *Journal of Early Christian Studies* 7, no. 1 (1999): 83–104.

Boyd, Susan A. "A 'Metropolitan' Treasure from a Church in the Provinces: An Introduction to the Study of the Sion Treasure." In Boyd and Mango, *Ecclesiastical Silver Plate in Sixth-Century Byzantium,* 5–38.

Boyd, Susan A., and Marlia Mundell Mango, eds. *Ecclesiastical Silver Plate in Sixth-Century Byzantium.* Washington, D.C.: Dumbarton Oaks Research Library and Collection, 1992.

Boys, Thomas. *Tactica Sacra: An Attempt to Develope, and to Exhibit to the Eye by Tabular Arrangements, a General Rule of Composition Prevailing in the Holy Scriptures.* London: Hamilton, 1824.

Breck, John. *The Shape of Biblical Language: Chiasmus in the Scriptures and Beyond.* Crestwood, N.Y.: St. Vladimir's Seminary Press, 1994.

Brenk, Beat. *The Apse, the Image, and the Icon: An Historical Perspective of the Apse as a Space for Images.* Wiesbaden: Reichert, 2010.

———. *Die frühchristlichen Mosaiken in S. Maria Maggiore zu Rom.* Wiesbaden: Steiner, 1975.

Brightman, F. E. "The *Historia Mystagogica* and Other Greek Commentaries on the Byzantine Liturgy." *Journal of Theological Studies* 9, no. 34 (1908): 248–67, and no. 35 (1908): 387–97.

Brock, Sebastian P. "An Early Syriac Life of Maximus the Confessor." *Analecta Bollandiana* 91 (1973): 299–345.

———. *Fire from Heaven: Studies in Syriac Theology and Liturgy.* Variorum Collected Studies Series. Aldershot: Ashgate, 2006.

Brown, Bill. "Thing Theory." *Critical Inquiry* 28, no. 1 (2001): 1–22.

Brown, Peter. *Power and Persuasion in Late Antiquity: Towards a Christian Empire.* Madison: University of Wisconsin Press, 1992.

———. "The Rise and Function of the Holy Man in Late Antiquity." *Journal of Roman Studies* 61 (1971): 80–101.

Brubaker, Leslie. *Inventing Byzantine Iconoclasm.* London: Bristol Classical Press, 2012.

Brubaker, Leslie, and John Haldon. *Byzantium in the Iconoclast Era, c. 680–850: A History.* Cambridge: Cambridge University Press, 2011.

———. *Byzantium in the Iconoclast Era (ca. 680–850): The Sources, an Annotated Survey.* Aldershot: Ashgate, 2001.

Buchwald, Hans. "Saint Sophia, Turning Point in the Development of Byzantine Architecture?" In Hoffmann, *Die Hagia Sophia in Istanbul,* 29–58.

Bull, Michael, and Les Bach, eds. *The Auditory Culture Reader.* Oxford: Berg, 2003.

Bush, Olga. "'When My Beholder Ponders': Poetic Epigraphy in the Alhambra." *Artibus Asiae* 66, no. 2 (2006): 55–67.

Butler, Judith. *Gender Trouble: Feminism and the Subversion of Identity.* New York: Routledge, 1999.

Calame, Claude. *Choruses of Young Women in Ancient Greece: Their Morphology, Religious Role, and Social Function.* Translated by Derek Collins and Janice Orion. Lanham, Md.: Rowman & Littlefield, 1997.

———. "From Choral Poetry to Tragic Stasimon: The Enactment of Women's Song." *Arion: A Journal of Humanities and the Classics* 3, no. 1 (1994–95): 136–54.

Cambi, Nenad, and Emilio Marin, eds. *Acta XIII Congressus internationalis archaeologiae christianae, Split-Poreč, 1994.* Split: Archeološki muzej; Rome: Pontificio istituto di archeologia cristiana, 1998.

Cameron, Alan. *The Greek Anthology: From Meleager to Planudes.* Oxford: Clarendon Press; New York: Oxford University Press, 1993.

———. "Isidore of Miletus and Hypatia: On the Editing of Mathematical Texts." *Greek, Roman, and Byzantine Studies* 31 (1990): 103–27.

———. *The Last Pagans of Rome.* Oxford: Oxford University Press, 2011.

———. "Poetry and Literary Culture in Late Antiquity." In Swain and Edwards, *Approaching Late Antiquity,* 327–54.

Cameron, Averil. *Procopius and the Sixth Century.* Berkeley: University of California Press, 1985.

Cappella Romana. *Byzantium in Rome: Medieval Byzantine Chant from Grottaferrata.* Edited by Ioannis Arvanitis and Alexander Lingas. Portland, Ore.: Cappella Romana, 2006. Two compact discs.

Cattoi, Thomas. "Liturgy as Cosmic Transformation." In *The Oxford Handbook of Maximus Confessor,* edited by Pauline Allen and Neil Bronwen, 414–38. Oxford: Oxford University Press, 2015.

Cavallo, Guglielmo, Jean Gribomont, and William C. Loerke. *Codex purpureus Rossanensis, Museo dell'Arcivescovado, Rossano calabro: Commentarium.* Rome: Salerno editrice; Graz: Akademische Druck- und Verlagsanstalt, 1987.

Charbonnier, Georges. *Le monologue du peintre.* Paris: Imprimerie Chantenay, 1959.

Chion, Michel. *The Voice in Cinema.* Translated by Claudia Gorbman. New York: Columbia University Press, 1999.

———. "Wasted Words." In Altman, *Sound Theory / Sound Practice,* 104–10.

Chuvin, Pierre. "Homère christianisé: Esthétique profane et symbolique chrétienne dans l'oeuvre de Paul le Silentiaire." *Cristianesimo nella storia* 30 (2009): 471–81.

———. *Mythologie et géographie dionysiaques: Recherches sur l'oeuvre de Nonnos de Panopolis.* Clermont-Ferrand (Puy-de-Dôme): ADOSA, 1991.

Ciccolella, Federica, ed. *Cinque poeti bizantini: Anacreontee dal Barberiniano Greco 310.* Alessandria: Edizioni dell'Orso, 2000.

———. "'Swarms of the Wise Bee': Literati and Their Audience in Sixth-Century Gaza." In Amato, Roduit, and Steinrück, *Approches de la troisième sophistique,* 80–95.

Cirillo, Ettore, and Francesco Martellota. *Worship, Acoustics, and Architecture.* Brentwood, Essex: Multi-Science Publishing, 2006.

Classen, Constance, ed. *The Book of Touch.* Oxford: Berg, 2005.

———. *The Color of Angels: Cosmology, Gender, and the Aesthetic Imagination.* London: Routledge, 1998.

———, ed. *Worlds of Sense: Exploring the Senses in History Across Cultures.* London: Routledge, 1993.

Classen, Constance, David Howes, and Anthony Synnott. *Aroma: The Cultural History of Smell.* London: Routledge, 1994.

Coakley, Sarah, and Charles M. Stang, eds. *Re-thinking Dionysius the Areopagite.* Chichester: Wiley-Blackwell, 2009.

Colish, Marcia L. *The Mirror of Language: A Study in the Medieval Theory of Knowledge.* Rev. ed. Lincoln: University of Nebraska Press, 1983.

Collins, George R. "The Transfer of Thin Masonry Vaulting from Spain to America." *Journal of the Society of Architectural Historians* 27, no. 3 (1968): 176–201.

Conomos, Dimitri E. *Byzantine Trisagia and Cheroubika of the Fourteenth and Fifteenth Centuries: A Study of the Late Byzantine Liturgical Chant.* Thessaloniki: Patriarchal Institute for Patristic Studies, 1974.

———. *The Late Byzantine and Slavonic Communion Cycle: Liturgy and Music.* Washington, D.C.: Dumbarton Oaks Research Library and Collection, 1985.

———. "Music for the Evening Office on Whitsunday." In *Actes de xve Congrès international d'études byzantines,* 453–69. Athens: Association internationale des études byzantines, 1979.

Constas, Nicholas. Introduction to *On Difficulties in the Church Fathers: The Ambigua,* by Maximus the Confessor, edited and translated by Nicholas Constas, vol. 1, Dumbarton Oaks Medieval Library, 28:vii–xxxii. Cambridge: Harvard University Press, 2014.

Conybeare, F. C., ed. *Rituale Armenorum: Being the Administration of the Sacraments and Breviary Rites of the Armenian Church.* Oxford: Clarendon Press, 1905.

Conybeare, F. C., and Oliver Wardrop. "The Georgian Version of the Liturgy of St. James." *Revue de l'Orient chrétien* 18 (1913): 396–410; 19 (1914): 155–73.

Coquin, René-Georges, ed. *Livre de la consécration du sanctuaire de Benjamin: Introduction, édition, traduction et annotations.* Cairo: Institut français d'archéologie oriental du Caire, 1975.

Corrigan, Kathleen Anne. *Visual Polemics in the Ninth-Century Byzantine Psalters.* Cambridge: Cambridge University Press, 1992.

Cuomo, S. *Technology and Culture in Greek and Roman Antiquity.* Cambridge: Cambridge University Press, 2007.

Ćurčić, Slobodan. "Architecture as Icon." In Ćurčić and Hadjitryphonos, *Architecture as Icon,* 3–37.

———. "Design and Structural Innovation in Byzantine Architecture Before Hagia Sophia." In Mark and Çakmak, *Hagia Sophia from the Age of Justinian to the Present,* 16–38.

Ćurčić, Slobodan, and Evangelia Hadjitryphonos, eds. *Architecture as Icon: Perception and Representation of Architecture in Byzantine Art.* Princeton: Princeton University Art Museum, distributed by Yale University Press, 2010.

Cutler, Anthony. "Structure and Aesthetic at Hagia Sophia in Constantinople." *Journal of Aesthetics and Art Criticism* 25 (1966): 27–35.

Cytowic, Richard E. *Synesthesia: A Union of the Senses.* Springer Series in Neuropsychology. New York: Springer, 1989.

Daim, Falko, and Jörg Drauschke, eds. *Byzanz—das Römerreich im Mittelalter.* Teil 2, pt. 1, *Schauplätze.* Mainz: Römisch-Germanisches Zentralmuseum, 2010.

Daniélou, Jean. *L'être et le temps chez Grégoire de Nysse.* Leiden: Brill, 1970.

Dann, Kevin T. *Bright Colors Falsely Seen: Synaesthesia and the Search for Transcendental Knowledge.* New Haven: Yale University Press, 1998.

Dark, Kenneth Rainsbury, and Jan Kostenec. "A New Archaeological Study of Hagia Sophia, Istanbul." In *Proceedings of the 22nd International Congress of Byzantine Studies, Sofia, 22–27 August 2011,* vol. 1, edited by Iliya Iliev, 213–37. Sofia: Bulgarian Historical Heritage Foundation, 2011.

Darmstädter, Ernst. "Anthemios und sein 'künstliches Erdbeben' in Byzanz." *Philologus* 88 (1933): 477–82.

Davies, Paul, and Deborah Howard. Introduction to Davies, Howard, and Pullan, *Architecture and Pilgrimage, 1000–1500,* 1–18.

Davies, Paul, Deborah Howard, and Wendy Pullan, eds. *Architecture and Pilgrimage, 1000–1500: Southern Europe and Beyond.* Farnham: Ashgate, 2013.

Day, Jo. "Introduction: Making Senses of the Past." In *Making Senses of the Past: Toward a Sensory Archaeology,* edited by Jo Day, 1–31. Carbondale: Southern Illinois University Press, 2013.

Deichmann, Friedrich Wilhelm. "Das Oktogon von Antiocheia: Heroon-Martyrion, Palastkirche oder Kathedrale?" *Byzantinische Zeitschrift* 65 (1972): 40–56.

———. *Ravenna, Hauptstadt des spätantiken Abendlandes.* 2 vols. Wiesbaden: F. Steiner, 1969–76.

de Grazia, Margreta, Maureen Quilligan, and Peter Stallybrass, eds. *Subject and Object in Renaissance Culture.* Cambridge: Cambridge University Press, 1996.

Deleuze, Gilles, and Félix Guattari. "On the Refrain." In *A Thousand Plateaus: Capitalism and Schizophrenia,* translated by Brian Massumi, 310–50. Minneapolis: University of Minnesota Press, 1987.

Dempsey, Charles. *The Portrayal of Love: Botticelli's "Primavera" and Humanist Culture at the Time of Lorenzo the Magnificent.* Princeton: Princeton University Press, 1992.

De Nuccio, Marilda, and Lucrezia Ungaro, eds. *I marmi colorati della Roma imperiale.* Venice: Marsilio, 2002.

Der Nersessian, Sirarpie. *L'illustration des psautiers grecs du Moyen Âge.* Vol. 2, *Londres Add. 19.352.* Bibliothèque des cahiers archéologiques 5. Paris: Klincksieck, 1970.

Derrida, Jacques. *Dissemination.* Translated by Barbara Johnson. Chicago: University of Chicago Press, 1981.

———. *On the Name.* Edited by Thomas Dutoit, translated by David Wood, John P. Leavey Jr., and Ian McLeod. Stanford: Stanford University Press, 1995.

Didi-Huberman, Georges. *Fra Angelico: Dissemblance and Figuration.* Translated by Jane Marie Todd. Chicago: University of Chicago Press, 1995.

———. "The Imaginary Breeze: Remarks on the Air of the Quattrocento." *Journal of Visual Culture* 2 (2003): 275–89.

D'Ippolito, Gennaro. *Studi nonniani: L'epillio nelle Dionisiache.* Quaderni dell'Istituto di filologia greca della Università di Palermo 3. Palermo: Presso l'Accademia, 1964.

Di Salvo, P. Bartolomeo. "Gli *Asmata* nella musica bizantina." *Bolletino della Badia Greca di Grottaferrata* 13 (1959): 45–50, 127–45; 14 (1960): 145–78.

Dobszay, László, ed. *Cantus Planus: Papers Read at the Seventh Meeting, Sopron, Hungary, 1995.* Budapest: Hungarian Academy of Sciences, 1998.

Dolezal, Mary-Lyon. "Illuminating the Liturgical Word: Text and Image in a Decorated Lectionary (Mount Athos, Dionysiou Monastery, cod. 587)." *Word and Image* 12 (1996): 23–60.

———. "The Middle Byzantine Lectionary: Textual and Pictorial Expression of Liturgical Ritual." 2 vols. Ph.D. diss., University of Chicago, 1991.

Doneda, Annalisa. "I manoscritti liturgico-musicali bizantini: Tipologie e organizzazione." In Escobar, *El palimpsesto grecolatino como fenómeno librario y textual,* 83–112.

Downey, Glanville. "Byzantine Architects: Their Training and Methods." *Byzantion* 18 (1948): 99–118.

———. *Constantinople in the Age of Justinian.* Norman: University of Oklahoma Press, 1960.

Doyle, Peter. *Echo and Reverb: Fabricating Space in Popular Music Recording, 1900–1960.* Middletown: Wesleyan University Press, 2005.

Duffy, Stephen. *The Dynamics of Grace: Perspectives in Theological Anthropology.* New Theology Studies 3. Collegeville, Minn.: Liturgical Press, 1993.

Dufrenne, Suzy. *L'illustration des psautiers grecs du Moyen Âge.* Vol. 1, *Pantocrator 61, Paris grec 20, British Museum 40731.* Paris: Klincksieck, 1966.

Duvernoy, Sylvie, and Orietta Pedemonte, eds. *Nexus VI, Architecture and Mathematics.* Turin: Kim Williams Books, 2006.

Eastmond, Antony, and Liz James, eds. *Icon and Word: The Power of Images in Byzantium; Studies Presented to Robin Cormack.* Aldershot: Ashgate, 2003.

Edgerton, Samuel Y. *The Mirror, the Window, and the Telescope: How Renaissance Linear Perspective Changed Our Vision of the Universe.* Ithaca: Cornell University Press, 2009.

Elkins, James. *On Pictures and the Words That Fail Them.* Cambridge: Cambridge University Press, 1998.

Elsner, Jaś, ed. *Art and Text in Roman Culture.* Cambridge: Cambridge University Press, 1996.

———. *Art and the Roman Viewer: The Transformation of Art from the Pagan World to Christianity.* Cambridge: Cambridge University Press, 1995.

———. "From the Culture of Spolia to the Cult of Relics: The Arch of Constantine and the Genesis of Late Antique Forms." *Papers of the British School at Rome* 68 (2000): 149–84.

———. "Iconoclasm as Discourse: From Antiquity to Byzantium." *Art Bulletin* 94, no. 3 (2012): 368–94.

———. "Introduction: The Genre of Ekphrasis." In "The Verbal and The Visual: Cultures of Ekphrasis in Antiquity," edited by Jaś Elsner, special issue, *Ramus* 31, nos. 1–2 (2002): 1–18.

———. "Late Antique Art: The Problem of the Concept and the Cumulative Aesthetic." In Swain and Edwards, *Approaching Late Antiquity,* 271–309.

———. "The Rhetoric of Buildings in the *De Aedificiis* of Procopius." In James, *Art and Text in Byzantine Culture,* 33–57.

Elsner, John. "The Viewer and the Vision: The Case of the Sinai Apse." *Art History* 17 (1994): 81–102.

Ergin, Nina. "The Soundscape of Sixteenth-Century Istanbul Mosques: Architecture and Qur'an Recital." *Journal of the Society of Architectural Historians* 67, no. 2 (2008): 204–22.

Escobar, Àngel, ed. *El palimpsesto grecolatino como fenómeno librario y textual.* Colección Actas, Filologia. Zaragoza: Institución "Fernando el Catolico," 2006.

Evangelatou, Maria. "Liturgy and the Illustration of the Ninth-Century Marginal Psalters." *Dumbarton Oaks Papers* 63 (2009): 59–116.

Evans, James Allan. *The Emperor Justinian and the Byzantine Empire.* Westport, Conn.: Greenwood Press, 2005.

Fantuzzi, Marco, and Roberto Pretagostini. *Struttura e storia dell'esametro greco.* 2 vols. Rome: Gruppo editoriale internazionale, 1995–96.

Farina, Angelo, and Regev Ayalon. "Recording Concert Hall Acoustics for Posterity." Paper presented at the 24th AES (Audio-Engineering Studies) Conference on Multichannel Audio, Banff, Alberta, June 26–28, 2003. http://www.ramsete.com/Public/AES-24/183-AES24.PDF, accessed May 16, 2010.

Fausti, Patrizio, Roberto Pompoli, and Nicola Prodi. "Comparing the Acoustics of Mosques and Byzantine Churches." Paper for the CAHRISMA Project (EU Contract ICA3-CT-1999-00007, Conservation of the Acoustical Heritage and Revival of Sinan's Mosques Acoustics, CAHRISMA, 2000–2003).

Ferguson, James G., Jr., and Robert B. Newman. "Gothic Sound for the Neo-Gothic Chapel of Duke University." *Journal of the Acoustical Society of America* 66, no. 1 (1979), S26.

Finamore, John. "Plotinus and Iamblichus on Magic and Theurgy." *Dionysius* 17 (1999): 83–94.

Findikyan, Michael Daniel. "Armenian Hymns of the Holy Cross and the Jerusalem Encaenia." *Revue des études arméniennes* 32 (2010): 25–58.

———. "The Armenian Ritual of the Dedication of a Church: A Textual and Comparative Analysis of Three Early Sources." *Orientalia christiana periodica* 64 (1998): 75–121.

Finke, Ronald A. *Principles of Mental Imagery.* Cambridge: MIT Press, 1989.

Fischer, M. "Marble from Pentelicon, Paros, Thasos, and Proconnesus in Ancient Israel: An Attempt at a Chronological Distinction." In *ASMOSIA VII: Actes du VIIe Colloque international de l'ASMOSIA, Thasos, 15–20 septembre, 2003,* Bulletin de correspondance hellénique, supplément 51:399–412. Athens: École française d'Athènes, 2009.

Fischer-Lichte, Erika, Christian Horn, Sandra Umathum, and Matthias Warstat, eds. *Performativität und Ereignis.* Tübingen: A. Francke, 2003.

Flood, Finbarr Barry. "Bodies and Becoming: Mimesis, Mediation, and the Ingestion of the Sacred in Christianity and Islam." In Promey, *Sensational Religion,* 459–93.

———. "From Icon to Coin: Potlatch, Piety, and Idolatry in Medieval Islam." In *Ritual, Images, and Daily Life: The Medieval Perspective,* edited by Gerhard Jaritz, 163–72. Vienna: LIT Verlag, 2012.

———. "Notes from the Field: Anthropomorphism." *Art Bulletin* 94, no. 1 (2012): 18–20.

———. "Presentation, (Re)animation, and the Enchantments of Technology." *Res: Anthropology and Aesthetics* 61–62 (2012): 229–36.

Forbes, John. *Studies on the Book of Psalms: The Structural Connection of the Book of Psalms, Both in Single Psalms and in the Psalter as an Organic Whole.* Edited by James Forrest. Edinburgh: T. & T. Clark, 1888.

———. *The Symmetrical Structure of Scripture, or The Principles of Scripture Parallelism Exemplified in an Analysis of the Decalogue, the Sermon on the Mount, and Other Passages of the Sacred Writings.* Edinburgh: T. & T. Clark, 1854.

Franses, Rico. "Lacan and Byzantine Art: In the Beginning Was the Image." In Betancourt and Taroutina, *Byzantium/Modernism,* 311–29.

———. "When All That Is Gold Does Not Glitter: On the Strange History of Looking at Byzantine Art." In Eastmond and James, *Icon and Word,* 13–24.

Fricke, Beate. "Tales from Stones, Travels Through Time: Narrative and Vision in the Casket from the Vatican." *West 86th: A Journal of Decorative Arts, Design History, and Material Culture* 21, no. 2 (2014): 230–50.

Friz, Anna. "Vacant City Radio." In Ripley, Polo, and Wrigglesworth, *In the Place of Sound,* 15–26.

Frolow, A. *La relique de la Vraie Croix: Recherches sur le développement d'un culte.* Archives de l'Orient chrétien 7. Paris: Institut français d'études byzantines, 1961.

Fumerton, Patricia, and Simon Hunt, eds. *Renaissance Culture and the Everyday.* Philadelphia: University of Pennsylvania Press, 1999.

Gade, Anders. "Acoustics in Halls for Speech and Music." In Rossing, *Springer Handbook of Acoustics,* 301–50.

Galadza, Daniel. "*Logikē Latreia* (Romans 12:1) as a Definition of the Liturgy." *Logos: A Journal of Eastern Christian Studies* 52, nos. 1–2 (2011): 109–24.

Galavaris, George. "Manuscripts and the Liturgy." In Vikan, *Illuminated Greek Manuscripts from American Collections,* 20–23.

Gallavotti, Carlo. "Note su testi e scrittori di codici greci." *Rivista di studi bizantini e neoellenici,* n.s., 24 (1987): 29–83.

Gavrilović, Zaga A. "Divine Wisdom as Part of Byzantine Imperial Ideology: Research into the Artistic Interpretations of the Theme in Medieval Serbia; Narthex Programmes of Lesnovo and Sopoćani." *Zograf* 11 (1982): 44–53.

Gell, Alfred. *Art and Agency: An Anthropological Theory.* Oxford: Clarendon Press, 1998.

Gnoli, Raniero. *Marmora romana.* Rome: Edizioni dell'elefante, 1971.

Goethe, Johann Wolfgang von. *Goethe's Literary Essays.* Selected and arranged by Joel Elias Spingarn. New York: Harcourt, Brace, 1921.

Golder, Herbert. Preface to *Arion: A Journal of Humanities and the Classics* 3, no. 1 (1994–95): 1–5.

Goldhill, Simon, and Robin Osborne, eds. *Art and Text in Ancient Greek Culture.* Cambridge: Cambridge University Press, 1994.

Golitzin, Alexander. *Et introibo ad altare dei: The Mystagogy of Dionysius Areopagita; With Special Reference to Its Predecessors in the Eastern Christian Tradition.* Thessaloniki: Patriarchikon Idruma Paterikōn Meletōn, 1994.

Gonzalez, Valérie. *Beauty and Islam: Aesthetics in Islamic Art and Architecture.* London: I. B. Tauris, 2001.

———. *Le piège de Salomon: La pensée de l'art dans le Coran.* Paris: Albin Michel, 2002.

Gonzalez-Senmartî, Antoni. "La ποικιλία como principio estilistico de las *Dionisiacas* de Nono." *Anuari de filologia* 7 (1981): 101–7.

Graf, Fritz. *Magic in the Ancient World.* Translated by Franklin Philip. Cambridge: Harvard University Press, 1997.

Greenhalgh, Michael. *Marble Past, Monumental Present: Building with Antiquities in the Mediaeval Mediterranean.* The Medieval Mediterranean 80. Leiden: Brill, 2009.

Griffith, Rosemary. "Neo-Platonism and Christianity: Pseudo-Dionysius and Damascius." *Studia patristica* 29 (1997): 238–43.

Grobe, Lars O., Oliver Hauck, and Andreas Noback. "Das Licht in der Hagia Sophia—eine Computersimulation." In Daim and Drauschke, *Byzanz—das Römerreich im Mittelalter, Teil 2, pt. 1, Schauplätze,* 97–111.

Grosdidier de Matons, José. *Romanos le Mélode et les origines de la poésie religieuse à Byzance.* Paris: Beauchesne, 1977.

Guidobaldi, Federico, and Alessandra Guiglia Guidobaldi. *Pavimenti marmorei di Roma dal IV al IX secolo.* Studi di antichità cristiana 36. Vatican City: Pontificio istituto di archeologia cristiana, 1983.

Guiglia Guidobaldi, Alessandra. "I marmi di Giustiniano: Sectilia parietali nella Santa Sofia di Costantinopoli." In Quintavalle, *Medioevo mediterraneo,* 160–74.

———. "I mosaici aniconici della Santa Sofia di Costantinopoli nell'età di Giustiniano." In *La mosaïque gréco-romaine VII: Actes du VIIème colloque international pour l'étude de la mosaïque antique, Tunis, 3–7 octobre 1994,* 2:691–702. Tunis: Institut national du patrimoine, 1999.

Guiglia Guidobaldi, Alessandra, and Claudia Barsanti, eds. *Santa Sofia di Costantinopoli: L'arredo marmoreo della grande chiesa giustinianea.* Studi di antichità cristiana 60. Vatican City: Pontificio istituto di archeologia cristiana, 2004.

Gumbrecht, Hans Ulrich. "The Charm of Charms." In *A New History of German Literature,* edited by David E. Wellbery, 1–7. Cambridge: Harvard University Press, 2005.

———. "Reading for the *Stimmung?* About the Ontology of Literature Today." *Boundary 2* 35, no. 3 (2008): 213–21.

———. *Production of Presence: What Meaning Cannot Convey.* Stanford: Stanford University Press, 2004.

———. *Stimmungen lesen: Über eine verdeckte Wirklichkeit der Literatur.* Munich: Hanser, 2011.

Hadot, Pierre. *Plotinus, or The Simplicity of Vision.* Translated by Michael Chase. Chicago: University of Chicago Press, 1993.

Hahn, Cynthia J. *Strange Beauty: Issues in the Making and Meaning of Reliquaries, 400–Circa 1204.* University Park: Pennylvania State University Press, 2012.

Hahn, Cynthia J., and Holger Klein, eds. *Saints and Sacred Matter: The Cult of Relics in Byzantium and Beyond.* Washington, D.C.: Dumbarton Oaks Research Library and Collection, 2015.

Halleux, Robert. *Le problème des métaux dans la science antique.* Paris: Société d'édition *Les belles lettres,* 1974.

Halporn, James W., Martin Oswald, and Thomas G. Rosenmeyer. *The Meters of Greek and Latin Poetry.* London: Methuen, 1963.

Hamburger, Jeffrey. "Speculations on Speculation: Vision and Perception in the Theory and Practice of Mystical Devotion." In Haug and Schneider-Lastin, *Deutsche Mystik im abendländischen Zusammenhang,* 353–408.

Hanke, Gregor Maria. *Vesper und Orthros des Kathedralritus der Hagia Sophia zu Konstantinopel: Eine strukturanalytische und entwicklungsgeschichtliche Untersuchung unter besonderer Berücksichtigung der Psalmodie und der Formulare in den Euchologien.* 2 vols. Ph.D. diss., Philosopisch-Theologische Hochschule St. Georgen, Frankfurt am Mein, 2002.

Harris, Simon. "The Byzantine Office of the Genuflexion." *Music and Letters* 77 (1996): 333–47.

———, ed. *The Communion Chants of the Thirteenth-Century Byzantine Asmatikon.* Amsterdam: Hardwood Academic Publishers, 1999.

Harris, Yolande. "The Building as Instrument." In Bandt, Duffy, and MacKinnon, *Hearing Places,* 404–11.

Harrison, R. M. *Excavations at Saraçhane in Istanbul.* Vol. 1. Princeton: Princeton University Press; Washington, D.C.: Dumbarton Oaks Research Library and Collection, 1986.

Harvey, Susan Ashbrook. *Scenting Salvation: Ancient Christianity and the Olfactory Imagination.* Berkeley: University of California Press, 2006.

Hauck, Oliver. "Computing the 'Holy Wisdom': Form•Z and Radiance as Analytic Tools for Historic Building Research." In Yessios, *Digital Media and the Creative Process,* 124–25. http://www.formz.com/jointstudy/JS2008/18Computing%20the%20Holy%20Wisdom.pdf, accessed June 3, 2010.

Haug, Walter, and Wolfram Schneider-Lastin, eds. *Deutsche Mystik im abendländischen Zusammenhang: Neu erschlossene Texte, neue methodische Ansätze, neue theoretische Konzepte.* Tübingen: Max Niemeyer, 2000.

Hautecoeur, Louis. *Mystique et architecture: Symbolisme de cercle et de la coupole.* Paris: A. & J. Picard, 1954.

Haven, Cynthia. "Finely Tuned." *Stanford Magazine,* January/February 2013, 46–53.

Heffernan, James A. W. *Museum of Words: The Poetics of Ekphrasis from Homer to Ashbery.* Chicago: University of Chicago Press, 1993.

Heidegger, Martin. *Poetry, Language, Thought.* Translated by Albert Hofstadter. New York: Harper & Row, 1971.

———. "The Thing." In *Poetry, Language, Thought,* 163–80.

Henrichs, Albert. "'Why Should I Dance?': Choral Self-Referentiality in Greek Tragedy." *Arion: A Journal of Humanities and the Classics* 3, no. 1 (1994–95): 56–111.

Hickmann, Ellen, Ricardo Eichmann, and Anne D. Kilmer, eds. *Studien zur Musikarchäologie III: Archäologie früher Klangerzeugung und Tonordnung; Vorträge des 2. Symposiums der Internationalen Studiengruppe Musikarchäologie im Kloster Michaelstein, 17.–23. September 2000.* Rahden: Leidorf, 2002.

Hinton, Stephen. "A Note on the Vineyard Style." *Stanford Live,* January 2013, 11–12.

Hoffmann, Volker, ed. *Der geometrische Entwurf der Hagia Sophia in Istanbul.* Bern: Lang, 2005.

———, ed. *Die Hagia Sophia in Istanbul: Bilder aus sechs Jahrhunderten und Gaspare Fossatis Restaurierung der Jahre 1847 bis 1849.* Bern: Peter Lang, 1999. Exh. cat.

Hopkinson, Neil. "Nonnus and Homer." In Hopkinson, *Studies in the Dionysiaca of Nonnus,* 9–42.

———, ed. *Studies in the Dionysiaca of Nonnus.* Cambridge: Cambridge Philosophical Society, 1994.

Howard, David M., and Jamie A. S. Angus. *Acoustics and Psychoacoustics.* 4th ed. Amsterdam: Focal, 2009.

Howard, Deborah, and Laura Moretti. *Sound and Space in Renaissance Venice: Architecture, Music, Acoustics.* New Haven: Yale University Press, 2009.

Howes, David, ed. *Empire of the Senses: The Sensual Culture Reader.* Oxford: Berg, 2005.

———, ed. *The Varieties of Sensory Experience: A Sourcebook in the Anthropology of the Senses.* Toronto: University of Toronto Press, 1991.

Hunter-Crawley, Heather. "Embodying the Divine: The Sensational Experience of the Sixth-Century Eucharist." In *Making Senses of the Past: Toward a Sensory Archaeology,* edited by Jo Day, 160–76. Carbondale: Southern Illinois University Press, 2013.

Huxley, George Leonard. *Anthemius of Tralles: A Study of Later Greek Geometry.* Greek, Roman, and Byzantine Monographs 1. Cambridge, Mass.: Eaton Press, 1959.

Iliadis, I. G. "The Natural Lighting in the Dome of the Rotunda in Thessaloniki." *Lighting Research and Technology* 37 (2005): 183–97.

Isar, Nicoletta. "*Chōra:* Tracing the Presence." *Review of European Studies* 1, no. 1 (2009): 39–55.

———. "Chorography (*Chora, Choros*)—a Performative Paradigm of Creation of Sacred Space in Byzantium." In Lidov, *Hierotopy,* 59–90.

———. "*Choros:* Dancing into the Sacred Space of Chora." *Byzantion* 75 (2005): 199–224.

———. "*Choros* of Light: Vision of the Sacred in Paulus the Silentiary's Poem *Descriptio S. Sophiae.*" *Byzantinische Forschungen* 28 (2004): 215–42.

———. *Chorós: The Dance of Adam; The Making of Byzantine Chorography, the Anthropology of the Choir of Dance in Byzantium.* Leiden: Alexandros Press, 2011.

———. "The Dance of Adam: Reconstructing the Byzantine *Choros.*" *Byzantinoslavica* 61 (2003): 79–204.

———. "The Iconic *Chōra:* A Space of Kenotic Presence and Void." *Transfiguration: Nordisk tidsskrift for kunst og kristendom* 2 (2000): 65–80.

———. "Undoing Forgetfulness: Chiasmus of Poetical Mind—a Cultural Paradigm of Archetypal Imagination." *Europe's Journal of Psychology* 1, no. 3 (2005). http://ejop.psychopen.eu/article/view/370/html.

Iser, Wolfgang. "The Reading Process: A Phenomenological Approach." In Tompkins, *Reader-Response Criticism,* 50–69.

Ivanovic, Filip. *Symbol and Icon: Dionysius the Areopagite and the Iconoclastic Crisis.* Eugene, Ore.: Pickwick Publications, 2010.

Jabi, Wassim, and Iakovos Potamianos. "Geometry, Light, and Cosmology in the Church of Hagia Sophia." *International Journal of Architectural Computing* 5, no. 2 (2007): 303–19.

Jakobs, Peter H. F. *Die frühchristlichen Ambone Griechenlands.* Bonn: Halbert, 1987.

James, Liz, ed. *Art and Text in Byzantine Culture.* Cambridge: Cambridge University Press, 2006.

———. "Color and Meaning in Byzantium." *Journal of Early Christian Studies* 11, no. 2 (2003): 223–33.

———. *Light and Colour in Byzantine Art.* Oxford: Clarendon Press, 1996.

———. "Senses and Sensibility in Byzantium." *Art History* 27, no. 4 (2004): 523–37.

James, Liz, and Ruth Webb. "'To Understand Ultimate Things and Enter Secret Places': Ekphrasis and Art in Byzantium." *Art History* 14, no. 1 (1991): 1–17.

Jauss, Hans Robert. *Toward an Aesthetic of Reception.* Translated by Timothy Bahti. Minneapolis: University of Minnesota Press, 1982.

Jay, Martin. *Downcast Eyes: The Denigration of Vision in Twentieth-Century French Thought.* Berkeley: University of California Press, 1993.

Jebb, John. *Sacred Literature; Comprising a Review of the Principles of Composition Laid Down by the Late Robert Lowth . . . in His Praelections and Isaiah: And an Application of the Principles So Reviewed, to the Illustration of the New Testament; in a Series of Critical Observations on the Style and Structure of That Sacred Volume.* London: Cadell & Davies; Edinburgh: W. Blackwood, 1820.

Jiménez, Raquel, Rupert Till, and Mark Howell, eds. *Music and Ritual: Bridging Material and Living Cultures.* Berlin: Ēkhō Verlag, 2013.

Johnson, Marcia K. "Reflection, Reality Monitoring, and the Self." In Kunzendorf, *Mental Imagery,* 3–16.

Johnston, Sarah Iles. "*Fiat Lux, Fiat Ritus:* Divine Light and the Late Antique Defense of Ritual." In Kapstein, *Presence of Light,* 5–24.

Jones, Ann Rosalind, and Peter Stallybrass. *Renaissance Clothing and the Materials of Memory.* Cambridge: Cambridge University Press, 2000.

Juriansz, Allan Russell. *King David's Naked Dance: The Dreams, Doctrines, and Dilemmas of the Hebrews.* Bloomington, Ind.: iUniverse, 2013.

Kalavrezou, Ioli. "Irregular Marriages in the Eleventh Century and the Zoe and Constantine Mosaic in Hagia Sophia." In *Law and Society in Byzantium, Ninth–Twelfth Centuries,* edited by Angeliki E. Laiou and Dieter Simon, 241–59. Washington, D.C.: Dumbarton Oaks Research Library and Collection, 1994.

Kaldellis, Anthony. "The Making of Hagia Sophia and the Last Pagans of New Rome." *Journal of Late Antiquity* 6, no. 2 (2013): 347–66.

———. *Procopius of Caesarea: Tyranny, History, and Philosophy at the End of Antiquity.* Philadelphia: University of Pennsylvania Press, 2004.

Kapitän, Gerhard. "The Church Wreck off Marzamemi." *Archaeology* 22, no. 2 (1969): 122–33.

———. "Elementi architettonici per una basilica dal relitto navale del vi secolo di Marzamemi (Siracusa)." In *XXVII corso di cultura sull'arte ravennate e bizantina,* 71–136. Ravenna: Edizioni del Girasole, 1980.

Kaplan, Michel, ed. *Le sacré et son inscription dans l'espace à Byzance et en Occident.* Byzantina Sorbonensia 18. Paris: Publications de la Sorbonne, 2001.

Kapstein, Matthew T., ed. *The Presence of Light: Divine Radiance and Religious Experience.* Chicago: University of Chicago Press, 2004.

Karabiber, Zerhan. "The Conservation of Acoustical Heritage." Workshop 4, CAHRISMA, Fifth Framework INCO-MED Programme of the European Commission. http://www.cyfronet.krakow.pl/~ncbratas/pdf /full_karabiber.pdf, accessed January 29, 2013.

Karampatzakes, Panagiotis. "Akoustikes metrēseis se 11 byzantinous naous tēs Thesalonikēs." Unpublished manuscript.

Kato, Shiro, Aoki Takayoshi, Kikue Hidaka, and H. Nakamura. "Finite-Element Modeling of the First and Second Domes of Hagia Sophia." In Mark and Çakmak, *Hagia Sophia from the Age of Justinian to the Present,* 103–19.

Kekelidze, Kornelis S. *Drevne-gruzinskij Archieratikon: Gruzinskij tekst.* Tbilisi: Losaberidze, 1912.

Kessler, Herbert L. "*Arca Arcarum:* Nested Boxes and the Dynamics of Sacred Experience." *Codex aqvilarensis: Revista de arte medieval* 30 (2014): 83–107.

———. *Old St. Peter's and Church Decoration in Medieval Italy.* Spoleto: Centro italiano di studi sull'alto Medioevo, 2002.

———. "Speculum." *Speculum* 86, no. 1 (2011): 1–41.

Kessler, Herbert L., and Marianna Shreve Simpson, eds. *Pictorial Narrative in Antiquity and the Middle Ages.* Studies in Art History 16. Washington, D.C.: National Gallery of Art, 1986.

Kessler, Herbert L., and Gerhard Wolf, eds. *The Holy Face and the Paradox of Representation.* Villa Spelman Colloquia 6. Bologna: Nuova Alfa, 1998.

Kessler, Herbert L., and Johanna Zacharias. *Rome, 1300: On the Path of the Pilgrim.* New Haven: Yale University Press, 2000.

Kiilerich, Bente. "The Aesthetic Viewing of Marble in Byzantium: From Global Impression to Focal Attention." *Arte medievale,* 4th ser., 2 (2012): 9–28.

Kleinbauer, W. Eugene. "Antioch, Jerusalem, and Rome: The Patronage of Emperor Constantius II and Architectural Invention." *Gesta* 45 (2006): 125–45.

Kleinbauer, W. Eugene, Antony White, and Henry Matthews. *Hagia Sophia.* London: Scala; Istanbul: Archaeology and Art Publications, 2004.

Kleinert, Annette. *Die Inkrustation der Hagia Sophia: Zur Entwicklung der Inkrustationsschemata im römischen Kaiserreich.* Münster: University of Münster, 1979.

Klepper, David Lloyd. "The Acoustics of St. Thomas Church, Fifth Avenue." *Journal of the Audio Engineering Society* 43, nos. 7–8 (1995): 599–601.

Knight, David J. "The Archaeoacoustics of a Sixth-Century Christian Structure: San Vitale, Ravenna." In Jiménez, Till, and Howell, *Music and Ritual,* 133–46.

———. "The Archaeoacoustics of San Vitale, Ravenna." M.A. thesis, University of Southampton, 2010. http://eprints.soton.ac.uk/169837/1.hasCoversheetVersion/KnightMPhilETHESIS.pdf.

Koetsier, T., and L. Bergmans, eds. *Mathematics and the Divine: A Historical Study.* Amsterdam: Elsevier, 2005.

Kominko, Maja. *The World of Kosmas: Illustrated Byzantine Codices of the Christian Topography.* Cambridge: Cambridge University Press, 2013.

Konidaris, Johannes. "Die Novellen des Kaisers Herakleios." In Simon, *Fontes Minores,* 5:33–106.

Kovaltchuk, Ekaterina. "The Encaenia of St. Sophia: Animal Sacrifice in a Christian Context." *Scrinium* 4 (2008): 161–203.

———. "The Holy Sepulchre of Jerusalem and St. Sophia of Constantinople: An Attempt at Discovering a Hagiographic Expression of the Byzantine Encaenia Feast." *Scrinium* 6 (2010): 263–338.

Kraus, Chris, Simon Goldhill, Helene P. Foley, and Jaś Elsner, eds. *Visualizing the Tragic: Drama, Myth, and Ritual in Greek Art and Literature; Essays in Honour of Froma Zeitlin.* Oxford: Oxford University Press, 2007.

Krautheimer, Richard. "The Constantinian Basilica." *Dumbarton Oaks Papers* 21 (1967): 115–40.

———. *Early Christian and Byzantine Architecture.* 4th ed. Revised by Richard Krautheimer and Slobadan Ćurčić. Pelican History of Art. New Haven: Yale University Press, 1986.

Kries, Douglas, and Catherine Brown Tkacz, eds. *Nova Doctrina Vetusque: Essays on Early Christianity in Honor of Frederic W. Schlatter, S.J.* American University Studies, ser. 7, Theology and Religion 207. New York: Lang, 1999.

Krueger, Derek. *Liturgical Subjects: Christian Ritual, Biblical Narrative, and the Formation of the Self in Byzantium.* Philadelphia: University of Pennsylvania Press, 2014.

———. "Liturgical Time and Holy Land Reliquaries in Early Byzantium." In Hahn and Klein, *Saints and Sacred Matter,* 11–31.

Kühnel, Bianca, Galit Noga-Banai, and Hanna Vorholt, eds. *Visual Constructs of Jerusalem.* Turnhout: Brepols, 2014.

Kuisma, Oiva. *Art or Experience: A Study on Plotinus' Aesthetics.* Commentationes Humanarum Litterarum 120. Helsinki: Societas Scientiarum Fennica, 2003.

Kumler, Aden, and Christopher R. Lakey. "*Res et significatio:* The Material Sense of Things in the Middle Ages." *Gesta* 51, no. 1 (2012): 1–17.

Kunzendorf, Robert, ed. *Mental Imagery.* New York: Plenum Press, 1991.

Kurke, Leslie. "Visualizing the Choral: Epichoric Poetry, Ritual, and Elite Negotiation in Fifth-Century Thebes." In Kraus et al., *Visualizing the Tragic,* 63–101.

Kuttruff, Heinrich. *Room Acoustics.* 5th ed. London: Spoon Press, 2009.

Lackner, Wolfgang. "Der Amtstitel Maximos des Bekenners." *Jahrbuch der österreichischen Byzantinistik* 20 (1971): 63–65.

———. "Zu Quellen und Datierung der Maximosvita (BHG³ 1234)." *Analecta Bollandiana* 85 (1967): 285–316.

Lafontaine-Dosogne, Jacqueline. *Itinéraires archéologiques dans la région d'Antioche: Recherches sur le monastère et sur l'iconographie de S. Syméon Stylite le Jeune.* Brussels: Éditions de Byzantion, 1967.

Laiou, Angeliki E., ed. *The Economic History of Byzantium: From the Seventh Through the Fifteenth Century.* 3 vols. Washington, D.C.: Dumbarton Oaks Research Library and Collection, 2002.

Laird, Martin S. *Gregory of Nyssa and the Grasp of Faith: Union, Knowledge, and Divine Presence.* Oxford: Oxford University Press, 2004.

Lakoff, George. *Women, Fire, and Dangerous Things: What Categories Reveal About the Mind.* Chicago: University of Chicago Press, 1987.

Lamberton, Robert. *Homer the Theologian: Neoplatonist Allegorical Reading and the Growth of the Epic Tradition.* Berkeley: University of California Press, 1986.

———. "The Neoplatonists and the Spiritualization of Homer." In Lamberton and Keaney, *Homer's Ancient Readers,* 115–33.

Lamberton, Robert, and John J. Keaney, eds. *Homer's Ancient Readers: The Hermeneutics of Greek Epic's Earliest Exegetes.* Princeton: Princeton University Press, 1992.

Langacker, Ronald W. *Foundations of Cognitive Grammar.* 2 vols. Stanford: Stanford University Press, 1987–91.

Larchet, Jean-Claude. "The Mode of Deification." In *The Oxford Handbook of Maximus the Confessor,* edited by Pauline Allen and Neil Bronwen, 341–59. Oxford: Oxford University Press, 2015.

Latour, Bruno. *We Have Never Been Modern.* Translated by Catherine Porter. Cambridge: Harvard University Press, 1993.

Lauritzen, Delphine. "La Muse d'Homère dans la *Description* de Jean de Gaza." *Il calamo della memoria* 5 (2012): 221–34.

Lavin, Marilyn Aronberg. *The Place of Narrative: Mural Decoration in Italian Churches, 431–1600.* Chicago: University of Chicago Press, 1990.

Lazzarini, Lorenzo. *Poikiloi lithoi, versiculores maculae: I marmi colorati della Grecia antica.* Pisa: Fabrizio Serra Editore, 2007.

Lehmann, Karl. "The Dome of Heaven." *Art Bulletin* 27 (1945): 1–27.

Leidwanger, Justin, and Sebastiano Tusa. "Marzamemi II 'Church Wreck' Excavation: 2014 Field Season." *Archaeologia Maritima Mediterranea* 12 (2015): 103–15.

Lethaby, W. R. *Architecture, Mysticism, and Myth.* 2nd ed. London: Percival, 1892. Reprint, Mineola, N.Y.: Dover, 2004.

Lidov, Aleksei, ed. *Hierotopy: The Creation of Sacred Spaces in Byzantium and Medieval Russia.* Moscow: Indrik, 2006.

Lingas, Alexander. "Festal Cathedral Vespers in Late Byzantium." *Orientalia christiana periodica* 63 (1997): 421–59.

———. "From Earth to Heaven: The Changing Musical Soundscape of Byzantine Liturgy." In Nesbitt and Jackson, *Experiencing Byzantium,* 311–58.

———. "Gregorios the Protopsaltes." *Grove Music Online.* Accessed March 12, 2010.

———. "The Liturgical Place of the Kontakion in Constantinople." In Akentiev, *Liturgy, Architecture, and Art in the Byzantine World,* 50–57.

———. "Performance Practice and the Politics of Transcribing Byzantine Chant." *Acta Musicae Byzantinae* 6 (2003): 56–76.

———. "Sunday Matins in the Byzantine Cathedral Rite: Music and Liturgy." Ph.D. diss., University of British Columbia, 1996.

Liturgie de l'Église particulière et liturgie de l'Église universelle: Conférences Saint-Serge, XXIIe Semaine d'études liturgiques, Paris, 30 juin–3 juillet 1975. Rome: Edizioni liturgiche, 1976.

Lonsdale, Steven H. "'Homeric Hymn to Apollo': Prototype and Paradigm of Choral Performance." *Arion: A Journal of Humanities and the Classics* 3, no. 1 (1994–95): 25–40.

Loosley, Emma. *The Architecture and Liturgy of the Bema in Fourth- to Sixth-Century Syrian Churches.* Boston: Brill, 2012.

Lopez-Lezcano, Fernando, Travis Skare, Michael J. Wilson, and Jonathan S. Abel. "Byzantium in Bing: Live Virtual Acoustics Employing Free Software." https://ccrma.stanford.edu/~nando/publications/hagia_sophia _lac2013.pdf, accessed July 10, 2013.

Louth, Andrew. *Denys the Areopagite.* London: Continuum, 2002.

———. *Maximus the Confessor.* London: Routledge, 1996.

———. "The Reception of Dionysius up to Maximus the Confessor." In Coakley and Stang, *Re-thinking Dionysius the Areopagite,* 43–53.

———. *St. John Damascene: Tradition and Originality in Byzantine Theology.* Oxford: Oxford University Press, 2002.

Lowden, John. "The Beginning of Biblical Illustration." In Williams, *Imaging the Early Medieval Bible,* 9–59.

———. *The Jaharis Gospel Lectionary: The Story of a Byzantine Book.* New Haven: Yale University Press; New York: Metropolitan Museum of Art, 2009.

Lund, Nils W. "Chiasmus in the Psalms." *American Journal of Semitic Languages and Literatures* 49, no. 4 (1933): 281–312.

———. "The Presence of Chiasmus in the New Testament." *Journal of Religion* 10, no. 1 (1930): 74–93.

Maas, Michael, ed. *The Cambridge Companion to the Age of Justinian.* Cambridge: Cambridge University Press, 2005.

MacDonald, William L. *The Pantheon: Design, Meaning, and Progeny.* London: Lane, 1976.

———. "Roman Experimental Design and the Great Church." In Mark and Çakmak, *Hagia Sophia from the Age of Justinian to the Present,* 3–15.

Macrides, Ruth, and Paul Magdalino. "The Architecture of Ekphrasis: Construction and Context of Paul the Silentiary's Poem on Hagia Sophia." *Byzantine and Modern Greek Studies* 12 (1988): 47–82.

Maguire, Henry. *Earth and Ocean: The Terrestrial World in Early Byzantine Art.* University Park: Pennsylvania State University Press, 1987.

Mainstone, Rowland J. *Hagia Sophia: Architecture, Structure, and Liturgy of Justinian's Great Church.* London: Thames & Hudson, 1988.

Majeska, George P. "Notes on the Archaeology of St. Sophia at Constantinople: The Green Marble Bands on the Floor." *Dumbarton Oaks Papers* 32 (1978): 299–308.

Mango, Cyril. *The Art of the Byzantine Empire, 312–1453: Sources and Documents.* Englewood Cliffs, N.J.: Prentice-Hall, 1972. Reprint, Toronto: University of Toronto Press, 1986.

Mango, Cyril, and Ernest J. W. Hawkins. "The Apse Mosaics of St. Sophia at Istanbul: Report on Work Carried Out in 1964." *Dumbarton Oaks Papers* 19 (1965): 113–51.

Mango, Marlia Mundell. *Silver from Early Byzantium: The Kaper Koraon and Related Treasures.* Baltimore: Walters Art Gallery, 1986.

Manovich, Lev. "The Poetics of Augmented Space." *Visual Communication* 5, no. 2 (2006): 219–40.

Mansfeld, Jaap, and Lambertus Marie de Rijk, eds. *Kephalaion: Studies in Greek Philosophy and Its Continuation Offered to Professor C. J. de Vogel.* Assen: Van Gorcum, 1975.

Manson, Thomas W. Review of *Chiasmus in the New Testament,* by Nils W. Lund. *Journal of Theological Studies* 45 (1944): 81–84.

Maranci, Christina. "The Architect Trdat: Building Practices and Cross-Cultural Exchange in Byzantium and Armenia." *Journal of the Society of Architectural Historians* 62, no. 3 (2003): 294–305.

———. "The Great Outdoors: Liturgical Encounters with the Early Medieval Armenian Church." In Pentcheva, *Aural Architecture.* Draft manuscript available at http://auralarchitecture.stanford.edu, accessed April 28, 2014.

———. "'Holiness Befits Your House' (Ps. 92 [93]: 5): A Preliminary Report on the Apse Inscription at Mren." *Revue des études arméniennes* 36 (2014–15): 243–63.

Marano, Yuri Alessandro. *Il commercio del marmo nell'Adriatico tardoantico (IV–VI secolo d.C.): Scambi, maestranze, committenze.* Ph.D. diss., University of Padua, 2008.

Marinis, Vasileios. *Architecture and Ritual in the Churches of Constantinople: Ninth to the Fifteenth Centuries.* Cambridge: Cambridge University Press, 2014.

Mark, Robert, and Ahmet Ş. Çakmak. *Hagia Sophia from the Age of Justinian to the Present.* Cambridge: Cambridge University Press, 1992.

Marrou, Henri Irénée. *A History of Education in Antiquity.* Translated by George Lamb. New York: Sheed & Ward, 1956.

Martellotta, Francesco, Ettore Cirillo, Antonio Carbonari, and Paola Ricciardi. "Guidelines for Acoustical Measurements in Churches." *Applied Acoustics* 70, no. 2 (2009): 378–88.

Mateos, Juan. *La célébration de la parole dans la liturgie byzantine.* Orientalia Christiana analecta 191. Rome: Pontificium Institutum Studiorum Orientalium, 1971.

Mathews, Thomas F. *The Early Churches of Constantinople: Architecture and Liturgy.* University Park: Pennsylvania State University Press, 1971.

McClanan, Anne L. *Representations of Early Byzantine Empresses: Image and Empire.* New York: Palgrave Macmillan, 2002.

McKenzie, Judith. *The Architecture of Alexandria and Egypt, c. 300 B.C. to A.D. 700.* New Haven: Yale University Press, 2007.

———. *The Architecture of Petra.* Oxford: Oxford University Press, 1990. Reprint, Oxford: Oxbow Press, 2005.

McKinnon, James W. *The Advent Project: The Later-Seventh-Century Creation of the Roman Mass Proper.* Berkeley: University of California Press, 2000.

———, ed. *Music in Early Christian Literature.* Cambridge: Cambridge University Press, 1987.

———. "Vaticana Latina 5319 as a Witness to the Eighth-Century Roman Proper of the Mass." In Dobszay, *Cantus Planus,* 403–14.

McKitterick, Rosamond, John Osborne, Carol M. Richardson, and Joanna Story, eds. *Old St. Peter's, Rome.* Cambridge: Cambridge University Press, 2013.

McVey, Kathleen E. "The Domed Church as a Microcosm: Literary Roots of an Architectural Symbol." *Dumbarton Oaks Papers* 37 (1983): 91–121.

———. "The Sogitha on the Church of Edessa in the Context of Other Early Greek and Syriac Hymns for the Consecration of Church Buildings." *ARAM* 5 (1993): 329–70.

———. "Spirit Embodied: The Emergence of Symbolic Interpretations of Early Christian and Byzantine Architecture." In Ćurčić and Hadjitryphonos, *Architecture as Icon,* 39–71.

Merleau-Ponty, Maurice. "Eye and Mind." In *The Merleau-Ponty Reader,* 351–78.

———. "The Intertwining—The Chiasm." In *The Visible and the Invisible,* edited by Claude Lefort, translated by Alphonso Lingis, 130–55. Evanston: Northwestern University Press, 1968.

———. *The Merleau-Ponty Reader.* Edited by Ted Toadvine and Leonard Lawlor. Evanston: Northwestern University Press, 2007.

Meyendorff, John. *Byzantine Theology: Historical Trends and Doctrinal Themes.* New York: Fordham University Press, 1974.

———. "Wisdom—Sophia: Contrasting Approaches to a Complex Theme." *Dumbarton Oaks Papers* 41 (1987): 391–401.

Miller, James L. *Measures of Wisdom: The Cosmic Dance in Classical and Christian Antiquity.* Toronto: University of Toronto Press, 1986.

Miller, Patricia Cox. *The Corporeal Imagination: Signifying the Holy in Late Ancient Christianity.* Philadelphia: University of Pennsylvania Press, 2009.

Milne, J. Grafton. "Relics of Graeco-Egyptian Schools." *Journal of Hellenic Studies* 28 (1908): 121–32.

Minetor, Randi. "J. R. Clancy Provides Custom Rigging Solutions for Bing Concert Hall at Stanford University." *LiveDesign,* February 11, 2013. http://livedesignonline.com/blog/j-r-clancy-provides-custom-rigging -solutions-bing-concert-hall-stanford-university.

Mitchell, W. J. T. *Picture Theory: Essays on Verbal and Visual Representation.* Chicago: University of Chicago Press, 1994.

Monna, Dario, and Patrizio Pensabene. *Marmi dell'Asia Minore.* Rome: Consiglio nazionale delle ricerche, 1977.

Moran, Neil. "The Choir of the Hagia Sophia." *Oriens Christianus* 89 (2005): 1–7.

———. "The Musical 'Gestaltung' of the Great Entrance Ceremony in the 12th Century in Accordance with the Rite of Hagia Sophia." *Jahrbuch der österreichischen Byzantinistik* 28 (1979): 167–93.

———. *Singers in Late Byzantine and Slavonic Painting.* Leiden: Brill, 1986.

Morris, Rosemary, ed. *Church and People in Byzantium.* Society for the Promotion of Byzantine Studies Twentieth Spring Symposium of Byzantine Studies, Manchester, 1986. Birmingham: Centre for Byzantine, Ottoman, and Modern Greek Studies, 1990.

Most, Glenn W. "Τὸν Ἀνακρέοντα μιμοῦ: Imitation and Enactment in the *Anacreontics.*" In Baumbach and Dümmler, *Imitate Anacreon,* 145–60.

Mouriki, Doula. "The Octateuch Miniatures of the Byzantine Manuscripts of Cosmas Indicopleustes." Ph.D. diss., Princeton University, 1970.

Müller, Alexander. *Die Carmina Anacreontea und Anakreon: Ein literarisches Generationenverhältnis.* Tübingen: Narr, 2010.

Müller-Wiener, Wolfgang. *Bildlexikon zur Topographie Istanbuls: Byzantion, Konstantinupolis, Istanbul bis zum Beginn d. 17. Jh.* Tübingen: Wasmuth, 1977.

Nagy, Gregory. *Homer the Preclassic.* Sather Classical Lectures 67. Berkeley: University of California Press, 2010.

Nasrallah, Laura Salah. "Empire and Apocalypse in Thessaloniki: Interpreting the Early Christian Rotunda." *Journal of Early Christian Studies* 13, no. 4 (2005): 465–508.

Necipoğlu, Gülru. "The Life of an Imperial Monument: The Life of Hagia Sophia After Byzantium." In Mark and Çakmak, *Hagia Sophia from the Age of Justinian to the Present,* 195–225.

Neer, Richard T. *The Emergence of the Classical Style in Greek Sculpture.* Chicago: University of Chicago Press, 2010.

Nelson, Robert S. *Hagia Sophia, 1850–1950: Holy Wisdom Modern Monument.* Chicago: University of Chicago Press, 2004.

———, ed. *Visuality Before and Beyond the Renaissance: Seeing as Others Saw.* New York: Cambridge University Press, 2000.

Nesbitt, Claire, and Mark Jackson, eds. *Experiencing Byzantium.* Farnham: Ashgate, 2013.

Neuhoff, John G., ed. *Ecological Psychoacoustics.* Amsterdam: Elsevier Academic Press, 2004.

———. "Ecological Psychoacoustics: Introduction and History." In Neuhoff, *Ecological Psychoacoustics,* 1–13.

Nightingale, Andrea Wilson. *Spectacles of Truth in Classical Greek Philosophy: Theoria in Its Cultural Context.* Cambridge: Cambridge University Press, 2004.

Noble, Thomas F. X. *Images, Iconoclasm, and the Carolingians.* Philadelphia: University of Pennsylvania Press, 2009.

Odorico, Paolo, Panagiotis A. Agapitos, and Martin Hinterberger, eds. *"Doux remède . . .": Poésie et poétique à Byzance.* Dossiers byzantins 9. Paris: Centre d'études byzantines, néo-hélleniques et sud-est européenes, 2008.

Oikonomides, Nicolas. "The Mosaic Panel of Constantine IX and Zoe in St. Sophia." *Revue des études byzantines* 36 (1978): 219–32.

O'Meara, Dominic J. "Geometry and the Divine in Proclus." In Koetsier and Bergmans, *Mathematics and the Divine,* 135–45.

Onasch, Konrad. *Lichthöhle und Sternenhaus: Licht und Materie im spätantik-christlichen und frühbyzantinischen Sakralbau.* Dresden: Verlag der Kunst, 1993.

Onians, John. "Abstraction and Imagination in Late Antiquity." *Art History* 3 (1980): 1–23.

Ousterhout, Robert G. "The Architecture of Iconoclasm: Buildings." In Brubaker and Haldon, *Byzantium in the Iconoclast Era (ca. 680–850): The Sources, an Annotated Survey,* 3–19.

———. "Holy Space: Architecture and the Liturgy." In Safran, *Heaven on Earth,* 81–120.

———. *Master Builders of Byzantium.* Princeton: Princeton University Press, 1999.

———. "The Sanctity of Place vs. the Sanctity of Building: Jerusalem vs. Constantinople." In Wescoat and Ousterhout, *Architecture of the Sacred,* 281–306.

Papacostas, Tassos. "The Medieval Progeny of the Holy Apostles: Trails of Architectural Imitation Across the Mediterranean." In Stephenson, *Byzantine World,* 386–405.

Parenti, Stefano. "The Cathedral Rite of Constantinople: Evolution of a Local Tradition." *Orientalia christiana periodica* 77 (2011): 449–69.

Peers, Glenn. "Breathless, Speechless Images: On the Chalke Gate Epigram." *Cahiers des études anciennes* 34 (1998): 109–12.

———. "Byzantine Things in the World." In Peers, *Byzantine Things in the World,* 41–86.

———, ed. *Byzantine Things in the World.* Houston: Menil Collection, 2014.

———. *Subtle Bodies: Representing Angels in Byzantium.* Transformation of the Classical Heritage 32. Berkeley: University of California Press, 2001.

Pensabene, Patrizio. "Le principali cave di marmo bianco." In De Nuccio and Ungaro, *I marmi colorati della Roma imperiale,* 203–21.

Pentcheva, Bissera V. "The Aesthetics of Landscape and Icon at Sinai." *Res: Anthropology and Aesthetics* 65–66 (2015): 194–211.

———, ed. *Aural Architecture in Byzantium: Music, Acoustics, and Ritual.* Aldershot: Ashgate, 2017.

———. "Cross, Tunic, Body: Theology Through the Phenomenology of Light." In Schreiner and Poletto, *La stauroteca di Bessarione.*

———. "Hagia Sophia and Multisensory Aesthetics." *Gesta* 50, no. 2 (2011): 93–111.

———. "Mirror, Inspiration, and the Making of Art in Byzantium." *Convivium* 1, no. 2 (2014): 10–39.

———. "Moving Eyes: Surface and Shadow in the Byzantine Mixed-Media Relief Icon." *Res: Anthropology and Aesthetics* 55–56 (2009): 222–32.

———. "The Performative Icon." *Art Bulletin* 88, no. 4 (2006): 631–55.

———. "Performing the Sacred in Byzantium: Image, Breath, and Sound." *Performance Research International* 19, no. 3 (2014): 120–28.

———. *The Sensual Icon: Space, Ritual, and the Senses in Byzantium.* University Park: Pennsylvania State University Press, 2010.

Pérès, Marcel, and the Ensemble Organum. *Chants de l'Église de Rome: Période byzantine.* Harmonia Mundi, 1998. Compact disc.

Perkams, Matthias, and Rosa Maria Piccione, eds. *Proklos: Methode, Seelenlehre, Metaphysik; Akten der Konferenz in Jena am 18.–20. September 2003.* Leiden: Brill, 2006.

Permjakovs, Vitalijs. "'Make This the Place Where Your Glory Dwells': Origins and Evolution of the Byzantine Rite for the Consecration of a Church." Ph.D. diss., University of Notre Dame, 2012.

Pitra, I. B., ed. *Iuris Ecclesiastici Graecorum Historia et Monumenta Iussu Pii ix. Pont. Max.* 2 vols. Rome: Typis Collegii Urbani, 1864–68.

Platt, Verity. "Viewing, Desiring, Believing: Confronting the Divine in a Pompeian House." *Art History* 25, no. 1 (2002): 87–112.

Potamianos, Iakovos. "The Mathematics of the Ideal Dome." In Weber and Amann, *Aesthetics and Architectural Composition,* 66–72.

Potamianos, Iakovos, and Wassim Jabi. "Interactive Parametric Design and the Role of Light in Byzantine Churches." In Bourdakis and Charitos, *Communicating Space(s),* 798–803.

Pott, Thomas. *La réforme liturgique byzantine: Étude du phénomène de évolution non-spontanée de la liturgie byzantine.* Rome: CLV–Edizioni liturgiche, 2000. Translated by Paul Metendorff as *Byzantine Liturgical Reform: A Study of Liturgical Change in the Byzantine Tradition.* Crestwood, N.Y.: St. Vladimir's Orthodox Seminary Press, 2010.

Pounds, Richard, Daniel Raichel, and Martin Weaver. "The Unseen World of Guastavino Acoustical Tile Construction: History, Development, Production." *APT Bulletin* 30 (1999): 33–39.

Preisendanz, Karl. *Anthologia palatina: Codex palatinus et Codex parisinus phototypice editi.* Leiden: A. W. Sijthoff, 1911.

Price, Monica T. *Decorative Stone: The Complete Sourcebook.* London: Thames & Hudson, 2007.

Promey, Sally M., ed. *Sensational Religion: Sensory Cultures in Material Practice.* New Haven: Yale University Press, 2014.

Quintavalle, Arturo Carlo, ed. *Medioevo mediterraneo: L'Occidente, Bisanzio e l'Islam; Atti del Convegno internazionale di studi, Parma, 21–25 settembre 2004.* I convegni di Parma 7. Milan: Mondadori Electa, 2007.

Ramsey, Boniface. *Ambrose.* London: Routledge, 1997.

Rasch, Jürgen J. "Die Kuppel in der römischen Architektur: Entwicklung, Formgebung, Konstruktion." *Architectura* 15 (1985): 117–39.

Reudenbach, Bruno. "Holy Places and Their Relics." In Kühnel, Noga-Banai, and Vorholt, *Visual Constructs of Jerusalem*, 197–206.

———, ed. *Jerusalem, du Schöne: Vorstellungen und Bilder einer heiligen Stadt.* Bern: Lang, 2008.

———. "*Loca sancta:* Zur materiellen Übertragung der heiligen Stätten." In Reudenbach, *Jerusalem, du Schöne,* 9–32.

Reznikoff, Iégor. "The Evidence of the Use of Sound Resonance from Paleolithic to Medieval Times." In Scarre and Lawson, *Archaeoacoustics,* 77–84.

———. "On Primitive Elements of Musical Meaning." *Journal of Music and Meaning* 3 (Fall 2004 / Winter 2005): sect. 2.

———. "Prehistoric Paintings, Sound, and Rocks." In Hickmann, Eichmann, and Kilmer, *Studien zur Musikarchäologie III,* 39–56.

Richir, Marc. "Commentaire de Phénoménologie de la conscience esthétique de Husserl." *Revue d'esthétique* 36, *Esthétique et phénoménologie* (1999): 15–27.

Riordan, William K. *Divine Light: The Theology of Denys the Areopagite.* San Francisco: Ignatius Press, 2008.

Ripley, Colin, with Marco Polo and Arthur Wrigglesworth, eds. *In the Place of Sound: Architecture, Music, Acoustics.* Newcastle: Cambridge Scholars, 2007.

Roberts, Michael John. *The Jeweled Style: Poetry and Poetics in Late Antiquity.* Ithaca: Cornell University Press, 1989.

———. *Poetry and the Cult of the Martyrs: The Liber Peristephanon of Prudentius.* Recentiores: Later Latin Texts and Contexts. Ann Arbor: University of Michigan Press, 1993.

Rocconi, Eleonora. "Theatres and Theatre Design in the Graeco-Roman World: Theoretical and Empirical Approaches." In Scarre and Lawson, *Archaeoacoustics,* 71–76.

Rosenmeyer, Patricia A. *The Poetics of Imitation: Anacreon and the Anacreontic Tradition.* Cambridge: Cambridge University Press, 1992.

Rossing, Thomas D., ed. *Springer Handbook of Acoustics.* New York: Springer, 2007.

Ruggieri, Vincenzo. "Consacrazione e dedicazione di chiesa secondo il *Barberinianus graecus 336.*" *Orientalia christiana periodica* 54 (1988): 79–118.

Russo, Eugenio. *Le decorazioni di Isidoro il Giovane per S. Sofia di Costantinopoli.* Rome: Viella, 2011.

Russo, Lucio. *The Forgotten Revolution: How Science Was Born in 300 BC and Why It Had to Be Reborn.* Berlin: Springer, 2004.

Saba, Matthew D. "Abbasid Lusterware and the Aesthetics of *'Ajab.*" *Muqarnas* 29 (2012): 187–212.

Safran, Linda, ed. *Heaven on Earth: Art and the Church in Byzantium.* University Park: Pennsylvania State University Press, 1998.

Salés, Luis. "Maximos of Constantinople: A Political-Circumstantial Assessment of the *Greek* and *Syriac Lives of Maximus the Confessor.*" Byzantine Studies Conference, New York, October 22–25, 2015. Abstracts, 83. http://www.bsana.net/conference/archives/byabstracts.html.

Sallis, John. *Chorology: On Beginning in Plato's "Timaeus."* Bloomington: Indiana University Press, 1999.

Scarre, Chris. "Sound, Place, and Space: Towards an Archaeology of Acoustics." In Scarre and Lawson, *Archaeoacoustics,* 1–10.

Scarre, Chris, and Graeme Lawson, eds. *Archaeoacoustics.* Cambridge: McDonald Institute for Archaeological Research, 2006.

Scarry, Elaine. *Dreaming by the Book.* New York: Farrar, Straus, Giroux, 1999.

———. "On Vivacity: The Difference Between Daydreaming and Imagining-Under-Authorial-Instruction." *Representations* 52 (1995): 1–26.

Schäfer, Christian. "Μονή, πρόοδος, und ἐπιστροφή in der Philosophie des Proklos und des Areopagiten Dionysius." In Perkams and Piccione, *Proklos: Methode, Seelenlehre, Metaphysik,* 340–62.

Schafer, R. Murray. *The New Soundscape: A Handbook for the Modern Music Teacher.* Scarborough, Ont.: Berandol Music; New York: Associated Music Publishers, 1969.

———. *The Soundscape: Our Sonic Environment and the Tuning of the World.* New York: Knopf, 1977. Reprint, Rochester, Vt.: Destiny Books, 1994.

Schibille, Nadine. "Astronomical and Optical Principles in the Architecture of Hagia Sophia in Constantinople." *Science in Context* 22 (2009): 27–46.

———. *Hagia Sophia and the Byzantine Aesthetic Experience.* Farnham: Ashgate, 2014.

———. "The Profession of the Architect in Late Antique Byzantium." *Byzantion* 79 (2009): 360–79.

Schneider, Wolfgang Christian. "'Abtun der Sorge und Tanz': Der 'Große Einzug' und die Kuppel der Hagia Sophia Justinians." In Altripp and Nauerth, *Architektur und Liturgie,* 143–61.

———. "Sorgefrei und im Tanz der Weisheit: Philosophie und Theologie im Kuppelrund der Hagia Sophia Justinians." *Castrum Peregrini: Zeitschrift für Literatur, Kunst- und Geistesgeschichte* 271–72 (2006): 52–90.

Schneider, Wolfgang Christian, and Rudolf H. W. Stichel. "Der 'Cherubinische Einzug' in der Hagia Sophia Justinians: Aufführung und Ereignis." In Fischer-Lichte et al., *Performativität und Ereignis,* 377–94.

Schreiner, Peter, and Valeria Poletto, eds. *La stauroteca di Bessarione: Atti delle giornate internazionali di studio la stauroteca di Bessarione.* Venice: Istituto veneto di scienze, lettere ed arti; Gallerie dell'Accademia; Istituto ellenico; Centro tedesco di studi veneziani, forthcoming.

Schriever, Daniel. "Memory, Architecture, Performance: Romanos the Melodist *On the Prodigal Son.*" Byzantine Studies Conference, New York, October 22–25, 2015. Abstracts, 86. http://www.bsana.net/conference /archives/byabstracts.html.

Schulz, Hans-Joachim. *The Byzantine Liturgy: Symbolic Structure and Faith Expression.* New York: Pueblo, 1986.

Schwarzenberg, Erkinger. "Colour, Light, and Transparency in the Greek World." In Borsook, Gioffredi Superbi, and Pagliarulo, *Medieval Mosaics,* 15–34.

Ševčenko, Nancy Patterson. "Illuminating the Liturgy: Illustrated Service Books in Byzantium." In Safran, *Heaven on Earth,* 186–228.

Shankland, R. S., and H. K. Shankland. "Acoustics of St. Peter's and Patriarchal Basilicas in Rome." *Journal of the Acoustical Society of America* 50, no. 2 (1971): 389–96.

Shaw, Gregory. "The *Chōra* of the *Timaeus* and the Iamblichean Theurgy." *Horizons* 3, no. 2 (2012): 103–29.

———. *Theurgy and the Soul: The Neoplatonism of Iamblichus.* University Park: Pennsylvania State University Press, 1995.

Shorrock, Robert. *The Challenge of Epic: Allusive Engagement in the "Dionysiaca" of Nonnus.* Leiden: Brill, 2001.

Simon, Dieter, ed. *Fontes Minores.* Vol. 5. Forschungen zur byzantinischen Rechtsgeschichte 8. Frankfurt: Klostermann, 1982.

Smith, Jonathan Z. *To Take Place: Toward Theory in Ritual.* Chicago: University of Chicago Press, 1987.

Smith, Mark M., ed. *Hearing History: A Reader.* Athens: University of Georgia Press, 2004.

Snow-Smith, Joanne. *The "Primavera" of Sandro Botticelli: A Neoplatonic Interpretation.* New York: Lang, 1992.

Sodini, Jean-Pierre. "Marble and Stoneworking in Byzantium: Seventh–Fifteenth Centuries." In Laiou, *Economic History of Byzantium,* 1:129–46.

Spanoudakis, Konstantinos, ed. *Nonnus of Panopolis in Context: Poetry and Cultural Milieu in Late Antiquity.* Berlin: De Gruyter, 2014.

Speck, Paul. " Γραφαῖς ἢ γλυφαῖς: Zu dem Fragment des Hypatios von Ephesos über die Bilder mit einem Anhang zu dem Dialog mit einem Juden des Leontios von Neapolis." In *Varia 1,* Poikila Byzantina 4:211–72. Bonn: R. Habelt, 1984.

Spyrakou, Evangelia. *Singers' Choirs According to the Byzantine Tradition.* Institute of Byzantine Musicology Studies 14. Athens: Institute of Byzantine Musicology, 2008.

Squire, Michael. *Image and Text in Graeco-Roman Antiquity.* Cambridge: Cambridge University Press, 2009.

———. "Making Myron's Cow Moo? Ekphrastic Epigram and the Poetics of Simulation." *American Journal of Philology* 131 (2010): 589–634.

———. "Reading a View: Poem and Picture in the Greek Anthology." *Ramus* 39 (2010): 73–103.

Stäblein, Bruno, and Margareta Landwehr-Melnicki, eds. *Die Gesänge des altrömischen Graduale: Vat. lat. 5319.* Monumenta Monodica Medii Aevi 2. Kassel: Bärenreiter, 1970.

Stapert, Calvin. *A New Song for an Old World: Musical Thought in the Early Church.* Grand Rapids, Mich.: William B. Eerdmans, 2007.

Steenberge, Laura. "We Who Mystically Represent the Cherubim." In Pentcheva, *Aural Architecture.*

Stephenson, Paul, ed. *The Byzantine World.* New York: Routledge, 2010.

Sterne, Jonathan. *The Audible Past: Cultural Origins of Sound Reproduction.* Durham: Duke University Press, 2003.

———. *MP3: The Meaning of a Format.* Durham: Duke University Press, 2012.

———. "Sonic Imaginations." In Sterne, *Sound Studies Reader,* 1–17.

———, ed. *The Sound Studies Reader.* New York: Routledge, 2012.

———. "Space Within Space: Artificial Reverb and the Detachable Echo." *Gray Room* 60 (2015): 110–31. doi:10.1162/GREY_a_00177.

Stichel, Rudolf H. W. *Einblicke in den virtuellen Himmel: Neue und alte Bilder vom Inneren der Hagia Sophia in Istanbul.* Edited by Helge Svenshon. Tübingen: Wasmuth, 2008. Exh. cat.

———. "Sechs kolossale Säulen nahe der Hagia Sophia und die Curia Justinians am Augusteion in Konstantinopel." *Architectura* 30 (2000): 1–25.

———. "Τὰ σὰ ἐκ τῶν σῶν: Kaiser Justinian am Altar der Hagia Sophia." In Altripp and Nauerth, *Architektur und Liturgie,* 163–74.

Stiegemann, Christoph, ed. *Byzanz, das Licht aus dem Osten: Kult und Alltag im Byzantinischen Reich vom 4. bis 15. Jahrhundert, Paderborn 2001.* Mainz: Philipp von Zabern, 2001. Exh. cat.

Stock, Augustine. "Chiastic Awareness and Education in Antiquity." *Biblical Theology Bulletin* 14, no. 1 (1984): 23–27.

Stornajolo, Cosimo, ed. *Le miniature della Topografia cristiana di Cosma Indicopleuste, codice Vaticano greco 699.* Milan: Hoepli, 1908.

String, Martin. *Untersuchungen zum Stil der Dionysiaka des Nonnos von Panopolis.* Ph.D. diss., University of Hamburg, 1966.

Strunk, W. Oliver. "The Byzantine Office at Hagia Sophia." *Dumbarton Oaks Papers* 9–10 (1956): 175–202.

Sumi, Akiko Motoyoshi. *Description in Classical Arabic Poetry: Wasf, Ekphrasis, and Interarts Theory.* Leiden: Brill, 2004.

Summers, David. *Vision, Reflection, and Desire in Western Painting.* Chapel Hill: University of North Carolina Press, 2007.

Svenshon, Helge, and Rudolf H. W. Stichel. "Neue Beobachtungen an der ehemaligen Kirche der Heiligen Sergios und Bakchos (Küçük Ayasofya Camisi) in Istanbul." *Istanbuler Mitteilungen* 50 (2000): 389–409.

———. "'System of Monads' as Design Principle in the Hagia Sophia: Neo-Platonic Mathematics in the Architecture of Late Antiquity." In Duvernoy and Pedemonte, *Nexus VI,* 111–20.

Swain, Simon, and Mark Edwards, eds. *Approaching Late Antiquity: The Transformation from Early to Late Empire.* Oxford: Oxford University Press, 2004.

Tachau, Katherine H. *Vision and Certitude in the Age of Ockham: Optics, Epistemology, and the Foundations of Semantics, 1250–1345.* Leiden: Brill, 1988.

Taft, Robert F. *The Byzantine Rite: A Short History.* Collegeville, Minn.: Liturgical Press, 1992.

———. "Christian Liturgical Psalmody: Origins, Development, Decomposition, Collapse." In Attridge and Fassler, *Psalms in Community,* 7–32.

———. *The Great Entrance: A History of the Transfer of Gifts and Other Pre-anaphoral Rites.* Orientalia Christiana analecta 200. 2nd ed. Rome: Pontificium Institutum Studiorum Orientalium, 1978.

———. "The Liturgy of the Great Church: An Initial Synthesis of Structure and Interpretation on the Eve of Iconoclasm." *Dumbarton Oaks Papers* 34–35 (1980–81): 45–76.

———. *Liturgy of the Hours in the East and West: The Origins of the Divine Office and Its Meaning for Today.* 2nd rev.
ed. Collegeville, Minn.: Liturgical Press, 1993.

———. "One Bread, One Body: Ritual Symbols of Ecclesial Communion in the Patristic Period." In Kries and
Tkacz, *Nova Doctrina Vetusque,* 23–50.

———. "On the Use of the Bema in the East-Syrian Liturgy." *Eastern Churches Review* 3 (1970): 30–39.

———. "Some Notes on the Bema in the East and West Syrian Traditions." *Orientalia christiana periodica* 34
(1968): 326–59.

———. *Through Their Own Eyes: Liturgy as the Byzantines Saw It.* Paul G. Manolis Distinguished Lectures. Berkeley: InterOrthodox Press, 2006.

Taylor, Rabun. "A Literary and Structural Analysis of the First Dome on Justinian's Hagia Sophia, Constantinople."
Journal of the Society of Architectural Historians 55 (1996): 66–78.

Tchalenko, Georges. *Églises syriennes à bêma.* Paris: Geuthner, 1990.

Theis, Lioba. "Lampen, Leuchten, Licht." In Stiegemann, *Byzanz, das Licht aus dem Osten,* 53–64.

———. "Zur Geschichte der wissenschaftlichen Erforschung der Hagia Sophia." In Hoffmann, *Hagia Sophia in
Istanbul,* 55–80.

Thiel, Andreas. *Die Johanneskirche in Ephesos.* Wiesbaden: Reichert, 2005.

Thodberg, Christian. "Alleluia." *Grove Music Online.* Accessed September 17, 2014.

———. *Der byzantinische Alleluiarionzyklus: Studien im kurzen Psaltikonstil.* Monumenta Musicae Byzantinae,
Subsidia 8. Copenhagen: E. Munksgaard, 1966. http://www.oxfordmusiconline.com/subscriber/article
/grove/music/40711.

Thomas, Edmund. *Monumentality and the Roman Empire: Architecture in the Antonine Age.* Oxford: Oxford University Press, 2007.

Thompson, Emily. *The Soundscape of Modernity: Architectural Acoustics and the Culture of Listening in America,
1900–1933.* 2002. Reprint, Cambridge: MIT Press, 2004.

Thunberg, Lars. *Man and the Cosmos: The Vision of St. Maximus the Confessor.* Crestwood, N.Y.: St. Vladimir's
Seminary Press, 1985.

Thunø, Erik. *Image and Relic: Mediating the Sacred in Early Medieval Rome.* Analecta Romana Instituti Danici, Supplementum 32. Rome: Erma di Bretschneider, 2002.

Tollefsen, Torstein. *Activity and Participation in Late Antique and Early Christian Thought.* Oxford: Oxford University Press, 2012.

Tompkins, Jane P., ed., *Reader-Response Criticism: From Formalism to Post-structuralism.* Baltimore: Johns Hopkins
University Press, 1980.

Torrance, Thomas F. *The Doctrine of Grace in the Apostolic Fathers.* Edinburgh: Oliver & Boyd, 1948. Reprint, Grand
Rapids, Mich.: Eerdmans, 1960.

Trilling, James. "The Image Not Made by Hands and the Byzantine Way of Seeing." In Kessler and Wolf, *The Holy
Face and the Paradox of Representation,* 109–28.

Troelsgård, Christian. *Byzantine Neumes: A New Introduction to the Middle Byzantine Musical Notation.* Copenhagen: Museum Tusculanum Press, 2011.

Tronzo, William. "The Prestige of St. Peter's: Observations on the Function of Monumental Narrative Cycles in
Italy." In Kessler and Simpson, *Pictorial Narrative in Antiquity and the Middle Ages,* 93–112.

Tzekakis, Emmanuel G. "Reverberation Time of the Rotunda of Thessaloniki." *Journal of the Acoustical Society of
America* 57, no. 5 (1975): 1207–9.

Uglione, Renato, ed. *Atti del Convegno nazionale di studi "Arma virumque cano . . .": L'epica dei Greci e dei Romani,
Torino, 23–24 april 2007.* Turin: Edizione dell'Orso, 2008.

Välimäki, Vesa, Julian D. Parker, Lauri Savioja, Julius O. Smith, and Jonathan S. Abel. "Fifty Years of Artificial Reverberation." *IEEE Transactions on Audio, Speech, and Language Processing* 20 (2012): 1421–48.

Van Liefferinge, Carine. "Homère erre-t-il loin de la science théologique? De la réhabilitation du 'divin' poète par Proclus." *Kernos: Revue internationale et pluridisciplinaire de religion grecque antique* 15 (2002): 199–210.

Van Nice, Robert L. *Saint Sophia in Istanbul: An Architectural Survey.* Washington, D.C.: Dumbarton Oaks Center for Byzantine Studies, 1965.

Vasiliu, Anca. *Eikōn: L'image dans le discours des trois Cappadociens.* Paris: Presses universitaires de France, 2010.

Vian, Francis. "Nonno ed Omero." *Koinonia* 15 (1991): 5–18.

Vicchi, Roberta. *Die Patriarchalbasiliken Roms: Peterskirche, San Giovanni in Laterano, San Paolo fuori le Mura, Santa Maria Maggiore.* Translated by Christiane Büchel. Antella: Scala, 1999.

Vikan, Gary, ed. *Illuminated Greek Manuscripts from American Collections: An Exhibition in Honor of Kurt Weitzmann.* Princeton: Princeton University Art Museum, distributed by Princeton University Press, 1973. Exh. cat.

Vosté, J.-M. *Pontificale iuxta ritum ecclesiae Syrorum occidentalium id est Antiochiae: Versio Latina.* Vatican City: Congregazione Pro Ecclesia orientali, 1941.

Waller, Steven J. "Intentionality of Rock-Art Placement Deduced from Acoustical Measurements and Echo Myths." In Scarre and Lawson, *Archaeoacoustics,* 31–40.

———. "Sound and Rock Art." *Nature* 363 (1993): 501.

Warburg, Aby. *The Renewal of Pagan Antiquity: Contributions to the Cultural History of the European Renaissance.* Introduction by Kurt W. Forster. Translated by David Britt. Los Angeles: Getty Research Institute, 1999.

———. "Sandro Botticelli's *Birth of Venus* and *Spring*: An Examination of Concepts of Antiquity in the Italian Early Renaissance." 1893. In *The Renewal of Pagan Antiquity,* 88–156.

Ward-Perkins, J. B. "Constantine and the Origins of the Christian Basilica." *Papers of the British School at Rome* 22 (1954): 69–90.

———. *Marble in Antiquity: Collected Papers of J. B. Ward-Perkins.* Edited by Hazel Dodge and Bryan Ward-Perkins. Archaeological Monographs of the British School at Rome 6. London: British School at Rome, 1992.

———. "Materials, Quarries, and Transportation." In *Marble in Antiquity,* 13–22.

———. "Nicomedia and the Marble Trade." In *Marble in Antiquity,* 61–105.

———. "The Roman System in Operation." In *Marble in Antiquity,* 23–30.

———. "The Trade in Sarcophagi." In *Marble in Antiquity,* 31–38.

Ware, Kallistos, bishop of Dioklea. "The Meaning of the Divine Liturgy for the Byzantine Worshipper." In Morris, *Church and People in Byzantium,* 7–28.

Wear, Sarah Klitenic, and John Dillon. *Dionysius the Areopagite and the Neoplatonist Tradition: Despoiling the Hellenes.* Aldershot: Ashgate, 2007.

Webb, Ruth. "Accomplishing the Picture: Ekphrasis, Mimesis, and Martyrdom in Asterios of Amaseia." In James, *Art and Text in Byzantine Culture,* 13–32.

———. "The Aesthetics of Sacred Space: Narrative, Metaphor, and Motion in *Ekphraseis* of Church Buildings." *Dumbarton Oaks Papers* 53 (1999): 59–74.

———. *Ekphrasis, Imagination, and Persuasion in Ancient Rhetorical Theory and Practice.* Farnham: Ashgate, 2009.

Weber, Ralf, and Matthias Albrecht Amann, eds. *Aesthetics and Architectural Composition: Proceedings of the Dresden International Symposium of Architecture 2004.* Mammendorf: Pro Literatur, 2005.

Weissbort, Daniel, and Astradur Eysteinsson, eds. *Translation—Theory and Practice: A Historical Reader.* Oxford: Oxford University Press, 2006.

Weitze, Christopher A., Claus Lynge Christensen, and Jens Holger Rindel. "Comparison Between In-Situ Recordings and Auralizations for Mosques and Byzantine Churches." http://www.odeon.dk/pdf/NAM%202002%20paper.pdf, accessed May 25, 2010.

Weitze, Christopher A., Jens Holger Rindel, Claus Lynge Christensen, and Anders Christian Gade. "The Acoustical History of Hagia Sophia Revived Through Computer Simulation." http://www.odeon.dk/pdf /ForumAcousticum2002.pdf, accessed November 24, 2015.

Welch, John W., ed. *Chiasmus in Antiquity: Structures, Analyses, Exegesis.* Hildesheim: Gerstenberg, 1981.

Welch, John W., and Daniel B. McKinlay, eds. *Chiasmus Bibliography.* Provo, Utah: Research Press, 1999.

Wescoat, Bonna D., and Robert G. Ousterhout, eds. *Architecture of the Sacred: Space, Ritual, and Experience from Classical Greece to Byzantium.* Cambridge: Cambridge University Press, 2012.

West, M. L. *Greek Metre.* Oxford: Clarendon Press, 1982.

Whitby, Mary. "The Occasion of Paul the Silentiary's Ekphrasis of S. Sophia." *Classical Quarterly* 35, no. 1 (1985): 215–28.

———. "Writing in Greek: Classicism and Compilation, Interaction and Transformation." In *Theodosius II: Rethinking the Roman Empire in Late Antiquity,* edited by Christopher Kelly, 195–218. Cambridge: Cambridge University Press, 2013.

Williams, John, ed. *Imaging the Early Medieval Bible.* University Park: Pennsylvania State University Press, 1999.

Wisniewski, Edgar. *Die Berliner Philharmonie und ihr Kammermusiksaal: Der Konzertsaal als Zentralraum.* Berlin: Gebrüder Mann, 1993.

Wolf, Gerhard. *Schleier und Spiegel: Traditionen des Christusbildes und die Bildkonzepte der Renaissance.* Munich: Fink, 2002.

Woodbridge, Richard G. "Acoustic Recordings from Antiquity." *Proceedings of the IEEE* 57, no. 8 (1969): 1465–66.

Woodfin, Warren T. *The Embodied Icon: Liturgical Vestments and Sacramental Power in Byzantium.* Oxford: Oxford University Press, 2012.

Woszczyk, Wiesław. "Acoustics of Hagia Sophia: A Scientific Approach to Humanities and Sacred Space." In Pentcheva, *Aural Architecture.* Draft manuscript, January 27, 2014, available at http://auralarchitecture .stanford.edu, accessed August 31, 2014.

———. "Active Acoustics in Concert Halls—A New Approach." *Archives of Acoustics* 36, no. 2 (2011): 1–14.

Woszczyk, Wiesław, Doyuen Ko, and Brett Leonard. "Virtual Acoustics at the Service of Music Performance and Recording." *Archives of Acoustics* 37, no. 1 (2012): 109–13.

———. "Virtual Stage Acoustics: A Flexible Tool for Providing Useful Sounds for Musicians." *Proceedings of the International Symposium on Room Acoustics,* ISRA, August 29–31, 2010, Melbourne, Australia, 1–8. Accessible at http://www.acoustics.asn.au/conference_proceedings/ICA2010/cdrom-ISRA2010/Papers/o1e .pdf.

Xydis, Stephan G. "The Chancel Barrier, Solea, and Ambo of Hagia Sophia." *Art Bulletin* 29 (1947): 1–24.

Yessios, Chris I., ed. *Digital Media and the Creative Process: Partnerships in Learning 16, 2007–08 Form•Z Joint Study Journal.* Columbus, Ohio: AutoDesSys, 2009.

Zara, Vasco. "Musica e architettura tra Medio Evo e età moderna: Storia critica di un'idea." *Acta musicologica* 77 (2005): 1–26.

Zchomelidse, Nino. *Art, Ritual, and Civic Identity in Medieval Southern Italy.* University Park: Pennsylvania State University Press, 2014.

Zintzen, Clemens, ed. *Die Philosophie des Neuplatonismus.* Darmstadt: Wissenschaftliche Buchgesellschaft, 1977.

Zwicker, Eberhard, and Hugo Fastl. *Psychoacoustics: Facts and Models.* Springer Series in Information Sciences 22. 1990. Reprint, Berlin: Springer, 2007.

INDEX

Page numbers in *italics* refer to illustrations.

Typeset by
CLICK! PUBLISHING SERVICES

Printed and bound by
PACOM

Composed in
ARNO AND META

Printed on
HANSOL MATT ART